HISTORICAL DICTIONARY

The historical dictionaries present essential information on a broad range of subjects, including American and world history, art, business, cities, countries, cultures, customs, film, global conflicts, international relations, literature, music, philosophy, religion, sports, and theater. Written by experts, all contain highly informative introductory essays of the topic and detailed chronologies that, in some cases, cover vast historical time periods but still manage to heavily feature more recent events.

Brief A–Z entries describe the main people, events, politics, social issues, institutions, and policies that make the topic unique, and entries are cross-referenced for ease of browsing. Extensive bibliographies are divided into several general subject areas, providing excellent access points for students, researchers, and anyone wanting to know more. Additionally, maps, photographs, and appendixes of supplemental information aid high school and college students doing term papers or introductory research projects. In short, the historical dictionaries are the perfect starting point for anyone looking to research in these fields.

HISTORICAL DICTIONARIES OF SPORTS

Jon Woronoff, Series Editor

Competitive Swimming, by John Lohn, 2010.
Basketball, by John Grasso, 2011.
Golf, by Bill Mallon and Randon Jerris, 2011.
Figure Skating, by James R. Hines, 2011.
The Olympic Movement, Fourth Edition, by Bill Mallon and Jeroen Heijmans, 2011.
Tennis, by John Grasso, 2011.
Soccer, by Tom Dunmore, 2011.

Historical Dictionary
of Soccer

Tom Dunmore

The Scarecrow Press, Inc.
Lanham • Toronto • Plymouth, UK
2011

Published by Scarecrow Press, Inc.
A wholly owned subsidary of The Rowman & Littlefield Publishing Group, Inc.
4501 Forbes Boulevard, Suite 200, Lanham, Maryland 20706
http://www.scarecrowpress.com

Estover Road, Plymouth PL6 7PY, United Kingdom

British Library Cataloguing in Publication Information Available

Library of Congress Cataloging-in-Publication Data

Dunmore, Tom.
  Historical dictionary of soccer / Tom Dunmore.
    p. cm. — (Historical dictionaries of sports)
  Includes bibliographical references.
  ISBN 978-0-8108-7188-5 (cloth : alk. paper) — ISBN 978-0-8108-7395-7 (ebook)
  1. Soccer—History—Dictionaries. I. Title.
  GV942.5.D86 2011
  796.334—dc22   2011010683

∞™ The paper used in this publication meets the minimum requirements of American National Standard for Information Sciences—Permanence of Paper for Printed Library Materials, ANSI/NISO Z39.48-1992.

Printed in the United States of America

Contents

Editor's Foreword

Soccer is clearly the world's most popular sport. Its popularity can be measured by the millions of ordinary people, young and not so young, men and women, who play it for fun, and the millions of fans who watch it on television. It is played nearly everywhere, in more than 200 countries, by thousands of amateur teams at all levels and thousands of professional teams. Soccer has become this popular because of its intrinsic merits as a game. A large part of soccer's appeal is the game's basic structure and the fact it can be played almost anywhere with a minimum amount of equipment (a ball and two goals or nets). While it is mostly a spectator sport (substantially more people watch the game than play it), it remains an active form of recreation for many.

So, obviously, a *Historical Dictionary of Soccer* was a must for this series, and the present volume does an excellent job of presenting the sport. Inevitably, more space is given to the professional aspects, but that is how the sport has evolved and that is what will interest most readers. But soccer's amateur beginnings are not forgotten, and its ascension (which could hardly have been expected by its founders) is traced in both the chronology and the introduction. The dictionary section contains more than a hundred entries on major players and professional teams, and dozens more on the major nations playing the sport. It also presents information on the various associations that promote and organize the sport, as well as those that provide key personnel, such as coaches and referees. Obviously, there is no end to what can be said about soccer, and this book is more a beginning than an end, so the bibliography points to further reading.

Most of our historical dictionaries are written by academics, but this new sports series engages the services of people active in the field. Moreover, this book represents the first time one of our historical dictionaries has been written by someone who runs a blog, namely Tom Dunmore. This gives him a good perspective on a sport that moves and changes so quickly, and an excellent point of view for knowing what is of interest to fans. So readers might want to check out www.pitchinvasion.net, which has been widely recognized by sports blog readers and writers and has won several global awards. Aside from that, Tom is an avid fan himself, and he is active in the supporters' association of the Chicago Fire Soccer Club. This historical dictionary is, therefore, an excellent guide for anyone who wants to know more about soccer worldwide.

Jon Woronoff
Series Editor

Preface

Selecting the entries for a historical dictionary of soccer was extremely difficult for one simple reason: soccer is the world's most popular sport, living up to its clichéd title, "the global game." Therefore, covering soccer in anything even remotely close to its entirety would require an extensive multivolume encyclopedia. Soccer is played around the world by millions in an organized fashion on teams, with countless millions more playing in recreational ad-hoc games in parks, school yards, beaches, or anywhere a ball can be kicked. Fully professional leagues exist in dozens of countries featuring thousands of different club teams. The sport's Switzerland-based global governing body, Fédération Internationale de Football Association (FIFA), counts over 200 nations as members, almost all of whom participate in the quadrennial FIFA World Cup competition, arguably the world's most-watched sporting event, closely matched only by the Olympic Games.

Due to the vast scope of this global game, it would be impossible to cover comprehensively in one volume every national team's history or major players, let alone each country's domestic club scene, and to do justice to the game's history in its organized form since the 1800s. Instead, looking at the broad sweep of the sport since its rules were codified in 19th-century Britain, the aim has been to produce a historical introduction to the key countries, club teams, competitions, players, coaches, rules, administrators, and other key parts of the game that have formed the sport of soccer as we know it today. This presentation is necessarily subjective in the areas covered, but I believe the selection of entries does provide a broad overview of the game's history while retaining a global perspective.

It is important to note that this volume refers to the game as "soccer" throughout the text. The formal name of the sport is Association Football, but it is known by many different names around the world and is rarely given its full name. In the country of the sport's formal origins, Great Britain, it is most commonly known simply as "football." In the United States and a few other English-speaking countries, it is known popularly as "soccer" to distinguish it from another game played at a professional level, also known as "football." Soccer, though, actually has its linguistic origins in Great Britain, where it was used to distinguish, in shorthand language, Association Football from other popular forms of football, particularly Rugby Football: soccer comes from the "soc" in Association. It was only when Association Football became by far the most popular code of football in England in recent decades that it began to be referred to much more often simply as football and much more rarely as soccer. The use of the name "soccer" remains appropriate in an American context due to the greater popularity of the competing game of football, and the name of the governing body in the United States is the United States Soccer Federation (USSF). I have, therefore, used "soccer" as the appropriate term for the sport for this volume published in the United States.

I would like to thank my wife, Monika, for her support and near-endless patience while I was compiling this book. I owe my mother, Mary, for everything but particularly in this case for giving in to my incessant demands and taking me to my first live professional soccer game in 1991—to this day the greatest I have ever attended—cementing my love of the sport. This book is dedicated to my late father-in-law, Franciscek Leja, for the (too few) conversations we had about a sport for we shared a passion, and for building me the perfect space in which to complete this work.

Acronyms and Abbreviations

Governing Bodies

AFC	Asian Football Confederation
CAF	Confederation of African Football
CONCACAF	Confederation of North, Central American and Caribbean Association Football
CONMEBOL	South American Football Confederation
FA; The FA	The Football Association
FIFA	Fédération Internationale de Football Association
IFAB	International Football Association Board
IOC	International Olympic Committee
MLS	Major League Soccer
NASL	North American Soccer League
OFC	Oceania Football Confederation
UEFA	Union of European Football Associations
USSF	United States Soccer Federation
WPS	Women's Professional Soccer

Members of the Fédération Internationale de Football Association (FIFA)

AFG	Afghanistan
AIA	Anguilla
ALB	Albania
ALG	Algeria
AND	Andorra
ANG	Angola
ANT	Netherlands Antilles
ARG	Argentina
ARM	Armenia
ARU	Aruba
ASA	American Samoa
ATG	Antigua and Barbuda

AUS	Australia
AUT	Austria
AZE	Azerbaijan
BAH	Bahamas
BAN	Bangladesh
BDI	Burundi
BEL	Belgium
BEN	Benin
BER	Bermuda
BFA	Burkina Faso
BHR	Bahrain
BHU	Bhutan
BIH	Bosnia and Herzegovina
BLR	Belarus
BLZ	Belize
BOL	Bolivia
BOT	Botswana
BRA	Brazil
BRB	Barbados
BRU	Brunei
BUL	Bulgaria
CAM	Cambodia
CAN	Canada
CAY	Cayman Islands
CGO	Congo
CHA	Chad
CHI	Chile
CHN	China PR
CIV	Côte d'Ivoire (Ivory Coast)
CMR	Cameroon
COD	Congo DR
COK	Cook Islands
COL	Colombia
COM	Comoros
CPV	Cape Verde
CRC	Costa Rica
CRO	Croatia
CTA	Central African Republic
CUB	Cuba
CYP	Cyprus
CZE	Czech Republic

DEN	Denmark
DJI	Djibouti
DMA	Dominica
DOM	Dominican Republic
DPR	Korea DPR
ECU	Ecuador
EGY	Egypt
ENG	England
EQG	Equatorial Guinea
ERI	Eritrea
ESP	Spain
EST	Estonia
ETH	Ethiopia
FIJ	Fiji
FIN	Finland
FRA	France
FRO	Faroe Islands
GAB	Gabon
GAM	Gambia
GEO	Georgia
GER	Germany
GHA	Ghana
GNB	Guinea-Bissau
GRE	Greece
GRN	Grenada
GUA	Guatemala
GUI	Guinea
GUM	Guam
GUY	Guyana
HAI	Haiti
HKG	Hong Kong
HON	Honduras
HUN	Hungary
IDN	Indonesia
IND	India
IRL	Republic of Ireland
IRN	Iran
IRQ	Iraq
ISL	Iceland
ISR	Israel
ITA	Italy

JAM	Jamaica
JOR	Jordan
JPN	Japan
KAZ	Kazakhstan
KEN	Kenya
KGZ	Kyrgyzstan
KSA	Saudi Arabia
KUW	Kuwait
LAO	Laos
LBR	Liberia
LCA	Saint Lucia
LES	Lesotho
LIB	Lebanon
LIE	Liechtenstein
LTU	Lithuania
LUX	Luxembourg
LVA	Latvia
MAC	Macau
MAD	Madagascar
MAR	Morocco
MAS	Malaysia
MDA	Moldova
MDV	Maldives
MEX	Mexico
MGL	Mongolia
MKD	Macedonia
MLI	Mali
MLT	Malta
MNE	Montenegro
MOZ	Mozambique
MRI	Mauritius
MSR	Montserrat
MTN	Mauritania
MWI	Malawi
MYA	Myanmar
NAM	Namibia
NCA	Nicaragua
NCL	New Caledonia
NED	Netherlands
NEP	Nepal
NIG	Niger

NIR	Northern Ireland
NOR	Norway
NZL	New Zealand
OMA	Oman
PAK	Pakistan
PAN	Panama
PAR	Paraguay
PER	Peru
PHI	Philippines
PLE	Palestine
PNG	Papua New Guinea
POL	Poland
POR	Portugal
PRK	Korea Republic
PUR	Puerto Rico
QAT	Qatar
ROU	Romania
RSA	South Africa
RUS	Russia
RWA	Rwanda
SAM	Samoa
SCO	Scotland
SEN	Senegal
SEY	Seychelles
SIN	Singapore
SKN	Saint Kitts and Nevis
SLE	Sierra Leone
SLV	El Salvador
SMR	San Marino
SOL	Solomon Islands
SOM	Somalia
SRB	Serbia
SRI	Sri Lanka
STP	São Tomé and Príncipe
SUD	Sudan
SUI	Switzerland
SUR	Suriname
SVK	Slovakia
SVN	Slovenia
SWE	Sweden
SWZ	Swaziland

SYR	Syria
TAH	Tahiti
TAJ	Tajikistan
TAN	Tanzania
TCA	Turks and Caicos Islands
TGA	Tonga
THA	Thailand
TKM	Turkmenistan
TLS	Timor-Leste (East Timor)
TOG	Togo
TPE	Chinese Taipei
TRI	Trinidad and Tobago
TUN	Tunisia
TUR	Turkey
UAE	United Arab Emirates
UGA	Uganda
UKR	Ukraine
URU	Uruguay
USA	United States
UZB	Uzbekistan
VAN	Vanuatu
VEN	Venezuela
VGB	British Virgin Islands
VIE	Vietnam
VIN	Saint Vincent and the Grenadines
VIR	U.S. Virgin Islands
WAL	Wales
YEM	Yemen
ZAM	Zambia
ZIM	Zimbabwe

Chronology

206 BCE–1368 AD   A game called *cuju* (meaning "kick ball," literally translated) is played under the Han dynasty in China, a precursor of modern soccer. A similar game known as *kemari* is meanwhile played in Japan, developing from cuju's introduction there.

1314   In England, King Edward II issues an edict to stop his subjects from playing a sport involving "great footballs in the fields of the public, from which many evils may arise."

1477   England's ruling monarch again attempts to ban the sport, with a statute issued that reads "No person shall practise any unlawful games such as dice, quoits, football and such games."

1580   The rules of an antecedent of soccer, known as *calcio*, are issued for the first time in Florence, present-day Italy.

1660–1685   Soccer attains royal patronage at the court of King Charles II in England.

1848   Establishment of "Cambridge Rules" of the game at Cambridge University, England, the world's first formalized rules of the game.

1857   24 October: Sheffield Football Club is founded, generally accepted as the world's oldest football club. The club establishes the Sheffield Rules of the game.

1862   Establishment of Notts County Football Club, currently the oldest existing Football League club in England.

1863   26 October: Formation of The Football Association (the FA), the governing body of soccer in England. First meeting is held at the Freemasons' Tavern in London. **8 December:** The FA sets down 14 rules that form the basis for today's Laws of the Game.

1867   The first recorded soccer game in South America takes place in Argentina.

1870   5 March: England plays Scotland in the first international game, though it is not recognized as such today by the Fédération Internationale de Football Association (FIFA), soccer's present-day world governing body. The game ends in a 1-1 draw.

1871   22 July: Englishman C. W. Alcock proposes the creation of a Challenge Cup competition, and The Football Association Challenge Cup (the F.A. Cup) is founded as a knockout tournament, now the world's oldest existing soccer competition. Wanderers Football Club from London wins the first edition.

1872   30 November: First FIFA-recognized international match takes place between England and Scotland, a 0-0 draw in Glasgow, Scotland, in front of 4,000 spectators.

1882   Representatives from the national associations of England, Scotland, Wales, and Ireland meet to form a common set of rules and propose an international board be formed to regulate these rules, jointly creating the International Football Association Board (IFAB). **May:** Wanderers win the F.A. Cup, the last amateur team to do so to this day.

1885   20 July: The Football Association legalizes a limited form of professionalism in English soccer. **28 November:** The first international match outside of Great Britain takes place—Canada beats the United States 1-0 in Newark, New Jersey.

1886   2 June: First official meeting of the International Football Association Board takes place.

1888   Establishment of the Football League in England, the world's first professional league, with 12 founding member clubs.

1889   Preston becomes the first winner of the Football League and wins the F.A. Cup in the same year, becoming known commonly as the "Invincibles."

1891   Several crucial rule changes are made, including the introduction of the penalty kick and allowing the referee to officiate from within the field of play—the referee had previously operated from the sidelines.

1892   A new league in England, the Football Alliance, merges with the Football League, resulting in the creation of two divisions in the combined league.

1895   23 March: First recorded women's soccer match takes place in England—a team representing the "North" beats a team representing the "South" 7-1.

1900   The German Football Association is founded.

1904   22 May: The foundation of world soccer's governing body, the Fédération Internationale de Football Association (FIFA), takes place in Paris, France. Robert Guérin is elected as the first president of FIFA.

1905   Alf Common is the first player to be transferred for more than £1,000 sterling, moving from Sunderland to Middlesbrough in England.

1906   4 June: English Football Association administrator Daniel Burley Woolfall is elected as the second president of FIFA.

1908   19–24 October: Great Britain wins the first official soccer competition at the Summer Olympic Games in London. Six teams enter the competition, with Denmark finishing in second place and the Netherlands third.

1912   29 June–4 July: At the Olympic Games in Stockholm, Sweden, Great Britain wins the men's Olympic Football Tournament for the second time in a row, defeating Denmark 4-2 in the final. The Netherlands come in third, the same finishing order as in the previous 1908 tournament.

1913   FIFA becomes a member of the International Football Association Board, alongside the English, Irish, Welsh, and Scottish Football Associations.

1916   2–17 July: The first continental competition for national teams, the Copa América, takes place in South America. During the tournament, South America's confederation, the South American Football Confederation (CONMEBOL), is officially formed. It is the first continental confederation of national associations recognized by FIFA to govern the sport in a region under FIFA's umbrella.

1920   The first women's international soccer game, between a French XI and English team Dick, Kerr Ladies, takes place in front of a crowd of 25,000 people. **28 August–5 September:** The first Olympic Games since 1912 takes place, with fourteen teams participating in the men's Olympic Football Tournament. Belgium wins the gold medal, Spain the silver medal, and the Netherlands the bronze medal.

1921   1 March: Frenchman Jules Rimet is elected as the third President of FIFA. **5 December:** Women are banned from playing on Football League grounds by The Football Association in England.

1923   28 April: The first F.A. Cup final to be held at Wembley Stadium in London takes place.

1924 25 May–9 June: The fourth Olympic Football Tournament takes place in Paris, France. It is won by Uruguay, defeating Switzerland 3-0 in the final to take the gold medal. Sweden takes third place and the bronze medal.

1928 27 May–13 June: Amsterdam in the Netherlands is the host city to the fifth Olympic soccer tournament as part of the 1928 Olympic Games. It is won by Uruguay, who defeat Argentina in the final, and marks the last time the winner of the Olympic men's title is considered to be world champions of the sport, due to the creation of the FIFA World Cup.

1930 13–30 July: The first FIFA World Cup takes place in Uruguay. Thirteen nations compete, and it is won by the hosts, Uruguay, who defeat Argentina 4-2 in the final. They are awarded the Jules Rimet Trophy, named after the FIFA president. The United States finishes third and Yugoslavia fourth.

1934 27 May–10 June: The second FIFA World Cup is held in Italy. The hosts defeat Czechoslovakia 2-1 after extra time. Germany finishes third and Austria fourth.

1938 4–19 June: Italy wins the third FIFA World Cup, held in France, beating Hungary 4-2 in the final. Brazil wins the third-place play-off 4-2 over Sweden.

1946 The Asian Football Confederation (AFC), the governing FIFA confederation in Asia, is founded.

1949 4 May: The entire team of the Italian club Torino A.C. is killed when its plane crashes into the hill of Superga returning from a game in Portugal, killing 18 players, several club officials, journalists following the team, and the crew of the plane.

1950 24 June–16 July: After a 12-year hiatus due to World War II, the FIFA World Cup returns and is played outside Europe for the first time since 1930, in Brazil. Uruguay wins the decisive final-group game against Brazil to become world champions for the second time, with the hosts finishing second, Sweden third, and Spain fourth.

1953 22 November: England's unbeaten record against overseas opposition at home ends with a 6-3 defeat to Hungary at Wembley Stadium in London.

1954 Rodolphe William Seeldrayers is elected as the fourth president of FIFA. **15 June:** In Basel, Switzerland, the Union of European Football Associations (UEFA) is founded. Henri Delaunay is selected as UEFA's first general secretary. **16 June–4 July:** West Germany wins the sixth edition of the FIFA World Cup held in Switzerland, beating Hungary 3-2 in the final. Austria takes third place and Uruguay fourth.

1955   April: The European Cup, a knockout tournament for champions of domestic European leagues, is founded by UEFA, later known as the UEFA Champions League. In the same month, the Inter-Cities' Fairs Cup (forerunner of the UEFA Europa League) is also founded. **9 June:** Arthur Drewry is elected as the fifth president of FIFA.

1956   The premier competition for national teams in Asia, the AFC Asian Cup, is founded. **13 June:** The first edition of the European Cup is won by Real Madrid, defeating Stade de Reims 4-3 in the final held at Parc des Princes in Paris.

1957   February: The first continental competition for African teams, the Africa Cup of Nations, takes place. It is organized by the newly founded Confederation of African Football (CAF), the governing body of soccer in Africa.

1958   6 February: The Munich air disaster occurs—a British European Airways plane crashes with the English champions Manchester United onboard, killing 23 passengers and most of the team. **8 June–29 June:** Brazil wins its first FIFA World Cup title, defeating the hosts, Sweden, 5-2 in the final. France wins the third-place play-off game, beating Germany 6-3.

1960   19 April–19 June: South America's premier continental international club competition, the Copa Libertadores, is staged for the first time, then known as the Copa de Campeones de América. It is won by Peñarol of Uruguay. **6–10 July:** The first continental competition for national teams in Europe, organized by the UEFA and initially called the UEFA European Nations' Cup, takes place and is won by the Soviet Union. The tournament is later renamed the UEFA European Football Championship.

1961   Englishman Sir Stanley Rous is elected as the sixth president of FIFA. The governing body of the sport in the Americas outside of most of South America, the Confederation of North, Central American and Caribbean Association Football (CONCACAF), is founded through a merger of two smaller regional confederations.

1962   30 May–17 June: The FIFA World Cup heads to South America for the second time, hosts Chile finishing third, and Brazil claiming their second World Cup title, beating Czechoslovakia 3-1 in the final. Yugoslavia finishes fourth.

1964   24 May: In Lima, Peru, 318 fans are killed and 511 injured, crushed against exit gates following a disturbance in the crowd, toward the end of an Olympic Games Football Tournament qualifier played between Peru and Argentina.

1966   The Oceania Football Confederation (OFC), the FIFA confederation governing soccer in the South Pacific region, is founded. **11 July–30**

July: England wins the FIFA World Cup for the first time as the host of the competition, beating Germany 4-2 in the final at Wembley Stadium. Portugal wins the third-place match 2-1 over the Soviet Union.

1969 The Women's Football Association is formed in England, with 44 member clubs. **29 September:** A plane carrying the champions of Bolivia, The Strongest, crashes in the Andes Mountains near La Paz, Bolivia, killing 25 members of the team and 49 other passengers on board.

1970 31 May–21 June: In Mexico, Brazil wins its third FIFA World Cup and is allowed to keep the Jules Rimet Trophy forever as a result, defeating Italy 4-1 in the final. West Germany wins the third-place play-off over Uruguay 1-0. Red and yellow cards are used for the first time in the FIFA World Cup finals.

1971 The ban on women playing on Football Association–affiliated stadiums in England is rescinded after 50 years.

1974 Brazilian João Havelange is elected as the seventh president of FIFA. **13 June–7 July:** West Germany wins the World Cup held on home soil, beating the Netherlands in the final 2-1. Poland wins the third-place play-off over Brazil 1-0.

1978 1–25 June: Argentina hosts the FIFA World Cup and wins it, defeating the Netherlands 3-1 in the final after extra time. Brazil wins the third-place play-off 2-1 over Italy.

1984 First UEFA Women's Championship competition takes place for national teams in Europe.

1986 31 May–29 June: Mexico hosts the FIFA World Cup for the second time, with Diego Maradona's Argentina defeating West Germany 3-2 in the final after extra time. France beats Belgium 4-2 in the third-place play-off.

1988 12 March: Ninety-four fans die following a stampede at a game in Nepal due to a major hailstorm, with supporters crushed against exit gates.

1989 15 April: Ninety-six fans are killed and 200 are injured at an F.A. Cup game in Sheffield, England, when supporters of Liverpool Football Club are crushed against steel fences after police allow too many fans to enter an already-packed section of the stadium.

1990 8 June–8 July: Italy hosts the FIFA World Cup for the second time. West Germany wins the tournament, beating Argentina 1-0 in the final. Italy wins the third-place play-off 2-1 over England.

1991 16–30 November: The inaugural FIFA Women's World Cup is held, hosted by China. It is won by the United States, beating Norway in the final. Sweden finishes third and Germany fourth.

1992 The Laws of the Game are changed so that the goalkeeper may no longer handle a pass from a teammate.

1993 10 April: A plane carrying Zambia's national team to a World Cup qualifier in Senegal crashes into the sea following a refueling stop on the coast of Gabon. Eighteen members of the team die.

1994 17 June–17 July: The United States hosts the FIFA World Cup for the first time, bringing record crowds to the tournament. The final is decided by a penalty shoot-out for the first time after a scoreless draw, with Brazil prevailing over Italy. Sweden wins the third-place play-off match 4-0 over Bulgaria.

1995 5–18 June: The second FIFA Women's World Cup takes place in Sweden. It is won by Norway, with Germany finishing as runners-up. The United States takes third place, and China comes in fourth.

1996 21 July–1 August: A women's soccer tournament takes place at the Summer Olympic Games in Athens for the first time as an official competition and is won by the United States, defeating China in the final 2-1.

1997 The International Football Association Board approves a revised version of the Laws of the Game, with the text modernized and cut in length by 30 percent.

1998 Joseph Sepp Blatter is elected as the eighth president of FIFA. **10 June–12 July:** France hosts their second FIFA World Cup and wins it for the first time, beating Brazil 3-0 in the final. Croatia wins the third-place play-off 2-1 over the Netherlands.

1999 19 June–10 July: The third edition of the FIFA Women's World Cup is held in the United States. The hosts win the tournament, defeating China in the final in a penalty shoot-out. Brazil finishes in third place and Norway fourth.

2000 5–14 January: The FIFA Club World Cup, then called the FIFA Club World Championship, is held for the first time in Brazil. Two Brazilian teams contest the final, with Vasco de Gama from Rio de Janeiro beating Corinthians of São Paulo in the final after a penalty shoot-out.

2002 31 May–30 June: The FIFA World Cup finals are held in Asia for the first time, with the Republic of Korea and Japan acting as cohosts. Brazil wins their fifth FIFA World Cup title, beating West Germany 2-0 in the final. Turkey takes third place after beating the Republic of Korea 3-2.

2003   20 September–12 October: The United States hosts the FIFA Women's World Cup for the second consecutive time. Germany wins the competition, defeating Sweden in the final. The United States finishes in third place and Canada in fourth.

2006   9 June–9 July: Germany hosts the World Cup, which is won by Italy over France in a penalty shoot-out after the final ends in a draw. Germany wins the third-place play-off, beating Portugal 3-1.

2007   23 September–13 October: China plays host to the FIFA Women's World Cup for the second time. Germany wins the tournament, beating Brazil 2-0 in the final. The United States finishes in third place and Norway in fourth.

2010   11 June–11 July: The FIFA World Cup takes place on the African continent for the first time, hosted by South Africa. It is won by Spain, claiming their first FIFA World Cup title. The Netherlands finish in second place, Germany in third, and Uruguay in fourth.

Introduction

Association Football, or "soccer," as it will be referred to in this volume (for the common North American name given to the game), is the world's most popular sport and one of the globe's best-known cultural practices. The pinnacle of the sport worldwide is the FIFA World Cup for men's national teams and the FIFA Women's World Cup for women's national teams, competitions organized by soccer's global governing body, Fédération Internationale de Football Association (FIFA), founded in 1904 and now boasting 207 member national associations. Both World Cup competitions are held every four years and each crowns one nation as the world champion in front of huge global television audiences: over half of the planet's population watched the 2010 FIFA World Cup final between Spain and the Netherlands held in South Africa. Similarly, professional club soccer games, such as the UEFA Champions League final in Europe, attract television audiences numbering in the hundreds of millions. World soccer today is a vast, commercialized, global industry, with huge salaries paid to the biggest stars due to the amounts of revenue generated through the sale of television rights, ticket sales, and sponsorship income.

The media spotlight on world soccer means certain club teams, players, and coaches are among the best-known names on the planet. Pelé, the Brazilian player who led his country to three FIFA World Cup titles between 1958 and 1970, became a global celebrity and rivaled peers, such as Muhammad Ali. Today, David Beckham is a global brand name as much as he is an English soccer player, and is worth millions of dollars. Soccer is now a vast employment industry: dozens of professional leagues exist in countries around the world, encompassing thousands of professional players, coaches, and administrators. Aside from the elite professional level, it is the breadth and depth of the number of participants and spectators of soccer games around the world that truly justifies why soccer is so often called "the global game." FIFA's 208 member nations number more than the United Nations or the International Olympic Committee can boast as members. FIFA's 2006 "Big Count," a global survey of soccer participation worldwide, found 270 million active participants in the sport, almost 4 percent of the world's population.

Intensely passionate fan bases of club and national teams embed the sport deeply into the social fabric in most countries.

At first glance, soccer, today a vast, commercialized modern game in the globalized 21st century with hundreds of millions of participants around the world, bears little resemblance to the provincial, amateur form of the game first codified in mid-19th-century Britain. Yet at its heart, soccer retains the same essence that it had at its modern birth: it remains a simple sport, with the game consisting of two teams trying to kick a ball into a goal at either end of a rectangular field bounded by lines. Indeed, so simple is the act of kicking a round object with some kind of target in mind that the game has antecedents that stretch back millennia—forms of the game played by numerous civilizations in ways largely lost to the sands of time—with the basics of the game invented many times over in many different parts of the world. It is the simplicity of the game of soccer that explains the remarkable rise of its popularity worldwide since the 19th century and the many forms in which it existed before then. Feet and a ball are all that is required for recreational play, and not a lot more for organized games, unlike the complex and more expensive equipment and facilities needed for other modern sports such as American football, cricket, or hockey.

It is no surprise, then, that organized games along the lines of modern-day soccer in its most basic element—a ball being kicked by competing parties—have been played for thousands of years. The first known organized games of anything close to the form of modern soccer came during the Han dynasty in China (206 BCE—220 AD) in a form of the game known as *cuju* (literally meaning "kick ball"). In this game, two teams played with a stitched leather ball (stuffed with fur, feathers, or hemp), attempting to propel the ball into goals at either end of a marked field, with use of the players' feet a central element of play. It was a game enjoyed by the army and the upper classes in China, all the way up to the royal household. Similar forms of the game soon spread to Korea, Japan, and the Malay Peninsula. Variations on cuju—with a hollow ball becoming more commonly used as time passed—continued to be played under later Chinese imperial dynasties until the establishment of the Ming dynasty in 1368 AD, when the game began to be neglected, eventually disappearing altogether.

In the 13th century, Japan's form of cuju, known as *kemari*, was the first sport in Japan to become standardized and organized, from its field of play to the equipment, techniques, costume, and customs attached to it. Kemari was a competitive game, but it was less like modern soccer than was the original form of cuju in China: the aim was not to shoot the ball into a goal, but for a circle of players to keep a hollow ball in the air as long as possible by kicking it upwards, a stylish and graceful pastime. It was a skilled game that relied on team play with coordinated movement based on close communication to keep the ball aloft, and intense technical ability required of the players. It became a prestigious and popular game. Yet it did not become a popular sport when Japan modernized: following the Meiji Restoration in 1868 and the vast industrialization of Japanese society, kemari became a niche sport for aristocrats, a remnant of the old ways and not the forerunner to soccer today.

Other varieties of ball games involving kicking had also developed: In Mesoamerica, including present-day Mexico and Honduras, ball games were the fulcrum of culture, though their games were more like volleyball than modern soccer, and these activities were eventually suppressed by Spanish invaders in the 16th century. In Florence, *calcio* was a sport played in the 16th and 17th centuries, a team game with 27 players on each side, trying to kick and throw a ball inside a large, sandy pit. None of those forms, though, led to the modern game as we know it. That form would develop in Great Britain in the 19th century, branching off suddenly and dramatically from folk forms of the game dating back in the British Isles to at least the days of the Roman Empire, when a ball sport, known as *harpastum*, was played. In later times, the roots of ball games played with the feet, at folk level, can be seen in their appearances in English literature from works by William Shakespeare and Sir Walter Scott. Across England in the Middle Ages and up to the 19th century, village fairs and festivals often featured huge crowds of participants attempting to kick, throw, and carry a ball from one side of town to the other, a wildly popular pursuit and an unruly, dangerous game often clamped down on by the royal authorities. The industrialization of Britain in the 18th and 19th centuries largely killed off these folk games, with rare exceptions, as life and leisure patterns changed dramatically with the vast urbanization of the country. That folk form of a team ball game perhaps remained present in the popular imagination of the working classes, but it would be in the upper classes of British society that soccer, as we know it today, would be first formalized into an organized, modern game in the mid-19th century. It was then adopted by the masses, first in Britain, then worldwide, to become "the global game" in the 20th century.

In England's elite public schools, a ball game that was the clear antecedent of modern forms of soccer began to be codified as early as the 18th century at Westminster School, with the crucial intervention of forward passing introduced at the school in the early 19th century. Other schools like Eton, in 1815, also began to write down rules to more clearly define a previously unruly game. These public-school games influenced the rule makers who created the basis for the formal Laws of the Game that provide the rules under which soccer is played today, and these founders learned the game as players or teachers at English elite public schools. The game developed there and was a part of a Victorian ethos of inventing organized play that taught certain values: schoolmasters stressed fair play, the subordination of self to the team, and a form of "muscular Christianity." Eventually, interplay between different schools and the broader development of the sport demonstrated a need for shared, accepted rules nationwide. In 1862, one of the first rule books for soccer, *The Simplest Game*, was written by schoolmaster J. C. Thring at Uppingham Grammar School in England. Thring had earlier been part of a committee at Cambridge University, in 1848, that had drawn up a code of rules.

Thring's rule book and other efforts, such as the Sheffield Rules from further north in Sheffield, England, did not gain national acceptance. It would be on 26 October 1863, at what turned out to be a momentous meeting of representatives from 12 London clubs at the Freeman's Tavern in central London, that the Laws of the Game followed today have their clearest originating moment. As it had become apparent that a single national rule book needed to be created and broadly accepted in England to facilitate play between different schools and club teams, representatives from 12 teams decided to sit down and work out a single code they would all agree to play under, and two months of meetings followed. There soon emerged, however, deep philosophical differences between the representatives on how the game should be played, in terms of what the rules would or would not allow: Blackheath Club, for example, favored allowing players to kick each other's shins ("hacking") as a legitimate method to stop opponents, but this was opposed by most of the rest of the group. Blackheath walked out on the discussion when the rules were formally adopted on 8 December 1863, but the other 11 clubs agreed to 14 rules that were called the "Laws of the Game." They formed The Football Association, the world's first national soccer governing body, whose decisions all clubs agreed to adhere to (though in practice it would be some years until this was overwhelmingly accepted nationwide). The form of the game to be known as "Association Football" had been born. Other competing football codes with different rule books would soon emerge, but it would be soccer—as it would be nicknamed to differentiate it from other forms such as Rugby Football—that became the world's most popular sport over the next century.

Now that the sport had commonly accepted rules in England, it also needed greater organization of its games on a consistent basis for the game to spread further. A crucial development in the history of the game came with the founding of the world's first nationally organized soccer competitions: first the F.A. Challenge Cup (now commonly known as the F.A. Cup) and later, the Football League. The former was first contested in 1871, organized by The Football Association following a suggestion at a Football Association meeting by F.A. Honorary Secretary Charles Alcock, who stated that it "is desirable that a Challenge Cup should be established in connection with the Association, for which all clubs belonging to the Association should be invited to compete." Three months later, the proposal was approved, and the first F.A. Challenge Cup began with 12 teams taking part, playing each other on a single-elimination basis leading up to a final game. The first competition was won by the Wanderers, defeating the Royal Engineers 1–0 in the final, in front of a crowd of 2,000 people at the Kennington Oval in London. The F.A. Cup, still contested today, crucially demonstrated the interest among the broader public for annual competitive contests in the early development of organized club soccer, and attracted a broader membership to the nascent governing body in England, The Football Association.

Interest in the sport of soccer continued to grow enormously across Great Britain, spurred by the success of the F.A. Cup, as growing crowds and greater numbers of clubs took part each year in the 1870s and 1880s. In the meantime, The Football Association had continued to adjust the Laws of the Game, changing the rules to establish 11-a-side play in 1870 and introducing a neutral referee to adjudicate disputed calls in 1871. Ten years later, the referee was given the power to send off a player from the field for "ungentlemanly behavior." By the mid-1880s, the basic structure of the game on the field was set as it has remained ever since, despite some modifications since by the new body formed to oversee the Laws of the Game: the International Football Association Board (IFAB) was founded in 1882 by representatives from the four national associations of the British Isles. The associations of England, Scotland, Wales, and Ireland founded the IFAB to determine a standard rule book to be applied in all official fixtures between and within each country, basing this off the agreed Football Association rules already in place in England. International matches between teams representing their countries had taken place as early as 30 November 1872, with a 0–0 tie between England and Scotland that spurred the creation of the Scottish Football Association, the world's second national governing body. National associations were soon created in Wales and Ireland as well. Shortly after that, the British Isles hosted regular international games between all four countries in what became an annual competition begun in 1883 and lasting until 1984, the International Championship. The formation of the IFAB greatly assisted this first form of international competition in laying down rules accepted across national boundaries.

Off the field, The Football Association also faced the need to make a momentous decision in the early 1880s: as the original amateur status of the game became the subject of controversy, a push for professionalism developed as soccer became commercialized and working-class players needed payment to play, particularly in northern England. As more money came into the game through growing crowds paying to attend games, club directors were tempted to pay players, particularly those from working-class backgrounds, who could not afford simply to play at their leisure every week and give up work, as upper-class players could. Notably, Preston North End in northwest England began recruiting top players from north of the border in Scotland. The club found convenient paid work for them in the town nearby to bypass rules against clubs paying players directly, often to the chagrin of southern upper-class clubs. Thinly veiled class snobbery was at the root of much of the debate. Several northern clubs pressured The Football Association to legalize professionalism and end such charades, threatening to break away from The Football Association in 1884 and form their own British Football Association incorporating Scottish clubs and players. Despite opposition from adherents to amateurism in the South, on 20 July 1885, The Football Association conceded an initial compromise to allow limited professionalism, permitting clubs to pay players who had either been born or lived within a six-mile radius of each club's ground for a minimum of two years. Despite these initial limitations, the dam to full professionalism had been burst, and soccer in England would never again be a minority pursuit played mainly by old boys from upper-class schools. The sport became a mass phenomenon with broad appeal to the working class, who began to dominate the game as players and spectators in larger and larger numbers while the game's commercial income increased in the late 19th century.

The opportunities to grow the sport provided by the introduction of professionalism, and the rising wage bills that it incurred for clubs, spurred the formation of the Football League in England in 1888, the idea of William McGregor, a director at the English club Aston Villa. On 2 March 1888, McGregor wrote to four fellow English clubs, Blackburn Rovers, Bolton Wanderers, Preston North End, and West Bromwich Albion, suggesting that "10 or 12 of the most prominent clubs in England combine to arrange home-and-away fixtures each season." Regularly scheduled competition was deemed to be crucial for clubs to bring in consistent cash flow, compared to the irregularity of friendly games and F.A. Cup runs. Six months later, on 8 September 1888, the Football League began play with 12 clubs taking part and is still in existence today, the world's oldest league, though now secondary to the Premier League in importance in England.

Outside of Great Britain in the late 19th century, soccer as an organized game began to be developed in countries around the world, taken to places as diverse as Argentina and Austria by British émigrés working as sailors, railway engineers, and in a myriad of other occupations in the various parts of Britain's formal and informal worldwide empire. In Argentina, for example, British immigrants set up the country's first soccer teams and leagues in the late 19th century. But the game soon took on a flavor it had never had before in Britain. In each country, soccer developed its own native ethos: Latin immigrants began playing the game in beguiling new ways, and it became the people's sport in Argentina. Meanwhile, the same impetus for greater organization and coordination on the rules and structure of soccer's competitive fixtures that had spurred the establishment of The Football Association, the Football League, and the International Football Association Board in Britain was becoming particularly evident outside the British Isles, and especially in continental Europe. There, the examples set by the British national associations were followed with similar organizations set up to oversee the development of soccer in numerous countries, such as in France. Those countries then desired to further international play and regulate the movement of players between clubs and countries, and initially looked to England for leadership in establishing an international governing body for the sport with broader powers than the simple rule-making basis of the International Football Association Board.

Yet entreaties from French soccer administrators to The Football Association for English help in forming an international association of nations in the early years of the 20th century fell on deaf ears across the channel. English administrators were unable to see the purpose of focusing on the sport's development outside the splendidly isolated British Isles. Ultimately, that English intransigence did not deter continental soccer administrators from establishing their own lasting solution. Led by the energetic Frenchman Robert Guérin, the federation of national associations that still governs the global game today was formed on 21 May 1904, known then, as now, by its French name: Fédération Internationale de Football Association (FIFA). The founding members, who represented their nation's soccer associations, came from France, Belgium, Denmark, the Netherlands, Sweden, Spain, and Switzerland. England's Football Association ended up joining FIFA, after all, in 1906, with Football Association administrator Daniel Burley Woolfall taking over from Guérin as president of FIFA the same year. Over the coming decades, FIFA would come to be the true governing body of soccer globally as it expanded its reach to other continents: from seven founding members in 1904, FIFA grew to more than 200 member national associations by the time of its centenary celebration in 2004, then boasting an income of more than $700 million and a public profile for its president, Sepp Blatter, as high in the public eye as many heads of state.

The key to the growth of FIFA in its wealth and power to direct the sport, and the central element forming the desirability for national associations to become and remain a part of what it calls its "FIFA Family," is the FIFA World Cup. Contested every four years since 1930 (with an enforced 12-year break due to the Second World War), the World Cup provides the bulk of FIFA's income through the sale of television and commercial rights to the competition, with much of that money flowing back to national associations, and much now stocking a very healthy FIFA bank balance. This commercial wealth is, however, a relatively recent development. It was not until 26 years after FIFA's founding in 1904 that the first World Cup took place, and it would not become a money-spinning phenomenon until television became a lucrative outlet for the games in the 1970s.

The origins of the World Cup owe much to the effort of a few administrators who persevered in attempting to create a global international competition despite the considerable challenges in terms of travel and organization in the first decades of the 20th century, long before air travel was feasible for teams. But it had been evident from FIFA's earliest years that the growth of the game in numerous countries, along with the competitive nature of the sport, demanded the creation of an international tournament to determine a world champion national team. The idea was discussed by FIFA as early as 1906, but their initial attempts to organize such a tournament failed. Meanwhile, the recently founded modern Olympic Games offered an obvious venue for such a soccer competition to take place instead, and FIFA agreed to allow international play under its regulation at the Olympics. After appearing as an exhibition competition at the 1904 Olympic Games in St. Louis, soccer first appeared as an official Olympic sport at the games held in London in 1908. The tournament was won by a Great Britain team made up of players from England, and the same nation prevailed again at the second Olympic Games Football Tournament, held at the 1912 Olympic Games in Stockholm, Sweden. Following a break for the First World War, soccer resumed play at the Olympic Games in 1920 with FIFA approval, the Olympic Games Football Tournament now recognized as the world championship for amateur national teams. The 1924 tournament was considered a success, as was the 1928 competition. Both were won by Uruguay, and both attracted huge crowds to the games. Yet soccer was not ideally suited for the Olympics: the amateur ethos of the Olympics did not mesh with the growing professionalism of world soccer, and this meant many of the world's best players did not participate in the championship. FIFA came under pressure to create a competition that would allow professionals to compete alongside amateurs, and, led by President Jules Rimet in the 1920s, FIFA saw an opportunity to create an independent showcase for soccer's growing popularity internationally, without being swallowed up by the Olympic Games.

Therefore, in the late 1920s, FIFA formed a committee to organize a world championship under its own independent auspices, open to all professionals and amateurs on national teams affiliated with FIFA. In 1929, it awarded hosting rights for what would be the inaugural FIFA World Cup in 1930 to reigning Olympic champions, Uruguay. It was fitting that the first World Cup took place in South America, as it was the continent that had pioneered international competition for national teams: in 1916, the South American Football Confederation (CONMEBOL) was founded as the world's first continental governing body affiliated with FIFA, and it established the first continental competition for national teams the same year, the Copa América. Uruguay won FIFA's favor as hosts for the first World Cup in part because of its willingness and ability to spend a large amount of money to stage the competition: they paid accommodation costs for the visiting teams and built a new stadium to host the games, Estadia Centenario, so named to mark the centenary of Uruguay's first constitution proclaimed in 1830. Despite Uruguay's financial help, the lengthy sea travel required to reach South America precluded some European nations from competing in the first World Cup, and England refused an invitation from Uruguay to appear at the competition (and would not play at a World Cup until 1950), feeling the competition was beneath their status in the international game. Once it kicked off, the quality of the games and the large crowds made the first FIFA World Cup an undoubted success, with hosts Uruguay eventually emerging as victors to the host nation's delight. FIFA had decided the World Cup would be staged every four years. So in 1934, the World Cup headed to Italy, then under the rule of dictator Benito Mussolini. Unfortunately for FIFA, the tournament was used as something of a showcase for his fascist regime, though the true quality of Italy's national team was evident in their win that year, and their successful defense of the World Cup four years later, in France. The World Cup's momentum, and the progress of world soccer as a whole, was stalled by the global conflagration of the Second World War. The tournament did not return until 1950, but it had established itself as a permanent part of the global soccer calendar in normal times.

World War II also interrupted the development of international competition among club teams that had begun to advance in the 1930s with the establishment of the Mitropa Cup in central Europe, which was contested by teams from several countries. It was only when postwar reconstruction was complete across Europe and international travel became increasingly easier due to the growth of air travel that continental club soccer in Europe became a prestigious and lucrative endeavor. The seeds for such competition that eventually resulted in today's lucrative UEFA Champions League had been sown by the Mitropa Cup and then further advanced by independent one-off games contested by leading European club teams in an effort to prove their standing across the continent in the early 1950s. The common introduction of floodlights to leading European stadiums in the 1950s proved a further boon as it allowed these intra-European games to take place during midweek evenings, thus not interfering with the weekend domestic league schedules. Taking advantage of this growing desire for international club competition in the mid-1950s, the recently founded European governing body for the sport, the Union of European Football Associations (UEFA), began to run a European Cup competition for leading club teams across the continent, adopting an idea developed by French newspaper editor Gabriel Hanot. The European Cup, now known as the UEFA Champions League, began play in 1955 and soon became the most prestigious prize in European soccer. It was dominated in its early years by Spanish giants Real Madrid, starring the likes of legendary Argentinean-born Alfredo di Stéfano. In South America, CONMEBOL followed suit with the establishment of the leading South American club competition, the Copa Libertadores, in 1960, which long competed with the European Cup (later, known as the UEFA Champions League) as the leading international club tournament, the winners of each squaring off from 1960 to 2004 in the Intercontinental Cup. Other continents soon had their own premier club competition: what is now the CONCACAF Champions League was founded in 1962 in the region of North America, Central America, and the Caribbean; Africa's CAF Champions League (as it is known now) began play in 1964; and its equivalent in Asia was established in 1967 (now known as the AFC Champions League). Oceania became the final region to found its current top level of continental play in 1987, with what is today called the OFC Champions League. The winners of each confederation's competition play each other in the FIFA Club World Cup, first contested in 2001.

The development of continental club competitions, and their spread around the world, reflected the growth of professional club soccer as a whole globally. New professional leagues were established in dozens of countries in the interwar period (such as in Spain in 1929 with the founding of La Liga) and following World War II (such as in Germany with the founding of the Bundesliga in 1963). New stadiums were built and crowds soared: in many countries, soccer became the unquestionable national sport, and national and club teams became seared into the fabric of everyday life for fans, and into broader culture, both nationally and locally. The media spotlight on the sport grew enormously, and by the 1960s, soccer players like George Best were becoming well remunerated international celebrities. The sport's commercialization continued unabated as its popularity rose.

Soccer's soaring popularity was based on an uncommon fanatic support that surrounded club and national teams by the 1960s. Perhaps more so than in any other sport in the world, soccer's fans are in many ways as important to the history of its development and to its part in each country's culture as players, media, and team management have been. This is manifested not only in ways that show supporters are the lifeblood of the sport's growth and development, but also in tragic incidents that have changed the course of the sport. The most obvious negative events involve death and injury to spectators, and the history of soccer has been littered all too often with dozens of deaths in stadiums in Europe, South America, and Africa. The vast majority of these stadium disasters have their root cause not in misbehavior by fans, as a clichéd view of soccer supporters as hooligans might have it, but by the all-too-repetitive failures of the authorities in providing a safe venue for large numbers of fans to enjoy the game. This might be because of inadequate stadium structures (such as at Ibrox Park in Glasgow, Scotland, in 1902, when new wooden stands proved unable to hold the crowd and collapsed), inadequate policing (with decisions made by police supervisors in Sheffield, England, in April 1989, leading to the deaths of 96 Liverpool supporters in the Hillsborough Disaster), or poor planning (the Soviet authorities allowing a game at Lenin Stadium in Moscow to go ahead in freezing conditions, with icy stands leading to a crush that killed 69 spectators in October 1982).

Some of these tragedies have transformed the game: in England, the Hillsborough Disaster led directly to the implementation of new regulations that made stadiums safer, and provided government funding for the building or redevelopment of dozens of English stadiums, a crucial step on the road to prosperity for the English Premier League, now the world's richest league. With this change, soccer has become a sport consumed by all classes in England, rather than the working-class dominance seen up until the end of the 1980s. This change has seen some poorer supporters priced out and some of the atmosphere in English stadiums lost, in exchange for a more sanitized and safer experience and a massive rise in the income for Premier League clubs, which has allowed the recruitment of many of the world's top players by English clubs.

Hooliganism by fans, however, has been directly to blame for some stadium disasters, a pursuit of a tiny majority of fans that has had hideous consequences for many innocent supporters and has at times threatened the future of the game itself in some countries. Most famously and tragically, at the European Cup final in May 1985, Liverpool fans charged toward fans of the opposing team, Juventus of Italy, leading to the collapse of a wall on those retreating fans and the deaths of 39 people. English clubs were banned for five years from European play by UEFA as a consequence. Hooliganism in England, as practiced by a small minority of fans of various clubs and the national team, reached its apogee in the early 1980s. In the country in which it had been first established, soccer became plagued by violence, or at least, the perception of violence: the media spotlight that was focused on rare incidents of true hooliganism often exaggerated just how pervasive the dangers were. Hooliganism was not a product of the game of soccer as an intrinsic practice, but of larger forces at work from society in general in 1970s and 1980s Britain. Youth subcultures that attached their identity to hooliganism were attracted to English soccer as an outlet for habitual violence, epitomized by the "casuals" style of the 1980s. Racist groups exploited the opportunity to foment trouble and attract recruits. Hooliganism soon appeared in numerous other countries around the world and is now more evident outside Britain, where it has become a seriously marginalized pursuit.

Fan culture and organization also manifested itself in marvelously positive ways for the sport of soccer. Standing, singing crowds in England gave games a vociferous atmosphere not seen in competing sports such as rugby and cricket in the mid-20th century. In continental Europe and South America in the 1970s and 1980s, the organization of support for club and national teams was taken even further in terms of visual displays at games by groups known, for their fanatic attitude, as "ultras." Ultras groups began creating extraordinarily colorful and elaborate *tifo* displays of support for their teams, with banners, flags, confetti, and streamers flooding stadiums. At times, ultras culture would, at its margins, cross over into hooliganism, but the vast majority of ultras have remained focused on positive support for their club teams. Meanwhile, in England from the 1980s on, fan groups began to play an important role in lobbying for better treatment by the authorities for supporters to avoid the conditions that led to tragedies like the Hillsborough Disaster. They also campaigned to remove racism from the sport, while developing their own self-made media outlets with the growth of fanzine print culture. As the sport became further commercialized in the 1990s, fan groups in England developed to the extent that many purchased their clubs from bankrupt ownership or even set up their own clubs. They did this, in part, to protest the marginalization they felt as fans of elite clubs like Manchester United. The founding of FC United of Manchester by Manchester United fans in 2005 is one example.

This fan initiative to claim a role in running clubs to protect them as community enterprises reflected just how deeply market forces had transformed the sport in the 1970s and 1980s. This had led both to enormous growth for the sport along with some alienation of hardcore fans and a growing risk of corruption as more money entered the game. The transformation of soccer's marketing and media coverage led to it becoming a key element of globalized culture as the game rapidly developed beyond the traditional strongholds of Europe and South America. FIFA played a key part in this process following the election of João Havelange as FIFA president in 1974, the Brazilian replacing stolid Englishman Sir Stanley Rous. It was no coincidence that Havelange hailed from Brazil, the country that had dominated the FIFA World Cup in the postwar period, with victories in 1958 in Sweden, 1962 in Chile, and 1970 in Mexico. Though England won its first and only World Cup in 1966, it came on home soil and it was elsewhere that the game was being taken in new directions on and off the field: international soccer was developing its first global stars, recognizable to millions worldwide regardless of their interest in the sport. Brazil's Pelé was the first of this phenomenon that has led to the global fame today of the likes of David Beckham, Cristiano Ronaldo, Marta, and Lionel Messi. Pelé's celebrity was due to his remarkable playing abilities as a prolific goal scorer and creative force with his bewitching touch on the ball, leading Brazil to those three FIFA World Cup triumphs in 12 years from 1958 to 1970. But in that span came a development that meant his fame eclipsed that of previous world greats such as Garrincha or Stanley Matthews, and that Havelange would grasp hold of to commercialize and globalize the World Cup: soccer's widespread availability to television viewers.

It was only in 1954 that the FIFA World Cup was broadcast for the first time on television in any form, and only in 1970 that it was broadcast in Technicolor and carried by satellite live worldwide. In that year, Pelé's magical Brazilian team, in their iconic yellow shirts, obtained rapt attention worldwide, culminating in their 4–1 win over Italy in the World Cup final. Meantime, FIFA was perfectly poised to take advantage of the growing global audience for the sport. Membership of FIFA had increased enormously in the postwar decades, fueled by the growing number of independent nations around the world in that era of de-colonization from imperial European rule in Africa and Asia. Membership of FIFA grew from 50 members in 1934, to 80 members in 1954, and to 141 members by 1974. Such was the growth that the need for regional groupings of national associations under the umbrella of FIFA quickly became obvious for easier organization of continental competition. Beyond the example first set in South America in 1916 with the formation of CONMEBOL, in the postwar era, FIFA confederations were set up in Europe (UEFA, founded in 1954), Asia (the Asian Football Confederation [AFC], founded in 1954), Africa (the Confederation of African Football [CAF], founded in 1957), and Oceania (the Oceania Football Confederation, OFC, founded in 1966). Each of these confederations was made responsible by FIFA for the development and promotion of soccer in its region and played a critical role in developing continental competitions for both clubs and countries, such as the UEFA European Football Championship and the Africa Cup of Nations. All enjoyed substantial television income, which was funneled back into developing the sport further in each region.

The international growth of the sport soon put pressure on FIFA to reflect its rapidly globalizing state in its own leadership and in its decisions on where to stage the FIFA World Cup, along with how many nations from each FIFA confederation would be allowed to take part in the increasingly prestigious and financially lucrative World Cup finals tournament. In the 1960s, this led to a wrenching conflict within the halls of FIFA that brought about the end of European administrative control of the global game. By the 1960s, the newly formed Confederation of African Football was providing FIFA with a growing number of member nations (rising from 18 in 1854 to 39 by 1974), yet still did not receive an automatic qualification spot for the FIFA World Cup finals tournament at the 1966 tournament. FIFA's resistance under President Sir Stanley Rous to awarding an African team an automatic slot, combined with his continued support for apartheid-era South Africa, led to a boycott by CAF of the 1966 FIFA World Cup in England. By 1970, FIFA had relented and awarded Africa one automatic qualification spot, but Rous' Eurocentric failure to adapt to the changing membership of FIFA led to his defeat and replacement by the Brazilian Havelange for the presidency of FIFA in 1974.

Havelange's election in part rested on his promise to expand the World Cup finals to accommodate more nations from the developing world, in order to reflect FIFA's global growth: while the combined number of FIFA members from Europe and South America had held steady between 1954 and 1974 at 43 nations, those from other parts of the world had risen from 37 in 1954 to 98 by 1974. Yet, at the 1974 World Cup, only 3 of the 16 competing teams hailed from outside Europe and South America. The World Cup, at least, went to a new continent, North America, in 1970, with Mexico hosting the finals. However, it would not be until the reign of Havelange's successor and protégé, Sepp Blatter, as FIFA president, that it would reach Asia and Africa: the former in a jointly hosted World Cup by Japan and the Republic of Korea in 2002, and finally to the latter in South Africa in 2010. By the time of its first visit to South Africa, the World Cup had been transformed from a relatively small event featuring mainly European and South American teams, as it had been until 1974, to a global extravaganza with 32 teams appearing in the finals (double the number from the 1966 World Cup). And these teams were spread more broadly around the FIFA confederations: at the 2010 World Cup, there were 13 nations represented from Europe, six from Africa, five from South America, four from Asia, three from North and Central America, and one from Oceania. The World Cup has yet to be won by a country from outside Europe or South America, but more and more of the world's elite players now hail from outside those two traditional powerhouse continents.

Still, despite the growing presence of players from outside Europe and South America among the global elite, the largest concentration of wealth and power in the sport remains in Europe. Therefore, club teams from the Premier League in England, La Liga in Spain, Serie A in Italy, and the Bundesliga in Germany pluck the best talents from other continents, often at very young ages. World soccer, as reflected in the World Cup's growth, has become a multibillion-dollar global industry, with teams in the top European leagues spending enormous sums to acquire and retain the best talent. This money comes from an enormously lucrative market for the sport worldwide. Consumption of the game is not limited to merely watching it on television or attending it in person: merchandising and marketing of teams, players, and tournaments is an industry in itself. Sports companies, such as Nike, spend millions to have the right to outfit teams, such as Manchester United, and sell millions of team jerseys in return. These jerseys, at least for club teams, are almost always bedecked with the name of a sponsoring company in addition to the logo of the manufacturer, usually printed across the front of the shirt. Chicago-based Aon Corporation, for example, committed to a $33 million annual deal with Manchester United to sponsor the team for four seasons, from 2010 on. This international arrangement speaks to the globalization of world soccer: the biggest club teams, especially those from the Premier League in England and La Liga in Spain, count millions of fans each worldwide, as well as their own substantial domestic followings.

Elite European clubs, in part thanks to the success of the richly rewarding UEFA Champions League, are now by far the richest in the world. In July 2010, Manchester United was valued as the most valuable sports property in the world, by *Forbes* magazine, at $1.84 billion, ahead of the NFL's Dallas Cowboys in second place, at $1.65 billion. Manchester United's revenue, like that of most of the biggest club teams in the world, comes from three main diverse streams: game day income from their stadium, Old Trafford, commercial income from items such as the sale of Manchester United jerseys, key chains, mugs and all manner of products, and television-rights income. This commercialization of the sport is a rapid and vast development over the past three decades. European clubs only began accepting shirt sponsorships in the late 1970s, and television rights to broadcast club games were sold for a pittance, if sold at all, until the late 1980s and early 1990s. That is when satellite television companies began paying premiums to win the exclusive broadcast rights and attract subscribers, resulting in billions of dollars of new revenue flowing into the game, inflating wages and enriching players, coaches, and agents. A spiral of increasing spending also led to rising ticket prices for fans, and soccer's fan base became more middle class and less working class in much of Europe. Draining dollars out of consumers of soccer has become a growing part of the business of the global game. Furthermore, the sudden, gushing flow of money into the game has opened new avenues for corruption to seep in from the highest levels on down, with match fixing and bribery of officials a constant global concern. The growing rewards of the sport also increase the incentives to attempt to cheat: doping scandals surfaced as far back as the 1960s in Italy, with random drug testing introduced by national and international authorities in an attempt to stymie the use of performance-enhancing drugs. The most high-profile doping case came at the 1994 FIFA World Cup, with Argentina's aging superstar Diego Maradona failing a drug test, which led to his expulsion from the competition.

The commercialization of international soccer and the influx of vast new income to the game also allowed new, safer stadiums to be built—albeit, often with more sanitized atmospheres—and a broad availability of games on television from leagues around the world for fans to watch wherever they live. This transformation of the sport was clearest in the original home of organized soccer, England. The English Premier League, which began play in 1992 as 22 elite clubs broken away from the Football League, became the richest league in the world a decade into its existence, mainly thanks to its lucrative, and initially exclusive, broadcasting rights deals with Sky Television. That revenue is shared among all Premier League clubs, with the rights to games sold collectively by the league: current television income is $3 billion for domestic rights and around $1 billion in international rights, both for a three-year period. In other leagues, television rights are often sold individually by teams: Barcelona, in Spain's La Liga (the top professional league in the country), currently has a $1.5 billion television contract with Spanish company MediaPro, for example. Despite this income, top European clubs are often heavily in debt: both Manchester United and Barcelona, for diverse reasons, are hundreds of millions of dollars in the red. In part, this is due to a freer market operating in European soccer than in American sports leagues, including the top tier of professional men's soccer in the United States, Major League Soccer. In that league, spending by clubs is tightly limited by a salary-cap system, in a long-term attempt to avoid the reckless spending by teams in the previous top-tier, outdoor American men's league, the North American Soccer League, which folded in 1984. In Europe, the free market essentially rules supreme in most leagues, such as England's Premier League, though in countries such as Germany, where clubs in the Bundesliga are majority owned by fans, more-sensible financial controls are in place. The future of the game is one that appears to be increasingly tied to the demands of high finance and global television, though many fan groups are meanwhile campaigning to keep the game oriented to their desire for the sport to belong to them and to serve their local communities.

The future of the sport will increasingly feature women's soccer as a visible part of the global game, following over a century of struggle by women to establish themselves in the sport as players, supporters, administrators, coaches, and commentators. Soccer is the fastest growing women's team sport in the world, and there are now hundreds of female professional players who play for elite professional teams in leagues like Women's Professional Soccer in the United States or the Bundesliga in Germany. The FIFA Women's World Cup is an event held every four years that now attracts considerable audiences on television worldwide, and today's stars such as the Brazilian Marta are globally famous and handsomely rewarded financially for their play, if not yet as richly remunerated as their male counterparts. The women's game has made vast strides on and off the field in the past two decades, with more women than ever before participating in the sport at both professional and amateur levels.

This recent growth has come after a century of stunted development from the late 19th century to the late 20th century, when women's soccer was effectively discriminated against by male-dominated authorities in most parts of the world. For example, in England, the popularity of women's soccer by 1920, epitomized by the nationwide fame of club team Dick, Kerr Ladies, threatened the male establishment in The Football Association, which banned women from playing at soccer stadia across the country. Only since the 1970s has that ban been lifted and women's soccer begun to recover from decades of restrictions and neglect by the authorities in England. By that decade, women's soccer was rapidly progressing around the world from the United States to Italy to China, aided by a cultural shift from the 1960s onward that saw women's participation in sport become less subject to formal and cultural discrimination.

Independent women's clubs and leagues began to organize competitions outside the structures regulating men's soccer, with nascent world championships set up in the 1970s. The governing authorities of men's soccer eventually took women's soccer under their umbrella, with the first FIFA Women's World Cup played in November 1991. By the end of the decade, the 1999 Women's World Cup in the United States made celebrities of the victorious American women's national team, playing in front of huge crowds in vast stadia and before millions of rapt viewers on television. In countries like Germany, the quality of women's soccer has improved enormously in the years since, with women's soccer rapidly advancing in fitness levels, the level of technique, and the intensity and sophistication of the coaching.

Whether played by men or women, the game—once called by J. C. Thring the "simplest game"—on the field of play in the 21st century retains its essence from its 19th-century origins, even as tactics, strategy, and rules have changed dramatically. Team formations that were once overwhelmingly offensive—19th-century teams lined up with more forwards than defenders—have now become defensively oriented, with fewer attackers and more defenders employed, and with the number of goals per game declining in professional play over the past century. Still, new, creative ways of play have sprung up to adapt and overcome defensive tactics, such as the "Total Football" of the Netherlands in the 1970s developed by coach Rinus Michels, with players moving more freely between positions, following the example set by Hungary in the 1950s. Individual geniuses in each decade, from Garrincha to Pelé to Johan Cruyff to Diego Maradona to Zinedine Zidane to Lionel Messi, have found new ways of unlocking even the tightest defenses, despite the increasing athleticism, size, and fitness levels of all players that has cut down on the space a creative player has to operate on the field. The ball remains an object able to be simply manipulated in amazing ways by the world's greatest talents. Similarly, though the focus of this volume is on the professional form of the game that has developed since the 19th century, participation in the sport globally continues to rapidly rise in both organized and unorganized forms. It remains a simple game to participate in, with more universal appeal than any other sport. Soccer as the world's sport remains today, for all its commercialization and orientation to the needs of television, full of enough magical mayhem in the run of play that it shows little sign of losing its momentum as the global game par excellence.

A

ADEMIR. B. 8 November 1922, Rio de Janeiro, Brazil. D. 11 May 1996. Ademir, as he was commonly known, was born Ademir Marques de Menezes, and was an outstanding forward for **Brazil** from 1945 to 1953. During that period, Ademir scored 32 goals in just 39 games for his country, and was the top scorer at the 1950 **FIFA World Cup**, scoring nine goals in only six games. He failed to score in the crucial last game of the competition, however, as Brazil lost to **Uruguay** 2-1, a result that made the Uruguayans World Cup winners for the second time and denied the Brazilians the title on home soil.

AFC ASIAN CUP. First contested in 1956, the AFC Asian Cup is the premier tournament for national teams in the **Asian Football Confederation (AFC)**. The winning team qualifies for the **FIFA Confederations Cup**. The first staging of the AFC Asian Cup was held in Hong Kong in 1956, and was contested by seven of the AFC's 12 affiliated nations. It has been held every four years since, apart from a three-year break in 2007. The competition has grown as the AFC has expanded its membership, with 24 teams entering the tournament for the 2007 edition. That year, the competition had more than one host nation for the first time: Indonesia, Malaysia, Thailand, and Vietnam all acted as host nations, causing considerable logistic problems with extensive travel between the nations. War-torn Iraq surprisingly won the AFC Asian Cup for the first time that year. The most successful nations in the AFC Asian Cup have been **Saudi Arabia**, **Iran**, and **Japan**, who have each won it three times.

AFC CHAMPIONS LEAGUE. The leading international club tournament organized by the **Asian Football Confederation (AFC)**, the AFC Champions League has been contested annually since its founding in 2002. The winning team qualifies for the annual **FIFA Club World Cup**. The number of clubs qualifying from each AFC member nation for the AFC Champions League is determined by each country's respective ranking in the confederation, based on the performance of its clubs in continental competition. The **Saudi Arabian** club Al-Ittihad has been the most successful team in the tournament's brief history, with three titles won up to the 2007–2008 season. Before the founding of the AFC Champions League, the AFC's premier club tournament was known as the Asian Champion Club Tournament, and prior to that, it was the long-running Asian Club Championship.

AFC U-19 CHAMPIONSHIP. The premier junior men's competition in Asia, organized by the governing **FIFA confederation** in the region, the **Asian Football Confederation (AFC)**, the AFC U-19 Championship is a biennial competition for national teams with players under the age of 19. The final stage consists of 16 teams, with the qualifying rounds open to all member nations of the AFC. It has been played since 1959, running on an annual basis until 1978. The most successful team has been the **Republic of Korea**, with 11 total championship victories, followed by Burma with seven titles, and Israel with six.

AFGHANISTAN. Soccer in Afghanistan and its national team is organized by the Afghanistan Football Federation (AFF), formed in 1933. Afghanistan affiliated with the **Fédération Internationale de Football Association (FIFA)** in 1948 and was a founding member of the **Asian Football Confederation (AFC)** in 1954. Afghanistan has never reached the **AFC Asian Cup** finals or the **FIFA World Cup** finals. It did not even enter the latter tournament's qualifying competitions between 1930 and 2002. Afghanistan made its only appearance in the **Olympic Games Football Tournament** in 1948, losing its single game 6-0 to Luxembourg in the preliminary round. Afghanistan's lack of success internationally is a result of its historically hampered domestic soccer organization, in part due to the difficult political and economic conditions of the country, especially after the **Russian** invasion in 1979. Under the rule of the Taliban regime from 1996 to 2001 in Afghanistan, players were banned from wearing shorts and short-sleeved jerseys, and games at the national stadium in Kabul were sometimes preceded by public executions. As a result of this domestic turmoil, Afghanistan did not play an international game between 1984 and 2002. After the fall of the Taliban, Afghanistan competed in the Asian Games football tournament in September 2002. Organization of the team has continued to prove problematic given the country's war-torn condition, and nine players absconded on a trip to **Italy** in 2004, prompting the AFF to disband the entire team. The team was reformed the next year, but all three FIFA World Cup qualification attempts since the fall of the Taliban have been unsuccessful.

AFRICA CUP OF NATIONS. The premier international tournament on the African continent, the Africa Cup of Nations has been organized by the governing body of soccer in Africa, the **Confederation of African Football (CAF)**, since 1957. The winner of the tournament earns the right to be CAF's entrant to the following **FIFA Confederations Cup**. The Africa Cup of Nations is held biennially in the African summer months, with 16 teams competing in the finals following a qualification tournament open to all member nations of CAF. The size of the competition has grown along with the membership of CAF as a whole since the Africa Cup of Nations was first held in Khartoum, Sudan, in 1957, with only three teams competing in the first finals tournament. Four teams had been initially scheduled to play in the inaugural 1957 competition, but **South Africa** refused to participate due to CAF's demand that they field a multiracial team. **Egypt** won the inaugural cup and has been the most successful team since, with a further five titles to their credit. **Ghana** and **Cameroon** have each won the tournament twice.

AJAX AMSTERDAM. Ajax Amsterdam is the most successful club team from the **Netherlands**, with 29 domestic league titles and four **UEFA Champions League** triumphs. Ajax was founded on 18 March 1900 in Amsterdam as "Football Club Ajax," succeeding two earlier failed attempts at forming clubs in Amsterdam known as "Union" and "Foot Ball Club Ajax" in the previous decade. They joined the top tier of the national Dutch championship in 1911, only to be relegated three years later. Ajax then returned to the first division in 1917, where they have remained ever since. Ajax won their first national championship the next year, though their golden age would come in the 1930s, when under legendary English manager Jack Reynolds, Ajax won five national championships in 10 years. They moved into the De Meer stadium in 1934, which remained their home for 60 years.

Ajax achieved world fame in the 1960s and 1970s as their domestic success blossomed into European glory: they won the UEFA Champions League (then known as the European Cup) in consecutive years from 1971 to 1973, led by the brilliant creative midfielder **Johan Cruyff** and playing a new attacking style of the game that became known as "**Total Football**" under coach **Rinus Michels**. In 1972, Ajax won the **Intercontinental Cup** for the first time. Ajax became known globally for their advanced youth training methods, developing a plethora of young players with outstanding technical skills, forming the heart of the Dutch national team that twice reached the **FIFA World Cup** final in the 1970s. Ajax won a further 11 national championships between 1975 and 2000, including a victory in the UEFA Champions League in 1995, followed by their second Intercontinental Cup title the same year. The next year, Ajax moved out of De Meer into the modern Amsterdam Arena, and, though still one of the leading three clubs domestically in the Netherlands, has not been as successful on the European stage in the past decade.

AKERS, MICHELLE. B. 1 February 1966, Santa Clara, California, United States. Michelle Akers is a former American international player. In 2002, she was named the FIFA Women's Player of the Century by the sport's global governing body, **Fédération Internationale de Football Association (FIFA)**, sharing the award with **Sun Wen** from **China**. She played for the **United States** from 1985 to 2000 as an attacking forward or midfielder, scoring 105 goals in 153 games for her country. Akers played in three **FIFA Women's World Cup** finals tournaments, scoring 12 goals in 13 games, and twice appearing in the final of the competition, in 1991 and 1999. The United States won both finals, giving Akers two FIFA Women's World Cup winners' medals. She also won a gold medal with the United States at the 1996 **Olympic Games Football Tournament**. Akers retired from playing in 2000.

AL-AHLY SPORTING CLUB. Founded in 1907 in the capital of **Egypt**, Cairo, Al-Ahly Sporting Club is probably the most successful and most popular club in Africa and across the Middle East today. In 2000, the **Confederation of African Football (CAF)** named Al-Ahly the African Club of the Century. This award was based on its unmatched title-winning success in Egypt and in continental competition. Domestically, Al-Ahly has won 34 national league championships since the founding of the Egyptian league in 1948, its only serious rivals being **Zamalek Sporting Club**. It has also dominated Africa's continental club competitions, with six titles in the **CAF Champions League** (originally known as the African Cup of Champions Clubs). Al-Ahly claims to have 50 million fans in Egypt and abroad, and its populist tradition stretches back to its name: "Ahly" translates into English as "national," with the club's origins lying in student unions rebelling against colonial rule from Great Britain. In 1925, membership in Al-Ahly's sporting club—whose best-known division soon came to be soccer—was restricted to Egyptians. Al-Ahly's popularity exploded in the 1950s following the founding of the Egyptian league in 1948, with Al-Ahly winning the first 10 titles contested, inspired by one of Egypt's finest players of all-time, El Fanagily. Its most successful manager has been **Portugal**'s Manuel José, with CAF Champions League wins in 2001, 2005, 2006, and 2008. It has appeared three times in the **FIFA Club World Cup**, a record for African teams, with its best result being third place in 2006.

AL-HILAL. **Saudi Arabia**'s most prominent and successful club team. Based in the country's capital, Riyadh, Al-Hilal has, by most accounts, been the most successful team in modern Asian football. Founded in 1957 and known as El-Olympy (Olympic Club) until 1958, its name was changed to Al-Hilal under a decree from Saudi King Saud Bin Abdul-Aziz Al-Saud.

They won their first trophy, the King's Cup, in 1961, and have garnered an average of more than one title a year since. Al-Hilal has dominated the Saudi Professional League since its formation in 1976, with 12 championship victories. The 1970s saw several big names, including **Brazil**'s legendary coach **Mário Zagallo** and superstar player **Rivelino**, attracted to Al-Hilal by the riches available in prosperous Saudi Arabia that filtered into the backing of the club. Many of Saudi Arabia's greatest players have enjoyed long spells with the club, including, in recent years, Sami Al Jabar and Mohamed Al-Deayea. Al-Hilal won two Asian Club Championship (now the **AFC Champions League**) titles in 1992 and 2000. The club plays in the nation's largest soccer stadium and home of the Saudi Arabian national team, the 67,000-capacity King Fahd Stadium. Their nickname is *Al-Zaeem*, meaning "the Boss," a name intended to reflect their strength in the region, though in the past decade, from 2001–2010, their rivals Al-Ittihad have been notably more successful, with six titles to Al-Hilal's three.

ALBANIA. The first Albanian club team, Vllaznia, was founded in 1920 with other clubs soon joining them, leading to the formation of the *Federata Shqiptare e Futbollit* (Football Association of Albania) as the governing body of soccer in Albania in 1930. Albania affiliated with the **Fédération Internationale de Football Association (FIFA)** in 1932 and was a founding member of the **Union of European Football Associations (UEFA)** in 1954. The first domestic Albanian championship was contested in 1930, featuring six teams. SK Tirana became the inaugural champions and has dominated Albanian soccer since, along with KS Dinamo Tirana, KS Vllaznia, and FK Partizani. Albania's national team played its first international match on 7 October 1946 against **Yugoslavia**, as the country's postwar Communist regime strengthened soccer's infrastructure in the country. Albania has never qualified for the **FIFA World Cup** or **UEFA European Football Championship** finals. Its best results have come in UEFA European Football Championship qualifiers. In December 1967, Albania's 0-0 draw with West **Germany** denied the West Germans qualification for the finals. Albania's most famous victory came in 2003, beating **Russia** 3-1 in their unsuccessful qualification campaign for the 2004 UEFA European Football Championship. Albania's highest-ever **FIFA ranking** is 62nd, which occurred in August 2006.

ALBERT, FLÓRIÁN. B. 15 September 1941, Hercegszántó, Hungary. Flórián Albert was a graceful, prolific goal-scoring forward for his native **Hungary** and Hungarian club team Ferencváros, and winner of the **European Footballer of the Year** award in 1967. Albert scored 31 goals in 75 games for Hungary between 1959 and 1974. He appeared in the **FIFA World**

Cup finals tournament on two occasions, in 1962 and 1966, scoring a total of four goals in seven games in the two competitions combined, as Hungary reached the quarterfinal stage on both occasions. He was the joint top scorer in the 1962 World Cup. Albert also won a bronze medal at the 1960 **Olympic Games Football Tournament** for his part in Hungary's third-place finish, scoring five goals in five games in the competition. With his club team Ferencváros, Albert won numerous Hungarian league championship winners' medals, and reached European glory with victory in the 1965 Inter-Cities Fairs Cup, the forerunner to the **UEFA Cup**. Albert retired in 1974, five years after a serious right leg injury limited his abilities on the field. In 2007, Ferencváros renamed their home stadium *Stadion Albert Flórián* (Flórián Albert Stadium) in Albert's honor.

ALCÁNTARA, PAOLINO. B. 7 October 1896, Iloilo City, Philippines. D. 13 February 1964. Paolino Alcántara was the first Asian player to appear for a European club, making his debut for **Barcelona** in **Spain** at the age of just 15, still the youngest player to date to play for the Spanish giants. He went on to have an extraordinary career for Barcelona, playing his entire career for the club and scoring a fantastic total of 357 goals in 357 games between 1912 and 1927. In that period, he won five Spanish championships and 10 Catalan championships with Barcelona. He remains the highest scorer in Barcelona's history. Alcántara's relatively slight appearance belied his potent striking ability. He had the ability to strike the ball with remarkable power and accuracy. Internationally, he briefly played for both the Philippines and Spain, taking up Spanish citizenship. He retired in 1927 to become a doctor and served on Barcelona's board of directors from 1931 to 1934.

ALTAFINI, JOSÉ. B. 24 August 1938, Piracicaba, Brazil. José Altafini, known as "Mazola" in his native **Brazil**, played for both the Brazilian and **Italian** national teams and was a prolific goal scorer. He spent most of his career playing in Italy after beginning his career with Palmeiras in Brazil and is best known for his sensational seven years at **AC Milan**, scoring 146 goals for the club in 246 total appearances. Altafini won two league championships with AC Milan, in 1959 and 1962, and most famously scored twice in the final of the 1963 **European Cup**, as AC Milan became the first Italian team to win Europe's premier club competition by beating **Benfica** 2-1. Altafini again appeared in the final of the same competition a decade later, playing for **Juventus** in their defeat to **Ajax Amsterdam**.

Altafini began his international career playing for Brazil, earning the nickname "Mazola" for his resemblance to the brilliant Italian forward **Valentino Mazzola**, and appeared at the 1958 **FIFA World Cup** for Brazil, when they won the competition for the first time. Altafini, only 19 at the time, played in Brazil's first three games of the competition, scoring twice in their opening game against **Austria**, but did not feature in the semifinals or final of the competition. Following his move to Italy after the World Cup in 1958, he began representing the Italian national team in the 1960s, playing two games at the 1962 World Cup for his adopted country. Altafini retired in 1976.

AMATEURISM. The vast majority of soccer is played on an amateur basis, with no monetary reward for players, but the overwhelming majority of media coverage of the game focuses on the elite professional level. Without the vast participation in soccer at amateur level, soccer would not have the status it does around the world, and its origins as an organized game also lie at the amateur level: soccer was first formalized and popularized by the avid amateurs of England's elite public schools in the mid-19th century. Soccer only became professional in England in the 1880s when it was legalized by the sport's governing body, **The Football Association**. This led to the formation of the first professional league in the world in 1888, the **Football League**. The decision to legalize professionalism was controversial, with some famous clubs such as **Corinthians** remaining stoutly amateur and a breakaway Amateur Football Association formed. Amateurism in soccer at the highest levels lasted in most countries around the world for decades longer than in Great Britain. The sport took root around the world in the first half of the 20th century, and most countries now have fully professional leagues. Amateur leagues continue to thrive worldwide with vast organizational apparatuses supporting them and funding sometimes coming via subsidy from the professional level.

ANDRADE, JOSÉ LEANDRO. B. 22 November 1901, Salto, Uruguay. D. 5 October 1957. José Leandro Andrade was a **Uruguayan** player who played a key role in his country's victory at the 1930 **FIFA World Cup**, held in Uruguay. He made 34 total appearances for his country. Andrade won two gold medals in the **Olympic Games Football Tournaments** of 1934 and 1938. Playing as a defensive midfielder for most of his career, he also starred for leading Uruguayan club teams **Nacional** and **Peñarol**, winning the national league championship on four occasions.

ARGENTINA. Argentina's national and club teams have proven to be among the most successful on the international stage, including global success in the **FIFA World Cup** and **Intercontinental Cup**. Soccer is by far the most popular sport in Argentina, with more than 3,000 club teams in existence, many with a fanatic culture of support that has developed since soccer was brought to Argentina in the mid-19th century by British immigrants working in the capital, Buenos Aires. The first recognized game took place on 20 June 1867, contested by two teams from the Buenos Aires Football Club, founded earlier that month by two British expatriates, Thomas and James Hogg. A key pioneer of the game was an immigrant from **Scotland**, schoolmaster Alexander Watson Hutton, who founded the Argentine Association Football League on 21 February 1893, renamed the "Argentine Football Association" (AFA) in 1903. In 1912, the AFA became the first national association from South America to join international soccer's global governing body, **Fédération Internationale de Football Association (FIFA)**. In 1934, after mergers with competing amateur organizations and several further name changes, the AFA's official name was changed to *Asociación del Fútbol Argentino* in Spanish, as it remains today.

The Argentinean national team played its first official match in 1901 against **Uruguay**, and has since been the most successful team in the South American continental championship, the **Copa América**, winning it for the first time in 1921 and winning 14 titles as of August 2010. Argentina's first appearance in the final of a global tournament came in 1928, when they lost to Uruguay in the **Olympic Games Football Tournament**. They lost again to the same country in the first World Cup finals two years later. They would not reach the final again for another 48 years, winning the World Cup on home soil in 1978, beating the **Netherlands** 3-1 after extra time in the final of the competition. Argentina would then reach the World Cup finals consecutively in 1986 and 1990 under the inspiration of the greatest-ever Argentinean player, **Diego Maradona**, winning the first final in **Mexico** and losing the second in **Italy**, both times against West **Germany**. Argentina has continued to rank among the global elite of national teams since, winning the 1992 **FIFA Confederations Cup** and finishing runners-up in 1995 and 2005. In 2009, **Lionel Messi** became the second Argentinean to be voted the **FIFA World Player of the Year**.

Argentina's club teams have been equally successful internationally. Professional club soccer began in Argentina in 1931 with the renegade *Liga Argentina de Football* won by **Boca Juniors**. The next season, **River Plate** and **Independiente** finished tied at the top of the league standings, with River Plate winning a play-off game 3-0 to decide the championship. Those three clubs have since dominated Argentinean soccer in the ensuing years, with 70 domestic league championships won between them: 33 for River Plate, 23 for Boca Juniors, and 14 for Independiente. On the continental stage, Independiente has been the most successful, winning seven **Copa Libertadores** titles, South America's leading continental club tournament. In global competition, Boca Juniors have won one Intercontinental Cup, Independiente has two titles in that competition, and River Plate has won it once.

Women's soccer has been slow to develop in Argentina, long hampered by cultural prejudice against female participation in the sport and a lack of organization by the governing AFA. A national league was set up in the 1990s, and Argentina qualified for its first **FIFA Women's World Cup** in 2003, though the team did not win a game at the tournament. The AFA has made active efforts in recent years to increase participation and improve the facilities for female players.

ARSENAL FOOTBALL CLUB. Arsenal Football Club, or Arsenal as they are usually referred to, is one of the leading professional clubs in **England**, currently playing in the **Premier League**, a competition they have won on three occasions since it began play in 1992. Previous to that, Arsenal won eight **Football League** championship titles, the highest level of league play in England before the inauguration of the Premier League. They have also won the **Football Association Challenge Cup** on 12 occasions. Arsenal was originally founded in 1886 at Woolwich Arsenal Armament Factory in south London, becoming known as Woolwich Arsenal when the club became professional in 1891. In 1913, they moved to north London, and began playing at Arsenal Stadium in the Highbury area of London, soon dropping the "Woolwich" part of their name. Arsenal achieved little success until the 1930s, when innovative manager Herbert Chapman took charge of the club, leading them to their first league title in 1931, with several more titles following that decade.

Further success ensued for Arsenal in the postwar period. Following their first European trophy in 1970, the 1971 season was a particular highlight, as Arsenal won the double of the league title and F.A. Cup. Arsenal next won the league in 1989, and then again in 1991, under manager George Graham. Another period of great success for Arsenal followed the arrival of French coach Arsene Wenger in 1996, with the club winning the league title and F.A. Cup double again in both 1998 and 2002. Arsenal then won the league two years later in 2004 without losing a game the entire season, with star striker **Thierry Henry** in particularly inspirational form. In 2006, Arsenal reached the final of the **UEFA Champions League** for the first time, though they lost at that stage to **Barcelona**. That same year marked the end of the club's long tenure at Arsenal Stadium, when they moved to the newly built Emirates Stadium, also located in north London.

AS SAINT-ÉTIENNE. Founded as a professional club in 1933, AS Saint-Étienne is one of **France**'s most famous club teams. It enjoyed particularly prominent success internationally in the 1970s. AS Saint-Étienne has won a joint record (tied with **Olympique de Marseille**) 10 French league championships, including four in the club's golden era of the 1970s, when they also won four French Cups. That same decade, they became the first French team to reach the final of Europe's premier international club competition, the European Cup (now the **UEFA Champions League**), losing 1-0 to **Bayern Munich** at Hampden Park in Glasgow, **Scotland**. Saint-Étienne has been less successful over the past three decades, with their last major trophy coming in 1981. They play at Stade Geoffroy-Guichard, opened in 1931 and host to games at the 1998 **FIFA World Cup**. *See also* KEÏTA, SALIF; MILLA, ROGER; PLATINI, MICHEL.

ASANTE KOTOKO. Asante Kotoko is a club based in Kumasi, **Ghana**, and was the leading team in that country and, arguably, in the entire African continent in the 20th century. Asante Kotoko, nicknamed the "Porcupine Warriors" due to the porcupine in their club logo, have garnered 21 national titles and two **CAF Champions League** titles to be crowned as Africa's best in both 1970 and 1983. They are based at Baba Yara Stadium, named after one of their former stars, a 40,000-capacity venue that played host to **Africa Cup of Nations** games in both the 2000 and 2008 tournaments.

ASIAN FOOTBALL CONFEDERATION (AFC). The governing body of soccer in Asia, the Asian Football Confederation is one of the six continental **FIFA confederations**. The AFC currently has 46 national member associations and is by far the largest of the FIFA confederations in terms of population size. The AFC was formed in 1946, and its headquarters are in Kuala Lumpur, Malaysia. Its responsibilities include regulating the game, promoting the grassroots development of soccer, and organizing major club, national team, and youth competitions, such as the **AFC Asian Cup** for national teams, the **AFC Champions League** for the leading club teams across the continent, and junior developmental tournaments such as the **AFC U-19 Championship**.

ASSISTANT REFEREE. The leading **referee** on the field has at least two assistant referees who provide advice for the referee when making decisions, as requested by the lead official. Two assistant referees run either touchline, using a flag or wireless communication through a headset to signal to the referee for infringements and to offer other assistance as required. A fourth official was added to international games by the **Fédération Internationale de Football Association (FIFA)** in 1991, initially serving as a reserve official in case of injury to one of the other referees, but now playing a role that has since taken on further responsibilities in managing the technical area for coaches on the touchline. The **Union of European Football Associations (UEFA)** has also tried the addition of two further assistant referees placed behind each goal line in an attempt to provide more accurate advice for the referee on disputed calls in the penalty area. *See also* LAWS OF THE GAME.

ASSOCIAZIONE CALCIO MILAN (AC Milan). One of **Italy**'s biggest clubs, commonly known as AC Milan, the *"Rossoneri"* (a nickname in reference to their famous red-and-black shirts) have impressive trophy counts, both domestically and internationally, and a hugely passionate fan base. AC Milan was founded in 1899 by British expatriates, originally as Milan Football and Cricket Club. The name was not changed to its present form, Associazione Calcio Milan, until 1939. By that time, AC Milan had established themselves as a leading force in Italian soccer and, in 1926, had taken up residence in what became the legendary **San Siro** stadium. But after three Italian league championships in their first decade of existence (1901, 1906, and 1907), AC Milan endured a 44-year wait for their fourth title, in 1951.

The 1960s would prove to be a golden era for the club, with Giovanni Trapattoni and **Gianni Rivera** leading the club to European glory. AC Milan won the European Cup (now known as the **UEFA Champions League**) in 1963, a **UEFA Cup Winners' Cup** title in 1968, and a second European Cup in 1969. That same year also saw AC Milan win the **Intercontinental Cup**. The next two decades saw far less success for AC Milan, and they were even relegated out of the top Italian division in 1980 as punishment after an investigation into match fixing and illegal betting by the Italian authorities in what was known as the *totonero* scandal. AC Milan made a resurgence in the 1990s backed by the money of chairman Silvio Berlusconi, an outspoken television mogul and future Italian prime minister. Since Berlusconi's takeover in 1986, AC Milan has won seven Italian championships and five UEFA Champions League titles. The club also won the Intercontinental Cup in 1989 and 1990 and became the first European team to win the **FIFA Club World Cup** in 2007. *See also* ALTAFINI, JOSÉ; BAGGIO, ROBERTO; BARESI, FRANCO; BECKHAM, DAVID; DESAILLY, MARCEL; GULLIT, RUUD; KAKÁ; LAUDRUP, BRIAN; LIEDHOLM, NILS; MALDINI, PAOLO; NORDAHL, GUNNAR; PAPIN, JEAN-PIERRE; RIJKAARD, FRANK; RIVALDO; RONALDINHO; RONALDO; SACCHI, ARRIGO; SCHIAFFINO, JUAN ALBERTO; SHEVCHENKO, ANDRIY; VAN BASTEN, MARCO; WEAH, GEORGE.

AUSTRALIA. Soccer is not the most popular sport in Australia, languishing behind cricket, rugby, and Australian Rules Football as a spectator sport. But soccer in Australia is a fast-growing sport, with almost half a million registered participants and a professional league, the A-League, which was established in 2005. Soccer in Australia is governed by Football Federation

Australia (FFA), which was known until 2005 as the Australian Soccer Association. Early administrative problems plagued the game after its introduction into Australia in the late 19th century, with the Australian Soccer Association suspended from the **Fédération Internationale de Football Association (FIFA)** in 1960 for unpaid fines. The association was reformed in 1961 and affiliated with FIFA in 1963 after paying the fines owed to soccer's international governing body. Australia's men's team, known as the "Socceroos," have appeared in two **FIFA World Cup** tournaments, with a **FIFA ranking** high of 14th achieved in September 2009. Australia fell at the first round of the FIFA World Cup finals tournament in 1974, their first appearance in it, and reached the last 16 in their next World Cup appearance in 2006 in **Germany**, exiting after losing 1-0 to eventual champion **Italy**.

Since 2005, Australia has been a member of the **Asian Football Confederation (AFC)**, though this is a geographic curiosity as the country is not part of the Asian continent. For many decades, Australia participated in the **Oceania Football Confederation (OFC)**, along with neighboring countries such as **New Zealand** and Papua New Guinea. Despite dominating the Oceanic region, Australia left the OFC to join the AFC, in part, because the OFC does not have a direct qualification spot to the World Cup, and to allow its club teams to compete in the more lucrative **AFC Champions League**. Australia's professional men's league, the A-League, was established in 2005, replacing the National Soccer League (NSL) as the nation's premier club competition, with eight founding members: Adelaide United, Central Coast Mariners, Melbourne Victory, Newcastle Jets, New Zealand Knights, Perth Glory, Queensland Roar, and Sydney FC. The New Zealand Knights have since been replaced by the Wellington Phoenix, and two expansion teams were added for the 2009–2010 season, Gold Coast United and North Queensland Fury.

AUSTRIA. Soccer is one of the most popular sports in Austria, first played there in 1890 by English gardeners in Vienna working for the famous Rothschild banking family. Four years later, the country's first clubs were formed in Vienna, and Austria's national association, the Austrian Football Association, or *Österreichischer Fußball-Bund* (ÖFB), was founded in 1904, affiliating with the **Fédération Internationale de Football Association (FIFA)** the next year. In 1954, Austria became a founding member of the **Union of European Football Associations (UEFA)**. Austria was one of the world's leading soccer nations for much of the period from 1930 to 1960, finishing fourth at the 1934 **FIFA World Cup** and in third place, their best-ever finish in seven appearances in the tournament, at the 1954 World Cup. They also won a silver medal at the 1936 **Olympic Games Football Tournament**.

Austria's national team in the 1930s, coached by the legendary **Hugo Meisl** and known as the *Wunderteam*, went to the 1934 World Cup as favorites and introduced an attractive, quick-passing style to international soccer. Austria, though, lost their semifinal to World Cup hosts, **Italy**, in poor playing conditions. Meisl passed away in 1937, and Austria was subsumed by Nazi **Germany** in the 1938 Anschluss, with many Austrians forced to play for Germany at the 1938 World Cup. Austria's top level of club team play is known as the Bundesliga, currently consisting of 10 teams. *See also* BICAN, JOSEF; HAPPEL, ERNST; SINDELAR, MATTHIAS.

B

BAGGIO, ROBERTO. B. 18 February 1967, Caldogno, Italy. Roberto Baggio is one of the greatest **Italian** players of all time and was the winner of both the **FIFA World Player of the Year** award and the **European Footballer of the Year** award in 1993 at the peak of his career. The next year, Baggio led Italy to the final of the 1994 **FIFA World Cup** and was generally regarded as their best-performing player in the tournament. Italy, however, lost the final game to **Brazil** on a penalty shoot-out, with Baggio famously missing the decisive penalty kick. Baggio played a total of 56 games for Italy, usually operating as a creative forward and scoring 27 goals for his country. He also played for Italy at the 1990 FIFA World Cup, where they finished in third place. Baggio played his club career for several Italian teams, his best period coming with **Juventus**, with whom he won the **UEFA Cup** in 1993 and the Italian league championship in 1994 before he was transferred to **AC Milan**, where he again won the Italian league championship in 1996. He also played for **Internazionale**, Bologna, and Brescia before his retirement from playing in 2004. Baggio was nicknamed the "Divine Ponytail" in a nod to his hairstyle and his Buddhist beliefs, and was known on the field for his stylish, skillful play.

BALL. The ball is the basic, ever-present element in all forms of soccer, from recreational to professional variants. In the professional modern global game under the auspices of the **Fédération Internationale de Football Association (FIFA)**, the **Laws of the Game** strictly define the limits on the shape, weight, size, and pressure of the ball to be used in professional games. Law 2 of the Laws of the Game states that the ball must be spherical and be "made of leather or other suitable material." Law 2 further specifies that the ball must have a circumference of no more than 28 inches and no less than 27 inches, weigh no more than 16 ounces and no less than 14 ounces at the start of a game, and have a pressure equal to 8.5 lbs. per sq. inch at sea level. At the recreational level, the simplicity of soccer means these requirements are rarely met, and balls are fashioned out of anything roughly round enough to play with. In professional soccer, the weight and texture of the ball has changed dramatically over the past century. From the 19th until the mid-20th century, balls were stitched leather laced together around a central bladder made out of animal skin, a material that had a tendency to gain weight in wet conditions or to burst completely, delaying the game. Plastic balls with valves were introduced in the 1950s to alleviate this problem, and white balls, able to be seen better on color television, were introduced at the 1970 **FIFA World Cup**. Ball design has since become an area of aesthetic competition between different ball manufacturers, with ever-more intricate cosmetic variants made to their look and feel. Slight changes to the ball's materials and surface continue to alter the game in subtle ways. New balls are usually released for major tournaments to maximize the ball's marketing potential for the manufacturer, at times, to the dissatisfaction of players not used to any changes that might result in unusual ball movement.

BALLON D'OR. The Ballon D'Or, or "Golden Ball" in English, is the name given in French by the magazine *France Football* to the player their panel of 96 journalists from around the world judges to have been the best in each calendar year. It has been awarded by *France Football* magazine since 1956 and has long been considered one of the most prestigious honors in the world game, though it was initially awarded only to European players. The first winner was **Stanley Matthews** of Blackpool and **England**. Until 1994, only players eligible for a European national team were nominated for the award, but from 1995 onward, the award was opened up to all players on European club teams. In 2007, this was opened up further to include all players of every nationality from all clubs around the world. In 2010, it was announced the Ballon D'Or was merging with the **FIFA World Player of the Year** award, creating the **FIFA** Ballon d'Or. Three players have won the award three times: **Johan Cruyff** of the **Netherlands**, **Michel Platini** of **France**, and **Marco van Basten** of the Netherlands. With 18 wins, clubs from the **Italian** league have provided the greatest number of Ballon D'Or award winners.

BANKS, GORDON. B. 30 December 1937, Sheffield, England. Gordon Banks was **England**'s **goalkeeper** for their victorious campaign at the 1966 **FIFA World Cup** and is considered among the greatest goalkeepers in soccer history. He used his agility to dominate the goal despite lacking outstanding size. He played 73 games for England, conceding only 57 total goals in those games. Banks played for England at the 1970 World Cup, making a famous save from **Pelé** in the first round, but missed England's defeat in the quarterfinals to West **Germany** due to sickness. His performances at club level in England were equally impressive, though Banks never played for a major English club. His only team honors were two League Cup trophies, with Leicester City in 1964 and Stoke City 1972, with Banks awarded the Footballer of the Year award in the latter season.

BARCELONA. Founded on 20 November 1899 by Swiss businessman Hans Gamper, Barcelona, from the Catalan region of **Spain**, has become one of the most popular and successful club teams in the world, with 170,000 members. Gamper began the club by putting a note in a local sports magazine in October 1899 calling for players, and he found 11 players to form the club with him by the next month. Englishman Gualteri Wild became the first president of the club, and the team had considerable success in its early decades, with numerous Catalan championship victories. Barcelona won one national Spanish league championship before the Second World War, in 1929, but it was in the postwar period that Barcelona established themselves as an all-powerful national force, winning seven Spanish league championships between 1945 and 1960. In 1957, Barcelona opened their legendary stadium, the breathtaking Camp Nou.

Yet, despite big name signings, including the legendary **Johan Cruyff**, the team would not achieve significant success in European competition until after 1979, with **Diego Maradona** starring for the club in the 1980s. Their glory years in the 20th century came in the 1990s, with Cruyff now as Barcelona's head coach, when they won six Spanish Championships and reached the pinnacle of the European game with a victory in the European Cup in 1992, beating Sampdoria at **Wembley Stadium**. The club would again win Europe's biggest prize, now renamed the **UEFA Champions League**, in 2006 and 2009, with a star-studded team playing attacking, aesthetically pleasing soccer, led by the likes of Brazilian **Ronaldinho** and Argentinean **Lionel Messi**. Messi, the 2009 **FIFA World Player of the Year**, played an instrumental role in the club's remarkable sweep of trophies during 2009, as Barcelona won the Spanish Championship, the Spanish Cup (the *Copa del Rey*), the Spanish Super Cup, the **UEFA Super Cup**, and the **FIFA Club World Cup**, an unprecedented set of achievements in a single year in global soccer by one team. *See also* ALCÁNTARA, PAOLINO; HENRY, THIERRY; HERRERA, HELENIO; KOCSIS, SÁNDOR; KUBALA, LÁSZLÓ; LAUDRUP, MICHAEL; MICHELS, RINUS; NEESKENS, JOHAN; RIJKAARD, FRANK; RIVALDO; ROMÁRIO; RONALDINHO; RONALDO; SIMONSEN, ALLAN; STOICHKOV, HRISTO; ZAMORA, RICARDO.

BARESI, FRANCO. B. 8 May 1960, Travagliato, Italy. Franco Baresi was an **Italian** player, and one of the finest defenders in the history of the sport. He played his entire club career for **AC Milan**, making his debut in 1978 and retiring in 1997 after appearing in more than 700 games for the team, including 531 of them in *Serie A*, Italy's top division, which AC Milan won six times with Baresi anchoring the team on defense. AC Milan also won three European Cup titles during Baresi's long tenure with the team, in 1989, 1990, and 1994 (in the latter year, known as the **UEFA Champions League**), along with two **Intercontinental Cup** titles, in 1989 and 1990. For the Italian national team, Baresi won a **FIFA World Cup** winners' medal in 1982, though he did not play in Italy's triumph at the tournament in **Spain**. He played for Italy again at the 1990 World Cup on home soil, where they earned third place. He captained Italy at the 1994 World Cup in the **United States**, playing in the defeat in the final to **Brazil** and missing a crucial penalty in the decisive penalty shoot-out. He retired from international soccer after 81 games for his country and with a reputation as one of the best defenders of all time.

BATISTUTA, GABRIEL. B. 1 February 1969, Reconquista, Argentina. Gabriel Batistuta is the all-time leading scorer for **Argentina**'s national team, having tallied 56 goals in just 78 games for his country between 1991 and 2002. He was a fast, powerful forward with a blistering and accurate shot. Batistuta appeared at three **FIFA World Cup** finals tournaments, though Argentina did not progress further than the quarterfinals with Batistuta on any of those occasions. His greatest international success came in 1993 when he played a major role in Argentina's victory in the **Copa América**. He scored twice in the final as Argentina defeated **Mexico** 2-1. At club level, the longest spell of Batistuta's career came playing for Fiorentina in **Italy** from 1991 to 2000, though his greatest honor came after he moved to AS Roma in 2000, winning the Italian league championship in 2001. He retired in 2005.

BAYERN MUNICH. Bayern Munich has by some distance been the most successful club from **Germany** on the domestic and international stages, with 21 German league championships and four **UEFA Champions League** victories to their credit. Bayern Munich was founded on 27 February 1900 by a dozen men led by Franz John, who broke away from the club team MTV 1879 Munich to form Bayern Munich. The club won one German championship in 1932 before the intercession of the Second World War. Bayern Munich only established themselves as a dominant force in German soccer after postwar reconstruction in the 1950s. In the 1960s, they began their ascent, winning the German Cup in 1966, 1967, and 1969, and achieved their first European success with victory in the **UEFA Cup Winners' Cup** in 1967, beating **Rangers Football Club** 1-0 in the final. By this point, Bayern Munich was in the top division of German soccer, and they won their first league championship in 1969, setting off on an unprecedented and unmatched run in German soccer history. Before the century was out, they would win a further 13 national league titles, five German cups, and three consecutive European Cup (now UEFA Champions League) titles from 1974 to 1976, when Bayern Munich was clearly the best team in Europe. The heart of their mid-1970s team was three of Germany's greatest-ever players, **goalkeeper Sepp Maier**, the imperious roving defender **Franz Beckenbauer,** and the stout, deadly forward **Gerd Müller**. Bayern Munich would crown this period with global success by also winning the **Intercontinental Cup** in 1976, defeating the South American champions Cruzeiro from **Brazil**. Bayern Munich continued to consistently win trophies domestically over the next three decades, often led by Germany's leading players, such as **Karl-Heinz Rummenigge** and **Lothar Matthäus**. Bayern Munich would finally reach the pinnacle of European soccer again in 2001, winning the UEFA Champions League on penalties in the final against **Spain's** Valencia. They followed this with their second Intercontinental Cup title, defeating the South American champions, **Boca Juniors**. A membership-based club, Bayern Munich currently has more than 140,000 registered members, and since 2005 has played at the ultramodern Allianz Arena, a 70,000-capacity 2006 **FIFA World Cup** venue. *See also* BREITNER, PAUL; DONOVAN, LANDON; KAHN, OLIVER; KLINSMANN, JÜRGEN; PAPIN, JEAN-PIERRE.

BEACH SOCCER. As the name indicates, beach soccer is an organized variant of soccer that is played on a surface composed of sand. At international level, the **Laws of the Game** specified under **Fédération Internationale de Football Association (FIFA)** auspices require the sand to be fine and at least 40 centimeters deep. The field is rectangular, with a required width between 26 and 28 meters at either goal line and with sidelines between 26 and 28 meters in length. The smaller playing area and softer surface of beach soccer in comparison to regular outdoor soccer produces more shots on goal, more goals on average per game, and encourages agile, acrobatic moves. Five players are on each team, and shoes are not allowed to be worn. The games last for 36 minutes each, with three referees officiating. Beach soccer has been played informally for decades but began to be seriously organized only in the 1990s, with the first professional beach soccer tournament held in Miami Beach, featuring teams from the **United States, Brazil, Italy**, and **Argentina**. The first beach soccer world championship was held in 1995 and was won by Brazil, and the success of these events led to the creation of the Pro Beach Soccer Tour in 1996, with teams traveling to four continents for games. A European Pro Beach Soccer league was launched in 1998, with considerable success. In 2005, FIFA took over organization of the game, and the first FIFA Beach Soccer World Cup was held that year. **France** won the first tournament, which, since then, has been held annually; Brazil has been dominant, with four straight victories from 2006 to 2009.

BECKENBAUER, FRANZ. B. 11 September 1945, Munich, Germany. Franz Beckenbauer is the only man to have both captained and coached a **FIFA World Cup** winning team, doing so with West **Germany** in 1974 and 1990 respectively. He is regarded as the greatest German player of all time, having established an innovative presence in the game by playing a consistently creative role from initially defensive positions on the field. Beckenbauer began his professional career with **Bayern Munich** in 1964, leading the club to the top tier of German soccer, the Bundesliga. He made his debut for West Germany the next year and played in the World Cup in 1966, taking home a runners-up medal after a 4-2 defeat in the final to **England**. Bayern Munich went on to achieve ever-greater success in the late 1960s with Beckenbauer anchoring the team, winning the West German Cup in 1966, 1967, and 1969, the **UEFA Cup Winners' Cup** in 1967 and, after Beckenbauer took over the team captaincy in 1968, the Bundesliga championship in 1969.

The 1970s would prove to be Beckenbauer's most glorious years as a player; he began to play a new role as a *libero*, not only organizing the team on defense but also bringing the ball forward to launch attack after attack. The German media saluted his overall dominance of the game by nicknaming him "*Der Kaiser*" (the Emperor). The 1970 World Cup saw West Germany fall 4-3 to **Italy** in the semifinals, but in 1974 on home soil, Beckenbauer captained his country to their second World Cup championship when they defeated the **Netherlands** 2-1 in the final. Beckenbauer and his teammates had preceded this with victory in the **UEFA European Football Championship** in 1972. In club soccer, Bayern Munich reached new heights with Beckenbauer playing a starring role, winning the Bundesliga three successive times from 1972 to 1974 and dominating the continent with **European Cup** titles in 1974, 1975, and 1976, followed by victory in the **Intercontinental Cup** that same year. Beckenbauer won the **European Footballer of the Year** award in both 1972 and 1976. In 1977, Beckenbauer moved to the riches of the **North American Soccer League** in the **United States**, winning the Most Valuable Player award in his first season with the New York Cosmos and going on to win the Soccer Bowl three times with the Cosmos. Beckenbauer returned to the Bundesliga for two seasons with Hamburg from 1981 to 1982, and then spent one last season back with the Cosmos preceding his retirement in 1983.

Just a year later, Beckenbauer was named head coach of the West German national team, replacing Jupp Derwall, whose team had failed at the 1984 UEFA European Football Championship. Beckenbauer led West Germany to the final of the 1986 World Cup in Mexico, where they lost to a **Diego Maradona**–inspired **Argentina** team, but they would win the World Cup for the third time four years later under Der Kaiser, beating England on penalties in the semifinals and taking revenge on Argentina 1-0 in the final. This made

Beckenbauer the first man to both captain and head coach World Cup–winning teams. Beckenbauer then moved into club management in the early 1990s before becoming an administrator. He led the hosting of the 2006 World Cup staged in Germany and joined the **FIFA Executive Committee** in 2007.

BECKHAM, DAVID. B. 2 May 1975, London, England. Though not considered one of the greatest players in the history of the sport, **England**'s David Beckham is certainly one of its most globally famous faces. Beckham achieved his greatest success with his first club, **Manchester United**, making his professional debut at the age of 17 in September 1992 against Brighton and Hove Albion in the Rumbelows Cup. He would not establish himself as a first-team player in the **Premier League** for Manchester United until 1995, but he proved to be integral to the team that went on to win the league championship and **Football Association Challenge Cup** double the next year in 1996. Under Scottish manager **Alex Ferguson**, Manchester United would hit its peak in 1999 when, with Beckham's visionary passing at the fulcrum of the midfield, Manchester United won the treble of the Premier League, the F.A. Cup, and the **UEFA Champions League**. This earned Beckham second place in **FIFA World Player of the Year** voting, a feat he would repeat in 2001 as Manchester United won the Premier League again. A sixth league title would come the next year, his final season with Manchester United.

Beckham moved on to **Real Madrid** in **Spain** in 2003, an enormously lucrative transfer financially for him, but leading to a less successful time on the field, as the Spanish giants won the league title just once in his four years there, in his final season in 2007. Beckham then moved to **Major League Soccer (MLS)** in the **United States** for another moneymaking contract with the Los Angeles Galaxy, twice joining **AC Milan** on loan in the MLS offseason. Internationally, Beckham has made more than 100 appearances for England since his debut in 1996, scoring in three separate **FIFA World Cup** finals tournaments. Beckham has been both adored and vilified as captain of the national team and its most famous player by the English public. His sending off for kicking Diego Simeone in the second round of the 1998 World Cup against **Argentina** led to considerable abuse for Beckham in the media and from fans. He came back, though, to score the decisive goal against Greece that sent England to the 2002 World Cup finals and earned him legendary status in England. Despite his considerable success on the field, Beckham is perhaps best known for his good looks and celebrity marriage to pop star Victoria Adams, which have earned him unprecedented sponsorship deals and celebrity fame in the world of soccer.

BELANOV, IGOR. B. 25 September 1960, Odessa, Soviet Union. Igor Belanov is a former Ukrainian player and star for the **Soviet Union** national team during the period that Ukraine was a part of the Soviet Union. He was the 1986 **European Footballer of the Year**, playing for outstanding teams at both club level with Dynamo Kiev and international level with the Soviet Union under innovative **Valery Lobanovski**, who coached both teams. That year, Dynamo Kiev won the **UEFA Cup Winners' Cup**, with Belanov's speed and power central to the club's European triumph, and he was the top scorer in the competition. Belanov also scored four goals at the **FIFA World Cup**, played that year in **Mexico**, as the Soviet Union reached the last 16 of the competition. Two years later, Belanov's Soviet Union reached the final of the **UEFA European Football Championship**, losing to the **Netherlands**, with Belanov missing a penalty in that game. The next year, Belanov was allowed to leave the Soviet Union and pursue his career in the West, moving to Borussia Mönchengladbach in West **Germany**. The move did not work out for Belanov, who soon left the club for a German second-division team, eventually returning to play in Ukraine, and then retiring in 1997.

BELGIUM. Soccer is the most popular sport in Belgium. The Royal Belgian Football Association (RBFA) was founded in 1895 and currently has 450,000 affiliated members, approximately 4 percent of the nation's population. The RBFA affiliated with the **Fédération Internationale de Football Association (FIFA)** in 1904 and was a founding member of the **Union of European Football Associations (UEFA)** in 1954. The RBFA organizes the Belgian national team and the domestic league. Belgium's national team, nicknamed the "Red Devils," has an impressive record in international play given the small size of the country, with a highest-ever **FIFA ranking** of 16th in 2003. Belgium's first international game came in 1904, with its strongest period of performance coming during the 1980s and 1990s when the country qualified for six straight **FIFA World Cups** led by star midfielder **Enzo Scifo**. Their best World Cup performance came at the 1986 tournament held in Mexico, where they lost in the semifinals 2-0 to eventual winner **Argentina**, and then lost again in the third-place play-off to **France** to finish in fourth place. Belgium reached the final of the 1980 **UEFA European Football Championship** after topping a first-round group that included **Italy**, **England**, and **Spain**, and then lost 2-1 to West **Germany**. The top echelon in Belgium's domestic league structure is currently known as the Jupiler Pro League, which was first organized by the RBFA in 1895. **Royal Sporting Club Anderlecht**, based in the capital, Brussels, is the most successful club in Belgian history, having won 29 domestic championships along with two **UEFA Cup** victories and two **UEFA Cup Winners' Cup** titles. *See also* HEYSEL STADIUM DISASTER; VAN HIMST, PAUL.

BELLOUMI, LAKHDAR. B. 29 December 1958, Mascara, Algeria. Lakhdar Belloumi was the African Footballer of the Year in 1981 and one of his continent's best performers on the international stage in the 1980s, appearing for his native Algeria at both the 1982 and 1986 **FIFA World Cups**. His most famous moment came at the 1982 World Cup when he scored the winning goal for Algeria against West **Germany**, though Algeria did not advance past the first-round stage of the competition. A creative playmaker, Belloumi spent almost his entire club career in his native Algeria, retiring in 1999 and pursuing a career as a coach. *See also* MADJER, RABAH.

BENFICA. Benfica, based in **Portugal**, is one of the most successful club teams in the history of European soccer. A multisport club founded in 1904, Benfica was an original member of Portugal's national league when it started play in 1933 and have since won the title 31 times. Their most glorious period came in the early 1960s under the coaching of Hungarian **Béla Guttmann** when they ended **Real Madrid**'s dominance of the European Cup (now the **UEFA Champions League**), winning the competition to be crowned Europe's best in both 1961 and 1962 while being inspired by their star creative force, the legendary **Eusébio**. Benfica has since reached another five European Cup finals, but have yet to win Europe's ultimate prize again, despite continued domestic success. Benfica is Portugal's most popular club, now boasting more than 200,000 paying club members around the world. Benfica play at the recently rebuilt 65,000-capacity Estádio da Luz, which also hosted the 2004 **UEFA European Football Championship** final.

BEST, GEORGE. B. 22 May 1946, Belfast, Northern Ireland. D. 25 November 2005. A Northern Irish star best known for his years playing for **Manchester United**, Best was one of the greatest talents in the history of the game. But his off-the-field issues prevented him from winning all of the honors that seemed destined for him when, at the age of 22 in 1967, he won the European Cup (now known as the **UEFA Champions League**) with Manchester United and took home the **European Footballer of the Year** award. In his six years with Manchester United, where he had arrived from across the Irish Sea at the age of 15, he also won two league titles and scored more than 100 goals. Blessed with remarkable balance, pace, and the ability to dribble past defenders from his usual wide midfield role, he also had a fierce shot and an excellent goal-scoring record for club and country.

Best's remarkable success on the field, combined with his good looks and the growth of celebrity culture in **England** in the 1960s, contributed to his downfall, one marked by addiction to alcohol and women. The retirement of Best's mentor at Manchester United, legendary manager **Matt Busby**, preceded his increasing distraction from the game. Gambling, drinking, and womanizing took over his life, leading him to regularly miss practice under the most intense media spotlight a British player had ever endured. Best quit Manchester United for good in 1974 at the age of 27 and later appeared in brief roles for various teams in England and the **United States** but never recaptured his glorious form of the late 1960s. Best died of a kidney infection at the age of 59 in November 2005, and the George Best Foundation has since been set up in his name to research alcoholism and liver disease.

BICAN, JOSEF. B. 25 September 1913, Vienna, Austria-Hungary. D. 12 December 2001. Josef Bican was a **Czech** and **Austrian** forward with an extraordinarily prolific goal-scoring record, finishing his career with 649 goals to his credit. Bican was known for his lightning speed and ability to score from an array of angles and ranges from goal. Born in Vienna, he represented both Austria and Czechoslovakia at international level with considerable success. In the 1930s, Bican played for Austria's "Wunderteam," perhaps the best team in the world that decade. He played at the 1934 **FIFA World Cup**, where Austria reached the semifinals and then lost to hosts **Italy** in a controversial game. He scored one goal in four games at the tournament. At club level, Bican earned an outstanding record as a goal scorer for Slavia Prague, scoring more than 300 goals for the club between 1937 and 1948. He also represented the Czechoslovakian national team after he became a Czech citizen. Bican retired as a player in 1955 and went on to have a long coaching career in the sport before his death in 2001.

BLATTER, JOSEPH S. B. 10 March 1936, Visp, Switzerland. Joseph Blatter, commonly known as "Sepp," is the current president of the **Fédération Internationale de Football Association (FIFA)**, world soccer's global governing body. A former Swiss amateur soccer player, Blatter gained experience as a sports administrator as general secretary of the Swiss Ice Hockey Federation in the 1960s and in international sport as an organizer of the 1972 and 1976 Olympic Games. Blatter began to work for FIFA in 1975 as its director of Technical Development Programmes, with promotions to general secretary in 1981 and chief executive officer in 1990. Blatter was elected the eighth FIFA president on 8 June 1998, replacing his close confidant **João Havelange** after a bitter campaign against his rival, Lennart Johansson. He was reelected as FIFA president in 2002 and again in 2006.

In his roles with FIFA, Blatter has played a critical part in the commercialization of world soccer, overseeing the massive growth in the value of television rights and marketing of the **FIFA World Cup** from 1986 up to the present day. As FIFA president, Blatter has led the introduction of the **futsal** world cup and the much-criticized **FIFA Club World Cup**. Blatter's reign has come under considerable attack for alleged corruption at the highest levels of FIFA and for a lack of transparency in FIFA's operations, as detailed in Andrew Jennings' investigative book *Foul! The Secret World of FIFA: Bribes, Vote Rigging and Ticket Scandals*.

BLOKHIN, OLEG. B. 5 November 1952, Kiev, Ukraine. Oleg Blokhin was the first-and-still-only Ukrainian player to win the **European Footballer of the Year** award, taking the accolade in 1975. He was the top goal scorer in the history of the **Soviet Union**'s league championship; playing for Dynamo Kiev, he scored 211 goals from 1969 to 1988. Blokhin also played 112 games for the Soviet Union, scoring 42 goals, and appeared at the **FIFA World Cup** finals tournaments in 1982 and 1986. After his retirement from playing, Blokhin coached several club teams before taking charge of the Ukraine national team and leading them to the quarterfinals of the 2006 World Cup. He resigned in 2007.

BOCA JUNIORS. Founded on 3 April 1905 in the *La Boca* working-class dockside area of **Argentina**'s capital, Buenos Aires, Boca Juniors are an enormously successful club team. They are winners of 23 Argentinean league championships, six continental titles in the **Copa Libertadores**, and three **Intercontinental Cup** titles. Only their fierce rivals, **River Plate**, have won more domestic honors in Argentina than have Boca Juniors. The club's famous blue-and-gold colors were chosen in 1907, inspired by a Swedish flag flying on a ship at the docks of La Boca. They won promotion to the first division in 1913 and claimed their first championship in 1919. When Argentinean football turned professional in 1931, Boca claimed the inaugural championship. In 1940, the club opened its legendary stadium, the Estadio Alberto J. Armando—much more commonly known as "*La Bombonera*" (The Chocolate Box)—famous for its colorful, vibrant, and intimidating atmosphere for opposing teams. Many of Argentina's greatest-ever players have played at the club, including **Diego Maradona**.

BONIEK, ZBIGNIEW. B. 3 March 1956, Bydgoszcz, Poland. Zbigniew Boniek was the creative force for **Poland** at three **FIFA World Cup** tournaments, including their best-ever finish in 1982 when they came in third place in the competition in **Spain**. Boniek played 80 times for Poland between 1976 and 1988, scoring 20 goals and establishing himself as the country's leading player of the 1980s. He was a quick, skillful player and able to beat defenders off the dribble. Following the 1982 World Cup, Boniek moved from Widzew Łódź in Poland to play for **Juventus** in **Italy**. Playing alongside greats such as **Michel Platini**, Boniek won prestigious international club honors with Juventus, including the 1984 **UEFA Cup Winners' Cup**, the 1985 **European Cup**, and the 1985 **Intercontinental Cup**. In 1986, he moved to play for Italian club AS Roma, retired in 1985, and went on to have a managerial career that included a brief spell in charge of Poland in 2002.

BORUSSIA DORTMUND. Borussia Dortmund's full name is "Ballspiel-Verein Borussia 1909 Dortmund," with the 1909 referencing the club's founding year. "Borussia Dortmund," as it is commonly called, is one of **Germany**'s leading clubs, enjoying particularly strong success over the past two decades. In that period, they won the German league title on three occasions, in 1995, 1996, and 2002, and won the **UEFA Champions League** and the **Intercontinental Cup** in 1997. Borussia Dortmund play at Signal Iduna Park, regularly attracting more than 80,000 fans per game. *See also* SAMMER, MATTHIAS.

BRAZIL. Football is the most popular sport in Brazil, with more than two million registered players in the country and an estimated 13 million total players. At the international level, Brazil is the most successful team in the history of the **FIFA World Cup** with a record five titles to their credit and, as of 2010, is the only country to have played in every single World Cup finals tournament. In 1970, Brazil, led by the legendary **Pelé**, considered by many to be the greatest soccer player of all time, was allowed to keep the **Jules Rimet Trophy** for being the first country to win the World Cup three times.

Like their great rivals, **Argentina**, soccer was brought to Brazil by **English** expatriates. A son of an English railway worker who had immigrated to Brazil, Charles Miller, brought a rule book and equipment from England to Brazil, and the game was quickly adopted by many others in his home city, São Paulo. In 1914, the Brazilian Football Confederation (in Portuguese, *Confederação Brasileira de Futebol* [CBF]) was formed, the national governing body of soccer in Brazil. In 1916, the CBF affiliated with the South American Football Confederation (CONMEBOL), and in 1923, it became a member of the **Fédération Internationale de Football Association (FIFA)**. Though moderately successful in international competition in the interwar period, winning the **Copa América** in 1919 and 1922 and finishing third at the 1938 World Cup, it would not be until after World War II that a new generation of Brazilian players took the country to the peak of the sport. Brazil hosted the 1950 World Cup, but in an upset that shocked the nation, lost at the legendary **Maracanã** stadium to **Uruguay** in the final game, in front of a crowd reportedly numbering more than 200,000 people.

The golden era of Brazilian soccer followed an overhaul of that team, with the brilliant talents of **Didi, Garrincha**, and Pelé mesmerizing the world with their sauntering, skillful style of play in their victorious 1958 World Cup campaign, beating the hosts, **Sweden**, 5-2 in the final. Brazil would repeat their victory at the FIFA World Cup held in **Chile** four years later, defeating Czechoslovakia 3-1 in the final, inspired by the brilliant Garrincha, joint top scorer in the tournament with four goals; Pelé only played in two games due to injury. The 1966 World Cup was a disappointment for Brazil: Pelé was brutally targeted by the **Portuguese** as Brazil exited in the first round. The 1970 World Cup in **Mexico**, though, would see Pelé and Brazil at their best, earning global fame with their flowing, fantastic soccer and sweeping aside **Italy** 4-1 in the final. Pelé and his teammates, especially **Rivelino, Tostão**, and **Jairzinho**, were outstanding throughout the competition as they etched into legend their exciting, fluid style of play. They are still considered perhaps the greatest national team of all time.

Despite sending outstanding teams to both the 1982 and 1986 World Cups, Brazil would not again reach the final until 1994, when they won the World Cup in the **United States**, defeating Italy again in the final. Their victory this time came through a penalty shoot-out, after a dour 0-0 draw that reflected Brazil's more pragmatic approach to play in the modern era of the game. Brazil reached the World Cup final in **France** once again in the 1998 competition on the back of several goals by sensational forward **Ronaldo**, but his mysterious illness before the last game against France hampered Brazil, who lost 3-0 to the hosts. Ronaldo and Brazil would return in force at the 2002 World Cup held in the **Republic of Korea** and **Japan**; Ronaldo was the top scorer in the competition with a total of eight goals and Brazil defeated **Germany** 2-0 in the final to take their fifth World Cup title. In the 2006 World Cup, Brazil lost to eventual winners France in the quarterfinals and fell at the quarterfinal stage again in the 2010 World Cup, this time losing to the **Netherlands**. *See also* ADEMIR; ALTAFINI, JOSÉ; CORINTHIANS; CUBILLAS, TEÓFILO; GRÊMIO FOOT-BALL PORTO-ALEGRENSE; HAVELANGE, JOÃO; KAKÁ; LEÔNIDAS DA SILVA; MARTA; RIVALDO; ROMÁRIO; RONALDINHO; SANTANA, TELÊ; SANTOS FUTEBOL CLUB; SANTOS, DJALMA; SANTOS, NÍLTON; SÃO PAULO FUTEBOL CLUB; SISSI; SÓCRATES; ZAGALLO, MÁRIO; ZICO.

BREITNER, PAUL. B. 5 September 1951, Kolbermoor, West Germany. Paul Breitner played 48 games for West **Germany** between 1971 and 1982, achieving considerable success with his country on the field while also generating notable controversy off the field. He twice appeared in the final of the **FIFA World Cup** with his country, scoring a goal on both occasions, in a winning effort in 1974 and a losing effort in 1982. West Germany won the 1974 final against the odds versus the **Netherlands,** with Breitner playing a crucial role in stifling the array of Dutch attacking prowess from his role at the left side of the defense. The 1974 triumph was Breitner's second major trophy with West Germany, having already won the 1972 **UEFA European Football Championship.** Breitner was a skillful player who proved adept enough to play on defense or midfield for both club and country, advancing into more central positions as the years progressed. He won numerous major honors at club level before his retirement in 1983, including five West German league championships with **Bayern Munich** in two spells during the 1970s and 1980s, as well as winning the 1974 **European Cup** with the West German club. Following that triumph, Breitner played in **Spain** from 1974 to 1977 with **Real Madrid,** twice winning the Spanish league title, then returning to West Germany. Breitner was at times a divisive figure for club and country, a free thinker with little regard for authority, sporting an Afro hairstyle, championing left-wing politics, and refusing to sing the national anthem before West Germany's games.

BULGARIA. Soccer was brought to Bulgaria, then part of the Ottoman Empire, by **Swiss** teacher George de Regibus in 1896. The sport was slow to develop in Bulgaria, with the first soccer club in the capital, Sofia, not founded until 1912. Soccer took off more broadly only in the 1920s. The governing body, the Bulgarian Football Union, was founded in 1923, affiliated with the **Fédération Internationale de Football Association (FIFA)** in 1924, and became a founding member of the **Union of European Football Associations (UEFA)** in 1954. Since the 1920s, Bulgaria has embraced the game as its national sport and has produced a number of talented national teams and individuals. They have appeared in the **FIFA World Cup** on seven occasions, with Bulgaria's best result a fourth-place finish in the 1994 World Cup held in the **United States.** The team was led by star forward **Hristo Stoichkov,** who was named **European Footballer of the Year** that year, the only Bulgarian to win the award to date. The top league in Bulgarian soccer is the Bulgarian A Professional Football Group, founded in 1948, with teams from the Bulgarian capital, Sofia, dominating the competition: CSKA Sofia has won 31 championships, Levski Sofia has won 26, and Slavia Sofia has won seven. *See also* FIFA WORLD CUP, 1994.

BUSBY, SIR MATT. B. 26 May 1909, Orbiston, Lanarkshire, Scotland. D. 20 January 1994. One of **English** soccer's leading club managers of all time, Sir Matt Busby led **Manchester United** to five domestic league championship victories, two **Football Association Challenge Cup** wins, and one

European Cup (now **UEFA Champions League**) title between 1945 and 1969. Ironically, Busby began his career in soccer playing for Manchester United's two main local rivals, Manchester City and **Liverpool**, where he became captain. He made one official playing appearance internationally for **Scotland**. During the Second World War, Busby made the transition from playing to management as a soccer coach in the army. In 1945, Busby was offered an assistant manager job with Liverpool but turned down the opportunity and became the head coach of Manchester United instead, joining the club after he left the armed forces in October 1945. Manchester United had a bomb-damaged stadium and considerable debts, but along with assistant manager Jimmy Murphy, Busby quickly led the club to success, winning the F.A. Cup in 1948 and the league championship in 1952.

Busby set up a superior youth development and scouting structure that developed a stream of impressive young talent, who became known as the "Busby Babes." His young team won the English league championship again in 1956 and 1957. On 6 February 1958, the airplane carrying Manchester United, which was traveling from a European Cup game, crashed in Munich, killing 23 people onboard. Eight players were among the dead, along with three club officials. Busby was severely injured and was twice given the last rites in hospital. Busby recovered and returned to the club in August 1958 faced with the daunting task of entirely rebuilding a devastated squad. His efforts bore fruit in the mid-1960s, as Manchester United again won league titles in 1965 and 1967. The following season, 10 years after the Munich disaster, they reached the final of the European Cup for the first time, beating **Benfica** 4-1 after extra time to become the first English team to win Europe's premier club competition. Busby retired in 1969, staying on as general manager to oversee new head coach Wilf McGuinness before returning temporarily as manager just a year later for the 1970–1971 season. He then retired permanently and became a club director and, later, president of Manchester United, before his death in 1994.

C

CAF AFRICAN YOUTH CHAMPIONSHIP. Contested since 1977, the CAF African Youth Championship, organized by the governing **FIFA confederation** on the continent, the **Confederation of African Football (CAF)**, is the leading youth soccer competition in Africa for national teams and has an age limit of 20. It is sometimes called the "Tessema Cup," in honor of **Ydnekatchew Tessema**, the president of CAF at the time of the tournament's creation. **Nigeria** has won the competition a record five times, with three wins each for **Egypt** and **Ghana**.

CAF CHAMPIONS LEAGUE. The CAF Champions League, organized by the region's governing **FIFA confederation**, the **Confederation of African Football (CAF)**, is the premier club tournament in Africa. The CAF Champions League, founded in 1964 and then known as the "African Champions' Cup," changed its name and expanded its format in 1997—mimicking the **UEFA Champions League**. It offers prize money totaling more than $1 million to the champion team. The winning club earns the right to compete in the **FIFA Club World Cup** as CAF's representative. Club teams from **Egypt** have been the most successful in the competition, winning a total of 12 championships, with **Al-Ahly Sporting Club** the all-time leading club, having won the tournament six times, and **Zamalek Sporting Club** in second place with five wins. Clubs from **Cameroon** and Morocco have each won the tournament five times.

CAF WOMEN'S AFRICAN CHAMPIONSHIP. The leading continental competition for women's national teams in Africa is the CAF Women's African Championship, organized by the governing body of soccer in Africa, the **Confederation of African Football (CAF)**. The two finalists in the tournament qualify as the representatives of CAF in the **FIFA Women's World Cup**. The competition was first organized outside of CAF's auspices in 1991 and was taken over by CAF in 1998, and since then, it has been played every two years. **Nigeria** won the first seven editions of the competition that were contested, with the eighth edition and most recent competition, in 2008, won by Equatorial Guinea. *See also* WOMEN'S SOCCER.

CAMEROON. One of Africa's strongest countries in world soccer, Cameroon's men's national team—known as the "Indomitable Lions"—have appeared at the **FIFA World Cup** on more occasions than any other African nation, with appearances in 1982, 1990, 1994, 1998, 2002, and 2010. In 1990, Cameroon, led by aging star **Roger Milla**, became the first African team to reach the quarterfinals of the World Cup. They have also won the **Africa Cup of Nations** four times, in 1984, 1988, 2000, and 2002. In 2000, they won the **Olympic Games Football Tournament** as well. Soccer in Cameroon is governed by the *Fédération Camerounaise de Football* (FCF), its national association, founded in 1959. The FCF affiliated with the **Confederation of African Football (CAF)** in 1963 and with the **Fédération Internationale de Football Association (FIFA)** in 1964. In 1961, the FCF began organizing a national league, the *Championnat du Cameroun de Football*, known for sponsorship purposes as the MTN Elite One. It is still the top level of the sport today. Cameroon's club teams, with five victories in the premier African club tournament, currently called the "**CAF Champions League**," have been surpassed only by **Egyptian** teams in continental competitions in Africa. The most successful of those clubs is Canon Yaoundé, founded in 1930 and based in the capital, Yaoundé, with victories in 1971, 1978, and 1980. Canon Yaoundé shares the record for championship titles in Cameroon with northern club Coton Sport FC de Garoua, each having won the *Championnat* 10 times.

CANADA. Soccer in Canada is governed by the Canadian Soccer Association (CSA), formed in 1912 and affiliated with soccer's global governing body, the **Fédération Internationale de Football Association (FIFA)**, in 1913 and with the regional governing body, the **Confederation of North, Central American and Caribbean Association Football (CONCACAF)**, in 1961. Soccer in Canada dates back to the mid-19th century, with the first-known game taking place in the late 1850s. Today, Canada does not have a fully professional league, and its strongest teams compete in or will soon be joining **Major League Soccer (MLS)** in the **United States**: Toronto FC (who joined MLS in 2007), the Vancouver Whitecaps (scheduled to join MLS in 2011), and the Montreal Impact (scheduled to join MLS in 2012). Though Canada has high levels of participation in soccer at the junior level, its national teams have made relatively little impact internationally. Canada's men's national team has qualified only once for the **FIFA World Cup**, losing all three games in the 1986 tournament held in **Mexico**. Canada has had more success in regional competition, winning the CONCACAF Championship in 1985 and the **CONCACAF Gold Cup** in 2000. Canada's women's national team has been considerably more successful than its men's team, consistently ranked among the top 10 international teams, and with a best finish in the

FIFA Women's World Cup of fourth place in 2003 in the United States. Canada's junior women's national team reached the final of the 2002 **FIFA U-20 Women's World Cup**, held in Canada.

CANNAVARO, FABIO. B. 13 September 1973, Naples, Italy. Fabio Cannavaro was the **FIFA World Player of the Year** in 2006, in recognition of his achievement in captaining **Italy** to victory at the 2006 **FIFA World Cup** in **Germany**. He also won the **European Footballer of the Year** award that year. Cannavaro, known for offering a formidable and composed presence in the center of defense for Italy since 1997 and holding the record number of appearances for his country, is the only defender to have won the FIFA World Player of the Year as of August 2010. He retired from international play in July 2006 following the 2010 World Cup in **South Africa**, having amassed 136 total appearances for his country. At club level, Cannavaro achieved his greatest success playing for **Real Madrid** in **Spain** from 2006 to 2009, twice winning the Spanish league championship. He also won the 1999 **UEFA Cup** playing for **Juventus** in his native Italy.

CHA, BUM-KUN. B. 22 May 1953, Hwaseong, Republic of Korea. Cha Bum-Kun is a coach from the **Republic of Korea** and was the country's leading player in the 1980s, enjoying a particularly successful club career in West **Germany**. A potent striker, he remains the all-time leading scorer for his national team. He played at the 1986 **FIFA World Cup** for the Republic of Korea, and he coached that team at the 1998 World Cup. Cha won two major international honors at club level as a player: winners' medals from the 1980 and 1988 **UEFA Cups** for West German clubs Eintracht Frankfurt and Bayer Leverkusen, respectively.

CHARLTON, BOBBY. B. 11 October 1937, Ashington, England. One of the greatest English players of all time, Bobby Charlton remains the leading all-time goal scorer for **England**, having totaled 49 goals in 106 games for his national team. Charlton played a key role in England's only **FIFA World Cup** triumph, when England hosted the competition in 1966. His importance for England in their World Cup triumph was recognized in his selection as **European Footballer of the Year** in 1966. Charlton was equally successful at club level for **Manchester United**. In more than two decades at the club, from 1953 to 1973, he scored 247 goals in 754 games.

Along with his excellent goal-scoring record (many of his goals came from his accurate, powerful long-range shooting), Charlton was an all-around talent who overcame considerable adversity to succeed. Along with the rest of the Manchester United team, which won the league title in the first season that he played regularly for the club in 1957, Charlton was on an airplane that crashed in Munich on 6 February 1958 returning from a **European Cup** match. Twenty-one of those onboard died, including several of Charlton's young teammates (known as the "Busby Babes" after manager **Matt Busby**), and Charlton himself was injured. He recovered from the trauma to become a dominant creative forward for Manchester United, playing a vital role as they won further league championships in 1965 and 1967. They were then crowned as European champions for the first time with victory in the 1968 European Cup, Charlton captaining a team including the brilliant **George Best**. Charlton tried his hand at club management, with limited success, after his retirement from playing in the 1970s and settled down as a director at Manchester United and as a global ambassador for club and country.

CHELSEA FOOTBALL CLUB. Chelsea Football Club, usually referred to simply as "Chelsea," is a club team located in west London, **England**. They were founded in 1905 and have been one of the leading teams in England since the 1950s, with four total domestic league championships, six victories in the **Football Association Challenge Cup**, two **UEFA Cup Winners' Cup** triumphs, and one **UEFA Super Cup** title. Since their purchase, in 2003, by Russian billionaire Roman Abramovich, who has made a considerable investment into the club, Chelsea has been one of the dominant forces in the English **Premier League**, most recently taking the title in 2010 under head coach Carlo Ancelotti and winning the F.A. Cup the same season. Chelsea plays its home games at Stamford Bridge, opened in 1877 and renovated several times since, with a current capacity of almost 43,000. *See also* GULLIT, RUUD; WEAH, GEORGE.

CHILE. Chile played host to the 1962 **FIFA World Cup**, the first time in 12 years that it had been held in South America. Chile finished in third place at the competition, still their best-ever finish at a World Cup competition in their eight total appearances. Chile has finished runners-up in the **Copa América**, South America's leading competition for national teams, four times: in 1955, 1956, 1979, and 1987. In 2000, Chile finished in third place in the men's **Olympic Games Football Tournament**. Soccer in Chile is organized by the *Federación de Fútbol de Chile*, founded on 19 June 1895 in the port city of Valparaiso. Chile affiliated with the **Fédération Internationale de Football Association (FIFA)** in 1913, and was a founding member of the **South American Football Confederation (CONMEBOL)** in 1916. The highest level of domestic soccer in Chile is the *Primera División*, founded in 1933, and the most successful club in it has been **Colo Colo**, based in Santiago, the capital of Chile. In 1991, Colo Colo won the **Copa Libertadores**, the leading club competition in South America. **Women's soccer** in Chile has developed rapidly in recent years: Chile hosted the 2008 **FIFA U-20 Women's World Cup** and a national women's soccer league was set up for the first time following that competition. *See also* FIGUEROA, ELÍAS; ZAMORANO, IVÁN.

CHINA. Despite being able to draw talent from the world's most populous country, China's men's national team has only qualified for the **FIFA World Cup** on one occasion, 1994, and lacks a high-performing elite professional league. Corruption from gambling is often linked to the game in China. Soccer, however, is enormously popular in China, with hundreds of millions of viewers tuning in their televisions for major international games. China has a rich history in the sport, with an antecedent of soccer, a game known as *cuju*, played regularly two thousand years ago. The sport in China is governed by the Chinese Football Association, founded in 1924 and affiliated with the **Fédération Internationale de Football Association (FIFA)** in 1931. It is also a member of the **Asian Football Confederation (AFC),** and China reached the final of the AFC's premier competition, the AFC Nations Cup, in both 1984 and 2004. China's women's national team has been far more successful than has its men's counterpart. Despite the historical cultural prejudice against women participating in soccer, China's women's team is among the elite globally. They were runners-up in both the 1996 **Olympic Games Football Tournament** and the 1999 **FIFA Women's World Cup**, losing on both occasions to the **United States**. China's star player during the 1990s, **Sun Wen,** won the FIFA Woman Player of the Century award jointly with American **Michelle Akers** in 2002.

CLOUGH, BRIAN. B. 21 March 1935, Middlesbrough, England. D. 20 September 2004. Known as much for his charisma as for his extraordinary record as a manager of Derby County and Nottingham Forest in **England,** Brian Clough has recently been the subject of both a best-selling novel and an international hit movie, *The Damned United.* Clough began his career in soccer as an outstanding professional player: a penetrating forward and prolific goal scorer for his hometown team Middlesbrough in the 1950s and nearby Sunderland in the early 1960s. Though he played for the England national team twice, Clough suffered a severe career-ending injury in December 1962 at the age of just 27, tearing the cruciate ligament in his knee. He moved into coaching first with Hartlepool United in 1965 and achieved enough success that he was soon appointed manager of second division Derby County in 1967. He brought along his assistant Peter Taylor, who played a crucial role for Clough in scouting players and identifying hidden talent. Clough and

Taylor soon turned Derby County into one of the strongest teams in England, winning the **Football League** championship in 1972.

Clough left Derby County the following year after a dispute with the club's board of directors, briefly taking over Brighton and Hove Albion on the south coast along with Taylor, then departing from Brighton and Taylor in 1974 for a short and disastrous spell in charge of Leeds United. Clough and Taylor reunited in charge of Nottingham Forest in 1977, leading the provincial club to the top of the English game. They won the Football League in 1978 and then, most remarkably, won successive **European Cup** titles in 1979 and 1980. Clough continued as manager of Nottingham Forest until 1993, though the club declined under his guidance in his final years in management due to his poor health and his drinking problem. The team was relegated at the end of 1993, and Clough retired from management that year.

CLUB DEPORTIVO GUADALAJARA. Commonly known by their nickname "Chivas," C.D. Guadalajara, based in the central city of Guadalajara in Mexico, is one of the most popular and successful **Mexican** club teams. The club was founded as an amateur team on 8 May 1906 by Edgar Everaert, a **Belgian** immigrant and store owner in Guadalajara. C.D. Guadalajara was enormously successful almost immediately and dominated amateur soccer in Mexico's Western League for three decades. The advent of a national professional league in Mexico in 1943 did not see the club dominate initially on the field, but they did pick up their enduring nickname, "Chivas" (translated as "goats" in English), when once called "*chivas brinconas*" ("jumping goats") during a game. In 1957, C.D. Guadalajara won their first national title and embarked on an extraordinary run of success: powered by stars such as Salvador Reyes, Jaime Gomez, and Juan Jasso, the club won seven consecutive national championships from 1957 to 1966. They earned a nationwide following in the process, along with continental glory, winning the 1962 CONCACAF Champions Cup (now known as the **CONCACAF Champions League**). C.D. Guadalajara has never approached that golden period of domination again but has since won further first division titles, in 1970, 1987, 1997, and 2006, and remains, arguably, Mexico's most popular club. On 30 July 2010, the club opened its new stadium, Estadio Omnilife, a state-of-the-art venue with a capacity of 45,000.

CLUB DEPORTIVO LOS MILLONARIOS. Usually referred to simply as "Millonarios," Club Deportivo Los Millonarios has been one of the strongest club teams in **Colombia** since the 1950s. The club, officially founded on 16 June 1946, plays in Bogotá, the capital of Colombia. In 1948, Millonarios joined Colombia's first national professional league. As Colombia's league was not affiliated with the **Fédération Internationale de Football Association (FIFA)** for its first six years, their riches could be paid in wages to recruit players instead of in transfer fees. Millonarios signed nine Argentineans, a Brazilian, a Chilean, and a Peruvian for their 1949 team. This included the legendary stars **Alfredo di Stéfano** and Adolfo Pedernera from **Argentina**. Millonarios won their first national championship that year, playing dazzling soccer that earned them the nickname *"Ballet Azul"* (ballet in blue, for the color of Millonarios' jerseys) and earning world fame with a global tour in 1952 after four successive championship victories. Colombia rejoined FIFA in 1954 and most of Millonarios' great foreign players returned home. Millonarios have claimed a total of 11 national league titles, though none since 1988. They play at Estadio El Campín, a 44,000-capacity stadium.

COACHES. Most professional soccer clubs have a head coach and assistant coach, with duties that can range from responsibility for team selection, team motivation, and team training to various administrative duties, depending on the club. Some clubs employ specialist coaches, such as a **goalkeeper** coach, to train players in only one position. The head coach, or manager, is the figure with overall responsibility for the team's performance on the field and for dealing with the media. In many countries today, coaches are required to hold a license achieved by passing a qualification course, a sign of the increasing professionalization and specialization of the position. In the earlier days of coaching, in the first couple of decades of the 20th century, the role of the head coach was less clear, and the coach often had little contact with players at the club. Herbert Chapman of **Arsenal Football Club** was one of the first innovators in this area, forging a close bond as a coach with his players and introducing new tactics that won the club several titles. Tactical and strategic innovation became an increasingly important part of coaching as the 20th century progressed. The likes of **Hungary**'s **Gusztáv Sebes** in the 1950s and **Rinus Michels** of the **Netherlands** two decades later revolutionized play on the field by developing an exciting, fluid system of play known as "**Total Football**," which demanded that players switch positions rapidly. Some innovations from coaches were negative tactically: in **Italy** during the 1960s, **Helenio Herrera** created at **Internazionale** a successful, but grinding, defensive system that stymied creative play on the field. As the role of coaching, in management of players and in responsibility for tactics on the field of play, has increased, along with the oversight of scouting and recruitment of players, so has the media spotlight intensified. It is a demanding, but highly rewarding, position, with top-level contemporary coaches, such as José Mourinho, becoming as famous as almost any professional player. At the amateur level, the coach remains the critical figure for the team, often responsible for a myriad of duties from organizing games to washing jerseys, as well as selecting the team. *See also* BECKENBAUER, FRANZ; BUSBY, SIR MATT; CLOUGH, BRIAN; CRUYFF, JOHAN; DICICCO, TONY; DORRANCE, ANSON; FERGUSON, ALEX; GUTTMANN, BÉLA; HAPPEL, ERNST; HERBERGER, "SEPP" JOSEPH; JACQUET, AIMÉ; LIPPI, MARCELLO; LOBANOVSKI, VALERY; MENOTTI, CÉSAR LUIS; PAISLEY, ROBERT; POZZO, VITTORIO; RAMSEY, SIR ALF; SACCHI, ARRIGO; SANTANA, TELÊ; SHANKLY, BILL; VOGTS, BERTI; ZAGALLO, MÁRIO.

COLO COLO. Colo Colo, whose formal name is Club Social y Deportivo Colo Colo, is the best-known club from **Chile**, boasting a record 28 national league titles in its history, and is the only Chilean team to have won the premier South American competition, the **Copa Libertadores**. Colo Colo was founded in 1925 and turned professional in 1933. They won their first national title in 1937. Colo Colo first reached the final of the Copa Libertadores in 1973, but lost on that occasion. They went on to win their first and only Copa Libertadores title 18 years later, in 1991, defeating Olimpia of **Paraguay** in the final. *See also* PUSKÁS, FERENC.

COLOMBIA. Soccer was introduced to Colombia at the turn of the 20th century by British railway engineers and sailors in Barranquilla on the Caribbean coast. It has since become Colombia's most popular sport, and Colombia has become one of the leading South American nations, if not in the elite class of **Argentina**, **Brazil**, or **Uruguay**. Soccer in Colombia is governed by the Colombian Football Federation (or *Federación Colombiana de Fútbol* in Spanish), founded in 1924 and affiliated with both the **Fédération Internationale de Football Association (FIFA)** and the **South American Football Confederation (CONMEBOL)** in 1936.

Soccer had been slow to develop in Colombia in the first half of the 20th century, but this rapidly changed in 1948 following a political upheaval after the assassination of populist leader Jorge Eliecer Gaitan. As a side effect, this threw the plans in place for Colombia's first professional league, *DiMayor*, due to start play that year, into chaos and saw its clubs suspended from FIFA. This freedom from FIFA regulation, ironically, allowed Colombia's leading clubs, such as **Club Deportivo Los Millonarios**, to recruit leading international players from other teams without paying a transfer fee: and with further income from the Colombian government, Millonarios signed several of the world's best players, including the brilliant Argentineans **Alfredo di Stéfano** and Adolfo Pedernera. A brief, golden era in the Colombian league followed. Colombia rejoined FIFA in 1954, with most of the leading international players leaving the country, as wages and the quality of players came back down to earth.

Colombia's national team and club teams achieved little in the 1960s and 1970s. Colombia appeared only once in a **FIFA World Cup** (in 1962, eliminated in the first round) until 1990. The country withdrew from plans to host the 1986 World Cup due to Colombia's poor economic state and crumbling, unsafe stadiums. But fueled by money from local drug cartels in the late 1980s, Colombian clubs such as Corporación América de Cali invested heavily in recruitment. Cali won several national titles and reached the final of the leading South American club competition, the **Copa Libertadores**, three times in a row, from 1985 to 1987, though they lost the final on each occasion. At the same time, the influx of drug money corrupted Colombian soccer: uncontrolled gambling on games took off, and the 1989 league championship was canceled by the Colombian Football Federation. Despite this, Colombia could call on remarkable talent for the 1994 World Cup and was picked by some analysts, including most notably **Pelé**, as a dark horse to win the competition, following a stellar qualifying campaign led by midfield maestro **Carlos Valderrama**. But their World Cup campaign would end with an early exit in the first round and a tragic death for Colombian defender Andrés Escobar, who was gunned down upon his return to Colombia in the city of Medellin for reasons that remain murky. Colombia reached the World Cup for the fourth time in 1998 in **France** but once again exited at the first-round stage and has not qualified for the World Cup since. In 2001, Colombia won their first major international competition with victory in South America's leading national team competition, the **Copa América**, held in Colombia.

CONCACAF CHAMPIONS LEAGUE. The leading annual international club tournament for the **Confederation of North, Central American and Caribbean Association Football (CONCACAF)** region, the CONCACAF Champions League was known as the CONCACAF Champions Cup from 1962 to 2008. It was rebranded and reorganized into a new format that year, taking a cue from the success of the **UEFA Champions League** in Europe. Until that point, the tournament had been for the league champions of each member nation in CONCACAF, but the new league format allowed leading countries such as the **United States** and **Mexico** to send more entrant clubs and expand the tournament. Twenty-four teams now entered at the initial stage and 16 participated in the lengthy group stage. The three leading club teams in the history of the competition in all its formats are all from Mexico: Club América and Cruz Azul have each won the trophy five times, and Pachuca has won it on four occasions.

CONCACAF GOLD CUP. The CONCACAF Gold Cup, contested biennially, is the premier regional competition for nations in the **Confederation of North, Central American and Caribbean Association Football (CONCACAF)** region. The winner of the CONCACAF Gold Cup tournament immediately prior to the quadrennial **FIFA Confederations Cup** tournament earns CONCACAF's berth in that competition. The CONCACAF Gold Cup was established in 1991 as a replacement for the CONCACAF Championship, which in the 1970s and 1980s was used to determine the region's entrant to the **FIFA World Cup** finals. The **United States** and **Mexico** have dominated the CONCACAF Gold Cup, winning every staging of the tournament except in 2003, when it was won by **Canada**. Due to the plethora of available high-quality stadiums, the tournament has been held in the United States every time, with Mexico cohosting with the United States in both 1993 and 2003.

CONCACAF UNDER-20 CHAMPIONSHIP. The CONCACAF Under-20 Championship was founded in 1962 and is the leading junior competition for national teams in the North, Central American and Caribbean region. It is organized by the **Confederation of North, Central American and Caribbean Association Football (CONCACAF)**. It serves as the qualifying campaign for the region's entrants to the **FIFA U-20 World Cup**. **Mexico** has been the dominant force in the competition, with 10 titles to its credit. **Canada** and Costa Rica have each won it twice, and El Salvador and Honduras have each won it once.

CONCACAF WOMEN'S GOLD CUP. The premier continental competition for women's national teams in the North, Central American and Caribbean region is the CONCACAF Women's Gold Cup, organized by the **Confederation of North, Central American and Caribbean Association Football (CONCACAF)**. It was founded in 2000, replacing the previous leading CONCACAF competition for women's national teams, the CONCACAF Women's Championship. It is now contested every two years, and has been won on all three occasions by the **United States**, with **Canada** twice finishing as runners-up. The CONCACAF Women's Gold Cup also serves as the qualifying event for the CONCACAF region in the **FIFA Women's World Cup**.

CONFEDERATION OF AFRICAN FOOTBALL (CAF). Commonly known as "CAF," the Confederation of African Football, one of the six **Fédération Internationale de Football Association (FIFA)** confederations, is the governing body of football on the African continent. CAF currently has 55 member national associations in Africa. Its administrative offices are in Cairo, **Egypt**. Six **FIFA World Cup** final places are designated for members of CAF, which runs a World Cup qualifying contest to determine the qualifiers. The **Africa Cup of Nations** is CAF's premier continental tournament for national teams. A new competition, the African Nations Championship, founded in 2009, is only for players based in the domestic continent. For African club teams, CAF organizes the **CAF Champions League** continental competition.

CAF was founded in 1957 by the national associations of Ethiopia, **Egypt**, **South Africa**, and Sudan. The Egyptian, Abdel Aziz Abdallah Salem, became the first president of CAF, and the new body organized the first Africa Cup of Nations in Khartoum, Sudan, in February 1957. All four founding members of CAF were invited, but South Africa abstained because their all-white apartheid-era national association refused CAF's demand that they field a multiracial team. South Africa was expelled from CAF as a result. Ethiopian **Ydnekatchew Tessema** was the president of CAF from 1972 until 1987 and helped achieve greater power for CAF within the global governing structure of FIFA. He actively supported the successful challenge of the South American **João Havelange** to the conservative presidency of **Sir Stanley Rous** in the 1974 FIFA presidential election. Havelange promised to expand the World Cup to include more African teams, and since then, CAF's number of automatic qualifiers has expanded from one in 1970 to five by 2010. During the same period, the Africa Cup of Nations has grown in its prestige, accepting professionals in 1980, and has become one of the world's major international competitions. CAF's influence on the sport globally has continued to expand under the long presidency of Issa Hayatou from **Cameroon**, and African teams and players have become increasingly prominent on the international stage. *See also* CAF AFRICAN YOUTH CHAMPIONSHIP; CAF WOMEN'S AFRICAN CHAMPIONSHIP.

CONFEDERATION OF NORTH, CENTRAL AMERICAN AND CARIBBEAN ASSOCIATION FOOTBALL (CONCACAF). The Confederation of North, Central American and Caribbean Association Football is the governing body of soccer in the Americas, except for South America, and one of the six regional confederations of national associations operating under the umbrella of the global governing authority, **Fédération Internationale de Football Association (FIFA)**. CONCACAF currently has 40 member national associations. It organizes club and national team competitions and training courses, and is charged with growing the sport of soccer in the region. CONCACAF runs the regional qualifying tournaments for the **FIFA World Cup**, **FIFA Women's World Cup**, and other international youth, **futsal**, and **beach soccer** competitions. The **CONCACAF Gold Cup** is the region's premier international tournament for male national teams and is held every two years. Similarly, the **CONCACAF Women's Gold Cup** is the region's top **women's** international competition and is staged every four years, doubling as CONCACAF's qualifying event for the FIFA Women's

World Cup. At club level, CONCACAF's most significant competition for the premier clubs from each national association in the region is the **CONCACAF Champions League**. The winner of this tournament gains entry to the **FIFA Club World Cup**. CONCACAF was formed in 1961 by a merger of two previous regional governing bodies, the Football Confederation of Central America and the Caribbean (CCCF) and the North American Football Confederation (NAFC). In recent decades, the region's international competition has been dominated by **Mexico** and the **United States**, by far the largest countries in CONCACAF, with both countries winning all but one iteration of the CONCACAF Gold Cup since its establishment in 1991. *See also* CONCACAF UNDER-20 CHAMPIONSHIP.

CONFEDERATION OF SOUTH AMERICAN FOOTBALL (CONMEBOL). The South American Football Confederation, recognized by **Fédération Internationale de Football Association (FIFA)** as the governing body of soccer in South America, is commonly referred to as "CONMEBOL." This is an abbreviation for its official names in Spanish, *Confederación Sudamericana de Fútbol*, and Portuguese, *Confederação Sul-Americana de Futebol*. CONMEBOL has 10 member national associations: **Argentina**, Bolivia, **Brazil**, **Chile**, **Colombia**, Ecuador, **Paraguay**, **Peru**, **Uruguay**, and Venezuela. CONMEBOL was the first confederation of national associations to be established in world soccer. It was founded at a meeting of delegates from Argentina, Brazil, Chile, and Uruguay at the headquarters of the latter's national soccer association on 15 December 1916. CONMEBOL organizes the main continental international tournaments in South America, including the **Copa América** for national teams and the **Copa Libertadores de América** for club teams. *See also* SOUTH AMERICAN YOUTH CHAMPIONSHIPS.

COPA AMÉRICA. Meaning "America Cup" in English, the Copa América, organized by the **South American Football Confederation (CONMEBOL)**, is the elite competition in South American soccer for international teams. It was first held in 1916, with all games played in Buenos Aires, **Argentina**, and was the world's first continental international championship. The inaugural tournament, organized as a mini-league with each of the four teams playing each other once, was won by **Uruguay**, finishing ahead of Argentina, **Brazil**, and **Chile**. The tournament has expanded along with the membership of CONMEBOL, with all 10 current members—Argentina, Bolivia, Brazil, Chile, **Colombia**, Ecuador, **Paraguay**, **Peru**, Uruguay, and Venezuela—appearing in the finals tournament each time. Between 1916 and 2007, the competition was held every two years; Argentina and Uruguay proved to be the most successful teams, winning 14 tournaments each. Brazil has won the Copa América eight times, with five of those wins coming since 1989. Paraguay and Peru have won it twice, and Bolivia and Colombia once each.

COPA LIBERTADORES DE AMÉRICA. The most important international club tournament in South America, the Copa Libertadores de América has been organized annually by the **South American Football Confederation (CONMEBOL)** since 1960. The tournament, inspired by the success of the **European Cup**, was first organized in 1955, though there had also been a South American precursor, the 1948 Copa de Campeones, held in **Chile** and featuring the champion club from seven South American countries. The first Copa Libertadores tournament in 1960 featured seven South American national champions and was won by **Peñarol** of **Uruguay**, who repeated the next year. **Santos** of **Brazil** won the next two tournaments, featuring **Pelé** in the 1963 final. **Argentina**'s first champions came when **Independiente** won the competition in 1964 and 1965. In 1966, the tournament was expanded to include runners-up in each country as well. Since 1998, even though not a member of CONMEBOL, clubs from **Mexico** have been invited to participate every year, largely to generate more television revenue for the tournament. Argentinean and Brazilian teams have dominated the tournament over the years, with the former boasting 22 champions and the latter 13. Uruguay, thanks largely to Peñarol's five titles, is in third place with eight championships. Two Argentinean clubs, Independiente and **Boca Juniors**, have been the most successful clubs as of August 2010 with seven and six titles respectively.

CORINTHIAN FOOTBALL CLUB. Corinthian Football Club was a famous amateur soccer club in **England** and a pioneer in the development of the sport in the 19th century. The team was founded in London in 1882, with many of their players representing England in their early international games against **Scotland**. Corinthian F.C. toured around the world and inspired the naming of "**Corinthians**" in **Brazil**. The club stuck to a strictly amateur ethos, refusing to join the professional **Football League** founded in 1888, and eventually aligned themselves with the Amateur Football Association. In 1939, Corinthian merged with another famous amateur team, Casuals Football Club, to form Corinthian-Casuals Football Club, which now still competes in the lower levels of the game in England.

CORINTHIANS. Sport Club Corinthians Paulista is better known simply as "Corinthians," a **Brazilian** club founded on 1 September 1910 and based in the city of São Paulo. They were first organized by a group of Brazilian laborers, who named the club after the famous British amateur team **Corinthian Football Club**, which had recently toured Brazil. Corinthians is one of the most successful clubs in Brazil. In 2000, they won the inaugural **FIFA Club World Cup** and have also won four Brazilian national championships and 26 state championships. *See also* RIVELINO, ROBERTO; RONALDO; SÓCRATES.

CORNER KICK. A corner kick is the way play is restarted when the **ball** has crossed over the goal line and was last touched by the defending team, without a goal having been scored. It is taken from the corner arc nearest to the point where the ball crossed the goal line, and all defending players must be at least 10 yards away when the ball is kicked. Another player must touch the ball before the kicker can touch it a second time, which prevents a player from dribbling the ball from a corner kick. A goal may be scored directly into the defending team's goal from a corner kick, though this rarely happens in practice. Law 17 of the **Laws of the Game** explains this rule, which was first introduced in 1872.

CORPORACIÓN DEPORTIVA AMÉRICA. Often known as "América de Cali," Corporación Deportiva América is one of **Colombia**'s leading professional club teams. The club was officially founded on 13 February 1927 in the western Colombian city of Cali, though their origins trace back to 1918. América de Cali turned professional in 1948, though they had to wait 31 years for their first national professional title in 1979. Many believed the club had been cursed by a former member of the club who had objected to the introduction of professionalism. Since that first victory in 1979, América de Cali has been remarkably successful, now boasting 13 national professional titles and reaching the final of South America's premier club competition the **Copa Libertadores** four times, in 1985, 1986, 1987, and 1996, though losing on each occasion. This success, however, was tainted by the club's connections to Cali drug cartels, and the **United States** controversially froze their assets for this reason. Their stadium is now known as "Estadio Olimpico Pascual Guerrero," named after a local poet who donated the land for its use, and has a capacity of almost 46,000.

CRUYFF, JOHAN. B. 25 April 1947, Amsterdam, Netherlands. Johan Cruyff is a renowned Dutch coach and former player, remembered as one of the greatest talents of the 20th century, alongside **Pelé** and **Diego Maradona**. A brilliant and stylish attacker who epitomized the concept of "**Total Football**," Cruyff was at his peak in the early 1970s, winning the **European Footballer of the Year** award in 1971, 1973, and 1974. Cruyff began his professional career in 1964 at the age of 17 with his local club, **Ajax Amsterdam**, and his genius was a key part of the team's rise from provincial also-ran to world power. In 1966, Ajax Amsterdam claimed the Dutch national championship, embarking on a run of success that saw them win five further domestic titles before Cruyff left the club in 1973 to play for **Barcelona** in **Spain**. The peak of his club career came with Ajax Amsterdam's three consecutive **European Cup** victories between 1971 and 1973. The club also won the **Intercontinental Cup** in 1972. But the high point of Cruyff's international fame came at the 1974 **FIFA World Cup** finals in West **Germany** when Cruyff led an underdog **Netherlands** team on a storming run to the final under his mentor and coach at both Barcelona and Ajax Amsterdam, **Rinus Michels**. Though the Netherlands lost in the final 2-1 to the hosts, West Germany, despite taking an early lead, their remarkably fluid, graceful, and razor-sharp play at the tournament has them remembered as one of the greatest teams of all time. Cruyff, though, would go on to play only a small number of games for the Netherlands after 1974. He never appeared in the World Cup finals again, ending his 11-year international career in 1977 with 33 goals in 48 appearances and missing the 1978 World Cup. At club level, Cruyff won the Spanish league in 1974 with Barcelona before moving to the **United States** for a generous payday in the **North American Soccer League** in the late 1970s. He then played his final years back in the Netherlands with Ajax Amsterdam and Feyenoord in the early 1980s, winning three further Dutch championships between 1982 and 1984.

Cruyff then retired from playing and took up a role as technical director at Ajax Amsterdam in 1985, leading the club to victory in the **UEFA Cup Winners' Cup** in 1987. He then mirrored his playing career with a move to Barcelona. There, he again claimed the UEFA Cup Winners' Cup trophy in 1989, a prelude to an outstanding period of achievement for the Catalonian club, as Cruyff's young team won the Spanish championship four times, from 1991 to 1994, and conquered Europe in 1992 with victory in the European Cup. Cruyff, suffering from heart trouble, left Barcelona in 1996 and took a 13-year break from coaching before taking an obscure but sentimental role as head coach of Catalonia's national team in 2009.

CUBILLAS, TEÓFILO. B. 8 March 1949, Lima, Peru. Teófilo Cubillas is **Peru**'s most outstanding player of all time, participating in three **FIFA World Cup** finals tournaments for his country, in 1970, 1978, and 1982. In 1970, Peru reached the quarterfinals of the competition, their best performance, going out to **Pelé**'s **Brazil**, with Cubillas scoring once in a gripping 4-2 defeat, his fifth goal in four games at the competition. A creative, attacking midfielder with a deft touch and a powerful shot, Cubillas scored 26 goals in 81 games for his country. In 1976, Cubillas scored two goals in the **Copa América** as Peru won the South American continental championship.

Cubillas was successful in club soccer as well, playing most of his career for his local club Alianza Lima before ending his career in the **United States**. He retired from playing in 1989.

CUJU. The first known organized ball game whose form was similar to that of modern-day soccer was played in China during the Han dynasty (206 BCE–220 AD). The game was known as *cuju*—literally meaning, "kick ball." Two teams attempted to shoot a stitched leather ball (stuffed with fur, feathers, or hemp) into a goal at each end of a marked field. Unlike some other ancient ball games, in cuju, use of the feet by players was a central element of the game. Cuju was played mainly by members of the army and the upper classes in China, all the way up to the royal household. Similar forms of the game soon spread across Asia to Korea, Japan (morphing into a different ball game, known there as "*kemari*"), and the Malay Peninsula. Variations on cuju—with a hollow ball becoming more commonly used as time passed—continued to be played under later Chinese imperial dynasties until the establishment of the Ming dynasty in 1368 AD, when the game began to be neglected, eventually disappearing altogether.

CZECH REPUBLIC. Both the Czech Republic and Slovakia are considered by the sport's global governing body, **Fédération Internationale de Football Association (FIFA)**, to be the successor and inheritor of Czechoslovakia's record in international soccer prior to their independent existences from 1993 onward. That record is an outstanding one, as Czechoslovakia twice finished runners-up at the **FIFA World Cup** in 1934 and 1962, won the **UEFA European Football Championship** in 1976 by defeating West **Germany** on penalty kicks in the final, and were victorious in the 1980 **Olympic Games Football Tournament**. Following the division of Czechoslovakia in 1993 into the Czech Republic and Slovakia, the former has continued a high level of performance, finishing as runners-up in the 1996 UEFA European Football Championship and making the semifinals at the 2004 UEFA European Football Championship. Success has also come at youth level with a victory in the 2002 **UEFA European Under-21 Championship** and a runners-up position at the 2007 **FIFA U-20 World Cup**. *See also* BICAN, JOSEF; KUBALA, LÁSZLÓ; MASOPUST, JOSEF; NEDVĚD, PAVEL; PLÁNIČKA, FRANTIŠEK.

CZECHOSLOVAKIA. *See* CZECH REPUBLIC.

D

DALGLISH, KENNY. B. 4 March 1951, Glasgow, Scotland. Kenny Dalglish was arguably the greatest Scottish player of the 20th century. Dalglish was a quicksilver attacking midfielder and forward with a golden goal-scoring touch. He won 13 league championship titles playing for **Glasgow Celtic** in **Scotland** and **Liverpool Football Club** in **England**. Dalglish was a key player in Liverpool's fantastic run of success in his tenure with the club from 1977 to 1989, garnering three **European Cup** triumphs in that period, in 1978, 1981, and 1984. Dalglish also had an exceptional record playing for Scotland, playing 102 games for his country and scoring 30 goals. He appeared at the 1974, 1978, and 1982 **FIFA World Cups**, scoring two goals in seven games. In 1985, Dalglish took over management of Liverpool while still playing a further season, and he has enjoyed a successful coaching career, winning English league titles with Liverpool in 1986, 1988, and 1990, and with Blackburn Rovers in 1995.

DESAILLY, MARCEL. B. 7 September 1968, Accra, Ghana. Marcel Desailly enjoyed an extraordinarily successful playing career for numerous club teams and for **France** for more than two decades from 1986 to 2006. He was a strong, powerful defender and defensive midfielder and a natural leader on the field. Desailly was born Odenke Abbey in Ghana but was adopted by a French diplomat, who changed his name and raised him in France from the age of four. He was a key player for France at the 1998 **FIFA World Cup**, their first World Cup victory, though Desailly was sent off against **Brazil** in the final with France already leading by two goals; they went on to win the game 3-0. Two years later, Desailly claimed another major honor with France as they won the 2000 **UEFA European Football Championship**. He played a total of 116 games for France, captaining the country at the 2002 World Cup, a less distinguished tournament for the French as they exited in the first round. At club level, Desailly enjoyed particularly strong success playing for **AC Milan** in **Italy** and **Olympique de Marseille** in France, winning the **UEFA Champions League** once with each club.

DI STÉFANO, ALFREDO. B. 4 July 1926, Buenos Aires, Argentina. Alfredo di Stéfano was an Argentinean player regarded as one of the best forwards of the 20th century. He played the majority of his career for **Real Madrid** in **Spain**, where he twice received the **European Footballer of the Year** award (in 1957 and 1959) and led the team to a remarkable run of five straight victories in the **European Cup** from 1956 to 1960. Di Stéfano began his playing career in his native **Argentina** at **River Plate**; he also spent some time on loan at fellow Argentinean club Huracan. In 1947, he finished top scorer in the Argentinean league and made his debut for the Argentina national team, with whom he won the South American continental championship that same year. In 1949, di Stéfano moved to Colombia and played for **Club Deportivo Los Millonarios.** Di Stéfano's goal-scoring exploits attracted increasing interest from the best clubs in Europe, with Spanish teams **Barcelona** and Real Madrid vying for his signature. The latter team ultimately won out, and he joined Real Madrid in 1953. Di Stéfano would spend 11 years in Madrid, scoring 216 goals in 262 games for the Spanish giants. The highlight of the club's remarkable success in European competition came at the 1960 European Cup final held in Glasgow, **Scotland**, where di Stéfano's Real Madrid team destroyed German team Eintracht Frankfurt 7-3. In his time with Real Madrid, the team also won eight domestic league championships. In this period, di Stéfano played for the Spanish national team as well (at this time, players were allowed to switch the countries they represented, di Stéfano previously having played for Argentina), for whom he scored 23 goals in 31 appearances. However, di Stéfano never appeared in a **FIFA World Cup** finals, missing the 1962 competition due to injury. Di Stéfano ended his playing career in 1966 after a short spell playing for Espanyol in Barcelona and went on to have a nomadic coaching career across South America and Europe.

DICICCO, TONY. B. 5 August 1948, Wethersfield, Connecticut, United States. An American soccer coach, Tony DiCicco managed the U.S. women's national team to an unmatched run of international success in the 1990s. A former player in the American Soccer League, DiCicco was an assistant coach for the United States during their victorious run at the inaugural **FIFA Women's World Cup** in **China** in 1991, taking over as head coach in 1994. In his five years as head coach of the United States, DiCicco compiled an unparalleled record, with the team winning 108 games, tying 8, and losing 8. In that period, they won the women's **Olympic Games Football Tournament** in 1996 and, most famously, the 1999 FIFA Women's World Cup on home soil, defeating China in a **penalty shoot-out** in the final. DiCicco then served as an interim commissioner of the short-lived Women's United Soccer

Association professional league, and took up a head-coaching role with the Boston Breakers in the **Women's Professional Soccer** league in 2007.

DICK, KERR LADIES FOOTBALL CLUB. Dick, Kerr Ladies was one of the most successful **women's soccer** teams during their existence from 1917 to 1965. They were based in Preston, a city in northern **England**. The team was formed during the First World War at a munitions factory in Preston called Dick, Kerr & Co Ltd, owned by W. B. Dick and John Kerr. The war presented a rare opportunity for women to enter areas of the workforce they were usually excluded from, such as munitions factories, with female workers becoming known as "munitionettes." At the Dick, Kerr munitions factory, women began to take part in informal games of soccer, with male colleagues, on their breaks and in their free time. Like the men, who had their own factory team, the women wanted more competition and set up their own factory team. On Christmas Day in 1917, the Dick, Kerr Ladies played a charity game in Preston, drawing more than 10,000 spectators and raising a large sum of money for donations to a local hospital. The crowds grew following the First World War: on Boxing Day in 1920, a crowd of 53,000 watched Dick, Kerr Ladies defeat St. Helen's Ladies 4-0 at Goodison Park in Liverpool. The team became famous nationwide, and stars like talented forward **Lily Parr** became nationally known figures. With other teams springing up around the country as well, a Women's Football Association was formed as the women's game seemed set to establish itself nationally.

Soon, though, a deathly blow was dealt to the development of women's soccer in England, in part due to the popularity of Dick, Kerr Ladies. Their success and fame challenged the conservative attitudes of the ruling members of English soccer's governing body, **The Football Association**, about the suitability of women playing the sport. As such, The Football Association's ruling council announced on 5 December 1921 that "the game of football is quite unsuitable for females and ought not to be encouraged," and requested that clubs belonging to its association refuse the use of their stadiums for women's soccer games, a ban that would last for 50 years. This forced Dick, Kerr Ladies to go abroad to play in front of the large crowds they could attract given they could no longer play at any large soccer stadium in England. They played on an extensive tour of the **United States** in 1922 and continued playing until they disbanded in 1965.

DIDI. B. 8 October 1928, Campos dos Goytacazes, Brazil. D. 12 May 2001. Born Valdir Pereira but better known by his nickname "Didi," Didi was a Brazilian player who starred for Brazil when they won the 1958 **FIFA World Cup** in **Sweden**. It was the second FIFA World Cup finals tournament Didi appeared in, previously playing at the 1954 World Cup in **Switzerland**. Didi played again for Brazil during their successful defense of the World Cup title in 1962, this time in **Chile**. A graceful and strong creator and goal scorer who usually played in midfield, Didi retired from playing in 1962, going on to have a long career as a coach, including managing **Peru** to the quarterfinal stage of the 1970 World Cup.

DINAMO ZAGREB. Dinamo Zagreb is a Croatian club based in the country's capital, Zagreb, whose rarely used official name is *Nogometni klub Dinamo Zagreb*. The club was founded in June 1945, merging three former popular clubs banned by the newly installed Communist regime, and was the champion of the league in the former **Yugoslavia** in 1948, 1954, 1958, and 1962. Since the breakup of Yugoslavia, Dinamo Zagreb has been a dominant force in Croatian soccer, winning the league on eight occasions since 1993. A disturbance at a Dinamo Zagreb game against a Serbian team in May 1990 is said by some to have played a role in prompting the start of the direct momentum toward Croatian independence. They play at Stadion Maksmir, a stadium built in 1912 and recently renovated with a capacity of around 40,000.

DONOVAN, LANDON. B. 4 March 1982, Ontario, California, United States. Landon Donovan is generally regarded as the best outfield player in the history of the U.S. national team. He currently plays at club level for the Los Angeles Galaxy in **Major League Soccer** and has played for **Bayern Munich** in **Germany**'s Bundesliga and for Everton in **England**'s **Premier League**. Donovan has played at the **FIFA World Cup** finals tournament on two occasions for the United States, and is the country's all-time leader in goals and assists. As of August 2010, he had scored 45 goals in 128 appearances for his country. Donovan is a quick, creative player able to play in midfield or at forward, with highly accomplished technical skills and an outstanding work rate.

DOPING. The use of drugs to enhance athletic performance in the sport of soccer is prohibited by the sport's international governing body, **Fédération Internationale de Football Association (FIFA)**, on the grounds that doping contravenes the ethics of sports, endangers athletes' health, and does not allow for fair competition. FIFA introduced doping controls in the 1970s following a series of doping scandals in several countries in the 1960s, including, most notably, **Italy**. Random drug testing takes place both in and out of competition. As of spring 2010, FIFA reported it had performed roughly 33,000 tests on players, with 0.03 percent returning positive results. The highest-profile positive test came at the 1994 **FIFA World Cup**, with **Diego**

Maradona of **Argentina** found to have traces of several banned substances in his blood; Maradona was immediately expelled from the competition.

DORRANCE, ANSON. B. 9 April 1951, Bombay, India. Elected to the U.S. National Soccer Hall of Fame in 2008, Anson Dorrance is the most successful coach in the history of American **women's soccer**, even though he has never coached a professional club. Dorrance was the coach of the U.S. women's national team from 1986 to 1994, during which time they won the inaugural **FIFA Women's World Cup** in 1991, held in **China**. In that eight-year period, the U.S. team coached by Dorrance won 66 games, tied 22, and lost just five, establishing itself as the dominant force in global women's soccer. Dorrance made his name as coach of the women's soccer program at the University of North Carolina, a position he took in 1979 and has held continuously since: in that time, his team, nicknamed the "Tar Heels," has won a remarkable 20 national championships out of the 28 ever contested, including an unprecedented nine straight from 1986 to 1994. During that period, North Carolina has won 633 games under Dorrance, losing only 21 and tying 33.

DREWRY, ARTHUR. B. 3 March 1891, England. D. 25 March 1961. Arthur Drewry was an English soccer administrator who became the interim president of the **Fédération Internationale de Football Association (FIFA)** in 1956 following the death in office of the previous president **Rodolphe William Seeldrayers**. Drewry was elected to a full term as FIFA president in June 1956, dying while still in office on 25 March 1961. During his tenure, Drewry oversaw the successful 1958 **FIFA World Cup** in **Sweden**. Drewry's greatest contribution to FIFA came before his tenure as president, when he was a leading force in returning the British national associations to membership of FIFA in 1946 with the aid of **Sir Stanley Rous**, the chairman of the **Football League**. Drewry was simultaneously the chairman of **The Football Association** while FIFA president. Drewry was also the selector of the **England** team that surprisingly lost to the **United States** at the 1950 World Cup.

DYNAMO KYIV. Dynamo Kyiv plays in Kyiv, Ukraine, and is the country's most successful-ever club. They were founded in 1927 and played in the Soviet league until the breakup of the Soviet Union in 1991. During that period, Dynamo Kyiv won the Soviet Union championship a record 13 times. That came despite the club suffering horrifically under the Nazi occupation of Ukraine during the Second World War, when numerous ex-players were executed or tortured after playing in a "death match" game against their Nazi occupiers. The club's golden era came under coach **Valery Lobanovski**, a former engineer who brought scientific and statistical analysis to the art of management, bringing home eight Soviet titles and two **UEFA Cup Winners' Cup** trophies in the 1970s and 1980s. The club's current home, Lobanovski Dynamo Stadium, is named after their legendary coach. In the 1990s, Dynamo Kyiv began playing in the Ukrainian Premier League and has dominated the competition with 13 league titles since 1993.

E

EGYPT. Egypt has been a traditional powerhouse in African soccer at both national and club team levels. Soccer was first played in an organized fashion in Egypt during the British occupation of the country from 1882 to 1923. The sport was particularly popular among colonial soldiers. The first known organized game took place in 1885. Egyptians quickly took up soccer themselves, and in the early 20th century, newly formed native clubs took on teams of foreigners representing colonial army units or companies, with the Anglo-Egyptian Cup established in 1916. Egypt was the first African nation to make a major mark on international soccer, as the Egyptian Football Association (EFA) became the first African affiliate of **Fédération Internationale de Football Association (FIFA)** in 1923. They were the only African country to appear at both the 1924 and 1928 **Olympic Games Football Tournaments**, registering particularly notable wins against **Hungary** (1924), **France** (1924), **Portugal** (1928), and **Turkey** (1928). Egypt reached the semifinals at the 1928 tournament, finishing in third place, and then became the first African team to take part in the **FIFA World Cup** in 1934, losing in the first round to Hungary. The first Egyptian national championship was organized in 1948 by the EFA with the support of King Farouk, an avid soccer fan. Two club teams, **Al-Ahly Sporting Club** and **Zamalek Sporting Club**, have dominated the domestic Egyptian championship, which has consistently been the strongest in Africa, as reflected in both clubs' success in African continental competition. Egypt has only qualified for one further World Cup since 1934, appearing in the 1990 World Cup in **Italy**, finishing at the bottom of their group with no victories. They have, though, been the most successful country in Africa's premier international tournament for national teams, the **Africa Cup of Nations**, with six titles.

ENGLAND. The originating country of soccer as an organized sport, England, in the 19th century, is where the ball game we now know as Association Football or soccer was first codified and where the first amateur and, later, professional clubs and competitions were established. The sport of soccer had its antecedent in folk forms of the game played in English towns and villages in the Middle Ages and was formalized into an organized game with defined rules in the mid-19th century, largely in elite public schools and universities. Within a few decades, the sport in England had become professionalized and popularized. There was considerable participation in soccer by the working classes in the late 19th century, and English emigrants established the game in numerous countries worldwide. England was the birthplace of the world's first soccer club in 1857; the world's first national governing body, **The Football Association**, in 1863; the world's first national cup tournament, the F.A. Cup in 1871; and the world's first league competition, the **Football League,** in 1888. England played against their northern neighbors **Scotland** in the world's first international game in 1870, and English administrators played a crucial role in establishing the **Laws of the Game** still followed worldwide under the auspices of the **International Football Association Board (IFAB)**, of which England is one of five members.

The world's richest league, the **Premier League**, was formed in 1992 by 22 clubs breaking away from the Football League. Several English club teams are among the world's most successful and famous, such as **Manchester United** and **Liverpool**. England's clubs have won Europe's premier club competition, the **UEFA Champions League**, on 11 occasions, a record bettered by only **Italy** and **Spain**, whose clubs have each won it 12 times. England's national team has won the **FIFA World Cup** on one occasion, when held for the first and only time in England in 1966, with England defeating West **Germany** 4-2 in the final held at **Wembley Stadium** in London, one of the world's most iconic stadiums. England has not reached the final of either the World Cup or the **UEFA European Football Championship** since, despite having more professional clubs and players than any other European nation. *See also* ARSENAL FOOTBALL CLUB; BANKS, GORDON; BECKHAM, DAVID; CHARLTON, BOBBY; CHELSEA FOOTBALL CLUB; CLOUGH, BRIAN; DICK, KERR LADIES FOOTBALL CLUB; KEEGAN, KEVIN; MATTHEWS, SIR STANLEY; MOORE, BOBBY; PAISLEY, ROBERT; PARR, LILY; RAMSEY, SIR ALF; ROUS, SIR STANLEY; SHEFFIELD FOOTBALL CLUB; WOOLFALL, DANIEL BURLEY.

ENGLISH PREMIER LEAGUE. *See* PREMIER LEAGUE.

ENYIMBA INTERNATIONAL FOOTBALL CLUB. Though Enyimba International Football Club, usually referred to simply as "Enyimba," was founded only in 1976, they have rapidly become one of the most successful teams in African soccer. Based in the southern city of Aba in **Nigeria**, Enyimba has twice won the premier African continental competition, the **CAF Champions League**, in 2003 and 2004. They have also won two African Super Cups, six Nigerian league championships, and two Nigerian FA Cups. They play at Enyimba International Stadium, a 15,000-capacity venue.

ERICO, ARSENIO. B. 30 March 1915, Asunción, Paraguay. D. 23 July 1977. Arsenio Erico was a **Paraguayan** striker and is commonly regarded as the greatest player his country ever produced. He played most of his career for **Independiente** in **Argentina**, amassing a phenomenal total of 293 goals in 325 games for the club, and is still tied today as the top scorer in the history of the Argentinean league with **Ángel Labruna**. He won two league titles with Independiente, in 1938 and 1939. Erico was known for his graceful yet effective jumping ability and his ability to dance with the ball, a creator of goals for his teammates as well as a prolific scorer. Erico retired in 1949 without ever having played an official game for Paraguay, though he featured regularly in unofficial games.

ESTADIO AZTECA. Estadio Azteca is the only **stadium** to have twice hosted the **FIFA World Cup** final, at the 1970 and 1986 tournaments hosted by **Mexico**. It is located in Mexico City, Mexico, and currently has a capacity of 105,000. It is the home stadium for both the Mexico national team and the famous club team Club América. Estadio Azteca's original capacity upon opening in May 1966 was 114,600, and it initially served as the main stadium for the 1968 Olympic Games. The stadium is located 7,200 feet above sea level, considered a considerable local advantage for the Mexican national team, who have a formidable record at the stadium.

ESTADIO DE CENTENARIO. Located in the capital city of **Uruguay**, Montevideo, Estadio de Centenario played host to the first **FIFA World Cup** final, held in 1930, in which Uruguay defeated **Argentina** 4-2. It also played host to both semifinals in that inaugural World Cup, along with seven first-round games. It was called a "temple of football" by then–**Fédération Internationale de Football Association (FIFA)** president Jules Rimet and was built specifically for the World Cup. The name, meaning "Centenary Stadium" in English, marked the 100th anniversary of Uruguay's constitution in 1930, and the **stadium** had an initial capacity of 100,000. Estadio de Centenario remains the home of the Uruguayan national team. With a reduced capacity of 60,000, the stadium is in need of major renovation. It is also home to Uruguay's two leading club teams, **Peñarol** and **Nacional**, though both teams play some home games at their own smaller stadiums.

ESTADIO SANTIAGO BERNABÉU. Estadio Santiago Bernabéu, commonly known simply as the "Bernabéu," is a **stadium** located in Madrid, **Spain**, and is home to club team **Real Madrid**. It played host to the final of the 1982 **FIFA World Cup**, along with two second-round games in the same tournament. The 1964 **UEFA European Football Championship** final took place there, and four **UEFA Champions League** finals have been played there. It currently has a capacity of 80,354, having undergone significant renovation in recent years.

ESTUDIANTES. Known as *Los Pincharratas* ("The Rat Stabbers") to their fans, Estudiantes is an **Argentinean** club based in the city of La Plata and boasts one of the best records in South American club competition. Founded in 1905, Estudiantes have won four domestic Argentine league championships and, more remarkably, four continental titles in the **Copa Libertadores**, with victories in 1968, 1969, 1970, and 2009. In 1968, they won the **Intercontinental Cup**, and were runners-up in the two following years. In 2009, Estudiantes reached the final of the 2009 **FIFA Club World Cup**, losing to **Barcelona**. During their remarkable run of success from 1968 to 1970 in South American and global club competition, Estudiantes were viewed as the epitome of the development of Argentine soccer into ultraphysical and defensive play, highly effective yet aesthetically displeasing. In recent years, the team has been built, in a different manner, around the stylish midfielder Juan Sebastián Verón, who led them to their first Copa Libertadores victory in 39 years, in 2009.

EUROPEAN CUP. *See* UEFA CHAMPIONS LEAGUE.

EUROPEAN FOOTBALLER OF THE YEAR. *See* BALLON D'OR.

EUSÉBIO FERREIRA DA SILVA. B. 25 January 1942, Maputo, Mozambique. Better known simply as "Eusébio," Eusébio Ferreira da Silva is **Portugal**'s greatest-ever player and arguably the greatest African-born player of all time. A mercurial and prolific goal-scoring forward, he led his club **Benfica** to their second **European Cup** title in 1962, scoring twice in the final against **Real Madrid**. Eusébio played for Benfica from 1960 to 1975, scoring a remarkable 320 goals in 313 Portuguese league games. Eusébio was equally deadly at the international level. He was the top scorer for his adopted country, Portugal, at the 1966 **FIFA World Cup**, where they finished in third place. He scored a total of 41 goals in 64 games for Portugal. Eusébio won the **European Footballer of the Year** award in 1965 and the European Golden Boot in 1968 and 1973, before spending the final years of his career in the **United States**.

F

FACCHETTI, GIACINTO. B. 1 July 1942, Treviglio, Italy. D. 4 September 2006. Giacinto Facchetti revolutionized the fullback defensive position. Regularly roaming forward and bringing a new attacking dimension to the role, he scored an unusual number of goals from that position. He starred for **Italy** at three **FIFA World Cup** tournaments, in 1966, 1970, and 1974. Facchetti captained his country on 70 of his 94 appearances, including in the final of the 1970 competition, when Italy lost to **Brazil**. He won the 1968 **UEFA European Football Championship** with his country. Facchetti was a stylish player who played his entire senior club career for **Internazionale** in Italy. He played a key part in the innovative defensive system installed by the club's coach, **Helenio Herrera**, known as "*catennacio*." He won four Italian league championships, two **European Cups**, and two **Intercontinental Cups** with Internazionale. Physically, Facchetti was a strong, very tall player with surprising speed, which assisted his forward runs. He was the runner-up in the voting for the 1965 **European Footballer of the Year** award. Facchetti retired in 1978 and later became the president of Internazionale.

FÉDÉRATION INTERNATIONALE DE FOOTBALL ASSOCIATION (FIFA). The Fédération Internationale de Football Association is the governing body of soccer worldwide. Headquartered in Zurich, **Switzerland**, and operating under Swiss law, FIFA had 208 member national associations as of August 2010. Since the first competition, held in 1930, FIFA has organized the **FIFA World Cup**, the world's leading international soccer tournament. The annual **FIFA Congress** of its member associations elects the organization's governing **FIFA Executive Committee**, including the president and general secretary. FIFA's statutes can be made or amended only by the congress and govern the regulations of the game in all member nations. FIFA is the most important single member of the **International Football Association Board (IFAB)**, which determines the **Laws of the Game** followed worldwide.

Members of FIFA are national associations responsible for organizing and supervising soccer in their respective countries under FIFA regulation. FIFA's statutes define a country as "an independent state recognized by the international community." Only one national association is permitted to be a member of FIFA per country, with an exception made for the four associations from the United Kingdom: associations from **England**, **Scotland**, Wales, and Northern Ireland are all separately affiliated with FIFA for historical reasons. There are six **FIFA confederations** recognized by FIFA who oversee the game in their continental regions: the **Union of European Football Associations (UEFA)** in Europe; the **Confederation of African Football (CAF)** in Africa; the **Confederation of North, Central American and Caribbean Association Football (CONCACAF)** in North America, Central America, and the Caribbean; the **Asian Football Confederation (AFC)** in Asia; the **Confederation of South American Football (CONME-BOL)** in South America; and the **Oceania Football Confederation (OFC)** in the Oceanic region.

FIFA was originally founded on 21 May 1904, in Paris, **France**. Representatives from six countries signed FIFA's foundation act: France, **Belgium**, Denmark, **Spain**, **Sweden**, and Switzerland. The next day, at the first FIFA Congress, French administrator **Robert Guérin** was elected the first president of FIFA. Notably not present at the founding proceedings were any English representatives, despite entreaties from Guérin to **The Football Association**. National associations were required to pay an affiliation fee to FIFA and to recognize that only FIFA had the right to organize an international competition. The first FIFA statutes were established at the congress, including regulations forbidding clubs or players to play simultaneously for different national associations, the recognition by all associations of a player's suspension by any other association, and an agreement that all matches would be played according to the Laws of the Game as established by the International Football Association Board. FIFA thus provided a structure for soccer to operate as an international sport.

Following further negotiations conducted by Baron Edouard de Laveleye on behalf of FIFA, the English Football Association became a member of FIFA in April 1905, a crucial coup for the nascent organization. An English administrator, the pragmatic **Daniel Burley Woolfall**, was elected as the second FIFA president the next year. Several other national associations soon joined: **Germany**, **Austria**, **Italy**, Scotland, Wales, and Ireland. Meanwhile, FIFA's initial attempt to organize an international competition in 1906 proved to be a failure. Soccer tournaments featuring several nations were successfully organized at the 1908 and 1912 **Olympic Games** with FIFA's assistance, but it would be some time before FIFA could organize its own world championship. Part of this was a result of FIFA's operation as an initially Euro-centric organization: expansion of its membership to other continents was critical for it to develop into a global governing body. This was partially achieved with the admission to FIFA of **South Africa**, **Argentina**,

Chile, and the **United States**, before the outbreak of the First World War in 1914 disrupted all international sporting cooperation.

FIFA's membership continued to grow rapidly, with dozens of new members joining in the 1920s. This, along with a growing demand for an international competition that would accept both professionals and amateurs (unlike the ethos of the strictly amateur Olympic Games), led to the founding of the FIFA World Cup in 1930 at the urging of FIFA President **Jules Rimet**. The first World Cup was held in **Uruguay** and was won by the hosts. It has been held every four years since aside from a break for World War II, becoming one of the world's leading global sporting events and a source of considerable commercial income for FIFA. In the 1960s, FIFA further modernized under the presidency of Englishman **Sir Stanley Rous**, when it accepted numerous new members from the decolonized nations of Asia and Africa. This did not occur without political controversy, as Rous resisted granting African nations direct qualification spots for the World Cup. This led to an African boycott of the 1966 World Cup and, ultimately, to Rous' defeat in the 1974 FIFA presidential election to Brazilian **João Havelange**.

Under João Havelange and his successor **Sepp Blatter**, since the 1970s, FIFA has dramatically increased its commercial presence, expanded its membership to more than 200 countries, and increased its revenue vastly, mainly thanks to lucrative television rights and sponsorship deals for its major tournaments. The men's World Cup finals tournament now includes 32 teams, with the 64 matches played at each competition providing considerable revenue from the sale of **television** rights and raising billions of dollars from broadcasters around the world. FIFA has further expanded its reach with the foundation of the **FIFA Women's World Cup** in 1991 and, for club teams, the **FIFA Club World Cup** in 2000, along with global junior competitions, such as the **FIFA U-20 World Cup** and **FIFA U-20 Women's World Cup**. As FIFA's income has grown, it has increasingly faced allegations of corruption at the highest levels, and FIFA was found guilty by a judge in New York of deceiving sponsors in the VISA-MasterCard scandal in 2006. FIFA, though, continues to expand its global presence, taking the World Cup to Africa for the first time in 2010, with the competition held in South Africa.

FIFA has, in the course of a little more than a century since its founding, grown from a small organization with influence in only northern Europe to become a large bureaucratic organization with annual revenue exceeding $1 billion and tight control on the direction of soccer globally. FIFA now annually spends hundreds of millions on its events (such as the FIFA Club World Cup), its staffing, and expansive headquarters in Switzerland, and in investment in the development of soccer around the world. FIFA's present power, in particular its control over where the World Cup is hosted, makes the position of FIFA president one of the most prominent in global sports administration, and FIFA presidential elections have become high-profile, contentious, and expensively contested affairs. FIFA has faced fierce criticism in recent years for its handling of the World Cup bidding process, and two members of the FIFA Executive Committee were suspended prior to the vote for the 2018 and 2022 World Cup hosting decisions in late 2010. *See also* Appendix A (Presidents of FIFA) and the separate entries for each FIFA president, BLATTER, JOSEPH SEPP; DREWRY, ARTHUR; GUÉRIN, ROBERT; HAVELANGE, JOÃO; RIMET, JULES; ROUS, SIR STANLEY; SEELDRAYERS, RODOLPHE; WOOLFALL, DANIEL BURLEY.

FENERBAHÇE SPOR KULÜBÜ. One of the leading three clubs in **Turkey**, Fenerbahçe's soccer team is part of a general sports club known as *Fenerbahçe Spor Kulübü* (Fenerbahçe Sports Club), founded on 3 May 1907 in Turkey's largest city, Istanbul. They play in Turkey's top league competition, Süper Lig, and have won the competition on 17 occasions, a Turkish record shared with rivals **Galatasaray Spor Kulübü**. Fenerbahçe's best performance in European club competition came in 2008 when they reached the quarterfinals of the **UEFA Champions League**, losing at that stage to eventual finalist **Chelsea Football Club**.

FERGUSON, ALEX. B. 31 December 1941, Glasgow, Scotland. Alex Ferguson was a Scottish player and is currently the most successful manager in the history of British soccer. Ferguson has won more than 30 trophies as **Manchester United** manager, including 12 **Premier League** titles, five **Football Association Challenge Cups**, and two **UEFA Champions League** triumphs. Ferguson was born in a working-class area of Glasgow and eventually played for six different Scottish clubs as a striker. He scored 170 goals in 317 career appearances. Ferguson began his managerial career with Scottish clubs Queen's Park, St. Johnstone, and Aberdeen, winning the Scottish league title, Scottish Football Association Cup, and **UEFA Cup Winners' Cup**, with the latter leading to his appointment as Manchester United manager in November 1986.

Ferguson's first three seasons as Manchester United manager did not bring any trophies, as the club continued to underachieve relative to the great success of the club under legendary manager **Matt Busby** in the 1960s. His position with the club was thought to be in doubt in the 1989–1990 season, but a successful F.A. Cup run that year bought Ferguson time and proved to be the springboard to a glorious period for the club. Ferguson's surprising purchase of the mercurial French forward Eric Cantona from rival Leeds United in the middle of the 1992–1993 season proved to be critical, as Manchester United won their first league championship for 26 years, inspired by Cantona's brilliant play.

Under Ferguson, Manchester United went on to win another four Premier League titles in the 1990s, dominating English football with a mix of home-grown stars like Ryan Giggs, **David Beckham**, and Paul Scholes, alongside experienced foreigners Cantona, Andrei Kanchelskis, and Roy Keane. Ferguson's greatest triumph came in 1999 when Manchester United won an unprecedented triple: the Premier League, F.A. Cup, and, most famously, the UEFA Champions League. In the final, Manchester United scored twice in added time to defeat **Bayern Munich** and win European club soccer's greatest prize for the second time in its history. Manchester United's roll of success continued in the next decade with Premier League titles won in 2000, 2001, and 2003 before a brief lull amid rumors of Ferguson's impending retirement between 2004 and 2006. But Ferguson successfully remodeled his team once again and won three successive Premier League titles in 2007, 2008, and 2009, sparked by the purchases of young stars such as England's Wayne Rooney and **Portugal**'s **Cristiano Ronaldo**. Ferguson also ended his hunt for a repeat of the 1999 UEFA Champions League triumph with another victory in 2008 when Manchester United defeated **Chelsea Football Club** in the final in Moscow, **Russia**. They returned to the final the next season, 2009, but were defeated by **Barcelona**.

FIELD. Apart from a ball, players, and a goal, the other absolute necessity for a game of soccer is a field of play, commonly called a "pitch" in **England**. Soccer is played recreationally on a variety of surfaces, from pristine grass to beaches to backstreets in cities around the world. At the professional level, outdoor soccer is played on grass or artificial turf fields that meet the specifications of the **Laws of the Game** for games played under **Fédération Internationale de Football Association (FIFA)** auspices. Grass fields must meet the requirements of the FIFA Quality Concept for Football Turf specifications, and likewise, artificial turf fields must match the International Artificial Turf Standard unless special dispensation is given by FIFA.

The standard field of play is rectangular, and lines mark its borders and specific areas inside the field. The two longer-sided lines are called the touchlines, and the two shorter sided lines are called the goal lines. The goal at each end of the field is centered on these lines. A line across the field at halfway divides the field into two, with a center mark in the middle and a circle of a 10-yard radius around it. It is from here that play is started and restarted each half and following a goal. The length of a field must be a minimum of 100 yards and no longer than 130 yards. The width of the field must be no shorter than 50 yards and no longer than 100 yards. Inside the field, markings bound two areas, the goal area and the penalty area. The goal area, marked by two lines, extends six yards from the inside of each goalpost. These two lines are joined by a line running parallel with the goal line. The penalty area is an 18-yard box marked by lines extending from the inside of each goal post, joined by a line running parallel with the goal line. Inside the penalty area, a penalty mark (frequently referred to as the "penalty spot"), from which a **penalty kick** is taken, is made 12 yards from the midpoint between the goalposts and equidistant to them. Flag posts are placed in each of the four corners of the field, with a one-yard quarter circle corner arc marked in front, inside the field of play.

A goal stands on the center of each goal line. Two upright posts anchored into the ground, standing eight yards apart, are met at the top by a horizontal crossbar. These must be white, and are usually made of metal or, less commonly now, wood. Nets are usually attached to the back of the goal to catch the ball, but this is not required in the Laws of the Game. Other forms of the professional game have different field requirements, such as **beach soccer**, played on a smaller field on sand, and **indoor soccer** or **futsal**, played on different surfaces and with different field dimensions. *See also* STADIUMS.

FIFA. *See* FÉDÉRATION INTERNATIONALE DE FOOTBALL ASSOCIATION.

FIFA CONFEDERATIONS. *See* ASIAN FOOTBALL CONFEDERATION (AFC); CONFEDERATION OF AFRICAN FOOTBALL (CAF); CONFEDERATION OF NORTH, CENTRAL AMERICAN AND CARIBBEAN ASSOCIATION FOOTBALL (CONCACAF); OCEANIA FOOTBALL CONFEDERATION (OFC); CONFEDERATION OF SOUTH AMERICAN FOOTBALL (CONMEBOL); UNION OF EUROPEAN FOOTBALL ASSOCIATIONS (UEFA).

FIFA CONFEDERATIONS CUP. Held every four years in the year prior to the **FIFA World Cup**, the FIFA Confederations Cup is a tournament contested by the reigning champions of each **FIFA confederation**, along with the current FIFA World Cup titleholder and the host nation of the next World Cup. The tournament is held in that host nation's country, with the competition thus serving as a dress rehearsal for the following year's World Cup competition. It has been organized since 1997 by the **Fédération Internationale de Football Association (FIFA)** and was held every two years from then until 2005, when it moved to a four-year schedule. Prior to 1997, it was twice organized and held by **Saudi Arabia**, with **Argentina** the inaugural winners in 1992 followed by Denmark in 1995. **Brazil** holds the record for most titles with three tournament victories, in 1997, 2005, and 2009.

FIFA CONGRESS. According to the statutes of the **Fédération Internationale de Football Association (FIFA)**, the FIFA Congress is the legislative body and ultimate authority of world soccer's governing body, FIFA. The FIFA Congress' main responsibilities include electing the FIFA president every four years, amending the FIFA statutes, deciding on applications for membership, and approving the budget and activities of FIFA. It also has the power to expel a **FIFA Executive Committee** member or a national association member. These national association members, now numbering more than 200, make up the body of the Congress, with each entitled to one vote regardless of the country's size or performance on the field. Several congresses have approved momentous decisions in the history of world soccer: the 1929 congress in Barcelona approved the establishment of the **FIFA World Cup**, first played a year later, while the 1946 congress approved the return of the four national associations of Great Britain to FIFA membership, and the 2003 Congress approved significant amendments to the FIFA statutes. Since 1998, the FIFA Congress has met on an annual basis.

FIFA CLUB WORLD CUP. First contested in 2000 in **Brazil**, the FIFA Club World Cup (originally named the FIFA Club World Championship) was launched by the **Fédération Internationale de Football Association (FIFA)** as an attempt to create a global competition crowning the world's best club team. The tournament features the winning teams from each **FIFA confederation**'s premier continental competition. It replaced the **Intercontinental Cup**, which had featured only the champions of the **UEFA Champions League** from Europe and the **Copa Libertadores** from South America. The FIFA Club World Cup was not contested between 2000 and 2005 after planned tournaments for both 2001 and 2003 were canceled, but has since become an annual event. It currently consists of the champions of each of FIFA's six confederations and a representative of the host nation (since 2007, the champion of the **Oceania Football Confederation [OFC]** plays a play-off against the host-nation team). From 2005 to 2008, **Japan** hosted the tournament, replaced by the United Arab Emirates for 2009 and 2010. The competition is often criticized for adding further matches and travel to an already congested international calendar for the world's leading club teams and players.

FIFA EXECUTIVE COMMITTEE. The governing body of **Fédération Internationale de Football Association (FIFA)**, the FIFA Executive Committee consists of 24 members elected by the **FIFA Congress**, FIFA's sovereign authority, in the year following every **FIFA World Cup**. The FIFA president chairs the FIFA Executive Committee, which also consists of eight vice presidents and 15 other ordinary members. It meets at least twice a year and is the main decision-making body of FIFA outside of the FIFA Congress. Members are appointed to four-year terms. Under its purview are the dates, locations, and rules of FIFA tournaments; appointments of FIFA delegates to the **International Football Association Board (IFAB)**; and the election of the FIFA general secretary.

FIFA U-20 WOMEN'S WORLD CUP. The FIFA U-20 Women's World Cup was first played in 2002, when it was the FIFA U-19 Women's World Cup and open to female players under the age of 19. It was the first global women's youth tournament played under the auspices of the sport's world governing body, **Fédération Internationale de Football Association (FIFA).** In 2006, the age limit for the competition was raised to 20, and it was renamed the FIFA U-20 Women's World Cup.

The first competition in 2002 was hosted by **Canada** and surpassed expectations in terms of the attendance and media attention the tournament generated with an average crowd of 11,351 attending the 25 games played, which featured 12 national teams. The final, at Commonwealth Stadium in Edmonton, saw a large crowd of 46,784 watch the host nation Canada defeated by the **United States** 1-0. The second FIFA U-19 Women's World Cup took place in Thailand in November 2004 and was won by **Germany**, which was also the defending senior **FIFA Women's World Cup** champion. The hosts, Thailand, went out in the first round. The third tournament, renamed the FIFA U-20 Women's World Cup with the age ceiling raised by one year, was hosted by **Russia** in 2006. The event did not prove to be popular, with an average crowd of just 1,644 attending the 32 games, and the tournament expanded to 16 teams from the previous 12 in 2004. It was won by North Korea, defeating **China** in the final 5-0 in a rain-drenched game. The 2008 FIFA U-20 Women's World Cup took place in **Chile**, a well-hosted event with 6,749 fans attending on average. The United States won the tournament for the first time since 2002, defeating the defending champion North Korea 2-1 in the final. The 2010 competition was won by host Germany, who defeated **Nigeria**, the first African team to reach the final. *See also* WOMEN'S SOCCER.

FIFA U-20 WORLD CUP. The FIFA U-20 World Cup is the leading global competition for national teams with male players under the age of 20 and is organized by the sport's global governing body, **Fédération Internationale de Football Association (FIFA).** The tournament was known as the FIFA World Youth Championship from its first staging in 1977 until 1995. Eight different countries have won the FIFA U-20 World Cup in the 17 competitions staged every two years since 1977, with **Argentina** holding the record, having won it six times. **Brazil** has won it four times, **Portugal** twice, and the Soviet Union, **Spain**, West **Germany**, **Yugoslavia**, and **Ghana** once each, the latter becoming the first African nation to take the title, in 2009. The current format sees 24 nations take part, with each **FIFA confederation** sending qualifying teams through various youth competitions. The host nation qualifies automatically. Numerous globally famous players have made their mark on the competition and won the Golden Ball award for best player, including **Diego Maradona** in 1979, Robert Prosinečki in 1987, and **Lionel Messi** in 2005.

FIFA WOMEN'S WORLD CUP. The FIFA Women's World Cup, held every four years and organized by the **Fédération Internationale de Football Association (FIFA)** for teams from its member national associations, is the premier international tournament for women's national teams. It currently features 16 teams in a finals tournament, with the first round dividing teams into four groups of four teams each. Each team plays each other team in its group once. The top two teams in each group progress to the quarterfinal stage, which is played in a single-game elimination format; **penalty shootouts** are used to determine a winner if the game is tied after regulation and overtime. The 2011 tournament, to be held in **Germany**, will follow this format, but in 2015, the competition will be expanded to include 24 teams in the finals tournament.

The FIFA Women's World Cup was first held in **China** in November 1991, with 12 countries taking part in the tournament. Some 510,000 fans attended the 26 games, at an average of 19,615 spectators per match. Norway and the **United States** played the final in front of a crowd of 65,000 at Tianhe Stadium in Guangzhou. The score was tied 1-1 at the end of the regulation 90 minutes; the winning goal for the United States came in extra time, scored by **Michelle Akers**, who was also the tournament's top overall goal scorer and won the Golden Shoe award for this feat. The Golden Ball award for the tournament's best player went to Carin Jennings, also of the United States. **Sweden** finished in third place, and Germany fourth.

The second FIFA Women's World Cup was held four years later in June 1995 in Sweden, with 12 teams again competing and all six **FIFA confederations** represented. Norway and Germany reached the final, the former making up for their disappointment in 1991 with a comprehensive 2-0 victory to take the title. Norway's Kirstin-Ann Aarones took the Golden Shoe for most goals scored, and her teammate Hege Riise was awarded the Golden Ball as the best player in the tournament. The United States finished in third place, and China in fourth.

The third FIFA Women's World Cup was held in the United States in 1999 and proved to be the best-attended event yet, capturing the broad imagination of the American public. An all-time high for the competition of 1,194,215 fans attended the 32 games at an average of 37,319 fans per game, with the number of teams in the tournament expanded to 16 from 12. An estimated television audience of 40 million viewers in the United States watched the host country win their second FIFA Women's World Cup title, defeating China in front of 90,185 fans at the Rose Bowl in Southern California. A penalty shoot-out decided the game in favor of the United States, who had also beaten Germany 3-2 in the quarterfinals and **Brazil** 2-0 in the semifinals. Despite their defeat in the final, China swept the individual awards, with **Sun Wen** winning the Golden Ball and the Golden Shoe as both the best player and highest scorer of the tournament, with seven goals to her name.

The next FIFA Women's World Cup was also held in the United States in 2003, though it had originally been scheduled to be hosted by China for the second time. However, due to the outbreak of Severe Acute Respiratory Syndrome in that country, the tournament was moved to the United States by FIFA just six months before it was due to start in September 2003. Despite the short notice, an aggregate 679,664 fans attended the 32 games held, at an average of 21,239 fans at each. The tournament saw an all-European final for the first time since 1995, as the semifinals saw Germany defeat the United States 3-0 and Sweden reach the final after a 2-1 win over **Canada**. Germany claimed their first FIFA Women's World Cup title with a dramatic overtime victory, winning 2-1 at the Home Depot Center in Los Angeles in front of a crowd of 26,137. Their star player, **Birgit Prinz**, won both the Golden Ball for best player and the Golden Shoe as the tournament's top scorer for her seven goals.

The 2007 FIFA Women's World Cup was held in China to make up for the 2003 competition's cancellation, with an impressive total turnout of 997,433 fans at the 32 games, at an average of 31,169 per game, the second highest figure in the tournament's history. Germany emerged as victors for the second successive tournament, defeating Brazil in the final 2-0 to become the first country to win consecutive FIFA Women's World Cup titles. Brazil had comprehensively outclassed the United States 4-0 in the semifinal, while Germany had brushed aside Norway 4-0 in the other semifinal. **FIFA Women's Player of the Year**, Brazil's **Marta**, won both the Golden Ball and the Golden Shoe as the tournament's best player and highest goal scorer, with seven goals. *See also* WOMEN'S SOCCER.

FIFA WORLD CUP. The FIFA World Cup is the international global championship for men's teams representing the member national associations of **Fédération Internationale de Football Association (FIFA)**, soccer's global governing organization. The FIFA World Cup, often referred to simply as the "World Cup," was first contested in 1930 and has been held on a quadrennial basis ever since, with the exceptions of 1942 and 1946 due to the Second World War and its aftermath. The FIFA World Cup, with an estimated one billion television viewers for the FIFA World Cup final in 2006, is the most popular sporting event in the world, its only rival being the Olympic Games. When the FIFA World Cup began in 1930, 13 countries entered the competition held in **Uruguay**; for the 2010 World Cup in **South Africa**, more than 200 countries entered the qualifying competition for the final stage, which consisted of a 32-team competition played over the course of 30 days, reflecting the growth of the competition.

Though FIFA was founded in 1904 and, at that point, declared an international tournament for its member national associations could only happen under its auspices, it would be another 26 years until the first FIFA World Cup opened in Uruguay. In the meantime, FIFA retained an uneasy relationship with the International Olympic Committee with the **Olympic Games Football Tournament** serving as the world's premier international soccer tournament, played under FIFA regulation. The considerable crowds and successes of the 1924 Olympic Games Football Tournament convinced FIFA it was time to organize their own event, especially as many professional players were excluded from competing in the Olympic Games due to its amateur ethos. In 1927, the **FIFA Congress** voted in favor of holding an international championship in 1930, with FIFA issuing invitations to its members to take part. Thirteen teams eventually appeared at the first World Cup in Uruguay in 1930.

Since then, qualification for the FIFA World Cup finals tournament has become an increasingly intense and difficult process. Each of the six regional **FIFA confederations** oversees its own qualifying tournament, with FIFA determining how many places in the finals tournament each confederation is awarded based mainly on past performance in the tournament, a criteria that favors the historically strongest countries from Europe and South America. For example, for the 2010 FIFA World Cup in South Africa, the **Union of European Football Associations (UEFA)** was awarded 13 berths in the finals tournament, while the **Oceania Football Confederation (OFC)** was given just one.

The World Cup's host nation, which automatically qualifies for the finals tournament, is selected by FIFA from its member nations who bid to stage the competition some years in advance. As of 2010, the FIFA World Cup has been hosted in 16 different countries across five continents, with **Italy**, **Mexico**, and **Germany** having hosted the tournament twice. Though initially staged in just a single city of the host nation in 1930, the World Cup is now played across several venues in numerous cities of the host nation in stadiums that must meet stringent FIFA requirements on stadiums, facilities, and security. The bidding process to host the tournament has become increasingly competitive despite the increasingly complex requirements, with a unique global spotlight guaranteed for the host country for the duration of the competition.

The 19 World Cup tournaments held between 1930 and 2010 have been won by eight different countries, with **Brazil** the most successful team, having won it a record five times, in 1958, 1962, 1970, 1994, and 2002. Italy has collected four World Cup trophies, in 1934, 1938, 1982, and 2006. Germany has won it three times, in 1954 and 1974 when known as West Germany, and again shortly after the reunification of the country in 1990. **Argentina** has twice won it, in 1978 and 1986, as has Uruguay, in 1930 and 1950. **France**, in 1998, and **England**, in 1966, have each won it once, both as hosts, and **Spain** won it for the first time in 2010. A complete summary of each tournament contested up to, and including, the 2010 FIFA World Cup in South Africa follows.

FIFA World Cup, 1930

Host Nation: Uruguay
Dates: 13 to 30 July 1930
Teams: 13
Matches: 18
Winner: Uruguay
Runners-Up: Argentina
Third Place: USA
Fourth Place: Yugoslavia
Golden Shoe: Guillermo Stábile (Argentina), 8 goals

Thirteen teams representing their countries traveled to **Uruguay** for the inaugural **FIFA World Cup** held in July 1930, the realization of FIFA President **Jules Rimet**'s vision of organizing a worldwide international tournament for national teams. Several countries had offered to host the competition, but Uruguay's promise to pay the travel and accommodation expenses was an important factor in FIFA's selection of them as hosts, since the tournament's financial viability was unknown.

Uruguay celebrated its centenary as an independent nation that year and finished the tournament as the first FIFA World Cup champions, beating neighbors **Argentina** 4-2 in the final held at **Estadio de Centenario** in the Uruguayan capital, Montevideo. The spectacular new **stadium** had been specially built for the competition, though it was not completed in time for the first few games of the competition to be played there; the initial matches were staged elsewhere in Montevideo, instead. Unlike later World Cup tournaments, all 18 games of the competition were staged in a single city, Montevideo, at this World Cup.

A total of 70 goals were scored in the tournament, at an average of 3.9 per match. This is a healthy figure, though many of the goals came in lopsided games that showed the gulf in class between the world's two strongest teams, Argentina and Uruguay, and the rest. Also, those two strongest teams had to travel the least, with the European competitors facing long boat trips that saw many teams pull out long before the tournament began. The eventual 13 competitors were divided into four groups for the initial stage of the competition, with one group of four teams and three groups of three teams. The top team in each group, after everyone had played each other once, advanced to the final stage of single-elimination games: Argentina, **Yugoslavia**, Uruguay, and the **United States**.

The semifinals demonstrated the two strongest teams' abilities to crush opponents who had traveled long distances, along with a divide in quality: Argentina destroyed the United States 6-1, with Uruguay taking care of Yugoslavia by the same score. The final of the tournament between Argentina and Uruguay was a closer affair than the 4-2 result in favor of the hosts indicates. Argentina, in fact, led 2-1 at halftime, thanks to goals from Carlos Peucelle and tournament top-scorer **Guillermo Stábile**. Then, a partisan crowd at Estadio de Centenario roared on Uruguay to score three unanswered second-half goals and become the first-ever FIFA World Cup champions.

FIFA World Cup, 1934

Host Nation: Italy
Dates: 27 May to 10 June 1934
Teams: 16
Matches: 17
Winner: Italy
Runners-Up: Czechoslovakia
Third Place: Germany
Fourth Place: Austria
Golden Shoe: Oldrich Nejedly (Czechoslovakia), 5 goals

The second **FIFA World Cup** took place in Europe for the first time, with the competition won for the second consecutive time by the host nation, this time **Italy**. Seventeen matches were played in the competition from 27 May to 10 June 1934, in a substantially larger format than four years previously. The prestige of the World Cup had grown since the first edition in 1930, with 32 teams applying to FIFA to take part, leading to the organization of a preliminary qualifying competition to cut down the contenders to 16 nations for the finals tournament. Italy themselves had to take part in the qualifying competition, successfully so, though all future hosts would receive automatic qualification to the finals tournament. Defending FIFA World Cup champions **Uruguay** refused to travel to Italy and defend their title, partly in retaliation for Italy's refusal to travel to Uruguay for the previous World Cup competition.

The expansion of the tournament meant more **stadiums** needed to be used in the tournament than in the first World Cup in 1930, and eight Italian cities hosted games. The 16 teams played in a straight knockout format, with hosts Italy defeating the **United States** 7-1 in the first round, the highest scoring game of the tournament. The advantages of playing close to home were demonstrated by the semifinals lineup, with all four teams coming from Europe: **Czechoslovakia** defeated **Germany** 3-1, and Italy beat an excellent **Austria** team 1-0. The final, held in Rome, proved to be a tightly fought game, hosts Italy coming out on top 2-1 over Czechoslovakia after extra time, with the score tied at 1-1 at the end of regulation. **Angelo Schiavio** scored the winning goal in the 95th minute, giving Europe its first World Cup champion, Italy.

FIFA World Cup, 1938

Host Nation: France
Dates: 4 to 19 June 1938
Teams: 15
Matches: 18
Winner: Italy
Runners-Up: Hungary
Third Place: Brazil
Fourth Place: Sweden
Golden Shoe: Leônidas da Silva (Brazil), 7 goals

The third **FIFA World Cup** was the second to be hosted in Europe, held in **France** from 4 to 19 June 1938, just a year before the outbreak of the Second World War. Eighteen matches were played in 10 different French venues, with a total of 376,177 spectators attending at an average of 20,898 fans per game. A total of 87 goals were scored, at an average of 4.7 per game, and the result of the tournament saw **Italy** claim their second successive FIFA World Cup title, defeating **Hungary** 4-2 in the final. A preliminary qualifying tournament featuring 37 countries had determined the 15 finalist countries, with defending champions Italy and host France automatically qualifying. There were notable absentees from the tournament with **Argentina** and **Uruguay** both refusing to play, because they believed South America had been snubbed in favor of Europe to host the tournament. Meanwhile, the stormy political situation in Europe prevented **Austria** and **Spain** from competing, and cast a pall over the tournament as a whole, with antifascist demonstrations timed on the streets of France to coincide with games featuring **Germany** and Italy.

This World Cup was uniquely structured with three rounds of single-elimination games leading up to the final, starting with a first round featuring 14 of the 15 teams, **Sweden** receiving a bye to the second round. **Switzerland** and Germany tied in the first game 1-1. A replay five days later determined who would go through, the Swiss winning 4-2. The Dutch East Indies made their only appearance in a World Cup, losing 6-0 to Hungary. France beat **Belgium** comfortably by three goals to one. Cuba and Romania tied 3-3. They also played a replay, won by Cuba 2-1. Italy won a close game with Norway 2-1, their winning goal in extra time coming from **Silvio Piola**. The game of the tournament came on 5 June, with **Brazil** beating **Poland** 6-5 in a thrilling encounter. **Leônidas da Silva** scored three goals for Brazil, and Poland's Ernest Wilimowski remarkably ended up on the losing team despite scoring four of his team's five goals. In the final first-round game, **Czechoslovakia** won by the deceptively comfortably score line of three goals to none over the **Netherlands**, all three goals coming in extra time after a 0-0 tie at the 90 minute mark.

In the first game of the second round on 12 June, Brazil tied with Czechoslovakia 1-1, needing a replay to go through and winning 2-1 in the second game two days later. Hungary beat Switzerland 2-0 in Lille, while in Antibes, Cuba was thumped 8-0 by Sweden, including a **hat-trick** for Tore Keller. Hosts France lost 3-1 to Italy, with two more goals for Italian Silvio Piola. In the semifinals held on 16 June, Hungary registered an emphatic victory over Sweden: despite conceding a goal in the first minute, they scored five unanswered goals to win 5-1, Gyulla Zsengeller scoring three goals. In the other semifinal, Brazil, who had sauntered through to that point with the brilliant Leônidas da Silva lighting up the tournament, made the curious decision to rest their star so he would be fresh for the final, presumably expecting an easy win over Italy. But the defending champions were not to be taken so lightly, going up 2-0 early in the second half thanks to goals from Gino Colaussi and **Giuseppe Meazza**, and a late goal from Romeu that made it 2-1 was little consolation for the beaten South Americans.

Leônidas da Silva went on to score two more as Brazil won the third-place play-off with Sweden on 19 June, taking his total for the tournament to seven goals, the best in the competition. The final was held the same day, and Italy outclassed the Hungarians, with Meazza, their creative hub, assisting on the Italians first three goals as they won 4-2. Silvio Piola and Gino Colaussi each scored twice. Italy's two successive championship victories in the FIFA World Cup were masterminded by their coach **Vittorio Pozzo**. Due to the Second World War, it would be 12 years before the next World Cup took place.

FIFA World Cup, 1950

Host Nation: Brazil
Dates: 24 June to 16 July 1950
Teams: 13
Matches: 22
Winner: Uruguay

Runners-Up: Brazil
Third Place: Sweden
Fourth Place: Spain
Golden Shoe: Ademir (Brazil), 9 goals

The Second World War prevented the **FIFA World Cup** from taking place in 1942 and 1946, but it returned in 1950, staged in South America for the first time since 1930, in soccer-crazy **Brazil** from 24 June to 16 July 1950. A vast new **stadium**, the **Maracanã**, was specially built in Rio de Janeiro for the tournament. Despite the poor economic conditions following the war, six European teams traveled to Brazil to make up almost half the odd-numbered field of 13 teams for the tournament. Hosts Brazil qualified automatically, but a number of leading countries withdrew from the tournament, including **Argentina** and **France** and, at the last minute, **Scotland**, India, and **Turkey**. The format for the tournament was changed from the straight knockout setup of the previous World Cup in 1938 to a two-stage group format—the teams were first divided into four groups, with the winners of each group advancing to a final round-robin format in a single group.

Due to the late withdrawals of several teams, the first-round groups were awkwardly divided into two groups of four teams, one group of three teams, and one group containing just two teams. Brazil, **Spain**, **Sweden**, and **Uruguay** each topped their groups. The biggest surprise came on 29 June 1950 in a result still remembered today: the **United States** upset **England** 1-0 in Belo Horizonte, **Joe Gaetjens** scoring the winning goal in a scrappy game. The result shocked England, appearing in the World Cup for the first time and presuming that as the leading force in the development of the game since the 19th century, they would easily beat an upstart soccer nation like the United States.

The final round of the tournament, the only time in World Cup history that the competition did not lead to a single-game final, contained a further surprise: heading into the final game of the round-robin four-team group that would determine the winner of the competition, Brazil was in prime position to claim their first title and was favored on home soil. They had crushed both Sweden (7-1) and Spain (6-1), while their opponents, Uruguay, had tied with Spain and just eked out a win over Sweden 3-2. The final game between the two was played at the Maracanã stadium in Rio de Janeiro, in front of a crowd officially registered at 174,000 but was probably more than 200,000, almost all of them cheering on the host nation. To the shock of all of Brazil, Uruguay, despite going down 1-0 to a goal by Friaca in the 47th minute, won the game thanks to a strike by **Juan Alberto Schiaffino** in the 66th minute and the winning effort by **Alcides Ghiggia** in the 79th minute. Such was the momentous impact of the game that language itself changed: a new word in Spanish, *Maracanazo*, was coined to refer to such a blow at the home stadium of Brazil, the Maracanã. For the second time, Uruguay received the **FIFA World Cup Trophy**, which had been renamed that year in honor of FIFA President **Jules Rimet**'s 25 years in charge of the global governing body of the sport, and was thus now known as the "**Jules Rimet Trophy**."

FIFA World Cup, 1954

Host Nation: Switzerland
Dates: 16 June to 4 July 1954
Teams: 16
Matches: 26
Winner: West Germany
Runners-Up: Hungary
Third Place: Austria
Fourth Place: Uruguay
Golden Shoe: Sándor Kocsis (Hungary), 11 goals

The 1954 **FIFA World Cup**, the fifth time the competition was contested, returned the tournament to Europe for the first time since the outbreak of World War II, with neutral **Switzerland** the safe choice selected by FIFA as hosts, especially as it also was the home base of FIFA. It was the first World Cup to be broadcast on **television**, taking the games to a new audience. The tournament ended with a surprising winner, West **Germany**, who defeated the favorites **Hungary** 3-2 in the final. Forty-five teams entered the initial qualifying stage to become one of the 16 countries taking part in the finals competition in Switzerland that lasted from 16 June to 4 July 1954, with the 26 games played in six different Swiss stadiums. The format of the tournament changed from the previous event in 1950. The first stage saw the 16 teams divided into four groups of four teams each, a complicated format meaning the two "seeded" teams in each group played only the non-seeds, with the top two in each group going through to the next round. From there, it would be a knockout round of single-elimination games.

The elimination rounds were full of high-scoring affairs: the hosts, Switzerland, lost by five goals to seven to Austria in the quarterfinals, with **Uruguay**, favorites Hungary and West Germany progressing to the semifinals. There, Hungary became the first team to beat Uruguay in any World Cup finals tournament, defeating them 4-2 after extra time. West Germany comfortably disposed of **Austria** 6-1 and then faced Hungary in the World Cup final. The two teams had played each other in the first-round group stage,

Hungary having demolished the West Germans 8-3. They also beat the **Republic of Korea** 9-0 and were in the midst of a remarkable unbeaten run that stretched to 31 games. They played a form of free-flowing soccer, centered around their brilliant captain and creative star, **Ferenc Puskás**, that was never before seen. Puskás, however, was injured in the first match against West Germany; though he returned for the final, held at Wankdorf stadium in Berne, and scored the opening goal in the game in the sixth minute, he was short of his best. Hungary scored a second goal in the eighth minute, but then what became known to West Germany as the "Miracle of Berne" began: the West Germans quickly tied up the game with goals from Max Morlock in the 10th minute and Helmut Rahn in the 18th minute. Inspirational leadership from the West German captain **Fritz Walter** saw them keep the usually rapacious Hungarians at bay for the rest of the game, and in the 84th minute, Rahn scored a winning goal that shocked the world and gave West Germany their first World Cup triumph.

FIFA World Cup, 1958

Host Nation: Sweden
Dates: 8 June to 29 June 1958
Teams: 16
Matches: 35
Winner: Brazil
Runners-Up: Sweden
Third Place: France
Fourth Place: West Germany
Golden Shoe: Just Fontaine (France), 13 goals

The **FIFA World Cup** was played in Europe for the second successive time in 1958, this time in the **Swedish** summer, with international **television** broadcasts of the games shown for the first time. The tournament is best remembered as the international coming-out of a 17-year-old star called **Pelé**. His **Brazil** team, which would dominate the next 12 years of international soccer, won their first World Cup title. Sixteen teams took part in the finals tournament, from an original field of 45 teams that entered the qualifying stage, with 35 matches played from 8 to 29 June 1958 across 12 Swedish stadiums, a then–record number of host stadiums for a World Cup. Another record was set by **France's Just Fontaine**, whose 12 goals scored remains the most a single player has ever scored in the FIFA World Cup.

The 16 teams in the tournament were divided into four groups of four teams each for the first stage, each team playing each other once, with the top two teams in each group qualifying for a single-elimination knockout phase. Of the eight qualifiers to this stage, free-scoring France and Brazil impressed most. The latter, lining up in an innovative 4-2-4 formation, had not only Pelé but also the mercurial dribbling genius **Garrincha** and the experienced **Didi**, the team's elegant creative force in midfield. These two teams met at the semifinal stage and goals galore flowed: Brazil won 5-2, inspired by a **hat-trick** from Pelé that revealed France's defensive frailties. In the other semifinal, defending champions West Germany were comprehensively beaten by hosts Sweden three goals to one, despite taking an early lead in the game. The final, held in front of 51,000 spectators at Råsunda Stadium in Solna (just north of the Swedish capital, Stockholm), was another high-scoring affair, with Brazil's class eventually telling. Sweden struck first, though, through **Nils Liedholm** in just the fourth minute, but Brazil quickly equalized in the ninth minute with a goal from Vava, who then scored again in the 32nd minute to give Brazil the lead 2-1 at halftime. Pelé gave his team further breathing room with Brazil's third goal in the 55th minute. **Mário Zagallo**, who would later coach Brazil to further World Cup glory, scored Brazil's fifth in the 68th minute to make it 4-1. Sweden got one back through Agne Simonsson in the 80th minute, but Pelé fittingly had the final word with a fifth and final goal for Brazil in the ninetieth minute, his country claiming the first of what would become many FIFA World Cup triumphs.

FIFA World Cup, 1962

Host Nation: Chile
Dates: 30 May to 17 June 1962
Teams: 16
Matches: 32
Winner: Brazil
Runners-Up: Czechoslovakia
Third Place: Chile
Fourth Place: Yugoslavia
Golden Shoe: Tied—Flórián Albert (Hungary), Valentin Ivanov (Soviet Union), Drazen Jerkovic (Yugoslavia), Leonel Sánchez (Chile), Vava (Brazil), Garrincha (Brazil), 4 goals

The **FIFA World Cup** returned to South America after the two previous championships in 1954 and 1958 had been held in Europe, with **Chile** selected as hosts. Their ability to stage the tournament was cast into severe doubt by a massive earthquake in the country on 22 May 1960. With a magnitude of 9.5, it was the most powerful earthquake ever recorded anywhere in the world to date, with thousands killed and widespread physical disaster. The Chilean authorities, though, encouraged a national spirit of rebuilding in time to stage the World Cup. New venues, including the sparkling Estadio Nacional in Chile's capital, Santiago, were built to provide fitting homes for the 32 matches played from 30 May to 17 June 1962, with the final seeing **Brazil** claim their second successive World Cup title.

The format of the tournament was the same as the 1958 FIFA World Cup, with a first-round stage featuring the 16 competing teams divided into four groups of four teams each, the top two qualifying for the single-elimination knockout phase. The backdrop to many of the games, the stunning Andes mountain range, was often far more beautiful than the soccer played on the field: one infamous game in the first round, between **Italy** and Chile, became known as the "Battle of Santiago," with the game degenerating into vicious foul play and two players being sent off. Brazil's **Pelé**, meanwhile, tore his thigh muscle in their second game, against Czechoslovakia, and did not appear in any further games in the tournament. But, armed with plenty of other remarkable talent, including the flamboyant **Garrincha** at the height of his powers, Brazil soon proved to be the class of the competition: in the quarterfinals, they easily disposed of **England** by three goals to one, Garrincha scoring twice.

In the semifinals, Brazil faced hosts Chile, a game they comfortably won 4-2 in front of 76,500 spectators in Santiago, with two more goals coming from Garrincha, who was proving to be the star of the tournament. It was an all-European affair in the other semifinal, with Czechoslovakia defeating **Yugoslavia** 3-1 thanks to two goals late in the game by Adolf Scherer. In the final, the Czech underdogs surprisingly took an early lead through a goal in the 15th minute by **Josef Masopust**, their captain and outstanding player. But Pelé's replacement, Amarildo, equalized just two minutes later, and Brazil took control of the game in the 69th minute with Zito scoring from an Amarildo pass. A third goal by Vava in the 78th minute sealed the game for Brazil, who claimed their second FIFA World Cup title.

FIFA World Cup, 1966

Host Nation: England
Dates: 11 to 30 July 1966
Teams: 16
Matches: 32
Winner: England
Runners-Up: West Germany
Third Place: Portugal
Fourth Place: Soviet Union
Golden Shoe: Eusébio (Portugal), 9 goals

England, where professional soccer had first developed in the 19th century, played host to the **FIFA World Cup** for the first time, from 11 to 30 July 1966, with 16 teams taking part and 32 matches played in the eighth edition of the competition. England won the tournament for the first time, defeating West **Germany** 4-2 in a controversial final. The competition was not without rancor or incident, beginning with the qualifying competition: though a record 70 countries entered the preliminary stage, 16 African nations withdrew to protest a FIFA ruling in 1964 that meant the African champion had to compete in a play-off against either the Asian- or Oceanic-zone winners to qualify for the finals tournament. They requested an automatic qualifying place, instead. Further controversy followed when just months before the tournament, the **Jules Rimet Trophy** was stolen from an exhibition, though was bizarrely recovered by a dog named "Pickles" a week later hidden under some bushes in London.

Once the tournament got under way, the first-round group stage saw the 16 teams divided into four groups of four teams. In group one, England did not impress due to a cautious approach in the first round despite topping their group. They started with a dour 0-0 draw with **Uruguay**, who also qualified from the group. They showed some improvement with 2-0 wins over **Mexico** and **France**, who were both eliminated. Group two saw **Argentina** and **Spain** progress comfortably at the expense of a disappointing Spain and an out-classed **Switzerland**. Three of the world's strongest teams featured in group three, with defending champions **Brazil** joined by **Portugal** and **Hungary**, along with **Bulgaria**, who lost all three games. But Bulgaria did have some impact: vicious foul play in their first game against Brazil injured **Pelé**, ruling him out for the second game and limiting him in their third against Portugal. In that game, Portugal's star **Eusébio** scored twice as Brazil was defeated by three goals to one, eliminating them from the tournament, with Portugal and Hungary progressing. Group four also sprang a surprise: two-time World Cup winners **Italy** lost twice, first against group winners, the **Soviet Union**, and then, most shockingly, losing to reclusive North Korea and eliminated from the competition, finishing above only Chile.

In the quarterfinals, England won a bitter, brawling game against Argentina 1-0, West Germany easily brushed aside Uruguay 4-0, and the Soviet Union won a close encounter with Hungary 2-1, inspired by the goalkeeping of **Lev Yashin**. The most exciting game of the round saw North Korea briefly threaten a massive upset over Portugal when leading 3-0 after just 25 minutes, before eventually losing 5-3. The Portuguese comeback was inspired by Eusébio's four goals. The semifinals were both close affairs. West Germany edged out the Soviet Union 2-1 after a surprisingly poor game by star Russian **goalkeeper** Lev Yashin. Meanwhile, **Bobby Charlton** scored twice as England played their best game of the tournament to beat a talented Portuguese team 2-1, with Portugal's Eusébio scoring again and ultimately ending up as the leading goal scorer in the competition with nine goals.

England had now found their rhythm under coach **Sir Alf Ramsey**. They had switched to a formation without wide wingers: a 4-4-2 formation favoring hard-working players, with their cool, dominant central defender and captain **Bobby Moore** leading from the back. West Germany, though, was a formidable foe in the final: their own captain and star defender **Franz Beckenbauer** was revolutionizing the role a defensive player could perform, roaming forward to spray passes around the field with incisive vision and even scoring four goals in the tournament. The game at **Wembley Stadium** proved to be controversial. The Germans took an early lead through a goal by Helmut Haller, but English forward Geoff Hurst soon equalized and the score was tied 1-1 at halftime. England took the lead when Martin Peters scored in the 78th minute, but Wolfgang Weber tied the game again just before full time, with the game going to extra time. In the 101st minute, the controversy came: English forward Geoff Hurst struck the ball off the underside of the crossbar, the ball then bouncing down onto the line as most observers saw it. The **assistant referee** (then known as the linesman) Tofik Bakhramov, though, adjudged the ball to have crossed the line and awarded a goal. England did not look back, and Hurst completed his hat-trick with England's fourth goal in the 120th minute. England had won their first FIFA World Cup title.

FIFA World Cup, 1970

> **Host Nation:** Mexico
> **Dates:** 31 May to 21 June 1970
> **Teams:** 16
> **Matches:** 32
> **Winner:** Brazil
> **Runners-Up:** Italy
> **Third Place:** West Germany
> **Fourth Place:** Uruguay
> **Golden Shoe:** Gerd Müller (West Germany), 10 goals

Brazil, blindingly brilliant in their yellow shirts in the ninth edition of the **FIFA World Cup** and the first to be broadcast in Technicolor around the world, won their third World Cup title in the tournament, hosted by **Mexico** from 31 May to 21 June 1970. It was the first time the tournament had been hosted in North America; all previous competitions had been held in either Europe or South America. FIFA rule changes introduced some new elements to the play, including the introduction of red cards and yellow cards and an allowance of two substitutes per game per team.

The first round of the competition divided the 16 teams into four groups of four teams each, with the top two from each group progressing to the quarterfinals. In group one, hosts Mexico qualified for the next round, finishing behind the **Soviet Union**, with **Belgium** and El Salvador both eliminated. Italy topped a tightly contested group two, Uruguay also qualifying, and **Sweden** and Israel going out of the tournament. Group three was perhaps the strongest, with Brazil winning all three games and defending champions **England** qualifying to the next round in outstanding form as well, beating both Romania and **Czechoslovakia**. Brazil beat England 1-0 in a classic game, with **Jairzinho** scoring the winning goal, though the game is often recalled mainly for a remarkable save by England **goalkeeper Gordon Banks** from a close-range **Pelé** header. In group four, 1966 World Cup finalists West **Germany** impressed with victories over all three opponents, **Bulgaria**, Morocco (the first African contestant since the Second World War), and **Peru**, who also qualified to the next round after surprising many with their potent attacking style of play.

In the quarterfinals, an open and exciting contest between Peru and Brazil saw the latter prevail by four goals to two, thanks to goals by **Rivelino**, **Tostão** (two), and Jairzinho. Italy began to show their quality as they eliminated hosts Mexico 4-1. Uruguay won a close game over the Soviet Union 1-0 that went to extra time, thanks to a goal in the 116th minute by Victor Esparrago. The game of the round was a rematch of the 1966 World Cup final between West Germany and England. The defending champions, led by the stylish **Bobby Moore** and the attacking midfielder **Bobby Charlton**, ran out to a 2-0 lead with goals from Alan Mullery in the 31st minute and Martin Peters in the 49th minute. But the West German captain and outstanding creative force **Franz Beckenbauer** got a goal back for his country in the 68th minute, and England, missing goalkeeper Gordon Banks through illness, quickly crumbled defensively, conceding a second to Uwe Seeler in the 76th minute and then succumbing to a winning goal from **Gerd Müller** in extra time. Müller, a lethal striker, was on his way to becoming the tournament's top scorer with 10 goals.

In the first semifinal, Uruguay took a surprise early lead over Brazil, but the best team of the tournament reasserted their superiority. Playing a brand of skillful, attacking soccer rarely seen before in the World Cup, Brazil came out 3-1 winners to advance to their fourth World Cup final. There, they faced Italy, who had beaten West Germany 4-3 in the other semifinal. That game was tied at 1-1 at the end of 90 minutes. Then, a frenetic extra-time period followed that saw six goals scored, with the winning goal for Italy coming in the 111th minute. The final proved to be a classic in front of an official attendance of 107,412 at **Estadio Azteca** in Mexico City. It was announced that the winner of the Italy and Brazil contest, with two FIFA World Cup titles each, would be allowed by FIFA to keep the **Jules Rimet Trophy** for their third triumph. Brazil was at their brilliant best, with potent passing moves that even the smooth defensive efficiency of Italy could not cope with. Pelé opened the scoring with a header from a Rivelino cross in the 18th minute. Roberto Boninsegna equalized for Italy in the 37th minute, but Brazil was unstoppable in the second half: goals from Gerson in the 66th minute, Jairzinho in the 71st minute, and Carlos Alberto in the 86th minute sealed a 4-1 win. That final goal epitomized Brazil's flair and fluid passing. The ball was passed around almost the entire Brazilian team before Pelé languidly laid it off for the final scoring shot. Brazil took home the Jules Rimet Trophy for good and earned a reputation as one of the greatest teams in FIFA World Cup history.

FIFA World Cup, 1974

Host Nation: West Germany
Dates: 13 June to 7 July 1974
Teams: 16
Matches: 38
Winner: West Germany
Runners-Up: Netherlands
Third Place: Poland
Fourth Place: Brazil
Golden Shoe: Grzegorz Lato (Poland), 7 goals

The 10th staging of the **FIFA World Cup** was held in West **Germany** from 13 June to 7 July 1974. It was won by the host nation, who defeated the **Netherlands** in the final. A new **FIFA World Cup Trophy**, still used now, was awarded to West Germany, as the previous one, the **Jules Rimet Trophy**, had been given permanently to **Brazil** in recognition of their achievement in becoming the first country to win three World Cup titles, in 1970. The force behind those triumphs, Pelé, had now retired from international soccer, but there was a magisterial replacement: the star of the tournament, the Netherlands' **Johan Cruyff**, was shining on the biggest stage in world soccer.

The format of the tournament changed substantially in 1974 from the previous edition of the World Cup in 1970, even though the same number of teams (16) took part. An initial group stage saw the 16 teams divided into four groups of four teams each, with the top two teams in each group progressing to the next stage. That was followed by a second group stage of four teams each, playing each other once, with the winner of each group progressing to the final. West Germany, though starting shakily, progressed into the second stage along with East Germany from group one in the first round.

Yugoslavia and **Brazil** went through from group two, with **Scotland**, despite not losing a game, and Zaire, losing all three games they played, eliminated. In group three, the Netherlands impressed with two wins and a draw against **Sweden**, who also qualified, with **Bulgaria** and **Uruguay** exiting from the tournament. The best first-round performance came from **Poland** in group four, as they won all three games, and Polish forward Grzegorz Lato started a scoring spree that would see him end the World Cup as its top scorer with seven goals. **Argentina** also qualified from group four, with 1970 World Cup finalists **Italy** and tournament first-timers Haiti bowing out.

The second group stage, which would determine the finalists, began with a statement of the Netherlands and their coach **Rinus Michels'** commitment to open, attacking soccer that became known as "**Total Football.**" They crushed Argentina 4-0, with Johan Cruyff scoring twice to open play in group A. Brazil won close games over both East Germany and Argentina, and which team out of Brazil and the Netherlands would reach the final came down to a game between the two teams on 3 July. Defending champions Brazil, not the power they had been in 1970, were no match for the Dutch, **Johan Neeskens** and Johan Cruyff scoring twice in the second half to send the Netherlands to their first World Cup final. There, they would face hosts West Germany, who had topped group B in a battle with Poland, after both had won their games against Sweden and Yugoslavia. This set up a decisive game between teams with a rivalry that extended deep into the history of the two nations. West Germany prevailed through a goal by **Gerd Müller** for a 1-0 win in pouring rain, with several outstanding saves from West German **goalkeeper Sepp Maier** proving to be the difference between the two teams.

The Netherlands entered the final as favorites due to the fantastic play that they had shown throughout the tournament, despite the home advantage for West Germany in front of an official crowd of 75,200 in Munich's Olympic Stadium. The Dutch scored early from the penalty spot after Cruyff had been fouled, Johan Neeskens scoring the penalty. The Netherlands controlled possession for much of the first half, but Paul Breitner scored a penalty to tie it up for West Germany after Bernd Hoelzenbein was taken down by Wim Jansen. With the ever-elegant **Franz Beckenbauer** at the heart of the West German team and **Berti Vogts** tightly playing Johan Cruyff defensively, Dutch frustration grew and Müller snatched a goal for the host nation in the 43rd minute that the Netherlands could not answer, giving West Germany its second World Cup title.

FIFA World Cup, 1978

Host Nation: Argentina
Dates: 1 to 25 June 1978

Teams: 16
Matches: 38
Winner: Argentina
Runners-Up: Netherlands
Third Place: Brazil
Fourth Place: Italy
Golden Shoe: Mario Kempes (Argentina), 6 goals

The 11th staging of the **FIFA World Cup** took place in **Argentina** from 1 to 25 June 1978. The host nation, led by a tournament-leading six goals from forward **Mario Kempes**, won their first World Cup title, with the **Netherlands** losing their second successive World Cup final. The tournament returned to South American soil for the first time since the 1962 World Cup in **Chile**, with 38 matches played across six venues in Argentina. There had been controversy leading up to the tournament due to the military coup in Argentina in 1976 that resulted in considerable political repression in the country. Some countries considered boycotting the competition, but in the end, no country withdrew. Two of the stars from the previous 1974 World Cup were missing, though, with both **Johan Cruyff** of the Netherlands and **Franz Beckenbauer** of West **Germany** failing to make the trip with their countries. A young **Diego Maradona** was also snubbed by Argentina's **coach César Luis Menotti**, who preferred to rely on the experienced and considerable talents of captain Daniel Passarella, the creative midfielder Ossie Ardiles, and the striking prowess of Mario Kempes.

The tournament was structured in the same way as the 1974 edition. The 16 teams were divided into four groups of four teams, each playing each other team in the group once, with the top two teams advancing. The second stage divided the remaining eight teams into two groups of four teams each, again every team playing each group member once, and the top team in the group going on to the final. The second team in each group would play in the third-place play-off. For the first time, FIFA introduced the **penalty shoot-out** into the FIFA World Cup rule book to break ties after extra time, though no game in this World Cup actually needed to be decided this way.

Surprisingly, in the first round, hosts Argentina did not win their group, finishing behind **Italy**, who defeated them 1-0 thanks to a goal by Roberto Bettega. The hosts did qualify in second place, however, after beating **Hungary** and **France**, who were both eliminated. One issue caused some controversy: Argentina kicked off every game in the evening, after the other games in the group were decided, meaning they had the advantage of knowing where they stood in the group each time. **Poland** won group two, finishing ahead of West Germany, who finished in second place, with Tunisia and **Mexico** going out of the tournament. Tunisia did, though, become the first African team to win a game at the World Cup, beating Mexico 3-1. Group three saw a surprise as **Austria** won the group with three-time World Cup champions **Brazil** coming in second place, perennial World Cup underachievers **Spain** finishing in third place, and **Sweden** last. **Peru** impressed by winning group four, comprehensively beating both **Scotland** and **Iran**, who both went out of the tournament, with an underwhelming start by the Netherlands, who finished second but still progressed to the next round.

In the second-round group phase, the Netherlands found their feet in group A, destroying Austria 5-1, tying with West Germany, and then beating Italy 2-1 despite going a goal down early on. A long-range strike from Arie Haan ensured that they topped the group and qualified for the final for the second consecutive World Cup. Group B was a tight battle between Brazil and Argentina. Both won their opening games, Brazil 3-0 over Peru and Argentina 2-0 over Poland, before playing each other to a 0-0 stalemate in the second game. Brazil then beat Poland 3-1 in their final group game, meaning Argentina, who had the advantage of playing their game after Brazil, knew they needed to beat Peru by at least four goals (a goals-for-and-against differential was the tie-breaking mechanism) to advance in first place over Brazil. Argentina easily achieved this by winning 6-0, with conspiracy theorists questioning the effort of Peru ever since. Brazil beat Italy in the play-off to finish in third place, ensuring they ended the tournament unbeaten but unhappy at failing to make the final.

The final took place on 25 June 1978 between Argentina and the Netherlands, with an official crowd of 71,483 spectators in attendance at Estadio Monumental Antonio Vespucio Liberti in Buenos Aires. A shower of pregame blue-and-white confetti from Argentine fans marked out the partisan support for the host country. Argentina was slow to come out as the atmosphere built; the Dutch later claimed the hosts had deliberately delayed the start of the game. When the game got under way, Argentina struck first through Mario Kempes in the 38th minute, but substitute Dick Nanninga struck an equalizer with his head for the Netherlands in the 82nd minute. The Dutch had a glorious chance to win the game and their first FIFA World Cup in the last minute of normal time, as Rob Rensenbrink struck the post with his shot. In extra time, Argentina took charge of the game, with Kempes scoring his sixth of the tournament to put them in the lead in the 105th minute, and Daniel Bertoni making it 3-1 and confirming a first World Cup title for Argentina with his goal in the 116th minute. A controversial FIFA World Cup ended with the hosts as champions and the Netherlands left embittered after a second consecutive defeat in the World Cup final.

FIFA World Cup, 1982

Host Nation: Spain
Dates: 13 June to 11 July 1982
Teams: 24
Matches: 52
Winner: Italy
Runners-Up: West Germany
Third Place: Poland
Fourth Place: France
Golden Shoe: Paolo Rossi (Italy), 6 goals

The 12th iteration of the **FIFA World Cup** was hosted by **Spain** from 13 June to 11 July 1982. A record 52 games took place, as the tournament was expanded from its previous number of 16 teams to 24 teams, allowing in more qualifying countries from Asia and Africa. **Italy** claimed their third World Cup title, defeating West **Germany** in the final, inspired by the tournament's top scorer, the Italian surprise-package striker **Paolo Rossi**. Attendance at the tournament's games topped two million for the first time, with 2,109,723 showing up for the games held in 14 Spanish stadiums.

A record 109 teams had entered the qualifying stage, with the **Netherlands**—finalists in the previous two World Cup tournaments in 1974 and 1978—the most surprising failure to make it to Spain. The 24 finalist teams were organized into a new format, with a first round of six groups of four teams, the top two in each group progressing to a second stage with four groups of three teams, with only the top team in each moving on to the semifinals.

In the first stage, **Poland** and Italy qualified from group one, though the Italians did not impress, drawing all three games and only edging past **Cameroon**, who they tied with on points, because they had scored one more goal than the African team. Controversy dogged group two: Algeria upset defending champions West Germany 2-1 in their first game but ultimately exited from the competition when the West Germans beat **Austria** 1-0 in their final game, which was played after Algeria's last game had been played. This sent West Germany and Austria through at the expense of Algeria and appeared to observers to be a conveniently arranged result. As a result, in future World Cups, the final round of games in the same group would be played at the same time. Group three saw **Belgium** and defending World Cup champions **Argentina** advance, **Hungary** exiting despite a record 10-1 win over hapless El Salvador. England dominated group four with three wins, **France** also qualifying, with **Czechoslovakia** and Kuwait eliminated. In group five, Northern Ireland surprised by qualifying in first place ahead of hosts Spain, who finished in second place, with **Yugoslavia** and Honduras bowing out. **Brazil** played some fantastic soccer to roll through group six with three wins, the **Soviet Union** qualifying with them, while **Scotland** and **New Zealand**—the latter competing in their first World Cup—exited the tournament.

In the second stage, Poland topped group one, advancing at the expense of Belgium and the Soviet Union. An all-West European group two was won by West Germany, edging out England and Spain. Group three brought the surprising demise of Brazil, who continued their superb form with a 3-1 trouncing of Argentina before their World Cup ended in disaster when a Paolo Rossi **hat-trick** gave Italy a 3-2 win over the Brazilians and a berth in the semifinals. They were joined there by France from group four, who beat both Austria and Northern Ireland to qualify with ease, their midfield spark Alain Giresse in superb form.

In the first semifinal, at the Camp Nou in **Barcelona**, Italy strolled to victory over Poland, winning 2-0 with Paolo Rossi scoring two more goals in his sensational run of form. The second semifinal, in Seville, proved to be one of the most memorable and controversial games in FIFA World Cup history. Pierre Littbarski opened the scoring with a goal for West Germany in the 17th minute, soon matched from the penalty spot by **Michel Platini** for the French. The match exploded when a brutal clattering challenge by West German **goalkeeper** Harald Schumacher on substitute Patrick Battiston left the Frenchman unconscious, a clear foul that to French astonishment was not called by the referee. The score remained tied at 1-1 at full time, but four goals followed in extra time. France went up by two from goals by Marius Tresor and Giresse before a remarkable West German comeback, tying the game through goals from **Karl-Heinz Rummenigge** in the 102nd minute and Klaus Fischer in the 108th minute. After 120 minutes, the score was tied at 3-3, and the game became the first in World Cup history to be decided by a **penalty shoot-out**. France seemed set for victory when Uli Stielike had West Germany's third penalty saved, but misses by Didier Six and Maxime Bossis for the French saw them exit. Harald Schumacher ended the game a West German hero despite his earlier violent challenge. An exhausted France lost the third-place play-off to Poland 3-2 in Alicante.

The final, held in front of a crowd of 90,000 fans at **Estadio Santiago Bernabéu** in the Spanish capital, Madrid, was a tepid game, with West Germany drained from the semifinal exertions. Three second-half goals, from Paolo Rossi in the 57th minute, Marco Tardelli in the 69th minute, and Alessandro Altobelli in the 81st minute, put Italy in full control, with only a late consolation strike coming for West Germany from Paul Breitner in the 83rd minute. Italy held on to win 3-1 and claimed their second World Cup title; their first since 1934. Paolo Rossi won the Golden Shoe as top scorer and the Golden Ball for best player of the tournament.

FIFA World Cup, 1986

Host Nation: Mexico
Dates: 31 May to 29 June 1986
Teams: 24
Matches: 52
Winner: Argentina
Runners-Up: West Germany
Third Place: France
Fourth Place: Belgium
Golden Shoe: Gary Lineker (England), 6 goals

Mexico became the first country to host the **FIFA World Cup** twice; the 1986 competition was played on Mexican soil just 16 years after its previous staging there in 1970. This only happened, though, because the originally chosen host nation for the 1986 competition, **Colombia**, pulled out of hosting the World Cup for economic reasons, in late 1982. Mexico was chosen as the replacement host by FIFA in May 1983. The run-up to the tournament was disrupted by a major earthquake in Mexico during September 1985, killing an estimated 20,000 people, but the tournament went forward as planned. **Argentina** emerged as victors of their second World Cup title just eight years after claiming their first in 1978 as hosts, **Diego Maradona** announcing himself as the world's best player, with five goals and five assists in the competition.

As in the 1982 World Cup, the 1986 tournament featured 22 teams who had qualified from 121 entrants to the preliminary competition. Along with the hosts, Mexico, and the World Cup title-holders, Argentina, who received automatic berths in the finals tournament, they made up the field of 24 countries. The first round followed the 1982 format of six groups of four teams each, but the previous second-round group phase was scrapped, replaced by a straight knockout from the 16 teams to qualify from the first round to the finals. Along with the top two finishers in each group from the first round, the four teams with the best records who finished in third place in their group in that stage also progressed to make up the 16 teams for the second round. The groups in the first round were seeded into four pots, with the hosts (Mexico), reigning World Cup champions (**Italy**), and the second- through fifth-place teams from the 1982 FIFA World Cup (West **Germany**, **Poland**, **France**, and **Brazil**) the top seeds.

Argentina topped group A in the first round, comfortably beating both **Bulgaria** and the **Republic of Korea**, who were both eliminated. They played a dour 0-0 draw against Italy, the defending champions, who qualified automatically in second behind Argentina. The hosts, Mexico, impressed in winning group B, beating a strong **Belgium** team and a weak Iraq team, who finished bottom of the group, and tying **Paraguay**, who finished in second place. The **Soviet Union** won group C, finishing ahead of France on goal differential, with weak teams from **Hungary** and **Canada** (the latter making their first World Cup appearance) going out of the competition. Brazil played some beautiful soccer as they won all three games to top group D, **Spain** finishing second, with neither Northern Ireland nor Algeria managing to win a game. Group E was dominated by Denmark, who won all three games, West Germany scraping through in second position with a win, a draw, and a loss, and **Uruguay** finishing above **Scotland** in third place. Group F was surprisingly won by Morocco, with **England** finishing in second place, Poland in third, and **Portugal** in fourth. Along with the top two teams in those six groups, Belgium, Bulgaria, Poland, and Uruguay also qualified for the next round as the best-placed third-place finishers from the six groups.

The second round of knockout games began with Mexico comfortably disposing of Bulgaria 2-0 on 15 June. The second game that day was the highlight of the round, with Belgium defeating the Soviet Union 4-3 after extra time. A talented Brazil team impressed with a 4-0 dismantling of Poland, while Argentina had one of their less impressive games of the tournament in a 1-0 win over Uruguay. Defending champions Italy fell to France 2-0, the brilliant **Michel Platini** at the heart of a stylish French team that had won the 1984 **UEFA European Football Championship**. Morocco, the first African team to advance beyond the first round of the World Cup, gave West Germany a considerable scare in their second-round game, the Europeans going through by only a single goal scored by **Lothar Matthäus** just three minutes from the end of the game. England comfortably beat Paraguay 3-0, Gary Lineker scoring twice on the way to becoming the winner of the Golden Shoe as the tournament's top scorer, ending with six goals to his credit. A strong Denmark team was beaten surprisingly easily by Spain 5-1, Spanish forward Emilio Butragueno scoring a **hat-trick**.

The quarterfinal stage featured some of the most exciting and dramatic games in World Cup history. It began with a classic encounter between two of the tournament favorites, Brazil and France. Careca put Brazil ahead in the 17th minute, but France equalized through Michel Platini in the 40th minute. Brazil's star player **Zico** missed a chance to score from the penalty spot in normal time, and the game ended in a **penalty shoot-out** won by France 4-3, their **goalkeeper** Joel Bats saving two Brazil kicks. Penalty kicks decided a game again following a dull 0-0 draw between West Germany and hosts Mexico, who exited in painful fashion, losing 4-1 in the penalty shoot-out. A memorable game then took place between Argentina and England, with the best and worst of Argentinean captain Diego Maradona on display: His first goal, opening the scoring in the game in the 51st minute, came from a clear and deliberate handball when Maradona lifted the ball over England goalkeeper Peter Shilton, an infringement remarkably missed by the match officials. But Maradona followed this with his second goal just three minutes later, brilliantly dribbling the ball almost the length of the field and slaloming past several hapless England defenders before stroking the ball past Shilton to make it 2-0 for Argentina. England got a goal back from another Gary Lineker strike but, despite further chances, was unable to tie the game. A third penalty shoot-out decided the final quarterfinal game, with a 1-1 tie between Spain and Belgium decided in the Belgians favor.

In the first semifinal, West Germany managed to nullify the electric talents of France's Platini, Jean Tigana, and Alain Giresse, with an early goal by Andreas Brehme followed by a late strike from **Rudi Völler**, giving the West Germans a 2-0 win. Diego Maradona continued to stamp his genius on the tournament in the second semifinal, scoring twice in the second half to overwhelm Belgium in a game that ended in a 2-0 win for Argentina. France claimed third place following a play-off game with Belgium that ended in a penalty shoot-out won by the French. In the final, with 114,600 officially in attendance at the **Estadio Azteca** in Mexico City, West Germany's Lothar Matthäus managed to keep a tighter leash on Maradona than any other defender had maintained in the tournament. Argentina, though, still managed to go up 2-0 in the first half with goals from José Brown in the 23rd minute and **Jorge Valdano** in the 55th minute. West Germany staged a spirited comeback in the second half, as **Karl-Heinz Rummenigge** scored in the 74th minute and Völler equalized for the West Germans in the 80th minute. But, as if on cue, Maradona awoke from a quiet game by playing a perfect pass through on goal for his teammate Jorge Burruchaga to score the goal that gave Argentina a 3-2 win and their second World Cup title. Fittingly, Diego Maradona was awarded the Golden Ball as the tournament's best player.

FIFA World Cup, 1990

Host Nation: Italy
Dates: 8 June to 8 July 1990
Teams: 24
Matches: 52
Winner: West Germany
Runners-Up: Argentina
Third Place: Italy
Fourth Place: England
Golden Shoe: Salvatore Schillaci (Italy), 6 goals

The 14th edition of the **FIFA World Cup** was held in **Italy** for the second time, 56 years after it had first hosted the tournament in 1934, with the tournament's 52 games kicking off on 8 June 1990. West **Germany** lifted the FIFA World Cup Trophy for the third time a month later on 8 July, beating defending World Cup champions **Argentina** in the final 1-0. Italy invested considerably in infrastructure for the tournament, with 10 stadiums receiving massive renovations and two entirely new arenas built for the World Cup games in Turin and Bari. The soccer itself at the World Cup was often defensive and dull, with a record low 2.2 goals scored per game, though the romance surrounding the staging of the games on the Italian peninsula won over a global audience with plenty of drama throughout the tournament.

The format of the competition was unchanged from the 1986 FIFA World Cup, with 24 teams taking part, separated into six groups of four for the first round. The top two teams in each group qualified for the next round, along with the four best third-place teams. The 16 remaining teams then played a straight knockout format until the final. The opening game of the first round in group B produced a considerable surprise: defending champions Argentina were beaten 1-0 by **Cameroon**, despite the African team having two players sent off. Cameroon followed that result by beating Romania, topping the group. Romania finished second and Argentina third, the latter only qualifying for the next round as one of the best third-place finishers, with the Soviet Union finishing in fourth place. In group A, Italy began in imperious form by winning all three games, with their unlikely star, striker **Salvatore Schillaci**, scoring twice in the first round on his way to winning the Golden Shoe as the top scorer in the tournament, ending up with six goals. **Czechoslovakia** finished in second place behind Italy, with **Austria** in third and the **United States** last, the Americans losing all three games. **Brazil** began in fantastic form in group C, winning all three of their games, Costa Rica surprisingly taking second place ahead of **Scotland**, who finished in third, with **Sweden** in fourth. West Germany piled on the goals in winning group D, beating **Yugoslavia**, who finished second, and the United Arab Emirates, who ended up last, along with a draw against **Colombia**, who qualified in second place. Group E saw Spain and Belgium progress automatically in first and second, with **Uruguay** in third and the **Republic of Korea** heading home after losing all three games. **England** only won one game in the first round but still topped group F ahead of the Republic of Ireland, who finished in second place, the Netherlands, who tied all three games and finished third, and **Egypt**, who finished last. Along with Argentina, the other best third-place teams to qualify for the second round were Colombia, Uruguay, and the Netherlands.

The second round started on 23 June with Cameroon beating Colombia 2-1 after extra time, and thus becoming the first African team to qualify for the quarterfinals of the FIFA World Cup. Veteran **Roger Milla**, who came on as a substitute, scored both of Cameroon's goals, the second after a howling error by eccentric Colombian goalkeeper Rene Higuita. Czechoslovakia easily beat Costa Rica 4-1, and then Brazil made a disappointingly early exit, losing to Argentina 1-0 despite having the better of the play. A bitter game between West Germany and the Netherlands ended with the West Germans going through 2-1, Frank Rijkaard from the Dutch team and **Rudi Völler** from West Germany both disgracefully sent off for spitting at each other. There was heartbreak for Romania, losing in a **penalty shoot-out** to the Republic of Ireland after a 0-0 tie, while hosts Italy cruised through 2-0 over Uruguay. Spain left a World Cup competition earlier than expected once again, losing 2-1 to an excellent Yugoslavia team after extra time, and England scraped past Belgium, the winning goal in a 1-0 game coming from David Platt in the 119th minute in extra time.

The quarterfinals kicked off on 30 June with a dull game between Yugoslavia and Argentina, the latter going through thanks to a victory in the penalty shoot-out after a 0-0 tie. Hosts Italy edged past the Republic of Ireland 1-0 later that evening, while the same score line saw West Germany advance past Czechoslovakia the next day. The final quarterfinal was the most dramatic, as England rather fortunately beat Cameroon 3-2 despite being down 2-1 until Gary Lineker's 83rd minute penalty tied it up. A second penalty from Lineker in extra time saw England go through. The semifinals both ended in 1-1 ties decided by penalty shoot-outs. Hosts Italy experienced heartbreak first, in front of almost 60,000 in Naples, when a Salvatore Schillaci first-half goal was canceled out by a Claudio Caniggia strike for Argentina in the 67th minute. Then, in the penalty shoot-out, the hero was Argentina's goalkeeper Sergio Goycochea, who saved two penalties, as he had also done in the previous round. West Germany and England then played to a 1-1 tie, Paul Gascoigne starring for the English and the West Germans inspired by **Lothar Matthäus**. Misses by both Chris Waddle and Stuart Pearce in a decisive penalty shoot-out saw England exit, eventually finishing in fourth place after losing the third-place play-off to Italy. The final was one of the worst in World Cup history: Argentina's **Diego Maradona** was unable to demonstrate the form that had led his country to victory in 1986, and his teammate Pedro Monzon earned an undesirable historical distinction as the first player to be sent off in a World Cup final. The sole goal in the game came from Andreas Brehme for West Germany from the penalty spot, after a foul by Argentina's Gustavo Dezotti, who was also sent off for his second yellow-card offense. West Germany's 1-0 win meant they had become the third team, after Brazil and Italy, to win three FIFA World Cup titles.

FIFA World Cup, 1994

Host Nation: United States
Dates: 17 June to 17 July 1994
Teams: 24
Matches: 52
Winner: Brazil
Runners-Up: Italy
Third Place: Sweden
Fourth Place: Bulgaria
Golden Shoe: Tied—Oleg Salenko (Russia), Hristo Stoichkov (Bulgaria), 6 goals

The 1994 **FIFA World Cup** was held in the **United States** from 17 June to 17 July 1994, with 24 teams taking part and playing a total of 52 games. A record aggregate 3,587,538 fans attended the games, also a record average attendance of 68,991 per match. Both records still stand today and justified the decision of FIFA to award the tournament to a country where soccer lagged well behind baseball, American football, basketball, and ice hockey as a major spectator sport. The United States did not have a professional outdoor first division soccer league at the time, though the World Cup staged there proved to be a spur toward the launch of **Major League Soccer** in 1996. The tournament itself proved to be exciting, with more goals scored than the previous World Cup held in Italy four years earlier, at an average of 2.7 goals per game compared to 2.2 in 1990. This came after FIFA introduced three points for a win in group play for the first time, up from two points previously, in order to encourage more attacking play. **Brazil** ended the competition as champions for the fourth time, beating **Italy** in the final through a **penalty shoot-out**.

The qualifying competition for the final tournament had seen a record 147 countries take part, with **England, France**, and reigning **UEFA European Football Championship** winners Denmark the most surprising teams to fail to qualify. Hosts the United States qualified automatically, taking their place in group A for the first round, which divided up the 24 teams into six groups of four teams, with the top two in each qualifying for the next round. Four best third-place finishers also went on to the second round to make up a field of 16 that then played single-match knockout rounds leading up to the final. Also in group A were Romania, **Switzerland**, and **Colombia**, the latter finishing last and facing tragedy when defender Andrés Escobar was shot dead on his return home after scoring a crucial own goal against the United States. Romania won the group ahead of Switzerland in second, the United States finishing third but still moving on to the next round as one of the best third-place teams. The

United States' game against Switzerland saw a game played indoors for the first time, at the Pontiac Silverdome in Pontiac, a suburb of Detroit. Group B was comfortably won by Brazil, Sweden taking second place, with **Russia** and **Cameroon** going out of the tournament. Amazingly, Russia's Oleg Salenko ended up as the tournament's joint top scorer due to his six goals in the first round, including a record five in one game as Russia beat Cameroon 6-1. **Germany** topped group C, **Spain** finishing in second place, and the **Republic of Korea** and Bolivia exiting. Group D saw controversy, as Argentinean star **Diego Maradona** failed a drug test after Argentina's first game and withdrew from the tournament. Argentina struggled through to the second round as one of the best third-place teams, finishing behind **Bulgaria** and an exciting **Nigeria** team, who won the group. In group E, all four teams ended up with four points with goals scored separating the teams as the tie breaker, leaving **Mexico** in first, **Italy** in second, the Republic of Ireland qualifying as one of the best third-place teams, and Norway bowing out. Group F was won by the **Netherlands**, **Saudi Arabia** coming in second, and **Belgium** another third-place qualifier, with Morocco losing all three games and finishing last.

The second round began on 2 July with a tight 3-2 win for Germany over Belgium, followed by Spain easily beating Switzerland 3-0. Saudi Arabia lost to Sweden 3-2 on 3 July before the game of the round between Romania and Argentina. The former won 3-2 thanks to a winning goal by their creative midfield force Gheorghe Hagi. On American Independence Day, the fourth of July, the United States lost 1-0 to Brazil but put in a strong performance against the eventual champions, their best display of the tournament. The other match that day saw the Netherlands beat the Republic of Ireland 2-0. The final second-round games took place on 5 July, Nigeria losing a heart-breaking game to Italy after taking an early lead. Italy's star **Roberto Baggio** scored twice, including a winning penalty kick in the 100th minute.

The quarterfinals took place on 9 and 10 July, beginning with a victory for Italy over Spain by two goals to one, Italy's illustrious Baggio scoring the winner in the 87th minute and sending Spain back home from a World Cup empty handed once again. The game of the round was between the Netherlands and Brazil in Dallas, with the Dutch fighting back to tie the game 2-2 after going down 2-0 in the first half, only to concede a winning goal by Brazil's Branco in the 81st minute. The surprise of the tournament came when reigning champions Germany were beaten 2-1 by Bulgaria in the third quarterfinal, despite the Germans taking the lead in the 47th minute. A tying goal by the electric **Hristo Stoichkov**, on his way to tying Oleg Salenko for the Golden Shoe as the tournament's top scorer, was followed by a winner from Iordan Letchkov to put Bulgaria through. They were joined in the semifinals by Sweden, who went through after a penalty shoot-out victory over Romania following a thrilling 2-2 tie.

The semifinals on 12 July were disappointing games. Bulgaria was beaten 2-1 by Italy in front of 74,110 at Giants Stadium in New Jersey, Roberto Baggio scoring twice and confirming himself as one of the tournament's outstanding players. Brazil beat Sweden 1-0 at the Rose Bowl in Pasadena, California, 91,856 in attendance, a goal by their supreme goal poacher **Romário** settling the game in the 80th minute. Romário would go on to win the Golden Ball award as the tournament's best player. In the third-place play-off that followed on 16 July, Sweden easily beat Bulgaria 4-0. The final took place on 17 July at the Rose Bowl, 94,194 officially attending the game. Italy and Brazil both played in a subdued style, Brazilian flair tempered by their pragmatic holding defensive midfielders Dunga and Zinho, while Italy was superbly marshaled from the back by the peerless **Franco Baresi**. No goals were scored, and the final became the first in World Cup history to be settled by a penalty shoot-out. There were four misses in the shoot-out, but the deciding error came from Italy's tired and injured Roberto Baggio, when he launched Italy's fifth kick over the crossbar, giving Brazil their fourth FIFA World Cup title.

FIFA World Cup, 1998

Host Nation: France
Dates: 10 June to 12 July 1998
Teams: 32
Matches: 64
Winner: France
Runners-Up: Brazil
Third Place: Croatia
Fourth Place: Netherlands
Golden Shoe: Davor Suker (Croatia), 6 goals

The 16th staging of the **FIFA World Cup** was held in **France** from 10 June to 12 July 1998, attended by 2,785,100 spectators at an average of 43,517 fans at each of the 64 games played in 10 different French stadiums. It was won by France, taking their first World Cup title after defeating **Brazil** in the final. A total of 32 teams took part, the largest ever number for the World Cup, as the field was expanded from the 24 that took part at the previous tournament in 1994. The qualifying competition to determine the final 32 teams featured a record 174 countries entering with 168 actually playing, and took place over 643 games in front of more than 15 million fans at games around the world. In the tournament itself in

France, 171 goals were scored, at an average of 2.7 a game, the same as in 1994. A new innovation in the rules meant that a goal scored in extra time during the knockout rounds was more valuable than ever before: it would now be known as the "Golden Goal," and the game would end immediately with the scoring team victorious.

Due to the expansion of the tournament, the format of the first round was changed from the setup in 1994. The 32 teams were broken down into eight groups of four teams who played each other once, and the top two teams from each group advanced to the first of four single-elimination rounds that led to the final on 12 July. The first round began on 10 June with defending World Cup champions Brazil opening group A with a 2-1 victory over **Scotland**. Brazil went on to qualify top of the group at the end of the first round despite their first World Cup group stage defeat since 1966, to Norway, who came in second place, while Morocco and Scotland exited the tournament. Group B was topped by **Italy**, with **Chile** in second and Austria and **Cameroon** going out. France won all three games to win group C, though they suffered a blow when playmaker **Zinedine Zidane** was sent off against **Saudi Arabia**. Fellow Europeans Denmark qualified in second place, with **South Africa** and Saudi Arabia both leaving the competition without winning a game. In group D, **Nigeria** beat **Spain** 3-2 in their opening match, the African country topping the group and the Spaniards exiting in third place. **Paraguay** qualified in second place behind Nigeria, and **Bulgaria** finished last. The **Netherlands** won group E and **Mexico** finished second, while both **Belgium** and the **Republic of Korea** failed to win a game. Group F was won by **Germany** ahead of the Netherlands, who finished in second place. Iran went out after finishing third, but beat the **United States** 2-1 in an encounter hyped up for the historical political overtones, the Americans failing to win a game in France during the tournament. Romania topped group D ahead of **England**, who finished in second place, while **Colombia** and Tunisia went home. This determined the last of the 16 qualifiers for the second round.

The knockout rounds began on 27 June in Paris with Brazil comfortably beating Chile 4-1. Italy beat Norway 1-0, and then Denmark surprisingly beat Nigeria by a comfortable score of four goals to one. Without the suspended Zinedine Zidane, serving a ban for his red card during the first round, France struggled to move past Paraguay until French defender Laurent Blanc scored the first Golden Goal in World Cup history to send the hosts to the next game. Germany edged past Mexico 2-1 with two late goals after being down 1-0, while the Netherlands beat Yugoslavia by the same score line. The most exciting game of the second round came in St. Étienne, where old rivals England and Argentina played a riveting game that ended 2-2. The incidents included a red card for **David Beckham**, a fantastic goal by young forward **Michael Owen**, and then a **penalty shoot-out** victory for Argentina, after both Paul Ince and David Batty missed penalties for England. In the final second-round game, Croatia beat Romania thanks to a goal by striker Davor Suker.

The quarterfinals began on 3 July with France again failing to impress but still advancing. They played to a 0-0 tie with Italy, before winning a penalty shoot-out 4-3, the Italians exiting the World Cup for the third consecutive time on penalty kicks. The second game that day offered up many more goals, with Brazil beating Denmark 3-2, thanks to a pair of strikes by **Rivaldo**. A sparkling Croatia team dismantled Germany, winning 3-0 in the third quarterfinal in Lyon. The final game of the round was a classic encounter between two high-quality teams, as the Netherlands beat Argentina 2-1, Dennis Bergkamp scoring a memorable winning goal in the 89th minute, deftly controlling a long pass and lashing it into the goal from a tight angle. In their semifinal against Brazil in Marseilles on 7 July, the Netherlands again scored a crucial late goal, this time from Patrick Kluivert in the 87th minute to tie the game 1-1, Brazil having taken the lead through their prolific striker **Ronaldo** in the 46th minute. With both teams afraid of conceding a Golden Goal, extra time was filled with cautious play and the game was decided by a penalty shoot-out, won by Brazil after misses for the Dutch by Phillip Cocu and Ronald de Boer. In the second semifinal, on 8 July in Stade de France in the northern suburbs of Paris, the hosts, France, finally played up to their potential with a 2-1 win over Croatia, with defender Lilian Thuram the unlikely scorer of France's two goals. Croatia's goal came from Suker, who would score again in the Croatian victory over the Netherlands in the third-place play-off, and end up as the tournament's top scorer with six goals.

The 1998 World Cup final took place on 12 July at the Stade de France, with 80,000 in attendance, but controversy dogged the game before kickoff even took place: Brazil sensationally dropped their star player, Ronaldo, from the initial lineups given to FIFA, a completely unexpected decision that immediately set off conspiracy theories and raised questions still unanswered today. But before the game began, Ronaldo was restored to the lineup, with rumors spreading that key Brazil and Ronaldo sponsor Nike had demanded his inclusion. Whatever the truth, Ronaldo, usually an electric force, was strangely subdued throughout the game, with France quickly taking charge in the first half thanks to two goals from Zinedine Zidane in the 27th and 46th minutes. Brazil had no answer for a French team that had found its stride after a slow start to the tournament. Emmanuel Petit added another goal in the 90th minute to end the game with a 3-0 win for the hosts. France had won their first FIFA World Cup.

FIFA World Cup, 2002

Host Nation: Republic of Korea/Japan
Dates: 31 May to 30 June 2002
Teams: 32
Matches: 64
Winner: Brazil
Runners-Up: Germany
Third Place: Turkey
Fourth Place: Republic of Korea
Golden Shoe: Ronaldo (Brazil), 8 goals

The 2002 **FIFA World Cup** was the first to be hosted by two nations, taking place in the **Republic of Korea** and **Japan** from 31 May to 30 June 2002. It was also the first to be hosted in Asia. A total of 2,705,197 fans attended the 64 games featuring 32 teams, at an average crowd of 42,268 per match. An entertaining tournament was won by **Brazil**, who claimed their record fifth World Cup title by defeating **Germany** in the final. One hundred sixty-one goals were scored in the tournament, at an average of 2.5 per match, slightly down from the rate at the previous 1998 World Cup. Qualification for the tournament had begun with 199 registered teams entering the competition, though only 193 actually took part in the record 777 games contested across the world. These games determined the 29 qualifiers who would join the automatic qualifiers at the World Cup, defending World Cup champions **France** and the two hosts, the Republic of Korea and Japan.

The first round of the tournament divided the 32 teams up into eight groups of four, playing against each other once, with the top two in each group going on to the knockout stage. From there, single elimination rounds would lead from the round of 16 to the final. In the first round, group A began play with a big upset, defending World Cup champions France losing to Senegal, appearing at the World Cup for the first time. France, a shadow of their 1998 selves, could not recover from that defeat, tying with Uruguay and then losing to Denmark to exit the competition in ignominy. Denmark won the group, with Senegal in second. **Spain** impressed by winning all three of their games to top group B, **Paraguay** finishing in second place, and **South Africa** and Slovenia exiting. Brazil dominated group C, victorious in their three games, with forward **Ronaldo** in outstanding form. **Turkey** squeezed through in second place ahead of Costa Rica and China. Group D was full of upsets, as hosts the Republic of Korea won the group, with the **United States** surprisingly beating **Portugal** 3-2 and finishing in second place, and the Portuguese and **Poland** eliminated. In group E, Germany and the Republic of Ireland qualified in first and second place at the expenses of **Cameroon** and **Saudi Arabia**. **Sweden** won group F, while **Argentina** was eliminated due to their loss to England, who went through in second, with **Nigeria** coming last. **Mexico** in first place and **Italy** in second qualified from group G, Croatia and Ecuador going out. Hosts Japan topped group H, **Belgium** in second place, with **Russia** and Tunisia eliminated.

The round of 16 began on 15 June with Germany defeating Paraguay 1-0 and England coasting past Denmark 3-0. Sweden and Senegal then put on an exciting game, the latter becoming the second African team to reach the quarterfinal stage of any FIFA World Cup by winning the game 2-1 after extra time. A **penalty shoot-out** then decided a 1-1 tie between Spain and the Republic of Ireland in Spanish favor, while the United States defeated their southern neighbors Mexico 2-0. Brazil beat Belgium by the same score line, Ronaldo scoring two more goals. Japan became the first of the hosts to go out, losing 1-0 in Miyagi to Turkey. The other host nation, the Republic of Korea, impressively defeated Italy 2-1 after extra time, thanks to a winning goal from a header by Ahn Jung-Hwan. Ahn happened to play for Italian club Perugia at the time, who pettily fired the Korean forward after the World Cup in retaliation for his goal against Italy.

The Republic of Korea, with a wave of national enthusiasm sweeping the host nation, then faced Spain in the quarterfinals in a controversial game that saw two apparent Spanish goals disallowed by the referee for questionable infringements. There was no score in the game, which was decided by a penalty shoot-out; a miss by Spain's Joaquin gave the Koreans victory. Germany won a tight game with the United States 1-0, and Turkey similarly beat Senegal by the same score line. England led Brazil 1-0 early on in Shizuoka, but Brazil fought back to win 2-1 thanks to goals from **Rivaldo** and **Ronaldinho**, despite the latter's red card in the 57th minute. The semifinals proved to be tightly fought games. In Seoul, Germany finally quelled the surprising Koreans' run in the competition, a lone goal by German midfielder Michael Ballack separating the two teams, though Ballack also received a suspension for the final for an accumulation of yellow cards. Brazil, thanks to yet another goal from the powerful play of Ronaldo, beat Turkey 1-0 in Saitama.

The 2002 World Cup final took place on 30 June in Yokohama, 69,029 in attendance at International Stadium Yokohama. Missing Ballack and facing a Brazil team inspired by their trio of talented attackers Rivaldo, Ronaldinho, and Ronaldo, Germany went down 2-0, with Ronaldo scoring two more to take his tally for the tournament to eight goals and take the Golden Shoe as the top scorer in the competition. Both goals went past German **goalkeeper Oliver Kahn**, who had enjoyed an outstanding tournament up to that point and was still awarded the Golden Ball as the tournament's best player. Turkey beat South Korea in the consolation play-off for third place, and Brazil lifted the FIFA World Cup Trophy for a record fifth time.

FIFA World Cup, 2006

Host Nation: Germany
Dates: 9 June to 9 July 2006
Teams: 32
Matches: 64
Winner: Italy
Runners-Up: France
Third Place: Germany
Fourth Place: Portugal
Golden Shoe: Miroslav Klose (Germany), 5 goals

The 18th staging of the **FIFA World Cup** was held in **Germany** from 9 June to 9 July 2006. Thirty-two teams took part, with the hosts having qualified automatically, and the other 31 progressing out of a qualifying tournament that saw 198 countries initially enter. Sixty-four games were played at the finals tournament in Germany, attended by 3,359,439 spectators, at an average of 52,491 per game, played at 12 different stadiums. One hundred forty-seven goals were scored in those 64 games, at an average of 2.3 per game, a lower goal-scoring ratio than in the previous World Cup in 2002. **Italy** won the tournament, claiming their fourth World Cup title, beating **France** in the final on 9 July, a game made particularly notable by **Zinedine Zidane**'s sending off for head butting Italian Marco Materazzi.

The 32 teams in the finals tournament were divided into eight groups of four teams, with the top two teams in each group qualifying for the round of 16, from which single-game elimination rounds led up to the final. Group A began play on 9 June with the hosts, Germany, winning 4-2 over Costa Rica and going on to win the group with further victories over **Poland** and Ecuador, who qualified in second place. Group B was won by **England, Sweden** finishing as runners-up with Trinidad and Tobago along with **Paraguay** going out. **Argentina** won group C, which was packed with quality teams and given the proverbial "Group of Death" moniker by the media. The **Netherlands** came in second, Côte d'Ivoire third, and Serbia and Montenegro fourth. Argentina was magnificent in a 6-0 demolition of the latter in Gelsenkirchen. **Portugal** strolled through group D, winning all three games over **Mexico** (who came in second), Angola, and **Iran** (who were both eliminated). Group E was won by Italy, advancing with **Ghana** at the expense of the **United States** and the **Czech Republic**. **Brazil** beat Croatia, **Japan**, and **Australia** in group F, the latter also qualifying for the next round in second place. In group G, **Switzerland**'s tight defense saw them win the group with no goals conceded in three games. They finished ahead of France, who took second place, the **Republic of Korea** and Togo going out.

The round of 16 kicked off on 24 June, with hosts Germany beating Sweden 2-0 in Munich. Argentina defeated Mexico 2-1 after extra time, thanks to a winning goal by Maxi Rodriguez. A trio of 1-0 score lines then followed: England beat Ecuador, Portugal defeated the Netherlands in an ill-tempered affair that saw four players sent off by referee Valentin Ivanov, and Italy defeated Australia through a penalty in the fifth minute of added time at the end of 90 minutes. A dull game between Switzerland and Ukraine petered out in a 0-0 tie, with the Ukrainians winning on a penalty shoot-out, as Switzerland went out of the competition without conceding a goal. Brazil beat Ghana 3-0 in Dortmund, while Spain exited earlier than expected from the World Cup once again despite taking a lead in the first half against France, goals from Frank Ribery, Patrick Vieira, and Zinedine Zidane sending the French through with a 3-1 win.

The first quarterfinal took place in Berlin on 30 June at the Olympic Stadium, 72,000 in attendance to see Germany tie with Argentina in normal time and the host nation go through on a penalty shoot-out after misses by Argentines Roberto Ayala and Esteban Cambiasso. Later that day, Italy easily beat Ukraine 3-0, with one goal from Gianluca Zambrotta and two from Luca Toni. England exited at the quarterfinal stage for the second-straight tournament, losing on penalty kicks to Portugal after a 0-0 tie with Wayne Rooney sent off in the second half. Misses by Frank Lampard, Steven Gerrard, and Jamie Carragher in the penalty shoot-out doomed England. Brazil then lost 1-0 to France, inspired by Zidane, who set up the goal for **Thierry Henry** in the 57th minute that proved decisive.

The first semifinal took place in Dortmund on 4 July, with the host nation, Germany, taking on Italy. No goals were scored in normal time, and, with the end of extra time approaching, it appeared the game would be decided by a penalty shoot-out, until Italy scored in the 119th minute through the unlikely source of defender Fabio Grosso, followed by a second for the Italians shortly after with a goal by Alessandro Del Piero. The following day, at the Allianz Arena in Munich, 66,000 saw France advance past Portugal 1-0, via a penalty from Zinedine Zidane following a foul on Thierry Henry by Ricardo Carvalho. Zidane was in inspired form, and would later be awarded the Golden Ball as the tournament's best player. Germany went on to win the consolation game for third place with Portugal 3-1; they could also console themselves with the Golden Shoe award given to their forward Miroslav Klose as the tournament's top scorer.

The final took place on 9 July, a tense, tight, and controversial game. Zinedine Zidane scored another penalty in the seventh minute following a foul on Florent Malouda by Marco Materazzi. But Italy equalized in the 19th minute through a powerful header by Materazzi from a corner kick, and their tight defense, led by their captain **Fabio Cannavaro**, kept Zidane in check for the remainder of normal time. Zidane finally exploded in the 110th minute but, this time in an unseemly and unexpected manner caught on **television**: an altercation off the ball with Materazzi incited the Frenchman to head butt the Italian in the chest, sending him sprawling to the ground. The fourth official, perhaps influenced by a television replay, informed the referee of the offense and Zidane was sent off, an ignominious end to a magnificent international career for the Frenchman. The game ended in a 1-1 tie, and the winner was determined by a penalty shoot-out: a miss for France by David Trezeguet, hitting the crossbar, resulted in victory for Italy, who claimed their fourth FIFA World Cup title.

FIFA World Cup, 2010

Host Nation: South Africa
Dates: 11 June to 11 July 2010
Teams: 32
Matches: 64
Winner: Spain
Runners-Up: The Netherlands
Third Place: Germany
Fourth Place: Uruguay
Golden Shoe: Thomas Müller (Germany), 5 goals

The World Cup headed to the African continent for the first time in 2010, with the 19th **FIFA World Cup** hosted by **South Africa** in June and July. It was won by **Spain**, who defeated the **Netherlands** in the final to claim their first World Cup title. Qualification for the 2010 World Cup began in August 2007 with a record total of 205 countries attempting to qualify for 31 places at the finals and South Africa qualifying automatically as hosts to make up the field of 32. The qualification campaign concluded in November 2009 with one of the most controversial moments in the history of World Cup qualification: **France** forward **Thierry Henry** deliberately handled the ball (unnoticed by the referee) while setting up William Gallas for the decisive goal. This gave France the win, in controversial fashion, in their play-off game against the Republic of Ireland to qualify for the World Cup at Irish expense. The games in South Africa at the World Cup were played at 10 stadiums in nine different cities, each noisily accompanied by the buzzing sound of plastic *vuvuzela* horns blown by thousands of fans at every game. The 64 matches attracted a total of 3.18 million spectators to the 64 games, the third highest total in World Cup history.

As in the previous three World Cup tournaments, eight groups of four teams each played in the first round, with the top two in each group qualifying for the second stage. In group A, France, who had reached the final in the 2006 FIFA World Cup and who were in open revolt against their coach, Raymond Domenach, were eliminated after failing to win a game. Hosts South Africa defeated France but were unable to win either of their other games against **Uruguay** and **Mexico**. The latter two qualified with Uruguay winning the group. Group B was won by a free-scoring **Argentina** team coached by their former star player Diego Maradona, the **Republic of Korea** qualifying in second place, with Greece and **Nigeria** eliminated. The **United States** won group C, the first time they had won a group in the first round of a FIFA World Cup, finishing ahead of **England**, who finished in second place, with Algeria and Slovenia going home. In group D, **Germany** qualified at the top of the group ahead of **Ghana**, who finished in second and were the lone African team to qualify for the second stage. **Australia** and Serbia were eliminated. The Netherlands won group E, Japan coming in second, with Denmark and **Cameroon** going out. **Paraguay** and Slovakia qualified from group F in first and second place, respectively. **New Zealand** finished third after tying all three games, and, in the biggest surprise of the opening stage, defending champions **Italy** came in fourth place, failing to win a game. **Brazil** won group G, **Portugal** coming in second place, with Côte d'Ivoire and North Korea (appearing at their first World Cup since 1966) eliminated. Spain topped group H, **Chile** coming in second, with **Switzerland** and Honduras heading home.

In the round of 16, Uruguay began play on 26 June by beating the Republic of Korea 2-1. The United States then lost to Ghana after extra time, a winning blast by Asamoah Gyan giving the Ghanaians a 2-1 win. The next day, Germany defeated England 4-1, the game marked by a wrongly disallowed goal for England's Frank Lampard, prompting FIFA to promise greater help for **referees** at future tournaments on goal-line calls. Argentina beat Mexico 3-1 with another refereeing controversy regarding a missed offside call on Carlos Tevez on Argentina's first goal. On 28 June, the Netherlands beat Slovakia 2-1, and Brazil beat Chile 3-0. Japan against Paraguay on 29 June ended scoreless; the game was decided by penalty kicks, the South Americans advancing at the expense of the Japanese.

The quarterfinals began on 2 July, with the Netherlands facing Brazil in the first game at Nelson Mandela Bay Stadium in Port Elizabeth. Despite going down a goal in the first half, the Dutch prevailed 2-1 thanks to two goals by Wesley Sneijder. Later that day, at Soccer City stadium in Johannesburg, Uruguay and Ghana tied 1-1, with Uruguay proceeding to the semifinals after winning in a **penalty shoot-out**. The game was marred by a controversial moment in the last minute of extra time, when Uruguayan forward Luis Suárez deliberately handled a ball on the goal line to stop a goal-bound shot. The referee called a penalty, but Ghana's Asamoah Gyan missed it. In the final two quarterfinal games on 3 July, Germany easily defeated a disorganized Argentina 4-0 in Cape Town, and Spain beat Paraguay 1-0 at Ellis Park Stadium, Johannesburg.

The first 2010 World Cup semifinal took place in Cape Town Stadium and was won 3-2 by the Netherlands over Uruguay, the Europeans resisting a late comeback by the South Americans. The next day, at Moses Mabhida Stadium in Durban, Spain controlled play against Germany and went through to the final with a 1-0 win, Carlos Puyol providing the lone goal with a thumping header. Uruguay then lost the third-place play-off to Germany on 10 July, but there was some consolation for them as their impressive forward **Diego Forlán** was awarded the Golden Ball by FIFA as the best player of the tournament.

Soccer City in Johannesburg played host to the final on 11 July, with 84,490 in attendance for the Netherlands against Spain. But, with the Dutch incessantly fouling the Spanish to try and break up their usual passing rhythm, it was referee Howard Webb who took center stage, giving out a record 14 yellow-card cautions, and one red card in extra time to Dutchman John Heitinga. By all accounts, Spain deserved the win in the face of a negative and cynical Dutch performance. The Spaniards achieved the win thanks to a neatly played goal deep into extra time in the 116th minute by Andrés Iniesta, which won Spain the FIFA World Cup for the first time.

FIFA WORLD CUP TROPHY. Two different trophies have been awarded by the **Fédération Internationale de Football Association (FIFA)** to the winners of the **FIFA World Cup** since it was first contested in 1930. From that tournament until 1970, the winners received the Jules Rimet Trophy, and, from 1974 to the present day, they have received the FIFA World Cup Trophy. The original Jules Rimet Trophy was initially known as the "Victory Trophy," and was renamed for **Jules Rimet**, the FIFA president who was the driving force behind the creation of the World Cup competition, in 1946. It was in 1928 that FIFA commissioned French sculptor Abel Lafleur to construct a trophy to be awarded to the winners of the first World Cup in 1930, and he produced a sterling silver and gold-plated trophy 35 centimeters high. The trophy proved to have a treacherous existence: during the Second World War, Ottorino Barassi, a FIFA vice president, hid the trophy in a shoe box under his bed. In 1966, it was stolen from a display in London ahead of the World Cup, that year in **England**, recovered only by chance thanks to a discovery in a park by a dog named "Pickles." In 1970, Brazil was awarded the trophy permanently for its third World Cup victory (as the first country to win it three times), but just 13 years later, it was stolen again in Rio de Janeiro, Brazil, and has never been recovered. The new FIFA World Cup Trophy, first awarded to West Germany as winners of the 1974 World Cup, was designed by Italian Silvio Gazzaniga and is 36.5 centimeters high, made out of 18-carat solid gold. The reigning champions retain the trophy between World Cups and are awarded a replica after returning it. The names of each winner since 1974 are engraved on the bottom side of the trophy.

FIFA WORLD PLAYER OF THE YEAR. An award made annually by soccer's world governing body, **Fédération Internationale de Football Association (FIFA)**, the FIFA World Player of the Year honor recognizes the best male and female player each year. Each national association affiliated with FIFA has two votes for each award, exercised by the respective head coaches and captains of their national teams. The men's award was first given in 1991, with **Germany**'s **Lothar Matthäus** the inaugural winner. **Brazilian** striker **Ronaldo** and **French** midfielder **Zinedine Zidane** jointly hold the record for most awards in the men's category, with three wins each. The women's award began in 2001, with the **United States' Mia Hamm** the first winner. Hamm won again the next year, with Germany's **Birgit Prinz** taking the following three awards. Brazil's **Marta** then began an unparalleled run from 2006 to 2009, winning four straight awards. In 2010, it was announced that the FIFA World Player of the Year award would be merging with the **Ballon d'Or** award and be renamed the "FIFA Ballon d'Or."

FIFA WORLD RANKING. Introduced in 1993, rankings of the national teams who are members of soccer's global governing body, **Fédération Internationale de Football Association (FIFA)**, are calculated on the basis of recent past performance in international play. The ranking has become a widely reported, and often criticized, indicator of world standing for each country. The rankings are used by FIFA for seeding purposes in **FIFA World Cup** qualification. Points are awarded and tallied for each team from FIFA-recognized international matches. After considerable early complaints about the convoluted method of calculation for the standings, the method used for the rankings was substantially revised in 2005 following a study by FIFA and external experts. The rankings now take into account the last four years of results for each country instead of eight years in the previous system, with factors such as the importance of the match, the strength of the opponent, and the recency of results weighted into account. Since the first rankings were released in 1993, **Brazil** has spent the most time at the number-one spot, followed by **Spain**, **Argentina**, and **France**. Despite the 2005 revision to the system, criticism of the rankings continues, and many fans view the alternative, independently produced World Football ELO rankings, to be a more realistic guide.

FIFA WORLD YOUTH CHAMPIONSHIP. *See* FIFA U-20 WORLD CUP.

FIGO, LUIS. B. 4 November 1972, Lisbon, Portugal. Luis Figo was named the **FIFA World Player of the Year** in 2001, a year after being named the **European Footballer of the Year**, those years representing the peak of his playing career that spanned 1989 to 2009. Figo played 127 games for **Portugal**'s national team, scoring 32 goals and appearing in several major tournaments. In 2006, Figo captained Portugal to fourth place at the **FIFA World Cup**, held in **Germany**. Figo, an athletic attacking winger with devastating dribbling ability with the ball, enjoyed a particularly successful club playing career in Portugal, **Spain**, and **Italy**. He won four Spanish league championships in Spain, first with **Barcelona** and then with **Real Madrid**, between 1995 and 2005, before going on to win four Italian league titles with **Internazionale** in Milan from 2005 to 2009. Following that, he retired shortly after a brief period of playing in Uzbekistan.

FIGUEROA, ELÍAS. B. 25 October 1946, Valparaíso, Chile. Elías Figueroa played at three **FIFA World Cup** finals tournaments for his native **Chile** and is regarded as one of the greatest Chilean players of all time. He was the South American Footballer of the Year on three occasions, 1974, 1975, and 1976. A composed defender and excellent distributor of the ball, Figueroa's club career spanned almost two decades. He made the bulk of more than 800 appearances for **Peñarol** in **Uruguay** and Internacional in **Brazil**.

FONTAINE, JUST. B. 18 August 1933, Marrakech, French protectorate of Morocco. Just Fontaine was a French player who still holds the record for scoring the most goals in a single **FIFA World Cup** tournament, having tallied 13 during the 1958 World Cup in Sweden. It was the only World Cup that Fontaine played in, participating in six matches for **France** as they finished third in the tournament. He scored four goals in a single game against West **Germany**. Fontaine scored a total of 30 goals in 21 international games for France between 1953 and 1960. He retired from playing in 1962 due to injury, having also scored prolifically at club level in France for Nice and Stade Reims. He then went on to have a long and successful career as a **coach**, most notably managing the national teams of both France and Morocco.

THE FOOTBALL ASSOCIATION (THE FA). The Football Association is the governing body of soccer in England (commonly known there as "football") and is responsible for the development and regulation of the sport at all levels in the country. The FA is headquartered at **Wembley Stadium** in London. It is a member of the **Union of European Football Associations (UEFA)** and **Fédération Internationale de Football Association (FIFA)**. The FA, established at a meeting that took place at the Freeman's Tavern in Great Queen Street, London, on 23 October 1883, was the first national soccer association ever established. Present were representatives from 12 clubs and schools from the south of England, and the aim of the meeting was to establish a set of common rules for the game to end the nationwide confusion over which rules would be in effect for any given game. One school, Blackheath, walked out of the meeting as they opposed a ban on "hacking" in the game. But 14 rules, reforming the established Cambridge Rules, were agreed to by the rest of the representatives under the charge of Ebenezer Cobb Morley, who had initiated the meeting by proposing a governing body for the sport be created. The creation of the FA did not result in its immediate acceptance as the ultimate authority in English soccer nationwide, with disputes (particularly from pioneering clubs in Sheffield, who had set their own rules in 1857) persisting into the late 1870s. But the formation of the **International Football Association Board (IFAB)** in 1882, with two representatives from each of the four associations of the United Kingdom, ended disagreements about the rules of the game and gave the FA control of the sport across England.

As soccer's popularity grew, the FA was faced with a considerable number of challenges and opportunities in the next few decades. It established the **Football Association Challenge Cup** in 1871; organized the world's first international games in the 1870s, between England and Scotland; finally accepted **professionalism** in 1885; oversaw the establishment of the world's first **Football League**; and eventually joined soccer's global governing body, FIFA, in 1906 after initially refusing to join the organization upon its founding in 1904. The FA's relations with the world of soccer outside the United Kingdom were characterized by English isolationism and a sense of superiority for several decades, with the FA withdrawing from FIFA in 1920 over a dispute on the membership of England's adversaries in the First World War. England did not participate in the first three World Cups in 1930, 1934, and 1938. The FA rejoined FIFA in 1946, and England played in the 1950 World Cup, surprisingly losing to the **United States**.

With the growth of the international game since then, The Football Association's primary public role now is its management of the **England** national team, which won the FIFA World Cup in 1966 on the only occasion it has been hosted by England. The national team has twice reached the semifinals of the **UEFA European Football Championship**. At club level, all professional teams in England are members of the FA. The **Premier League**, which broke away from the Football League in 1991, is the preeminent competition in England, and the FA is a "special shareholder" in the league, with veto power over the selection of the chairman, chief executive officer, and on matters pertaining to relegation and promotion in and out of the Premier League.

The Football Association's role in the development of **women's soccer** has been highly problematic, as the FA forbade the playing of games by women at Football League grounds between 1921 and 1971. The FA now organizes a national women's team, which reached the final of the **UEFA Women's Championship** for the first time in 2009, and runs domestic club competitions for women, including the FA Women's Premier League and the FA Women's Cup. Participation by women in English soccer has grown rapidly in the past two decades, and a new, fully professional Women's Super League is set to be launched by the FA in the summer of 2011.

THE FOOTBALL ASSOCIATION CHALLENGE CUP (F.A. CUP). The Football Association Challenge Cup, commonly called the F.A. Cup, is an annual tournament for clubs in **England** run by **The Football Association** and is the oldest soccer competition in the world. It is open to entry to both amateur and professional clubs, with more than 700 teams entering at the qualifying stages. Elite clubs in England's top leagues join later, in the tournament's "proper" rounds, with random draws made for each round. Single-elimination games determine who proceeds from each round, culminating in a final between two teams held at London's famous **Wembley Stadium**. Due to the random draw and single-game format, the F.A. Cup has become known for its production of surprising results and Cinderella stories, with numerous examples of unlikely smaller teams knocking off England's leading club teams. The winner of the F.A. Cup qualifies for the **UEFA Europa League** in European competition.

The F.A. Cup was founded in 1871, 16 teams participating in the first tournament, which ran through the English season into 1872; the Wanderers beat the Royal Engineers in front of a crowd of 2,000 at the Kennington Oval in London. It has been contested every season since, with the number of entrants increasing steadily to more than 700 in recent seasons, and elite teams from the **Premier League** have increasingly dominated the final stages in the past two decades. **Manchester United** boasts the most victories in the competition, with 11 wins in 18 appearances in the final.

FOOTBALL LEAGUE. The Football League, based in **England** and founded in 1888, was the world's first professional soccer league. Today, it is divided into three divisions comprising 24 clubs each, for a total of 72 teams in the league. The Championship is the top division, followed by League

One and League Two respectively. For sponsorship purposes, it is currently known as the "Coca-Cola Football League." The top and bottom clubs in each division are promoted and relegated in a pyramidal structure following each season, which sees each team play each other once at home and once away. The Football League is part of the larger pyramid of English soccer, with the top teams in the league's highest division, the Championship, promoted to the highest level of English soccer, the **Premier League**, and the bottom two tiers in the Football League's lowest division, League Two, relegated out of the league to the level below, the Football Conference.

The original inspiration for the foundation of the Football League in 1888 came from the chairman of Aston Villa, William McGregor. He saw the need to bring a system of more-ordered fixtures between teams competing in a myriad of cup competitions, especially since **The Football Association** had allowed professionalism just three years earlier, guaranteeing a continual stream of revenue from gate receipts each year. Twelve clubs made up the league for its inaugural season in 1888, and a second division was introduced in 1892 as it expanded to 28 teams. A third division was added in 1920, and in 1921, regional divisions were added to create a structure encompassing 88 clubs by 1923. This became 92 clubs in 1950, with a four-division system introduced in 1958 and the regional element removed. Until 1992, the Football League was the highest level of English club soccer, but that year, 22 clubs in the Football League's top division broke away to form the Premier League, tempted by a more lucrative **television** deal and autonomy from lower league teams. This reduced the Football League to three divisions and diminished its importance, though their crowds still remain larger than those of any other lower league system in Europe.

FORLÁN, DIEGO. B. 19 May 1979, Montevideo, Uruguay. **Uruguay**'s Diego Forlán won the Golden Ball as the best player of the 2010 **FIFA World Cup**, when he led Uruguay to fourth place in the competition, scoring five goals in the process. Forlán is a gifted forward who can both create and score goals and is notably deadly with his delivery from set plays. He began his senior club career with **Independiente** in **Argentina** in 1998, moving to join **Manchester United** in **England** in 2002 and spending two relatively unsuccessful years there. Forlán then moved to **Spain** and played first for Villareal and then for Atlético Madrid, scoring goals prolifically. Forlán's father, Pablo Forlán, starred for Uruguay at the 1966 and 1974 World Cup finals tournaments.

FOULS. A foul is called for numerous types of infringements during play as outlined in Law 12 of the **Laws of the Game**. There are seven such offenses outlined, such as tackling an opponent in a manner deemed by the **referee** to be careless, reckless, or using excessive force. The opposing team is awarded a direct **free kick**, indirect free kick, or **penalty kick** when a foul is called by the referee, depending on the type of offense committed and where it takes place on the field of play. For example, a reckless tackle on an attacking player in the penalty area is a foul, and a penalty kick is awarded. *See also* INTERNATIONAL FOOTBALL ASSOCIATION BOARD.

FOURTH OFFICIAL. *See* ASSISTANT REFEREE.

FRANCE. Soccer is one of the most popular sports in France, a country whose teams have achieved considerable success in international competition. Soccer in France is governed by the *Fédération Française de Football* (FFF) or, in English, the French Football Federation, which oversees the professional and amateur forms of the game. The FFF was a founding member of the **Fédération Internationale de Football Association (FIFA)**, the establishment of which was spearheaded by Frenchman **Robert Guérin**, who became its first president and was also the organizer of the French national team. In 1954, the FFF was a founding member of the **Union of European Football Associations (UEFA)**, Europe's **FIFA confederation**, meaning France's teams enter into UEFA's national team and club team championships for men, women, and juniors. According to FIFA figures from 2006, France has more than four million soccer players, almost two million of whom are registered with the FFF at 20,062 club teams.

The French men's national team has been one of the most successful in Europe, with 12 appearances in the **FIFA World Cup** with a win in the tournament in 1998 on home soil under the inspirational leadership of one of the world's greatest-ever players, **Zinedine Zidane**. Eight years later, France finished runners-up in the 2006 World Cup held in **Germany**, losing to **Italy** in a contentious game that ended with a **penalty shoot-out** after Zidane had been sent off in extra time. France's two previous best World Cup performances had come with third-place finishes in 1958, French forward **Just Fontaine** setting a record with 13 goals in the tournament, and in 1986, captained by the brilliant attacking midfielder **Michel Platini**. The French national team has also performed strongly in European continental competition, twice winning the **UEFA European Football Championship**, in 1984 and 2000, led by Platini in the former year and Zidane in the latter year. The French national team also won the men's **Olympic Games Football Tournament** in 1984 and the **FIFA Confederations Cup** in both 2001 and 2003. The French women's national team has been less successful, though, at junior level, France's Under-20 women's national team finished in fourth place at the **FIFA U-20 Women's World Cup** in 2008.

In domestic club football in France, the leading divisions, Ligue 1 and Ligue 2, contain 20 professional clubs each. Ligue 1 and Ligue 2 are run by *Ligue de Football Professionnel* (LFP), founded in 1944, operating under the authority of the FFF. A system of promotion and relegation between Ligue 1 and Ligue 2 sees the lowest-finishing clubs in the former replaced by the highest-finishing clubs in the latter each season. The French professional season typically runs from August to May. In Ligue 1, each team plays each other team twice during the season, at their home stadium and at their opponent's stadium, for a total of 38 games. The team that accrues the most points in the course of a season is crowned as the champion and automatically earns the right to enter the **UEFA Champions League**. Runners-up in Ligue 1 may also enter the UEFA Champions League as well, depending on how many participation spots France is awarded by UEFA (for the 2009–2010 season, France was awarded three entrants based on past performance by French clubs in European competition). The French league is considered one of the strongest in Europe, though French clubs have not been as successful in European competition as their peers in **Italy, England, Spain**, and **Germany**. Only one French team, **Olympique de Marseille**, has ever won the UEFA Champions League. That victory came in 1992–1993, with Olympique de Marseille beating **Red Star Belgrade** in the final. This triumph was later tarnished as not long after, Olympique de Marseille were found to have fixed matches in that season in Ligue 1 and were stripped of their domestic championship though not their UEFA Champions League title.

The top level of women's club football in France, governed by the FFA, is known as the *Championnat de France de football feminine*, or commonly the *Division 1 Féminine*. Twelve clubs participate in the league, founded in 1974. The lowest finishing two teams each year are relegated to the *Division 2 Féminine*. The champion of *Division 1 Féminine* earns entry into the **UEFA Women's Champions League**. In recent years, similar to men's Ligue 1, the league has been dominated by Olympique Lyonnais. *See also* AS SAINT-ÉTIENNE; DESAILLY, MARCEL; GIRESSE, ALAIN; HENRY, THIERRY; JACQUET, AIMÉ; KOPA, RAYMOND; PAPIN, JEAN-PIERRE; RIMET, JULES; TIGANA, JEAN; WOMEN'S SOCCER.

FRANCESCOLI, ENZO. B. 12 November 1961, Montevideo, Uruguay. Enzo Francescoli was **Uruguay**'s leading player in the 1980s and 1990s, and was the South American Footballer of the Year in 1984 and 1995. He played 73 national team games for Uruguay between 1982 and 1997, playing as the creative fulcrum of the team from midfield and scoring 17 goals. Francescoli's long club-playing career took him around the world, starring for **River Plate** in **Argentina**, Racing Club Paris in **France**, and Cagliari in **Italy** among many teams in a highly productive career. Francescoli played at the **FIFA World Cup** for Uruguay on two occasions, in 1986 and 1990, and won three **Copa América** titles with his country, in 1983, 1987, and 1995. Francescoli retired in 1997.

FREE KICK. A free kick is awarded to a team for an infringement in play by the opposing team as defined in the **Laws of the Game**. The type of infringement committed determines whether the free kick is allowed to be shot directly into the opponents' goal (a direct free kick) or must subsequently touch another player first before a goal can be scored (an indirect free kick). More-serious offenses, such as a deliberate handball, result in a direct free kick, while less-serious infringements, such as impeding the progress of an opponent, result in an indirect free kick. All free kicks must be taken with the ball stationary, and the kicker must not touch the ball again until another player has touched it after the kick. All opponents must be at least 10 yards from the spot of the ball (where on the field the infringement took place) when the free kick is taken. A special type of direct free kick, the **penalty kick**, is awarded if an offense that would normally result in a direct free kick occurs inside the penalty area while the ball is in play. *See also* FOULS; INTERNATIONAL FOOTBALL ASSOCIATION BOARD.

FUTEBOL CLUBE DO PORTO. Commonly known as "FC Porto," or simply "Porto," Futebol Clube do Porto, from the northern city of Porto, is one of the three biggest clubs in **Portugal**. The club was founded on 28 September 1893 by a wine merchant, António Nicolau de Almeida, who had discovered the sport of soccer in England while on business trips. Porto achieved considerable success throughout the 20th century, but its most glorious period came in the 1980s, with considerable credit given to their **coach** José Maria Pedroto (who died of cancer in 1984). He laid the groundwork that led to their *annus mirabilis* in 1987: following victory in the Portuguese championship in 1986, they won the European Cup (now known as the **UEFA Champions League**), the **UEFA Super Cup**, and the **Intercontinental Cup** all in the same year. Porto then entered a period of mediocrity in European competition by those standards but emerged again as a surprisingly strong force in 2003, winning the **UEFA Cup** under the coaching of José Mourinho, who then led them to victory in the UEFA Champions League the following year. Mourinho soon departed to manage **Chelsea Football Club**, but Porto still won a second Intercontinental Cup at the end of 2004.

FUTSAL. A form of soccer played indoors on a hard surface with five players per side, futsal has grown enormously in popularity in recent decades, particularly in South America. The premier global tournament is the FIFA

Futsal World Championship, organized by **Fédération Internationale de Football Association (FIFA)** and held every four years. FIFA has taken an increasingly prominent role in promoting and structuring futsal worldwide since taking over control of the world championship in 1989, a tournament organized before then by the previous world governing body of futsal, *Federación Internacional de Fútbol de Salón* (FIFUSA). In both men's and women's futsal, **Brazil** has traditionally produced the strongest teams. There have been large crowds in Brazil's high-quality futsal league and unmatched participation in a form of the sport that encourages skillful play due to the greater weight of the ball and the tight confines of the playing field.

Unlike other forms of **indoor soccer**, futsal courts are bordered by lines and do not allow the ball to be bounced off walls, thus slowing down play and putting an emphasis on accurate passing, close control, and dribbling skills. The name futsal is an abbreviation for *futebol de salão* in Portuguese and *fútbol de salón* in Spanish, roughly meaning "soccer played inside a hall." Popularized in **Uruguay** in the 1930s, futsal soon spread to the rest of South America, leading to the formation of its first world governing body, FIFUSA, in 1971. That body organized the first world championship in 1982, won by Brazil. By the end of the 1980s, FIFA took over global administration of the sport by convincing most nations to abandon FIFUSA. Since then, **Spain** and Brazil have vied for dominance of the sport in the men's game, with the latter having won four FIFA Futsal World Championship titles to the former's two.

G

GAETJENS, JOE. B. 19 March 1924, Port-au-Prince, Haiti. D. ? Joe Gaetjens is remembered today for a single goal he scored for the **United States**, against **England** at the 1950 **FIFA World Cup**, giving the Americans an upset 1-0 victory over the favored English. Gaetjens made all of his three appearances for the United States at that World Cup, having been plucked out of obscurity playing for Brookhatten in the American Soccer League. He had been living in the United States for a only few years, having been born in Haiti and moving to New York as a college student in the mid-1940s. Following the 1950 World Cup, Gaetjens did not earn fame or fortune for his accomplishment, instead he played out a low-key career and retired to his native Haiti. There, he became a victim of political repression in the country, arrested by the secret police in July 1964 due to his family's connections to opponents of François Duvalier's regime. Gaetjens disappeared and was presumed to have been killed by the secret police, though his body has never been found.

GALATASARAY. Galatasaray is one of the biggest professional club teams in **Turkey** and the most successful Turkish team in European competition. They are based in Istanbul and played at Ali Sami Yen Stadium until the end of 2010, when they moved to Türu Teleriom Arena. The club was founded in 1905 by students from a school in Galatasaray and began play in the Istanbul Football League, later joining Turkey's first professional national league, the Turkish Super League, when it was founded in 1959. They have won the Turkish Super League a joint-record 17 times (matched only by their fierce rivals **Fenerbahçe**). In 2000, Galatasaray became the first Turkish team to win a European competition, with victory in the UEFA Cup (now the **UEFA Europa League**). They have made 20 appearances in Europe's premier club competition, the **UEFA Champions League**, reaching the semifinals in 1989, when it was known as the European Cup.

GARRINCHA. B. 28 October 1933, Pau Grande, Brazil. D. 20 January 1983. Born Manuel Francisco dos Santos, but universally known as "Garrincha" (the "little bird"), Garrincha is the only rival for **Pelé** as **Brazil**'s most talented player of all time. Inventive, unpredictable, and impudent, Garrincha astonished spectators and humiliated opponents with his devilish dribbling technique, swerving and drifting past defenders seemingly at will. Garrincha overcame considerable obstacles to reach the top of the world's game, growing up in a deprived area and overcoming the physical impediment of having one leg a full two inches shorter than the other. He began his professional career with Botafogo in 1953, staying there for 12 seasons and scoring 232 goals in 581 appearances, and winning the Rio de Janeiro state championship three times. It was his performances for Brazil, playing a key part in Brazil's first two **FIFA World Cup** victories in 1958 in **Sweden** and 1962 in **Chile**, that earned Garrincha worldwide fame. He carried a particularly heavy load in the 1962 triumph, after injury early in the tournament restricted Pelé's contribution, scoring four goals to finish as joint top scorer. He played 50 times for Brazil, 43 of those games won, six drawn, and the only loss coming in his final appearance for his country, against **Hungary**, at the 1966 FIFA World Cup in **England**, when a poor Brazil team tumbled out in the first stage. Garrincha's life off the field was as eventful as his career on it; a heavy drinker, not always able to sensibly manage his fame and fortune, he died at the age of just 49 from cirrhosis of the liver, in 1983. He is remembered alongside Pelé as the greatest talent Brazil has produced.

GENTO, FRANCISCO. B. 21 October 1933, Guarnizo, Spain. Francisco Gento, a quick and skillful outside left midfielder, was a star player for **Spain** and **Real Madrid**. He played a total of 761 games in his career, scoring 253 goals, and was a key part of Real Madrid's golden team of the late 1950s and 1960s, winning a remarkable total of six **European Cup** trophies and 12 Spanish national league titles. Gento played for the Spanish national team on 44 occasions, appearing in the World Cups of 1962 and 1966, though Spain failed to advance beyond the first round on either occasion. He retired from playing in 1971 and then embarked on a low-key coaching career at lower-league Spanish clubs.

GERMANY. Soccer is an enormously popular sport in Germany, a country that has been among the elite in both men's and women's competitive soccer over the past century. Separate teams represented East Germany and West Germany from 1945 to 1989. Germany has been officially credited by the world's governing body, **Fédération Internationale de Football Association (FIFA)**, with the results of West Germany during those years, including their **FIFA World Cup** victory of 1954. Since reunification of the country, the sport has been run nationwide by the German Football Association (in German, *Deutscher Fußball-Bund* [DFB]). The DFB was founded in 1900 and was an inaugural member national association of both FIFA in 1904 and of European soccer's governing body, the **Union of European Football Associations (UEFA)**, in 1954. According to FIFA, there are more than 16 million soccer players in Germany, a bit more than six million of them at 26,837 registered clubs with the DFB.

Germany's men's national team has won three FIFA World Cups and has made 18 appearances in the FIFA World Cup finals tournament up to and including the 2010 World Cup in South Africa, where Germany finished in third place. Their first title came at the World Cup held in **Switzerland** in 1954, when West Germany surprised the world with a victory in the final against favorites **Hungary**, led by their inspirational captain **Fritz Walter**. That game, held in the Swiss city of Berne, became known as the "Miracle of Berne" to West Germans and proved an enormous boon for soccer in the country, as well as becoming a symbol of successful West German reconstruction following the Second World War. In 1966, West Germany reached the final of the World Cup held in **England** but lost to the hosts in the final 4-2, England's third goal a controversial decision by the **referee** still remembered and debated by fans of both sides today. Eight years later, led by **Franz Beckenbauer**, West Germany again won the World Cup and again upset the tournament favorites in the final, defeating the **Netherlands** 2-1 in the 1974 tournament held on German soil, in Munich. West Germany then reached the final of the World Cup in both 1982, losing to **Italy**, and 1986, defeated by **Diego Maradona's** team from **Argentina**. Crowning a remarkable run of reaching four finals in five FIFA World Cup tournaments, now-unified Germany won the 1990 FIFA World Cup hosted by Italy, taking revenge on Maradona's Argentina in the final. Germany has reached the World Cup final only once since 1990, in 2002 at the World Cup held in **Japan** and the **Republic of Korea**, finishing as runners-up for the fourth time after a loss to **Brazil**. Germany hosted the next World Cup in 2006, reaching the semifinals, where they lost to eventual winners Italy 2-0 after extra time; Germany finished third after beating **Portugal** in the third-place play-off. In 2010 at the World Cup in **South Africa**, Germany once again finished in third place in the competition, after losing to **Spain** in the semifinals and defeating **Uruguay** in the third-place play-off game. Germany has also been successful in European continental competition, winning the **UEFA European Football Championship** three times, in 1972, 1980, and 1996.

At club level, the highest level of play in men's competition is the Bundesliga, founded in 1963 as Germany's first fully professional league. Eighteen clubs compete in the Bundesliga each season, with a system of promotion and relegation interchanging clubs at the bottom of the Bundesliga with teams from the second-tier league, 2nd Bundesliga, each year. **Bayern Munich** has been by far the most successful club in the Bundesliga, with 21 league titles to their credit, and they have also been the most successful German club in European competition. The Bundesliga consistently enjoys the highest-average crowds among European leagues each season and is known for its fan-friendly stadiums and ownership system that means each club (with a couple of historical exceptions) must be majority owned by the club's fan base.

Women's soccer in Germany is played by a relatively large number of girls and women, and the German national women's team has been enormously successful, led by stars such as **Birgit Prinz**, a three-time **FIFA World Player of the Year**. A DFB census in 2006 found more than one million female competitive soccer players. The women's national team has twice won the **FIFA Women's World Cup**, in 2003 and 2007, and finished runners-up in the tournament in 1995. Germany has one of the strongest women's leagues in the world. *See also* BORUSSIA DORTMUND; BREITNER, PAUL; HERBERGER, "SEPP" JOSEPH; KAHN, OLIVER; KLINSMANN, JÜRGEN; MAIER, SEPP; MATTHÄUS, LOTHAR; MOHR, HEIDI; MÜLLER, GERHARD; RUMMENIGGE, KARL-HEINZ; SAMMER, MATTHIAS; SEELDRAYERS, RODOLPHE WILLIAM; SEELER, UWE; VOGTS, BERTI; VÖLLER, RUDI.

GHANA. One of the leading African nations in international competition, soccer in Ghana is governed by the Ghana Football Association (GFA), founded in 1957 and affiliated the next year with the **Fédération Internationale de Football Association (FIFA)** and the **Confederation of African Football (CAF)**. Ghana's men's national team, known as the "Black Stars," has achieved considerable success in world soccer since it began play as "Ghana" following independence from the United Kingdom in 1957. They have won the **Africa Cup of Nations** four times, in 1963, 1965, 1978, and 1982. Ghana has twice appeared at the FIFA World Cup, at the two most recent stagings in 2006 and 2010. Its best performance came in the latter competition, losing at the quarterfinal stage on penalty kicks to **Uruguay**. The growing quality of Ghanaian soccer is illustrated by its success in recent global youth competitions, where it won the 1991 and 1995 FIFA U-17 World Cup competitions and the 2009 **FIFA U-20 World Cup** (as well as finishing as runners-up in that competition in both 1993 and 2001). Ghana's women's national team is also proving to be successful at youth level, reaching the semifinals of the 2010 **FIFA U-20 Women's World Cup**.

In domestic soccer, the GFA organizes the elite men's professional competition, the GLO Premier League. Its two leading clubs are two of Africa's oldest and strongest teams, Hearts of Oak and **Asante Kotoko**, who have both won Africa's top international club competition, the **CAF Champions League**. There is no professional women's league in Ghana. *See also* DE-SAILLY, MARCEL; PELÉ, ABÉDI.

GHIGGIA, ALCIDES. B. 22 December 1926, Montevideo, Uruguay. Alcides Ghiggia scored perhaps the most famous goal in the final game of any **FIFA World Cup** finals tournament. He had the winning strike for **Uruguay** against **Brazil** in 1950 that gave the Uruguayans a shocking 2-1 victory and their second World Cup title. Brazil, playing at home in their newly built **Maracanã** stadium, which held more than 200,000 fans that day, were heavily favored to win and took an early lead in the game. But, after an equalizer for Uruguay from **Juan Alberto Schiaffino**, Ghiggia, a skinny, tricky winger, wrong-footed Brazil's **goalkeeper** and put in what proved to be the winning goal in the 79th minute. Such was the shock for Brazil that the game immediately inspired a new word in Brazil, the "*Maracanazo*." At club level, Ghiggia began his career with **Peñarol** in his native Uruguay before moving to **Italy** and playing for both AS Roma and, briefly, **AC Milan**. He also appeared for Italy's national team on five occasions in the late 1950s, retiring in 1968 after spending his final years back in Uruguay playing for Danubio Fútbol Club in his native city of Montevideo.

GIRESSE, ALAIN. B. 2 September 1952, Langoiran, France. Alain Giresse, a gifted, creative midfielder, was a key part of **France**'s exceptional team of the early 1980s. He, alongside **Michel Platini** and **Jean Tigana**, was part of the French team that won the 1984 **UEFA European Football Championship**. He also played at the 1982 **FIFA World Cup**, where France finished in fourth place, and the 1986 World Cup, where France finished in third. Giresse scored three goals in 12 World Cup finals games. At club level, Giresse played the vast majority of his career for Bordeaux, retiring in 1988. He has since pursued a globe-trotting career as a **coach**.

GLASGOW CELTIC. Along with fierce local rivals **Rangers Football Club**, Celtic, founded by a Marist monk called "Brother Walfrid" in 1887 as a charitable club to alleviate poverty in Glasgow's East End, has dominated professional club soccer in **Scotland** since the 19th century. The club began play at their legendary home in the Parkhead area of Glasgow, Celtic Park, in 1893, and they won their first Scottish League Championship that year. In 1903, the club began to wear their distinctive green-and-white hooped jerseys. They have won a remarkable 42 Scottish League Championships and 34 Scottish Cups, and, in 1967, they became the first team from Great Britain to win the **European Cup**, crowned as the best in Europe after a 2-1 win over

Italy's **Internazionale** in Lisbon, **Portugal**. The same year, under legendary manager Jock Stein, Celtic won every competition they entered: the Scottish League, the Scottish Cup, the League Cup, the Glasgow Cup, and the European Cup. Unlike their rivals Rangers, Celtic has never had a sectarian employment policy of any kind, and their most famous manager, Jock Stein, was a Protestant. Celtic and Rangers, who, together, are known as the "Old Firm," have long had a troubled and dark rivalry underpinned by religious overtones, as Celtic has traditionally been the team of Catholics in Glasgow, and Rangers, the team of Protestants. Sectarian violence has thus dogged many of their encounters, though, in recent times, Celtic has taken steps to clamp down on religious bigotry, as have Rangers. *See also* DALGLISH, KENNY.

GOAL. According to the **Laws of the Game**, the game of soccer is determined by the number of goals scored, with the team scoring the greater number declared the winner. If an equal number of goals, or none at all, are scored in a game, the game is officially ruled a tie, even if a **penalty shoot-out** is used after the game to determine a victor. A goal is scored when the ball crosses the goal line between the goalposts and under the goal crossbar. The entire ball must cross the goal line, with no infringement of the Laws of the Game by the attacking team ruled to have taken place on the play. *See also* FOULS; GOAL KICK; INTERNATIONAL FOOTBALL ASSOCIATION BOARD; PENALTY KICK.

GOAL KICK. A goal kick is the method used to restart play after the ball, last having touched a player on the attacking team, has passed over the goal line without a **goal** being scored. Any player on the defending team can restart play from a goal kick by kicking it from the goal area, and the ball must travel outside the penalty area. Though any player may take the kick, the vast majority of goal kicks are taken by the **goalkeeper**. These rules governing the goal kick are laid out in Law 17 of the **Laws of the Game**. *See also* INTERNATIONAL FOOTBALL ASSOCIATION BOARD.

GOALKEEPER. The goalkeeper position is a specialized role in soccer. The goalkeeper is the only player on the field permitted to handle the ball during play on the **field**. Each team must have one goalkeeper on the field at all times. The goalkeeper is usually the last stationed defensive player on a team and is allowed to handle the ball within his own team's penalty area. Until 1910, the **Laws of the Game** allowed the goalkeeper to handle the ball anywhere within his team's defensive half of the field. Goalkeepers may play the ball outside their own penalty area in the same manner as other players, without use of their hands. Goalkeeping demands vastly different skills than other positions on the field, and the equipment goalkeepers use is also specialized; most goalkeepers wear gloves along with distinctively colored shirts to differentiate them from the rest of their team. With less running required than in other positions, goalkeeping careers often last longer than do those of outfield players. Some of the best-known goalkeepers include **Lev Yashin** of **Russia**, **Sepp Maier** of **Germany**, and **Dino Zoff** of **Italy**. *See also* BANKS, GORDON; KAHN, OLIVER; PLÁNIČKA, FRANTIŠEK; SCHMEICHEL, PETER.

GORDILLO, RAFAEL. B. 24 February 1957, Almendralejo, Spain. Rafael Gordillo appeared for **Spain** at two **FIFA World Cup** finals tournaments and three **UEFA European Football Championships** in the 1980s. Known for his charismatic play on the field, he was one of the outstanding Spanish players of his generation. He played a total of 75 games for Spain, scoring three goals. He usually played a left-sided position on the wing and was able to surge forward and support the attack. At club level, Gordillo most notably appeared for **Real Madrid** from 1985 to 1992, winning the Spanish league championship on five occasions and the **UEFA Cup** once with the club, in 1986. He retired in 1996.

GRÊMIO FOOT-BALL PORTO-ALEGRENSE. Grêmio Foot-Ball Porto Alegrense, usually referred to simply as "Grêmio," was founded on 15 September 1903 in Porto Alegre, **Brazil**, and has long been one of the leading club teams in Brazilian soccer competition. They were founded in a Porto Alegre restaurant by a group of Portuguese and German immigrants. Grêmio has been very successful in state competitions, winning the *Campeonato Gaúcho* (the league for the state of Rio Grande do Sul) 35 times. Grêmio won the national Brazilian championship for the first time in 1981 and then achieved international fame by winning the premier South American club competition, the **Copa Libertadores**, in 1983. They then proceeded on to win the **Intercontinental Cup** the same year. Grêmio won the Copa Libertadores again in 1995 and the Brazilian championship for the second time in 1996. Since 1954, Grêmio has owned and played at Estádio Olímpico Monumental in Porto Alegre, renovated in 1980, with a current capacity of 45,000.

GUÉRIN, ROBERT. B. 28 June 1876. D. 1952, France. Frenchman Robert Guérin was the first president of soccer's global governing body the **Fédération Internationale de Football Association (FIFA)**, founded in 1904. At the start of the 20th century, as soccer was spreading fast from its origins in **England** across the European continent and beyond, Guérin was the driving force behind the creation of a world governing body to harmonize the **Laws**

of the Game and facilitate international play. Guérin was the chairman of the *Union des Sociétés Françaises de Sports Athlétiques* (USFSA) in **France**, and a journalist at *Le Matin* newspaper, giving him the necessary connections to develop the idea. Guérin and others approached the English **Football Association** and the **International Football Association Board (IFAB)** to attempt to win British support for the foundation of such a body, but received a tepid response. Guérin was undeterred and drafted a treaty for a foundation agreement in early 1904, inviting interested national associations from the **Netherlands, Switzerland**, Denmark, **Belgium, Sweden**, France, and, representing **Spain**, which did not yet have a national association, FC Madrid. That treaty was signed by those associations in July 2004, and Guérin was elected as the first president of FIFA. Ten articles creating the FIFA statutes were established. An annual subscription fee was instituted, the IFAB's Laws of the Game were adopted, and an intent to create an international championship was stated, though it was 26 years until the **FIFA World Cup** was finally established. Guérin would remain as president of FIFA for two years, successfully drawing new national associations into membership of FIFA including, most crucially, the British national associations. An unsuccessful attempt to stage an international tournament in 1906 precipitated Guérin's departure from the leadership of FIFA, and he was succeeded by **Daniel Burley Woolfall** of England.

GULLIT, RUUD. B. 1 September 1962, Amsterdam, Netherlands. Ruud Gullit is a Dutch **coach** and former star player for the **Netherlands**. He was captain of his country when they won their first major trophy, the 1988 **UEFA European Football Championship**. Gullit played for three club teams in the Netherlands before moving to **Italian** giants **AC Milan** in 1987. He filled numerous positions on the field due to his size, strength, technical ability, and versatility, most often operating as a goal-scoring midfielder. He was named the **European Footballer of the Year** in 1998. With AC Milan, Gullit won the *Serie A* league championship in 1988, 1992, and 1993, along with the European Cup in 1989 and 1990. He then moved to fellow Italian club Sampdoria and ended his playing career with **Chelsea Football Club** in **England**, where he became a player-manager in 1996. He later went on to coach Feyenoord in the **Netherlands** and the Los Angeles Galaxy in the **United States** without notable success. He also became a well-known **television** pundit and ambassador for Dutch soccer around the world.

GUTTMANN, BÉLA. B. 13 March 1900, Budapest, Hungary. D. 28 August 1981. Béla Guttmann was a Hungarian player and **coach**, who is better remembered in the latter role for his time managing **Benfica** in **Portugal**, who he led to the pinnacle of European club soccer. After winning the Portuguese championship with Benfica in 1960, Guttmann led Benfica to victory in the **European Cup** for the first time the following year, defeating **Barcelona** in the final. Guttmann's Benfica then repeated that triumph the next year, this time defeating **Real Madrid** in the final 5-3, with a starring role played by the team's outstanding creative forward, **Eusébio**. Guttmann's contract was not renewed by the club, however, as they rejected his request for a pay rise. Guttmann continued his managerial career at several clubs, though never matched his remarkably successful short period in charge of Benfica.

H

HAMM, MIA. B. 17 March 1972, Selma, Alabama, United States. Probably the most famous player in the history of **women's soccer**, Mia Hamm won the first two **FIFA Women's Player of the Year** awards in 2001 and 2002, and doubtless would have won many more at her peak in the 1990s had the award existed then. In that decade, she won two **FIFA Women's World Cups** with the **United States**: the inaugural tournament held in **China** in 1991 and the well-known 1999 edition in her native United States. It was there, in front of all-time record crowds for women's soccer, that Hamm became a nationally known figure when the United States won the trophy on penalties in front of more than 90,000 fans at the Rose Bowl in California and before a national television audience approaching 20 million viewers. Hamm had made her debut at the age of just 15 for the U.S. national team in 1987 and ended her international career 17 years later in 2004 after a record 158 goals in 275 appearances. She also won gold medals with the United States in the 1996 and 2004 **Olympic Games Football Tournaments**. Hamm played in the first professional women's league in the United States, the WUSA, winning the championship in 2003 with the Washington Freedom. She has dedicated her retirement to the promotion of the Mia Hamm Foundation, founded in memory of her brother, who died of complications from a bone marrow transplant.

HANDBALL. In soccer, the **Laws of the Game** in organized games and general custom in other forms rule that only the **goalkeeper** is legally allowed to handle the ball and only within his penalty area. Any other player judged to have deliberately handled the ball is penalized by the award of a direct **free kick** or, if the offense occurred in the penalty area, a **penalty kick**, to the opposing team. The infringing player may also be given a yellow or red card (for stopping a goal-scoring chance by handling the ball). This strict restriction on the use of hands by players in soccer is important to its differentiation from most other organized forms of football, such as rugby football, Gaelic football, and American football. Soccer split from rugby as a distinct sport in the 19th century, in part, over a disagreement about how players would be allowed to handle the ball, with carrying the ball by hand outlawed by the founding clubs of **The Football Association**. Catching the ball with hands was later ruled out in 1866, touching the ball at all by an outfield player was outlawed in 1869, and goalkeepers were restricted to handling the ball only in their team's penalty area in 1910, setting the rules that stand today.

HAPPEL, ERNST. B. 29 November 1925, Vienna, Austria. D. 14 November 1992. Ernst Happel is one of the most successful managers of all time. He followed an excellent playing career with an outstanding **coaching** record in several countries. As a player, he participated on the **Austria** team that reached the **FIFA World Cup** semifinals in 1954. As a manager, Happel won 17 titles with 10 different club and international teams, including the **European Cup** with both Feyenoord in 1970 and Hamburg in 1983. As an international manager, he took the **Netherlands** to the 1978 World Cup final, where they lost to **Argentina**, and finally took over his native Austria in 1991, but died the next year of cancer. The largest **stadium** in Austria was renamed the "Ernst-Happel-Stadion" in his honor following his death.

HAT-TRICK. "Hat-trick" is a term used to refer to the scoring of three goals by one player in a single game, which is an unusual feat. The term's origins lie in other professional sports, namely cricket and ice hockey, but it is now commonly used in amateur and professional soccer.

HAVELANGE, JOÃO. B. 8 May 1916, Brazil. João Havelange oversaw a massive modernization and commercialization of world soccer following his election as the seventh president of soccer's global governing body, the **Fédération Internationale de Football Association (FIFA)**, on 11 June 1974. He would be reelected to six terms as president, spanning 24 years. Havelange spent his entire life in sport. He was a swimmer at the 1936 Olympic Games and a water polo player at the 1952 Olympic Games before he began a career in soccer administration. He became the head of **Brazil**'s national soccer federation in 1958. That year saw Brazil win the **FIFA World Cup** for the first time, and Havelange benefited by association to the country's amazing run of three world championships in the space of 12 years, with further wins in 1962 and 1970, led by **Pelé**. Havelange courted the support of the world's developing nations in his bid to replace the then–English president of FIFA, **Sir Stanley Rous**, in the early 1970s, making almost 100 trips abroad in the two years preceding the 1974 election. He successfully courted the support of Asian and African national associations by promising to include more places for teams from those continents at the World Cup by expanding it from 16 to 24 teams and providing investment and support for the development of soccer infrastructure in both continents. Crucially, Havelange also promised to exclude the Football Association of **South Africa** from FIFA membership as long as it continued to apply apartheid to its national soccer structure.

Once in power, Havelange both led and benefited from the new revenue streams available to sporting bodies controlling the rights to major global tournaments such as the FIFA World Cup, which under his tenure eventually expanded from 16 to 32 teams. FIFA itself expanded its staff tenfold at its administrative headquarters in Zurich, Switzerland, while 50 new national associations also joined FIFA. New world championships for **women's soccer**, **indoor soccer**, and junior soccer were instituted, along with the **FIFA Confederations Cup**. Havelange summed up the commercialization of global soccer under his reign at FIFA: "When I arrived, I found an old house and $20 in the kitty. On the day I departed 24 years later, I left property and contracts worth over $4 billion." Some have accused Havelange of raiding that kitty during his time in office: investigative journalist Andrew Jennings' book *Foul! The Secret World of FIFA*: *Bribes, Vote-Rigging and Ticket Scandals* details a cash-for-contracts scandal involving FIFA's marketing partner, ISL. In 1998, Havelange stepped down from the FIFA presidency and successfully lobbied for **Sepp Blatter** as his hand-picked successor over Lennart Johansson in a controversial election at the **FIFA Congress** on 8 June 1998. On the same day, Havelange was made honorary FIFA president for life.

HENRY, THIERRY. B. 17 August 1977, Les Ulis, France. Thierry Henry is one of **France**'s greatest-ever players and most famous at club-team level for his successful spell playing for **Arsenal Football Club** in **England**'s **Premier League**. Henry played for Arsenal in London from 1997 to 2007, scoring a club record 226 goals in 370 appearances while winning the Premier League title with them in both 2002 and 2004. He was the runner-up in the voting for the **FIFA World Player of the Year** in the latter year. At club level, Henry has played for Monaco in France, **Juventus** in **Italy**, **Barcelona** in **Spain**, and Red Bull New York in the **United States**. For France, Henry had scored 51 goals in 123 games as of August 2010 and won winners' medals at both the 1998 **FIFA World Cup** and the 2000 **UEFA European Football Championship**. Henry's remarkable goal-scoring record at club and country level only hints at his talent level: he is a fast, athletic forward with a remarkable ability to create goal-scoring opportunities for others as well as finishing regularly himself.

HERBERGER, "SEPP" JOSEPH. B. 28 March 1897, Mannheim, Germany. D. 28 April 1977. Joseph Herberger, better known as "Sepp," was a German player and manager best known for coaching West **Germany** to victory in the 1954 **FIFA World Cup**, a seminal event in the history of postwar West Germany. Herberger ran the West German national team for 28 years, spanning the prewar and reconstruction eras from 1936 to 1964. A former amateur player who played three times for the German national team in the early 1920s, Herberger studied for a coaching diploma and worked for four years in the early 1930s at the West Germany Sports Association. He took over the West German team in 1936. Known as an authoritative and disciplined **coach**, his first major tournament was not a success as the joint Austro-German team (following the annexation of Austria by Nazi Germany) he managed fell in the first round of the 1938 World Cup in **France**.

The Second World War then ended international play for Germany for more than a decade, with Herberger renamed as national team coach of the western side of the divided nation in 1950. Herberger had to build the West Germany team from scratch, playing their first postwar international exhibition game later that year and heading to **Switzerland** for the 1954 World Cup as outsiders. They were crushed 8-3 by the world's most-feared team, **Hungary**, in their second game, as Herberger surprisingly rested several key players. But, with the team led by legendary captain Fritz Walter, Herberger's decision paid off as his rested players beat **Turkey** 7-2 in the decisive final group game. They then reached the final to face Hungary again in the Swiss city of Bern. Despite going down 2-0 early on to the favored Hungarians, the Germans came back through goals from Max Morlock and Helmut Rahn, with Rahn scoring again in the dying minutes to make West Germany world champions for the first time. Herberger would forever be immortalized as the orchestrator of what became known in West Germany as the "Miracle of Bern," and the victory would be seen as a key cultural healing moment for West German society in the postwar reconstruction era.

HERRERA, HELENIO. B. 10 April 1910, Buenos Aires, Argentina. D. 9 November 1997. Helenio Herrera was a famous soccer **coach** from **Argentina**, best known for his first spell in charge of **Internazionale** in Milan, **Italy**, from 1960 to 1968. In that period, he led Internazionale to victories at the highest level of European competition in the **European Cup**, in 1964 and 1965, along with three victories in the Italian championship. Internazionale also won the **Intercontinental Cup** in 1965 and 1966. He had previously made his name as a coach in **Spain**, taking both Atlético de Madrid and **Barcelona** to domestic championship glory. Prior to coaching, Herrera was a player in **France** for several clubs. But it was his period in Italy with Internazionale that saw him revolutionize the game from a managerial perspective: his team played a new style of pragmatic defense that was dour but extremely effective at blunting the opposition's attacks and led to a wave of teams copying his tactics, which became known as "*catenaccio*." Herrera also coached the national teams of Italy, France, and Spain, including the latter at the **1962 FIFA World Cup**, though without notable success. Herrera retired from coaching in 1981 and died in 1997.

HEYSEL STADIUM DISASTER. Before the start of the **European Cup** final on 29 May 1985 in **Belgium** at Heysel Stadium, Brussels, a wall collapsed inside the **stadium**, leading to the deaths of 39 spectators and more than 600 injuries. Most of those who died were supporters of **Juventus**, the team that was playing that day against **Liverpool**, with fans of both teams in attendance in large numbers. The disaster occurred when a group of Liverpool fans stampeded toward Juventus supporters, the retaining wall in sector Z of the stadium collapsing as Juventus fans attempted to escape. Some 32 Italians, four Belgians, two French people, and one person from Northern Ireland died as a result. The game took place despite ongoing rioting, with Juventus winning 1-0. Following the disaster, the Belgian authorities were criticized for inadequate crowd-control procedures, and the poor state of Heysel Stadium was regarded as a contributory factor. A week after the disaster, European soccer's governing body, the **Union of European Football Associations (UEFA)**, attributed all blame to the English club and banned clubs from **England** indefinitely from participating in its competitions. This ban was lifted for all English clubs, except Liverpool, after five years. Liverpool was banned from UEFA competition for one extra year. *See also* HOOLIGANISM.

HIDEGKUTI, NÁNDOR. B. 3 March 1922, Budapest, Hungary. D. 14 February 2002. Nándor Hidegkuti was a Hungarian player and coach, best known for his instrumental role in **Hungary**'s outstanding national team in the 1950s, known as the "Magical Magyars." Hidegkuti made his debut for Hungary in 1945, going on to play 69 games for his country and scoring 39 goals before his retirement from international duty in 1958. Hidegkuti revolutionized the game tactically by playing as a deep-lying central forward, dropping back to play a creative role as well as barreling forward to convert goal-scoring opportunities himself. This tactical innovation baffled opponents, including England in an infamous 6-3 victory for Hungary over **England** at **Wembley Stadium** in November 1953 when Hidegkuti scored a hat trick. That win came in the midst of a four-year unbeaten streak for Hungary with Hidegkuti playing a starring role throughout, a run that finally came to an end for the Magical Magyars with a disappointing defeat in the 1954 **FIFA World Cup** final to West **Germany**. Following his retirement from playing, Hidegkuti had a long, roaming career as a club **coach**, most notably and successfully with **Egyptian** club **Al-Ahly Sporting Club**. *See also* PUSKÁS, FERENC; SEBES, GUSZTÁV.

HILLSBOROUGH STADIUM DISASTER. On 15 April 1989, a crush occurred at Hillsborough Stadium in Sheffield, **England**, that killed 96 people in the crowd. All were **Liverpool** supporters in attendance for their team's game in the **Football Association Challenge Cup** semifinal that day against Nottingham Forest. That game was abandoned after six minutes. Fans were crushed on the terracing of the stadium, enclosed around the field by steel fencing. An inquiry into the disaster by Lord Chief Justice Taylor found that the chief cause of the crush was the failure by the police authorities of providing adequate crowd control and safety procedures. The pens containing supporters on the terrace were severely overcrowded and became more so as police opened up an exit gate to let in more people from outside the stadium. A crush barrier collapsed, and fans tried to climb over the steel perimeter fencing to escape the crush. Some fans were freed by other fans who pulled them from the upper tier of the stand. Lord Justice Taylor determined that the police had been at fault for failing to close the tunnels leading to the overcrowded stand, for failing to adequately handle the crowd outside the stadium, and for their slow reaction to the events. Taylor's second report led to the vast modernization of stadiums across England. *See also* HOOLIGANISM.

HONG, MYUNG-BO. B. 12 February 1969, Seoul, Republic of Korea. Myung-Bo Hong is regarded to be among the greatest Asian players of all time, playing 136 times for the **Republic of Korea** and appearing at four consecutive **FIFA World Cup** competitions, in 1990, 1994, 1998, and 2002. The 2002 tournament was the apex of Hong's career, as he led the joint hosts to a semifinal place and fourth-place finish in the competition. Hong, a consistent and commanding defender, played much of his career for **Pohang Steelers** before ending his career in the **United States** playing for the Los Angeles Galaxy. He retired in 2004.

HOOLIGANISM. The term "hooliganism" is typically used to refer to violence or disorder associated with soccer fans. It can either be used to mean "spontaneous acts of isolated aggression" or, more properly, "large-scale, organized fighting." The latter often takes place between fans of rival teams (and sometimes even between groups of fans of the same team) far away from any stadium and can include prearranged meetings to deliberately set up a pitched battle that may involve weapons such as knives, guns, or bats. A gang of soccer hooligans is commonly known as a "firm," a term that first became prominent in the 1960s in **England**, where crowd disorder became commonplace. It became a well-known element of English soccer culture in the 1970s and 1980s before it began to fade out from the late 1980s on after the **Heysel** and **Hillsborough stadium disasters**. Sensational coverage of hooliganism by fans of English clubs and the national team often led to a spiral of further disorder, with tabloid newspaper press coverage giving hooligans further notoriety. As many European and South American fans mimicked the style of English hooliganism, it became known as the "English disease." Incidents of hooliganism are now far-more common in many other countries than in England itself, which has seen a vast decline of soccer-related violence over the past two decades. Media attention on hooliganism has turned it into a subject of common pop-culture consumption, with innumerable fictional and autobiographical books and movies available describing and depicting the phenomenon, often in sensationalist fashion.

HUNGARY. Hungary produced some of the best players and strongest teams in world soccer from the 1930s to the 1950s, reaching the **FIFA World Cup** final in both 1938 and 1954, though losing on both occasions. Hungary has won the **Olympic Games Football Tournament** on three occasions, in 1952, 1964, and 1968, and finished runners-up in 1972. A country of a bit more than 10 million inhabitants, Hungary has 127,226 registered players at 2,778 club teams, according to a 2006 survey by the **Fédération Internationale de Football Association (FIFA)**.

Soccer in Hungary is governed by the Hungarian Football Federation (in Hungarian, *Magyar Labdarúgó Szövetség*, MLSZ), founded in 1901. Hungary affiliated with FIFA in 1906 and was a founding member of the **Union of European Football Associations (UEFA)** in 1954. No Hungarian team has won a UEFA club competition, while the sole national team success for Hungary came at youth level, with a **UEFA European Under-19 Championship** victory in 1984. Domestically, Hungary's top club league is the Hungarian National Championship, or *Nemzeti Bajnokság I* (NBI) in Hungarian, founded in 1901. The most successful team in the league's history is Ferencvárosi Torna Club, usually known simply as "Ferencváros," with 28 titles. **Ferenc Puskás** is Hungary's most famous player and was at the heart of the Hungarian team in the early 1950s considered to be one of the greatest of all time internationally. That team played the game in a new form, based on fluid passing and positioning, under coach **Gusztáv Sebes**. Hungary's most famous international game came in November 1953 with a 6-3 victory over **England** in London at **Wembley Stadium**, shocking the home crowd. Hungary was, at that point, on the way to a four-year unbeaten streak, from 1950 to 1954, including winning a gold medal at the 1952 Olympic Games Football Tournament. Sebes' Hungary continued the streak into the **1954 FIFA World Cup**, where they beat West **Germany**, the **Republic of Korea**, **Brazil**, and **Uruguay** on the road to the final. But there, Hungary was denied the ultimate triumph in world soccer, as West Germany surprisingly defeated Hungary with a 3-2 win. In recent decades, Hungary's teams have been unable to match that period of success, with the golden age of Hungarian soccer long past.

I

INDEPENDIENTE. One of **Argentina**'s strongest clubs domestically, behind only **River Plate** and **Boca Juniors** in national championship victories, Independiente has been the most successful South American team on the international stage, with two **Intercontinental Cup** titles and seven **Copa Libertadores** wins. Independiente was founded in 1904 by a group of Buenos Aires shop workers who were frustrated by their employers' not letting them play for their official shop team. It was officially registered as a club in March 1905. Their most successful period came from 1972 to 1975, with four straight Copa Libertadores victories, a period that also included their first victory in the Intercontinental Cup, beating **Ajax Amsterdam** of the **Netherlands** in a two-game series in 1973. They would win the same title again a bit more than a decade later in 1984, this time defeating **Liverpool** of **England**. *See also* ERICO, ARSENIO; FORLÁN, DIEGO.

INDOOR SOCCER. Indoor soccer is a form of the game played in an enclosed arena with a wall surrounding the field and play continuing when the ball rebounds off the wall. This makes it a much faster-paced game than regular outdoor soccer and other variants of the game played indoors, such as **futsal**, where stoppages are more frequent because of the ball going out of play. Indoor soccer is particularly popular in the **United States**, where it was briefly the preeminent form of the professional game in the 1980s. Indoor soccer is a substantially different game from traditional professional soccer. The field and the size of the goals are smaller than they are in regulation outdoor soccer, play lasts for a shorter duration, and the number of players per team is usually less, normally six per side (including a **goalkeeper**) rather than 11 per side. Different rules apply in the indoor variant, such as the allowance of unlimited substitutions and no offside rule. Indoor soccer is now usually played on an artificial-turf field. Two well-known indoor-soccer leagues are the Major Indoor Soccer League in the United States and the Masters Football League in the United Kingdom.

INFRINGEMENTS. *See* FOULS.

INTERCONTINENTAL CUP. Contested between the winners of the leading continental club competitions in Europe and South America tournaments from 1960 until 2004, the Intercontinental Cup—also known as the "European/South American Cup" or "Toyota Cup"—was the precursor of today's **FIFA Club World Cup.** From 1960 to 1979, it was contested over two games—one each in Europe and South America—with hard-fought contests often taking place. After Toyota took over sponsorship of the tournament in 1980, the cup was a one-off game contested in **Japan.** Five teams won the competition three times: **Boca Juniors**, **Peñarol**, and **Nacional** from South America, and **AC Milan** and **Real Madrid** from Europe.

INTERNATIONAL FOOTBALL ASSOCIATION BOARD (IFAB). The IFAB is the body responsible for issuing the **Laws of the Game** followed worldwide as the rules of the sport of soccer. The IFAB consists of four representatives from soccer's global governing body **Fédération Internationale de Football Association (FIFA)** and one each from the national associations of **England**, Northern Ireland, **Scotland**, and Wales. The statutes of FIFA state that all members of FIFA must apply the Laws of the Game as established by the IFAB in all games they organize.

The Laws of the Game established by the IFAB have their roots in the mid-19th century attempts by English soccer administrators to create accepted standards for the sport to avoid disputes over the rules due to regional variations. The Cambridge Rules had first established written laws of the game in 1848, and 15 years later, **The Football Association (the FA)** modified and adopted these. In order to standardize these rules beyond England, the FA invited the recently formed Scottish, Irish, and Welsh national associations to join them in agreeing to a uniform international code. The four associations decided to form the IFAB in 1882, with the first meeting of the board taking place on 2 June 1886 in London, and it initially consisted of two representatives each from England, Scotland, Ireland, and Wales.

FIFA accepted the IFAB's Laws of the Game at its establishment in 1904 but did not become a participant on the board until 1913. It now joins with representatives from the four British associations at an annual general meeting to study and vote on possible alterations to the Laws of the Game. The text of the laws is rarely altered dramatically, the most recent major change coming in 1997 when a simplification of the laws resulted in a 30 percent reduction of the text. FIFA explains the conservatism of the IFAB as crucial to soccer's permanent popularity: "The attraction of the game of football resides in its simplicity. And as guardian to its Laws, the IFAB seeks to preserve the original seeds on which football has blossomed so spectacularly." The IFAB has at times been criticized for moving too slowly in adapting laws to embrace new technology, such as to help adjudicate goal-line calls.

INTERNATIONAL SOCCER. Games between teams representing their countries date back to the 19th century. The first international game was played on 30 November 1872 between **England** and **Scotland** on a cricket field in the town of Partick, Scotland. The result was a 0-0 tie in front of an estimated 4,000 people. Today, the **FIFA World Cup** final is the pinnacle of the international game, with the 2006 game in **Germany** watched by a total of 600 million viewers on television and 69,000 in person at the Olympic Stadium in Berlin. The FIFA World Cup, held every four years, has become the most-watched sporting event in the world. Some 208 national soccer associations are affiliated with the organizers of the FIFA World Cup, the **Fédération Internationale de Football Association (FIFA)**, who oversee competition worldwide between teams of players selected by these associations to represent their countries in both the men's and women's games. The **FIFA Women's World Cup,** founded in 1991, is the peak of the international game for women, with the women's **Olympic Games Football Tournament** also highly regarded. The men's Olympic Games Football Tournament is less prestigious because of strict limitations agreed to between FIFA and the International Olympic Committee, the governor of the Olympic Games, on the number of players over the age of 23 allowed to participate in the tournament, to restrict its status as a potential competitor to the FIFA World Cup.

The six regional **FIFA confederations** also run their own prominent international competitions for national teams in their respective regional areas. The best known such competition is run by the **Union of European Football Associations (UEFA)**, the **UEFA European Football Championship**, founded in 1954 and held every four years. The first to be organized, though, was started substantially earlier by the **South American Football Confederation (CONMEBOL)** in 1916, the **Copa América**. In Africa, the **Confederation of African Football (CAF)** has organized the **Africa Cup of Nations**, the premier tournament for national teams affiliated with their confederation, since 1957. The **Asian Football Confederation** runs the **AFC Asian Cup**, founded in 1956 and contested every four years. In Oceania, the **Oceania Football Confederation (OFC)** runs the **OFC Nations Cup**, and in the North American, Central American and Caribbean region, **the Confederation of North, Central and Caribbean Football Association (CONCACAF)** organizes the **CONCACAF Gold Cup** for its affiliated member nations. The winners of each of these confederation championships are invited to take part in the **FIFA Confederations Cup**, organized by FIFA and held every four years. All FIFA confederations also organize qualifying competitions between international teams to determine the entrants for the FIFA World Cup finals tournament. Exhibition games, frequently referred to as "friendlies," regularly take place between national teams, arranged by their respective national associations using dates for international play scheduled by FIFA.

INTERNAZIONALE. One of the most successful clubs in **Italy**, Internazionale was founded in Milan in 1908 by dissident members of the Milan Cricket and Football Club (forerunners of their legendary rivals, **AC Milan**) who wanted to include foreign players on their team—hence the name. Their first, and still most, legendary player was **Giuseppe Meazza**, scorer of a magnificent 287 goals in 408 games for the team between 1927 and 1940. He, along with three other Internazionale players, would win the 1934 **FIFA World Cup** with Italy. Internazionale's **stadium**, the San Siro (shared with AC Milan), was renamed the "**Stadio Giuseppe Meazza**" in his honor in 1979. Internazionale's greatest international success came in the mid-1960s under their innovative manager **Helenio Herrera**, whose defensive tactical strategy became popularly known as "*catenaccio*" and was copied across Italy. Using this ultracautious style of play, Internazionale won both the European Cup and the **Intercontinental Cup** in successive years, 1964 and 1965. The decades following did not see Internazionale reach similar heights, often playing in the shadow of AC Milan, though a run of four-straight Italian championships, from 2006 to 2009, established them as the leading club in Italian soccer once again. This was followed by victory in the 2010 **UEFA Champions League**. *See also* FACCHETTI, GIACINTO; FIGO, LUIS; KLINSMANN, JÜRGEN; LIPPI, MARCELLO; MATTHÄUS, LOTHAR; PASSARELLA, DANIEL; RONALDO; RUMMENIGGE, KARL-HEINZ; SAMMER, MATTHIAS; SCHILLACI, SALVATORE; SUÁREZ, LUIS; ZAMORANO, IVÁN.

IRAN. Soccer is a very popular sport in Iran, introduced to the country by British sailors at port cities and by British oil workers at refineries across the country in the first decade of the 20th century. Soccer in Iran has been governed since 1920 by what is now known as the "Football Federation Islamic Republic of Iran" (FFIRI), an affiliate of the **Fédération Internationale de Football Association (FIFA)** since 1945 and of the **Asian Football Confederation (AFC)** since 1958. The FFIRI organizes the national teams and national leagues, including the highest level of the sport in Iran, the Iran Pro League, founded in 1973. The most successful team has been Esteghal Tehran Football Club, who play at the 100,000-capacity Azadi Stadium in the capital of Iran, Tehran.

Iran's men's national team is *Team Melli*, which has been a powerhouse in Asian soccer, currently boasting the joint best record along with **Saudi Arabia** in the continent's leading men's national team competition, the **AFC Asian Cup**, with three victories (1968, 1972, and 1976). Iran has also appeared in the **FIFA World Cup** on three occasions, in 1978, 1998, and 2006, though it has won only one game in those three appearances, failing to advance past the first round each time. Iran has been very successful in the Asian Games Football Tournament, winning the Gold Medal in both 1998 and 2002.

Women's soccer in Iran developed quickly in the 1970s, but its growth was stalled following the Iranian Revolution in 1979 and the imposition of a blanket ban on women playing the sport. Women's soccer has been revived in the past 15 years, with Iran's women's national team, *Team Melli Zanan*, beginning play in 2005 and finishing second at the West Asian Football Federation Women's Championship in 2007, though failing to qualify for the 2010 AFC Women's Asian Cup.

ITALY. Soccer, or *"calcio,"* as it's called in Italian, is the most popular sport in Italy, and national and club teams have been among the most successful in the history of the sport. According to **Fédération Internationale de Football Association (FIFA)** calculations from 2006, Italy has more than 1.5 million registered players on more than 16,000 clubs who play under the authority of the sport's governing body, the Italian Football Federation, known in Italian as *Federazione Italiana Gioco Calcio* (FIGC), founded in 1898. The FIGC oversees the Italian national men's and women's teams, along with the national league and cup competitions for club teams. The FIGC affiliated with FIFA in 1905, and was a founding member of the **Union of European Football Associations (UEFA)** in 1954.

Italy's men's national team has appeared in 16 **FIFA World Cup** finals tournaments, with victories in 1934, 1938, 1982, and 2006. That record is second to only that of **Brazil**, who have twice beaten them in World Cup finals, in 1970 and 1994, the latter in a heart-breaking **penalty shoot-out** defeat for the Italians. In 1990, Italy hosted the World Cup for the second time (having first hosted it in 1934), reaching the semifinals and losing at that stage on penalty kicks to **Argentina**. In continental competition, Italy has won one **UEFA European Football Championship**, in 1968, and finished runners-up in 2000, losing to **France**. They also won the **Olympic Games Football Tournament** held in **Germany** in 1936. Italy's women's national team has been less successful, never having won an official competition. Italy's soccer league system is a pyramidal structure of several interconnected leagues, the top level being the professional *Lega Calcio*, which is divided into two divisions, the lower tier *Serie B* and the upper tier *Serie A*. The most successful Italian club teams have been **AC Milan**, **Internazionale**, and **Juventus**. *See also* BAGGIO, ROBERTO; BARESI, FRANCO; CANNAVARO, FABIO; FACCHETTI,

GIACINTO; LIPPI, MARCELLO; MALDINI, PAOLO; MAZZOLA, VAL-
ENTINO; MEAZZA, GIUSEPPE; MONTI, LUIS; MORACE, CAROLINA;
PIOLA, SILVIO; POZZO, VITTORIO; RIVA, LUIGI; RIVERA, GIANNI;
ROSSI, PAOLO; SACCHI, ARRIGO; SCHIAVIO, ANGELO; SCHILLACI,
SALVATORE; STADIO GIUSEPPE MEAZZA; SUPERGA AIR DISAS-
TER; TIFO; ZOFF, DINO.

J

JACQUET, AIMÉ. B. 27 November 1941, Sail-sous-Couzan, France. Aimé Jacquet is a French **coach** and former player. He was the manager of the **France** national team when they won the 1998 **FIFA World Cup**, the country's first triumph in the tournament. Previously an assistant coach with the national team, Jacquet took over as head coach of France following the country's failure to qualify for the 1994 FIFA World Cup. He led the country to the semifinals of the 1996 **UEFA European Football Championship**, where they lost in a **penalty shoot-out** to the **Czech Republic**. In the buildup to the 1998 FIFA World Cup, held in France itself, Jacquet received considerable media criticism for his perpetual lineup changes. However, once the tournament began in June 1998, a French team inspired by midfielder **Zinedine Zidane** swept through the first-round group stage. They then beat **Paraguay** in the second round, **Italy** in the quarterfinals through a penalty shoot-out, and Croatia by two goals to one to meet **Brazil** in the final. There, Jacquet's team controlled the game from the start, easily beating the surprisingly subdued defending World Cup champions 3-0. Following the 1998 FIFA World Cup, Jacquet stepped down as head coach, taking on a role as France's technical director until 2006 and overseeing a further international title win for France at the 2000 UEFA European Football Championship.

JAIRZINHO. B. 25 December 1944, Rio de Janeiro, Brazil. Born Jair Ventura Filho but universally known as "Jairzinho," he was an outstanding force for **Brazil**'s national team from 1964 to 1982. He played a total of 81 games for his country, scoring 33 goals and establishing himself as a winger with the ability to beat defenders with ease and contribute both goals and assists. Jairzinho starred in Brazil's legendary 1970 **FIFA World Cup** triumph, scoring in every game of the tournament and finishing with a total of seven goals to his credit. He also appeared for Brazil at the 1966 and 1974 World Cup finals tournaments. At club level, Jairzinho played most of his career for Botafogo. He retired in 1982. *See also* PELÉ.

JAPAN. Soccer in Japan is governed by the Japan Football Association (JFA), founded in 1921 and affiliated with world soccer's governing body **Fédération Internationale de Football Association (FIFA)** in 1929. The JFA is responsible for oversight of the game at all levels and, in particular, the national team. Japan's men's national team has played in the **FIFA World Cup** finals tournament four times, in 1998, 2002, 2006, and 2010. Japan's development as a soccer nation was long hampered by the absence of a professional men's league, though a team representing Japan did win the bronze medal for third place at the 1968 **Olympic Games Football Tournament**. But it was not until 30 years later that Japan reached the FIFA World Cup finals tournament for the first time, losing all three of their games in **France** at the 1998 World Cup. Fours year later, Japan cohosted the first FIFA World Cup to be held in Asia along with the **Republic of Korea**. They reached the second round, where they lost to **Turkey**. In the 2006 World Cup, Japan went out at the first stage and, in 2010, were eliminated in the second round of the World Cup held in **South Africa**. Japan's top level of professional club soccer is the J-League, founded in 1991. The champion of the J-League each season goes on to participate in the **Asian Football Confederation**'s **(AFC)** premier continental tournament, the **AFC Champions League**. *See also* KASHIMA ANTLERS; KEMARI; NAKATA, HIDETOSHI.

JULES RIMET TROPHY. *See* FIFA WORLD CUP TROPHY.

JUVENTUS FOOTBALL CLUB. Juventus Football Club, based in Turin, **Italy**, and usually known simply as "Juventus," is one of the world's leading club teams. It was founded on 1 November 1897 and won its first Italian championship in 1905. Owned by the rich and powerful Agnelli family, it became the leading club in Italy in the 1930s and has claimed a total of 27 Italian league championships. Juventus has also achieved considerable success in European competition, winning three **UEFA Cups** (1977, 1990, and 1993), one **UEFA Cup Winners' Cup** in 1984, and, most importantly, one European Cup in 1985, along with a win in its successor competition, the **UEFA Champions League**, in 1996. The 1985 triumph was inspired by one of its greatest players of all time, Frenchman **Michel Platini**, but was overshadowed off the field at the final by the deaths of 39 fans in the **Heysel Stadium Disaster**. *See also* ALTAFINI, JOSÉ; BAGGIO, ROBERTO; BONIEK, ZBIGNIEW; CANNAVARO, FABIO; HENRY, THIERRY; LAUDRUP, MICHAEL; LIPPI, MARCELLO; MONTI, LUIS; NEDVĚD, PAVEL; ROSSI, PAOLO; SCHILLACI, SALVATORE; SÍVORI, OMAR; ZIDANE, ZINEDINE; ZOFF, DINO.

K

KAHN, OLIVER. B. 15 June 1969, Karlsruhe, West Germany. Oliver Kahn was an imperious **goalkeeper** for **Bayern Munich** at club level and for **Germany** at international level. He won the Golden Ball as best player at the 2002 **FIFA World Cup**, where he also collected a runners-up medal with Germany, after an outstanding tournament. Kahn was the goalkeeper for Germany when they won the 1996 **UEFA European Football Championship**. He played a total of 86 games for his country, between 1994 and 2006. At club level, he began his career for his local team Karlsruher SC, joining German giants Bayern Munich in 1994, with whom he played the rest of his career until his retirement in 2008. Kahn won numerous major honors with Bayern Munich, including the German league championship on eight occasions, and winners' medals in both the **UEFA Champions League** and the **FIFA Club World Cup** in 2001.

KAKÁ. B. 22 April 1982, Brasília, Brazil. Kaká, born Ricardo Izecson dos Santos Leite but universally known as "Kaká," is a gifted **Brazilian** attacking midfielder. In 2007, Kaká was the **FIFA World Player of the Year**, the fifth Brazilian player to win the award. He also won the **European Footballer of the Year** award the same year. He began his professional senior career playing for **São Paulo Futebol Club** in Brazil from 2001 to 2003, before moving to **AC Milan** in **Italy** and playing there until 2009. He won the Italian league championship in 2004, the **UEFA Champions League** in 2007, and the **FIFA Club World Cup** the same year. In 2009, Kaká was expensively recruited by **Real Madrid** in **Spain** and left AC Milan. Kaká has also enjoyed considerable success on the international stage with his national team, winning the 2002 **FIFA World Cup** with Brazil in the competition jointly staged that year by the **Republic of Korea** and **Japan**.

KASHIMA ANTLERS. Japan's national club championship, the J-League, has been won more times by Kashima Antlers than any other team, with seven titles to their credit since the J-League began play in 1993. Kashima Antlers were originally formed in 1947 as an amateur team attached to Sumitomo Metal Industries in Osaka. They moved to Kashima in 1975 and played as a semiprofessional club until the formation of the J-League in 1993. Two years previously, legendary Brazilian player **Zico** had joined the club to assist its application to become a founding member of the new, professional J-League, and he led Kashima Antlers to a surprising runners-up finish in its inaugural season. Zico retired in 1994, but remained as a technical advisor to the team, who won their first J-League crown in 1996. In 2000, Kashima Antlers enjoyed the greatest season in Japanese professional soccer history, winning an unprecedented triple of the J-League championship, the J-League Cup, and the Emperor's Cup, led by Brazilian coach Toninho Cerezo. Another championship followed the next year, then a fallow period followed, lasting until 2007. They have won three successive championships since then, in 2007, 2008, and 2009, under another Brazilian coach, Oswaldo de Oliveira. The Antlers play at Kashima Stadium, a 41,000-capacity venue built for the start of the J-League in 1993, which also was host to three games at the 2002 **FIFA World Cup**.

KEEGAN, KEVIN. B. 14 February 1951, Doncaster, England. Kevin Keegan is one of **England**'s greatest-ever players, winner of the 1978 and 1979 **European Footballer of the Year** awards, and an outstanding goal-scoring attacking player. He later became a well-known manager. Keegan began his career with Scunthorpe United in the 1960s but reached the peak of the English game following a move to **Liverpool Football Club**, where he starred for the northern club from 1971 to 1977. There he won three **Football League** championships and one **Football Association Challenge Cup** winner's medal domestically, along with two **UEFA Cups** and one **European Cup** in European competition. Following Liverpool's European Cup triumph in 1977, Keegan transferred to play for Hamburg in West **Germany**, winning two German league championships before returning to play in England in 1980 and finishing his career with Southampton and then Newcastle United. He retired from playing in 1984. Keegan also made 63 appearances for the England national team, scoring 23 goals, but played for his country in a particularly unproductive period, appearing only briefly in one **FIFA World Cup** finals tournament in 1982 in **Spain**, England exiting at the group stage in the first round.

Following a break from the sport in the late 1980s, Keegan began his managerial career with his former club Newcastle United in 1992. He led them to promotion to the **Premier League** and took them to contention for the championship while becoming known for his charismatic style of coaching, before suddenly departing in 1997. Keegan returned to management with Fulham the next year in 1998 and then took over as England's **coach** in 1999, a short and unsuccessful spell ending in 2000. He then coached at Manchester

City, managing them from 2001 to 2005 and retiring from soccer altogether that year.

KEÏTA, SALIF. B. 6 December 1942, Bamako, Mali. Salif Keïta, a Mali-born prolific goal-scoring forward who played the bulk of his professional career in **France**, was one of the best African players of his generation. His greatest period of success came playing for **AS Saint-Étienne**, with whom he scored 125 goals in 149 appearances while winning three French league championships in the period 1967–1972. In 1970, Keïta won the African Player of the Year award and, in 1972, led his country Mali to the runners-up position in the **Africa Cup of Nations**. He scored 11 goals in 13 games for Mali. Keïta retired in 1980 after a short but productive spell playing for the New England Tea Men in the **North American Soccer League** in the **United States**. Keïta returned to Mali in 1986 and was the president of the Mali Football Association from 2005 to 2009.

KEMARI. *Kemari*, which was played in Japan, is an ancient antecedent of the sport of soccer. It originated as a variant of the ancient ball game *cuju*, which was played in **China**. In the 13th century, Kemari became the first standardized, organized sport, from its field of play to the equipment, techniques, costume, and customs attached to it, in Japan. Kemari was a competitive game but less like modern soccer than the original form of cuju in China: the aim was not to shoot the ball into a goal, but for a circle of players to keep a hollow ball in the air as long as possible by kicking it, a stylish and graceful pastime. It was a skilled game that relied on team play, with coordinated movement based on close communication to keep the ball aloft, and intense technical skills were required to succeed. Kemari became a prestigious and popular game. Yet it did not become a modern sport when Japan modernized: following the Meiji Restoration in 1868 and the vast modernization of Japanese society, kemari became a niche sport for aristocrats, a remnant of the old ways.

KEMPES, MARIO. B. 15 July 1954, Bell Ville, Argentina. Mario Kempes, one of the greatest players ever produced by **Argentina**, played for his native country on 43 occasions, scoring 20 goals. A predatory and lethal striker, Kempes appeared in three **FIFA World Cup** finals tournaments in 1974, 1978, and 1982, scoring six goals in 17 games. All six goals came at the 1978 World Cup, where Kempes was the top scorer as Argentina won the World Cup for the first time. He won the South American Footballer of the Year award that year as a result. Kempes also enjoyed a successful career in club soccer, particularly for Valencia in **Spain**, winning the **UEFA Cup Winners'**

Cup in 1979 and 1980. Since retirement from playing, Kempes has **coached** teams in Indonesia, **Albania**, Venezuela, and Bolivia.

KLINSMANN, JÜRGEN. B. 30 July 1964, Göppingen, Germany. Jürgen Klinsmann was a lethal striker for **Germany** and several leading European club teams. He was a tireless, technically brilliant forward and an outstanding finisher, scoring 48 goals in 107 international games for Germany. He played in the **FIFA World Cup** on three occasions, taking home a winners' medal from the 1990 tournament in **Italy** after starring for West Germany in their victory, scoring three goals in the competition. Klinsmann won another major honor with Germany at the 1996 **UEFA European Football Championship** in **England**. At club level, he played for teams in Germany, Italy, **France**, and England, winning the Footballer of the Year award in the latter country while playing for Tottenham Hotspur in 1995. He won the **UEFA Cup** twice, with **Internazionale** in 1991 and **Bayern Munich** in 1995. Since his retirement as a professional player in 1998, he has managed Germany—taking them to third place at the 2006 FIFA World Cup—and Bayern Munich. *See also* MATTHÄUS, LOTHAR; VÖLLER, RUDI.

KOCSIS, SÁNDOR. B. 21 September 1929, Budapest, Hungary. D. 22 July 1979. Sándor Kocsis was a **Hungarian** player who starred for his national team and for **Barcelona** in **Spain**. Kocsis played for the legendary Hungarian team of the 1950s, considered by many to be the best national team ever not to win the **FIFA World Cup**, appearing alongside the likes of the brilliant **Ferenc Puskás** on a team nicknamed the "Mighty Magyars." Kocsis was a prolific goal-scoring forward, scoring a remarkable 75 goals in 68 appearances for Hungary and winning a gold medal at the 1952 **Olympic Games Football Tournament** with his country, as well as a runners-up medal at the 1954 World Cup in **Switzerland**. At club level, he won three Hungarian league championships playing for Honvéd FC and two Spanish league championships playing for Barcelona, where he scored 151 goals in 235 games. Kocsis retired from playing in 1965, pursued a brief **coaching** career cut short by illness, and died in a fall from a fourth-floor hospital window in 1979 at the age of 49.

KOPA, RAYMOND. B. 13 October 1931, Nœux-les-Mines, France. Raymond Kopa, born Raymond Kopaszewski, was a star for **France**'s national team, mainly in the 1950s. Kopa was named the **European Footballer of the Year** in 1958 following his role in inspiring France to third place at the 1958 **FIFA World Cup** held in **Sweden**. In his club career, Kopa was a key player for **Spanish** team **Real Madrid** when they won three straight **UEFA**

Champions League titles (then known as the European Cup) in 1957, 1958, and 1959 during their great run of success. Kopa then returned to France to play for Stade Reims and retired from play in 1967.

KOREA, THE REPUBLIC OF. Soccer in the Republic of Korea is overseen by the Korean Football Association, who affiliated with the **Fédération Internationale de Football Association (FIFA)** in 1948. Soccer, in its modern form, was first played in the Republic of Korea in the late 19th century, brought there by British sailors. The Korean men's national team has reached the **FIFA World Cup** finals tournament eight times, with its best finish being fourth place in 2002, the furthest a country from Asia has ever gone in the World Cup. The 2002 World Cup, held in the Asian continent for the first time, was cohosted by the Republic of Korea and **Japan**. The Republic of Korea national team has also had some success in continental competition, winning the **AFC Asian Cup** in 1956 and 1960, and finishing as runners-up in 1972, 1980, and 1988. According to FIFA's survey in 2006, the Republic of Korea has more than one million players, the vast majority unregistered, with 31,127 at 100 registered clubs. The highest level of play in Korean club soccer is the K-League, the country's only professional league. The winners gain entry into the **AFC Champions League**, Asia's top club competition. *See also* CHA, BUM-KUN; HONG, MYUNG-BO; POHANG STEELERS.

KUBALA, LÁSZLÓ. B. 9 June 1927, Budapest, Hungary. D. 17 May 2002. László Kubala was a **Hungarian** player and one of the top strikers in the history of the sport. His greatest period of play came for **Barcelona** in **Spain**, scoring 243 goals in 329 games for the club between 1950 and 1961 and winning four Spanish league championship titles. In an era when **Fédération Internationale de Football Association (FIFA)** regulations were much looser on national representation, Kubala remarkably appeared for the national teams of **Czechoslovakia**, **Hungary**, and Spain, though he never competed in a **FIFA World Cup** finals tournament. Kubala was an all-around forward, able to create chances as well as score goals with his exceptional pace, passing skills, and dribbling ability. Following his retirement in 1967, he went on to have a long **coaching** career spanning four continents around the world.

L

LABRUNA, ÁNGEL. B. 28 September 1918, Buenos Aires, Argentina. D. 20 September 1983. Ángel Labruna was a member of **Argentinean** club team **River Plate**'s superb forward line of the 1940s, known as "*la máquina*" (the machine). Labruna scored a total of 293 goals for River Plate over two decades, from 1939 to 1959, winning numerous championship medals. He also appeared for Argentina's national team on 37 occasions, scoring 17 goals, and played at the 1958 **FIFA World Cup** in **Sweden** at the age of 40. He won the 1955 **Copa América** with Argentina. Labruna retired in 1961, later managing River Plate in two separate periods and taking the team to further success.

LAUDRUP, BRIAN. B. 22 February 1969, Vienna, Austria. Though born in Austria, Brian Laudrup was the son of a Danish international player. Brian, as well, went on to play for Denmark, on 82 occasions scoring 21 goals and often appearing alongside his older brother, **Michael Laudrup**. In 1992, he helped lead Denmark to their surprising title run at the **UEFA European Football Championship**. Laudrup was a gifted attacking player with a habit of scoring spectacular goals. He played for Denmark at the 1998 **FIFA World Cup**, reaching the quarterfinal stage (their best-ever result) but losing there 3-2 to **Brazil** despite a superb volleyed goal from Laudrup. In club soccer, Laudrup had a globe-trotting career, playing in Denmark, **Germany**, **Italy**, **Scotland**, **England**, and the **Netherlands** for various clubs. He won league titles with Brøndby in Denmark, **AC Milan** in Italy, and **Rangers Football Club** in Scotland. Laudrup retired in 2000.

LAUDRUP, MICHAEL. B. 15 June 1964, Frederiksberg, Denmark. Michael Laudrup was one of the finest European players of his generation and the most-talented attacking player ever produced by his native Denmark. He played 104 times for his country, scoring 37 goals, and represented Denmark at both the 1986 and 1998 **FIFA World Cup** tournaments. The latter resulted in Denmark's best-ever finish at a World Cup finals competition, with Laudrup leading Denmark to the quarterfinals, where they lost to Brazil 3-2. However, Laudrup missed Denmark's first major championship victory in 1992 at the **UEFA European Football Championship** after falling out with team management. He was known for his outstanding technical abilities on the ball, able to dribble, pass, and shoot at a level rarely seen. Laudrup won league championships in three countries, with **Juventus** in **Italy**, both **Barcelona** and **Real Madrid** in **Spain**, and **Ajax Amsterdam** in the **Netherlands**. Laudrup retired in 1998 and has managed clubs in Denmark, Spain, and **Russia** since. *See also* LAUDRUP, BRIAN.

LAW, DENIS. B. 24 February 1940, Aberdeen, Scotland. Denis Law, a prolific goal-scoring striker who appeared at the 1974 **FIFA World Cup** and who scored 30 goals in 55 games for his country, was a star player for **Scotland** and **Manchester United**. For Manchester United, Law made his debut in 1962 and left the club in 1973, playing for the club in one of its strongest periods of success and scoring 237 goals in 404 games. He was nicknamed "The King" by Manchester United fans. In 1964, Law was named the **European Footballer of the Year**. He had moved to Manchester United after a relatively unsuccessful spell in **Italy**, playing for Torino, having moved there from Manchester City in 1961. He returned to Manchester City after leaving Manchester United in 1973 and retired from playing the next year.

LAWS OF THE GAME. Since 1886, the laws that govern the game have been the responsibility of the **International Football Association Board (IFAB)** and are applied to all games played under the auspices of soccer's global governing body, **Fédération Internationale de Football Association (FIFA)**. There are 17 Laws of the Game. Each year, the IFAB holds an annual general meeting to decide whether to accept or reject proposed alterations of the laws. The members of the IFAB are **The Football Association**, the Scottish Football Association, the Football Association of Wales, and the Irish Football Association, which have one vote each, along with FIFA, which has four votes. *See also* ASSISTANT REFEREE; CORNER KICK; FOULS; FREE KICK; GOAL; GOAL KICK; PENALTY KICK; PENALTY SHOOT-OUT; REFEREE; THROW-IN.

LEÔNIDAS DA SILVA. B. 6 September 1913, Rio de Janeiro, Brazil. D. 24 January 2004. Leônidas da Silva was a star player for **Brazil** at two **FIFA World Cup** finals competitions in 1934 and 1938, and the top scorer in the latter tournament with seven goals. He tallied an impressive eight goals in five total World Cup games. Known as the "Black Diamond," Leônidas was the first Brazilian to become a national superstar in his country, presaging the later fame of the likes of **Garrincha** and **Pelé**. Unusually agile, Leônidas was reportedly the inventor of the bicycle kick. He retired from international play in 1946, having scored 21 goals in 19 games for Brazil.

LIEDHOLM, NILS. B. 8 October 1922, Valdemarsvik, Sweden. D. 5 November 2007. Nils Liedholm was known as *"Il Barone"* (the Baron) in **Italy**, for his long and outstanding career as a player and **coach** in that country, and was a pioneering force in **Swedish** soccer abroad. Liedholm was an attacking midfield player who began his career as an amateur in his native Sweden. He joined Italian club **AC Milan** in 1949, becoming the third Swede to sign with the club that year. His compatriots were **Gunnar Nordahl** and Gunnar Gren, and the three formed a formidable attacking force soon nicknamed "Gren-No-Li" by adoring media and fans. Liedholm made 394 appearances for AC Milan, scoring 81 goals and winning four Italian league titles with the club in 1951, 1955, 1957, and 1959. He was known for his accurate passing and supreme fitness along with a graceful, unhurried style, rarely making mistakes in the run of play. At international level, Liedholm helped lead Sweden to international glory with victory at the 1948 **Olympic Games Football Tournament**, in which they won all four games they played. He did not represent his country for several years after that due to the Swedish national association's ban on professional players playing for the national team, but this was lifted in time for him to play for Sweden at the 1958 **FIFA World Cup** at the age of 36, where he helped them reach the final of the competition, losing there to **Brazil**. Liedholm took up a highly successful coaching career following his retirement from playing in 1961, which brought him two further Italian league championship medals, with AC Milan in 1979 and AS Roma in 1983.

LILLY, KRISTINE. B. 22 July 1971, New York City, United States. Kristine Lilly is an American player who currently holds the global record for the most appearances for a national team, appearing for the **United States** women's team a total of 345 times as of July 2010. She has played in all five **FIFA Women's World Cup** finals tournaments held so far, in 1991, 1995, 1999, 2003, and 2007, the only player to have done so. Lilly has two FIFA Women's World Cup winners' medals from the U.S. victories in 1991 and 1999. Lilly has also participated in three **Olympic Games Football Tournaments**, winning gold medals with the United States in 1996 and 2004. She currently plays for the Boston Breakers in the **Women's Professional Soccer** league in the United States. *See also* WOMEN'S SOCCER.

LIMA NATIONAL STADIUM DISASTER. Some 318 fans were killed on 24 May 1964 at a game in Lima, **Peru**, the worst recorded disaster at a soccer game worldwide. In addition, more than 500 fans were seriously injured. Victims were crushed against the stadium's closed exit gates toward the end of an **Olympic Games Football Tournament** qualifying match between **Argentina** and host nation Peru, after a crowd disturbance sparked by a disallowed goal for Peru turned into a stampede out of the stadium when police fired tear gas into the crowd. *See also* HOOLIGANISM.

LINESMAN. *See* ASSISTANT REFEREE.

LIPPI, MARCELLO. B. 12 April 1948, Viareggio, Italy. Marcello Lippi is a highly successful Italian **coach** at both international and club team levels. He managed **Italy** to their fourth **FIFA World Cup** victory in the 2006 World Cup and coached them at the 2010 World Cup, where they were disappointingly eliminated in the first round. A former player for Sampdoria in Italy, Lippi made his name coaching **Juventus** in the mid-1990s. He won five domestic championships with them in two spells between 1994 and 2004, having spent one season, 1999–2000, as manager of **Internazionale** in Milan. With Juventus, Lippi won the **UEFA Champions League** in 1996. They finished runners-up in 1997, 1998, and 2003. Lippi then took over the Italian national team in 2004, leading them to their surprising title win in **Germany** at the 2006 World Cup. Lippi left the job following that competition but returned to the position in 2008, leaving the post again following the 2010 World Cup.

LIVERPOOL FOOTBALL CLUB. Liverpool Football Club, based in the northwest of **England**, is one of the world's best-known club teams, having won a combined five European Cup and **UEFA Champions Leagues** along with 18 domestic English league championships. As of August 2010, Liverpool had won more trophies in English football than any other club. Liverpool was founded on 15 March 1892 by John Houlding, who had recently split from the club he had shepherded in its early years, Everton. Liverpool took over tenancy from Everton at Anfield, a **stadium** in the Anfield district of Liverpool that has been their home ever since. Everton then moved to nearby Goodison Park, and have been bitter rivals of Liverpool ever since.

Liverpool quickly achieved considerable success, joining the **Football League** in 1893 and going on to win five first-division championships in the first half of the 20th century. They struggled in the 1950s, relegated to the second division of the Football League. Liverpool was launched into its glorious decades of success following the appointment of **Bill Shankly** as manager in 1959, who moved from Huddersfield Town to replace Phil Taylor. Anfield was in a dreadful state at the time, with Shankly later saying "it was the biggest toilet in Liverpool" when he first arrived. Shankly soon led a transformation in the quality of the playing staff, and the club was promoted to the first division in 1962 and won the championship for the sixth time in 1964, along with the **Football Association Challenge Cup** the following year. Under Shankly, they went on to win a total of three league championships, two F.A. Challenge Cups, and the club's first European trophy, the UEFA Cup.

Shankly's successor, his assistant **Bob Paisley**, built on the foundation in place and led Liverpool to even greater success in his 15 years as manager: the club won six more league championships and most significantly, three European Cups in 1977, 1978, and 1981, establishing themselves as the best team in Europe. They would win a further European Cup in 1984 under Paisley's successor, his own assistant Joe Fagan. Tragedy would strike Liverpool in Fagan's second year in charge, 1985, with the **Heysel Disaster** at the 1985 European Cup final against Juventus, shortly after which Fagan retired. Liverpool were held partially responsible for the crowd violence that led to the deaths of 39 fans at Heysel, and were—along with all other English clubs—banned indefinitely from European competition (other English clubs were readmitted in 1990, and Liverpool a further year later). Despite this, Fagan's replacement, player-manager Kenny Dalglish, led the club to further success on the field, winning the league championship and F.A. Cup double in 1986. But the 1980s would end with further tragedy at a Liverpool match, with the **Hillsborough Disaster** killing 96 Liverpool fans during their F.A. Cup semifinal match with Nottingham Forest at Sheffield Wednesday's stadium, Hillsborough.

The 1990s were less successful for Liverpool, as their rivals **Manchester United** won several league championships. The past decade has seen the club near the top of the **Premier League** standings each season without ever winning the title. However, they have enjoyed considerable success in other competitions in recent years under their manager until 2010, Rafael "Rafa" Benitez, including a surprising UEFA Champions League victory in 2005, when they beat **Milan** on penalties in the final after coming back from a three-goal deficit at halftime led by captain Steven Gerrard. Liverpool's efforts to move to a new stadium have been hampered by financial problems largely due to the debt-laden purchase of the club by Americans George Gillett and Tom Hicks in February 2007.

LOBANOVSKI, VALERY. B. 6 January 1939, Kiev, Soviet Union. D. 13 May 2002. Valery Lobanovski was a Ukrainian soccer **coach** and is famous for his spells in charge of club team Dynamo Kiev and the national teams of the **Soviet Union** and Ukraine. Lobanovski was formerly a player in the Soviet league, mainly with Dynamo Kiev, whom he coached after retirement and after a spell in charge of Dnipro Dnipropetrovsk. Lobanovski led Dynamo Kiev, with victory in the 1975 **UEFA Cup Winners' Cup**, to become the first team from the Soviet Union to win a major European competition. Lobanovski trained his players with a sophisticated combination of a focus on technical ability, collective movement, and intense fitness. In the 1980s, Lobanovski coached the Soviet Union in the 1986 **FIFA World Cup**, losing in the second round to **Belgium**. He took the Soviets to the final of the 1988 **UEFA European Football Championship**, where they lost to the **Netherlands**. At the same time, Lobanovski continued to have success coaching Dynamo Kiev, winning the UEFA Cup Winners' Cup again in 1986 and reaching the semifinals of the 1987 **European Cup**, employing many of the same players also starring for his Soviet Union national team. Following the breakup of the Soviet Union, Lobanovski went abroad to coach both the United Arab Emirates and Kuwait before returning for a briefly successful spell in charge of Dynamo Kiev and a less successful period coaching Ukraine, failing to qualify for the 2002 World Cup. Lobanovski passed away in May 2002.

M

MADJER, RABAH. B. 15 February 1958, Hussein Dey, Algeria. Rabah Madjer scored two of the most notable goals in world soccer during the 1980s and was one of the leading African players that decade. His first famous goal came for Algeria at the 1982 **FIFA World Cup** when he scored the first of Algeria's two goals in their stunning victory over West **Germany** in the first round. Madjer also played for Algeria at the 1986 World Cup and was part of their victorious team at the 1990 **Africa Cup of Nations**. He totaled 29 goals in 87 games for his country from 1978 to 1992, playing as a forward. At club level, Madjer played in Europe throughout the 1980s and scored a memorable goal for **Futebol Clube do Porto** from **Portugal** in the final of the 1987 **European Cup**. Madjer impudently back heeled the ball into the goal to tie the game for the Portuguese club against **Bayern Munich** in the 78th minute, and they went on to win the match 2-1. Madjer received the African Footballer of the Year award that year. He retired in 1993, eventually **coaching** the Algerian national team in two different spells. *See also* BELLOUMI, LAKHDAR.

MAIER, SEPP. B. 28 February 1944, Metten, Germany. Sepp Maier was a legendary **German goalkeeper**, playing more than 478 league games for club team **Bayern Munich** in the 1960s and 1970s and appearing in three **FIFA World Cup** tournaments for his national team. An agile and resilient goalkeeper known as the "Cat from Anzing," Maier won almost every major international honor with club and country. Playing for Bayern Munich, Maier reached the pinnacle of the club game, winning four German league championships (in 1969, 1972, 1973, and 1974) and three consecutive **European Cup** titles in 1974, 1975, and 1976 along with an **Intercontinental Cup** win in 1976. With West Germany, Maier won the **UEFA European Football Championship** in 1972 and followed this two years later with victory in the FIFA World Cup held in his home country. Maier was selected as the German Footballer of the Year on three occasions, in 1975, 1977, and 1978. In 1979, Maier was in a serious car crash that ended his playing career.

MAJOR LEAGUE SOCCER (MLS). Major League Soccer is the highest-level men's professional league in the **United States**. It began play in 1996, fulfilling a promise made to the **Fédération Internationale de Football Association** by the U.S. Soccer Federation to build off the 1994 World Cup held in the United States by launching a top-tier outdoor professional league. None had existed in the country since the North American Soccer League had folded in 1984. MLS launched in 2006 with 10 teams and has since established itself as a lasting presence in American soccer, expanding to 16 teams by 2010, including one in **Canada**. MLS is expected to reach 20 total teams by 2012. Numerous world-famous players have played in MLS since 1996, including **Lothar Matthäus**, **David Beckham**, and Cuauhtémoc Blanco. Unlike many European leagues, MLS crowns its annual champion through a short end-of-season competition known as the "MLS Cup Playoffs," with the top teams from the regular season competing in a knockout competition to win the MLS Cup. The regular-season league champion receives the Supporters' Shield trophy. *See also* DONOVAN, LANDON; MCBRIDE, BRIAN; STOICHKOV, HRISTO.

MALDINI, PAOLO. B. 26 June 1968, Milan, Italy. Paolo Maldini was a star Italian player and one of the best defenders **Italy** has produced, with an illustrious club career for **AC Milan** and international career for his national team. Maldini played at four **FIFA World Cups** for his country, including the 1994 World Cup final, where Italy lost to **Brazil** on a **penalty shoot-out**. Maldini appeared a total of 126 times for Italy. Maldini played his entire club career for AC Milan, a period spanning 25 years from 1984 until his retirement from playing in 2009. During that time, he was a key player in a remarkable run of success for the club: they claimed the **UEFA Champions League** five times, the Italian championship seven times, and the **FIFA Club World Cup** once. Paolo Maldini's father, Cesare Maldini, also played for AC Milan and Italy.

MANCHESTER UNITED. One of the most successful and famous clubs from **England**, Manchester United was founded by a group of railway workers in 1878 as Newton Heath L&YR Football Club. They joined the **Football League** in 1892, but were dogged by serious financial problems for their first decade. Then, their captain Harry Stafford found new investors, principally John Henry Davies, who invested significant money and a new era for the club began in 1902 under a new name, "Manchester United." Success soon followed, with Manchester United winning their first league championship in 1908, their first **Football Association Challenge Cup** in 1909, and another league title in 1911. The previous year, they had moved into what remains their now legendary stadium, Old Trafford, though the club would achieve only limited success in the next few decades, not winning the league championship again until 1952. Following that, under the stewardship of manager **Sir Matt Busby**, Manchester United embarked on two decades of domestic success that would see them crowned as Europe's best in 1968. Busby and the club, though, also had to overcome tragedy: Busby's brilliant young team, champions in 1956 and 1957, and known as the "Busby Babes," were tragically stricken by the **Munich Air Disaster**. The club's plane crashed on its way back from a European Cup game, killing eight players and severely injuring Busby himself. Busby rebuilt the club with the fantastic talents of **George Best**, **Bobby Charlton**, and **Denis Law**, who were at the heart of the Manchester United team that went on to win the league championship in 1965 and 1967. They then became the first English team to lift the European Cup in 1968 with a 4-1 win over **Benfica** at **Wembley Stadium**. The club could not continue that level of success after the retirement of Busby in 1969 (he returned for a short spell in 1971), falling into the shadow of rivals **Liverpool Football Club** for the next two decades.

Alex Ferguson, appointed as manager in 1986, did not return Manchester United to their former glory during his first few years in charge, but his first trophy win in the 1990 F.A. Cup proved to be the catalyst for a new era of glory eclipsing even Busby's achievements in terms of titles won. European success quickly followed with victory in the 1991 **UEFA Cup Winners' Cup**, and then a 28-year wait for an English league championship was broken in 1993 by a Manchester United team inspired by Ferguson's acquisition of French forward Eric Cantona, who provided the club a dash of flair as they won the **Premier League**. Manchester United then won the league and F.A. Cup double in 1994 and won a further nine league titles in the next 15 seasons. The year 1999 proved to be Manchester United's annus mirabilis: they won the treble of the league championship, F.A. Cup, and their first **UEFA Champions League** (formerly the European Cup) since Busby's triumph in 1968. In 2008, Manchester United won the UEFA Champions League again as well as the **FIFA Club World Cup** title, which crowned a remarkable period of two decades of success under Alex Ferguson and made Manchester United one of the world's best-known clubs. *See also* BECKHAM, DAVID; FORLÁN, DIEGO; OWEN, MICHAEL; RONALDO, CRISTIANO; SCHMEICHEL, PETER.

MARACANÃ. The Estádio Jornalista Mário Filho, commonly known as the "Estádio do Maracanã" or simply the "Maracanã," is **Brazil**'s best-known **stadium**. It played host to several matches at the **1950 FIFA World Cup**, just weeks after its opening. Its official opening capacity was 183,000, making it then the largest soccer stadium in the world by some distance. The Maracanã hosted the final game of the tournament, in which an estimated

220,000 fans crammed into the stadium, far exceeding the official capacity, to see hosts Brazil surprisingly beaten by **Uruguay**, who, as a result, won the fourth FIFA World Cup. Owned by the state government of Rio de Janeiro, the Maracanã plays host to games featuring local club teams Flamengo, Fluminese, Botafogo, and Vasco de Gama. It has been the scene of numerous historically noteworthy events, including **Pelé**'s 1,000th goal in 1969; the 1989 **Copa América** final which saw Brazil beat Uruguay; and the inaugural **FIFA Club World Cup** final in 2000. The Maracanã is slated to be the venue for the 2014 **FIFA World Cup** final, with the tournament to be held in Brazil. It has been renovated in recent years, resulting in its capacity being reduced to 88,992. It will also be the venue for the 2016 Summer Olympic Games opening and closing ceremonies.

MARADONA, DIEGO. B. 30 October 1960, Lanús, Argentina. Diego Maradona is **Argentina**'s greatest-ever player and the only rival to **Pelé** as the greatest player of all time worldwide. Maradona played for Argentina from 1977 until 1994, captaining his country to its second **FIFA World Cup** championship in 1986. Maradona led his country to the World Cup final again four years later in **Italy**, where they lost to West **Germany** in a **penalty shoot-out**. He scored 34 goals in 91 games for his country. Maradona retired in 1997 and later went on to manage Argentina, taking them to the 2010 World Cup finals.

Maradona made his debut for Argentina at the age of 17 on 3 April 1977, but he was not selected by **coach César Luis Menotti** for the World Cup in 1978, won by Argentina on home soil. Maradona instead led Argentina to victory in the **FIFA World Youth Championship** in 1979. Maradona did play at the next World Cup in **Spain** in 1982, scoring twice against **Hungary** in the first round, but was then sent off against **Brazil** in the second round as Argentina went out of the competition.

The 1986 World Cup in **Mexico** would prove to be the peak of Maradona's career internationally. Despite being only 5 foot 5 inches tall, Maradona was able to physically dominate opponents with his strength, while his remarkable ball-control skills allowed him to dribble past opponents with uncanny ease. These skills were no better demonstrated than at the 1986 World Cup. Famously, Maradona's second goal against **England** in the 1986 World Cup quarterfinals saw him dribble the ball past half-a-dozen English players across the length of the field before slotting the ball into the goal. This goal was later crowned in a vote held by the **Fédération Internationale de Football Association (FIFA)** as the greatest goal of all time in the World Cup. Maradona has also been a highly controversial figure, as his other goal in the same quarterfinal game illustrated: he clearly handballed the ball past England **goalkeeper** Peter Shilton, an offense unseen by the referee. Maradona later claimed it was the "hand of God." Following the win over England, Maradona went on to score two more as Argentina beat **Belgium** in the semifinals and then led Argentina to a 3-2 win over West Germany in the final. He ended the tournament with five goals and five assists and as the undoubted best player in the competition.

The mid-1980s were also the peak of Maradona's club career. He had begun his club career in his native country, making his professional debut for Argentinos Juniors at the age of just 15 on 20 October 1976. He moved to **Boca Juniors** in 1981 and then on to Europe with **Barcelona** in **Spain** the next year for a world-record fee of almost $10 million. His greatest club success came following a move to Italian club Napoli in 1984: Maradona rejuvenated the southern Italian club, who won the *Serie A* league championship in 1987 and 1990 and the **UEFA Cup** in 1989.

Personal problems also began to plague Maradona at this stage of his career, as his cocaine addiction became widely known. He was suspended for 15 months in 1991 for failing a drug test, testing positive for cocaine use. After his suspension, Maradona played for Sevilla in Spain in 1992 and 1993, then joined Newell's Old Boys back home in Argentina, appearing for his national team again in the 1994 World Cup finals in the **United States**. Maradona scored in Argentina's opening game against Greece, but was then found to have failed a drug test for the use of the illegal drug ephedrine and sent home.

Maradona retired in October 1997, playing his final game for Boca Juniors against **River Plate**. His personal problems worsened in retirement, as he ballooned in weight, leading to a stomach-stapling surgery in 2005. He became a famous television host in Argentina, until he was surprisingly chosen by the Argentinean FA to take over as manager of the national team in 2008. Under his stewardship, Argentina struggled to qualify for the 2010 World Cup finals, and a vitriolic outburst by Maradona against the media led to a two-month suspension from soccer by FIFA, which ended in January 2010. At the 2010 World Cup in **South Africa**, Maradona's Argentina cruised through the opening round, but a 4-0 defeat to Germany eliminated them and led to Maradona's departure from the national team coaching job in August 2010.

MARTA. B. 19 February 1986, Dois Riachos, Brazil. Marta Vieira da Silva, commonly known simply as "Marta," is a **Brazilian** four-time **FIFA World Player of the Year**, one of the most successful, talented, and famous female soccer players of all time. As a child, Marta was discouraged from playing the sport because **women's soccer** was severely frowned upon culturally in Brazil. But, employing her undeniable talent, Marta moved to Rio de Janeiro at the age of 14, going on to play two seasons for famed club Vasco da Gama before their women's team was dissolved, and then playing one season for Sao Martins. She made her first mark on the world stage playing for Brazil at the 2002 **FIFA U-20 Women's World Cup** and then appeared at the **FIFA Women's World Cup** in 2003, held in the **United States**, Brazil reaching the quarterfinals. The next year, Marta led Brazil to the final of the women's **Olympic Games Football Tournament**, losing to the United States, a result repeated in the same tournament four years later in 2008. Her Brazilian team also fell at the final hurdle in the 2007 Women's World Cup, this time **Germany** denying Marta glory in the final of the competition. Marta's individual genius, though, had been recognized worldwide: she won both the Golden Ball, awarded to the tournament's best player, and the Golden Boot as the competition's top scorer. Marta's skill, speed, athleticism, and creative play, along with a lethal finishing ability, were unmatched in the women's game. This was recognized in her four consecutive FIFA World Player of the Year awards from 2006 to 2009, earning her international fame. At club level, in 2004, Marta moved to Europe to play for **Swedish** club team Umeå IK, winning several titles before joining the new professional league in the United States, **Women's Professional Soccer**, in 2009 to play for the Los Angeles Sol. There, she won the regular-season title, but the Los Angeles Sol lost the Women's Professional Soccer championship game to Sky Blue FC from New Jersey.

MASOPUST, JOSEF. B. 9 February 1931, Most, Czechoslovakia. Josef Masopust was a star player for **Czechoslovakia** in the 1950s and 1960s. He was a midfielder who twice appeared in the **FIFA World Cup** for his national team, in 1958 and 1962. In the latter year, Czechoslovakia reached the final of the World Cup, Masopust scoring the first goal in a 3-1 defeat to **Brazil**. He was named as **European Footballer of the Year** later that year. Masopust scored a total of 10 goals in 63 games for his country between 1954 and 1966, while playing most of his club career for Dukla Prague. Masopust retired in 1970 and went on to have a career in **coaching**, including a period in charge of the Czechoslovakia national team in the 1980s.

MATTHÄUS, LOTHAR. B. 21 March 1961, Erlangen, Germany. One of **Germany**'s greatest players of all time and a **FIFA World Player of the Year** in 1991, Lothar Matthäus retired in 2000 from playing after a 21-year career in which he won every major honor while making a total of 150 appearances for his country, a national record. Matthäus began his professional career with Borussia Mönchengladbach before moving on to **Bayern Munich**, playing most of the rest of his career at the German giant and winning a total of seven domestic German league championship winners' medals. Matthäus also spent four years at **Internazionale** in **Italy**, from 1988 to 1992, winning the *Serie A* league title once. It was during this period that Matthäus reached his peak: he captained West Germany to victory in the 1990 **FIFA World Cup** in Italy, his tireless, creative midfield play winning him the **European Footballer of the Year** award that year and the **FIFA World Player of the Year** award the following year. Matthäus played in a remarkable total of five World Cup tournaments for Germany, also claiming runners-up medals at the 1982 and 1986 World Cups in **Spain** and **Argentina**, respectively. Matthäus won the **UEFA European Football Championship** in 1980 with West Germany. He retired from playing in 2000 following a short spell playing for the New York MetroStars in **Major League Soccer** in the **United States**. He has since begun a **coaching** career, though has yet to win a major honor or coach a top European club.

MATTHEWS, SIR STANLEY. B. 1 February 1915, Hanley, England. D. 23 February 2000. Sir Stanley Matthews is among the greatest English players of the 20th century and was the first winner of the **European Footballer of the Year Award** in 1963, at the age of 48. Matthews played professional soccer until the age of 50. He remains the oldest player to appear in England's top professional division and the oldest player to play for the **England** national team. He made his debut for his local club, Stoke City, in 1932, and first played for England two years later, at the age of 19. Matthews was a fast, attacking player known for his tricky dribbling skills and close ball control. Following the Second World War, Matthews moved on to play for Blackpool, where he won his only major team honor, the 1953 **Football Association Challenge Cup**, now known as the "Matthews Cup Final." He returned to play for Stoke City in 1961, remaining there until retirement in 1965 and receiving a knighthood from the Queen shortly before the end of his career as a player. He ended his England career with 54 appearances and 11 goals. Following his playing career, Matthews had two fairly unsuccessful terms as a team manager, for Port Vale in England and Hibernians in Malta.

MAZZOLA, VALENTINO. B. 26 January 1919, Cassano d'Adda, Italy. D. 4 May 1949. Valentino Mazzola was a famous Italian playmaker for Torino at club level and for **Italy** at national-team level. His life and career were tragically cut short by the **Superga Air Disaster** in 1949. Mazzola died, along with almost the entire Torino first team, at the age of just 30, when his team's plane crashed. He was by then considered one of the greatest players in the world, having captained Torino to five Italian league championships in the 1940s in seven years with the club, from 1942 to 1949, and scoring 102 goals for the club in the process. Mazzola's goal-scoring record was all the more remarkable coming from an attacking midfield position. Mazzola was equally adept as a defensive workhorse when needed, and he was known as an inspirational captain, famous for rolling up his sleeves as a sign for his players to increase their intensity on the field. Mazzola played 12 games for Italy, scoring four goals. His son, Sandro Mazzola, also later became an Italian national team player.

MCBRIDE, BRIAN. B. 19 June 1972, Arlington Heights, Illinois, United States. Brian McBride is a forward from the **United States** who has appeared for his country at the **FIFA World Cup** finals tournament three times, scoring three times in 10 games and helping the United States reach the quarterfinal stage of the 2002 World Cup. At club level, the peak of McBride's career came playing for Fulham in **England**'s **Premier League** from 2004 to 2008, becoming the captain of the team, and earning a reputation as a tough, uncompromising target forward. McBride's strength, work rate, and aerial ability earned him awards as Fulham's player of the year in both 2005 and 2006. McBride returned to the United States to play for the Chicago Fire of **Major League Soccer** in 2008, returning from national team duty the same year. He retired at the end of the 2010 Major League Soccer season.

MEAZZA, GIUSEPPE. B. 23 August 1910, Milan, Italy. D. 21 August 1979. Giuseppe Meazza was one of **Italy**'s greatest players, appearing mainly at club level for **Internazionale** in Milan during the 1920s and 1930s and winning three league championships with the team. He most famously starred for his country at the 1934 and 1938 **FIFA World Cups**. Italy won both competitions, Meazza captaining his country to their second victory in 1938. Meazza was a goal-scoring attacking midfielder. He scored more than 200 goals for Internazionale and 33 for Italy in 53 appearances. The home **stadium** of Internazionale and **AC Milan** is named the "**Stadio Giuseppe Meazza**" in his honor.

MEISL, HUGO. B. 16 November 1881, Maleschau, Bohemia. D. 17 February 1937. Meisl was a crucial innovative force in European soccer in the first half of the 20th century. Few have contributed so much to so many spheres of the sport: he was a **referee**, a **coach**, an administrator, and an innovator in the sport. A former international referee who learned his trade in Vienna, Meisl took charge of **Austria**'s national team in 1912, leaving in 1914 for five years of service in the First World War and returning to the post in 1919. Along with Englishman Jimmy Hogan, Meisl put together the Austrian *Wunderteam*, regarded by many as the best in Europe in the interwar era. They played a brand of attractive attacking soccer, devastating many top-class teams, such as **Scotland**, **Germany**, and **Hungary**, in the early 1930s, inspired by the brilliance of playmaker **Matthias Sindelar**. Between April 1931 and June 1934, the *Wunderteam* lost just three out of 31 games. However, despite being favorites for the title, the 1934 **FIFA World Cup** would not crown Austria's glory years: they lost to hosts **Italy** in the semifinals of the competition in a rain-soaked, bruising encounter that was not suited to Meisl's skillful team.

Meisl's Austria would go on to win a silver medal two years later at the 1936 **Olympic Games Football Tournament**, losing again to Italy, this time in the final. Meisl would retire the next year, dying just weeks later of a heart attack at the age of only 55. As well as a legacy of tactical innovation on the field as a coach, Meisl was also general secretary of the Austrian Football Association, and from that position, he was able to put into action his innovative idea for an international club competition, the first of its kind and forerunner of today's moneymaking **UEFA Champions League**. The tournament Meisl founded was known as the "**Mitropa Cup**," and featured many of the strongest teams from central continental Europe. First played in 1927 and remaining in some form until 1992, it left a lasting legacy for Meisl's record of innovation in the sport.

MENOTTI, CÉSAR LUIS. B. 5 November 1938, Rosario, Argentina. César Luis Menotti, nicknamed "*El Flaco*" (The Thin One), led **Argentina**, who hosted the tournament, to their first **FIFA World Cup** title in 1978. The victory, Argentina beating the **Netherlands** 3-1 in the final, crowned a magnificent career for Menotti. He began his **coaching** career in 1971 after a successful playing career mainly in Argentina's domestic league. After just two years, he led Huracan to their first-ever league title in 1973, which earned him the opportunity to manage the Argentinean national team at the age of just 46, after the country's poor showing at the 1974 World Cup. Menotti was fortunate to have at his disposal one of the greatest crops of talent ever seen in world soccer: with captain Daniel Passarella and the prolific scoring forward Mario Kempes providing the spine of the team, Menotti put together a disciplined team playing fluid attacking football. Menotti also had at his disposal the remarkable young talent **Diego Maradona**, but despite playing him in Argentina's national team at the age of just 16 in 1977, Menotti controversially left him out of the 1978 World Cup winning team.

Menotti would manage Maradona the next year at the **FIFA World Youth Championship**. Argentina claimed their first title in that competition as well, with Maradona leading a team playing swashbuckling soccer. Menotti would taste failure managing Argentina at the 1982 World Cup, their second-round exit leading to the end of his tenure coaching his national team. He immediately teamed up again with Maradona at club level, coaching **Barcelona**, but despite some success in Spanish cup competition, the club did not win the league title, and Menotti moved on to a meandering career around the world, alternating between broadcasting, coaching, and teaching soccer.

MESSI, LIONEL. B. 24 June 1987, Rosario, Argentina. A star attacking player for **Argentina**, Lionel Messi was the 2009 **FIFA World Player of the Year**, having played a key role for **Spanish** club team **Barcelona** when they won an unprecedented five domestic and international titles, including the **UEFA Champions League** and the **FIFA Club World Cup**. In his youth, Messi overcame a hormonal growth deficiency with the help of Barcelona, who signed him at the age of 13 and paid for treatment for his condition, recognizing his remarkable talent. He soon graduated from Barcelona's youth team and made his debut for the first team in 2004. He starred for his country at the **FIFA U-20 World Cup** the next year. In 2006, at the age of 18, Messi became the youngest Argentinean to play in the **FIFA World Cup**. Messi is considered by many to be the successor to Argentina's greatest player of all time, **Diego Maradona**. Though blessed with a similar ability to beat players, despite his slight stature, Messi, unlike his idol, Maradona, is quiet and composed off the field. He possesses a remarkable vision for creative passing as well as accurate finishing. At the 2010 World Cup, Messi played for Argentina with Diego Maradona as coach but exited in disappointing fashion at the quarterfinal stage following a 4-0 defeat to **Germany**.

MEXICO. Soccer is the most popular sport in Mexico, a country of a little more than 100 million people, with 324,595 registered players and 8,155,000 unregistered players, according to the **Fédération Internationale de Football Association (FIFA)** count in 2006. Following the 2010 **FIFA World Cup**, Mexico had appeared in a total of 14 World Cup finals tournaments and has hosted it twice, in 1970 and 1986. It has never progressed past the quarterfinal stage of the tournament. Mexico's best results in FIFA competition have been victories in the 1999 **FIFA Confederations Cup** and the 2005 FIFA Under-17 World Cup. Mexico has been a dominant force in its regional FIFA confederation, the **Confederation of North, Central American and Caribbean Association Football (CONCACAF)**, winning seven continental titles. Soccer in Mexico is governed by the Mexican Football Federation, in Spanish, the *Federación Mexicana de Fútbol Asociación* (FEMEXFUT), which was founded in 1927 and affiliated with FIFA in 1929 and with CONCACAF in 1961. *See also* CLUB DEPORTIVO GUADALAJARA; ESTADIO AZTECA; SÁNCHEZ, HUGO.

MICHELS, RINUS. B. 9 February 1928, Amsterdam, Netherlands. D. 3 March 2005. Named the Coach of the 20th Century by world soccer's global governing body **Fédération Internationale de Football Association (FIFA)**,

Rinus Michels was a Dutch player and is best known as a successful, innovative tactician as a manager. Michels began his professional soccer career as a player for **Ajax Amsterdam**. He scored 121 goals in 269 games for the club and made five appearances for the Dutch national team. A few years after his retirement from playing, in 1965, Michels took over as manager of Ajax Amsterdam, taking a mediocre team and leading them to the Dutch championship in 1966. They would win the title again in 1967, 1968, and 1970 under Michels, and then became the first Dutch team to win the **European Cup** in 1971, with a team built around the genius of **Johan Cruyff** within a fluid, attacking structure of team play formulated by Michels that became known as "**Total Football**." That style of play was based on intelligent movement and creative roles for every player on the team, with Michels fortunate to work with players with exceptional talent and alongside the inimitable Cruyff at both Ajax Amsterdam and the **Netherlands**, and including the likes of **Johan Neeskens** and Johnny Rep.

Following the 1971 European Cup triumph with Ajax Amsterdam, Michels moved to **Barcelona** (bringing Cruyff with him shortly after), winning the Spanish league in 1974. That same year, Michels coached the Netherlands at the **FIFA World Cup** in West **Germany**, comfortably cruising to the final with his team playing at a level rarely before seen in the World Cup. In the final, though, the Netherlands were upset 2-1 by the hosts, West Germany. Michels went back to club coaching with several teams but returned as national team manager of the Netherlands for the 1988 **UEFA European Football Championship**, leading a new golden generation of Dutch players to glory as the country claimed their first international title.

MILLA, ROGER. B. 20 May 1952, Yaoundé, Cameroon. Roger Milla is one of the most famous African players of all time, playing in three **FIFA World Cup** tournaments for his native **Cameroon**. Most notably, he scored four goals at the 1990 World Cup in **Italy** as Cameroon reached the quarterfinal stage, at that time, the furthest an African team had ever gone in the World Cup. Milla played for Cameroon from 1978 to 1994 and was twice voted African Footballer of the Year, in 1976 and 1990. Milla twice won the **Africa Cup of Nations** with Cameroon, in 1984 and 1986, the joint top-scorer in both competitions with four goals in each and adjudged as the best player of the tournament in the latter year. He played the early part of his club career in Cameroon, winning the national league in 1972 and 1973 with club team Léopards de Duala before moving on to play the bulk of his career in **France**, including a productive goal-scoring spell for **AS Saint-Étienne** from 1984 to 1986. In 1994, the year of his retirement from Cameroon's national team, Milla became the oldest player to score in a World Cup finals tournament, with a goal for his country at the competition in the **United States**.

MITROPA CUP. The first major international club tournament, the Mitropa Cup was established in 1927, the brainchild of Austrian **Hugo Meisl**, and held annually until 1992, apart from a break in the 1940s due to the Second World War. It was officially called "*La Coupe de l'Europe Centrale*" in French. The competition initially featured countries from central Europe, then arguably the strongest region of European soccer, with two teams from each of **Hungary, Czechoslovakia, Yugoslavia**, and **Austria** entering in the first two seasons of the competition. In 1929, Yugoslavia was replaced by Italy, and, in 1934, the competition was expanded to include four teams from each country. Yugoslavia rejoined in 1937 along with Romania and **Switzerland**. The tournament was highly prestigious in the interwar period and played an important role as a precursor to the **European Cup**, established in 1955. The Mitropa Cup continued in the postwar period, but was overshadowed by the new Europe-wide tournaments such as the European Cup and was discontinued in 1992. *See also* WOMEN'S SOCCER.

MOHR, HEIDI. B. 29 May 1967, West Germany. Heidi Mohr was arguably the greatest European female soccer player of the 20th century. She played for **Germany** from 1986 to 1996 in international play, scoring 83 goals in 104 games. Mohr won two **UEFA Women's Championships** with Germany. She twice appeared at the **FIFA Women's World Cup**, scoring 10 goals in 12 total games as Germany finished in third place in 1991 and second place in 1995.

MONTI, LUIS. B. 15 May 1901, Buenos Aires, Argentina. D. 9 September 1983. Luis Monti not only played in two different **FIFA World Cup** finals tournaments for two different countries—**Argentina** and **Italy**—but also has the rare distinction of playing in the final of the competition on each occasion. Monti began his career in the 1920s in his native Argentina, going on to represent that country at the 1930 World Cup and playing in all four of their games. They lost in the final to hosts **Uruguay**. Monti then continued his career playing in Italy for **Juventus**. He soon began playing for Italy instead of Argentina at international level. Italy also recruited Monti's fellow Argentineans Raimundo Orsi and Enrique Guaita to play for them. Italy won the 1934 World Cup, Monti playing a critical role as the midfield fulcrum of the team, starting in their victory in the final of the competition, a 2-1 win over **Czechoslovakia**. He retired in 1939 and went on to have a career in **coaching** in both Italy and Argentina.

MOORE, BOBBY. B. 12 April 1941, Barking, England. D. 24 February 1993. Robert Moore, better known as "Bobby," was an **England** international defender who captained his country to victory in the 1966 **FIFA World Cup** and played in two other World Cup finals tournaments, in 1962 and 1970. He was an imperious and cultured defender, considered one of the best ever at his position by contemporaries such as **Pelé**. Moore began his professional club career playing for London team West Ham United, making his debut at the age of 17 in 1958. In 1962, he made his debut for England, playing in the 1962 World Cup, where England reached the quarterfinal stage. With West Ham United, Moore received domestic honors, winning the **Football Association Challenge Cup** in 1964, and then European glory with victory in the **UEFA Cup Winners' Cup**. Four years later, Moore was magnificent as England won the World Cup for the first time, on home soil. A curious incident occurred in **Mexico** before the beginning of the 1970 World Cup when Moore was arrested for allegedly stealing a bracelet from a jewelry store, a charge he was later completely cleared of. Despite this, Moore was again outstanding in that World Cup, including in a tight 1-0 loss to **Brazil** in the first-round group stage, but England was eliminated in the quarterfinals by West **Germany**. Moore played his last game for England in 1974 and ended his long tenure with West Ham United the same year, finishing his career in England with Fulham and then playing briefly in the **United States** for the San Antonio Thunder and the Seattle Sounders in the **North American Soccer League**. Moore retired from playing in 1978 and had an unremarkable career in coaching before his death from bowel cancer in February 1993.

MORACE, CAROLINA. B. 5 February 1964, Venice, Italy. Carolina Morace is a former star player for **Italy**'s female national team and a pioneering force in **women's soccer**. She first played for Italy's national women's team in 1978 at the age of just 14, appearing in several **UEFA Women's Championship** tournaments and one **FIFA Women's World Cup**, the inaugural competition staged in 1991. At that tournament, Italy reached the quarterfinals, and Morace scored a total of five goals, including a **hat-trick** against Chinese Taipei. Morace scored a total of 105 goals in 150 games for Italy, and won 12 titles at club level in the Italian national women's league. Morace achieved particular notoriety in Italy for becoming the first female coach of a men's professional team, briefly managing lower league club Viterbese. She also coached Italy's women's national team for several years and, in 2009, took charge of **Canada**'s women's national team.

MORENO, MANUEL JOSÉ. B. 3 August 1916, Buenos Aires, Argentina. D. 26 August 1978. José Manuel Moreno was an **Argentinean** player best known for his performances for **River Plate** in the 1930s and 1940s and for Argentina's national team, scorer of 19 goals in 34 games for his country. During that time, Moreno won five national league championships in Argentina, and three **Copa América** titles, in 1941, 1942, and 1947 respectively. In the 1950s and 1960s,

Moreno played for several clubs abroad, winning further league championships in **Mexico, Chile,** and **Colombia.** He retired in 1961, entering a career in **coaching** that included a short spell in charge of Argentina's national team.

MÜLLER, GERHARD. B. 3 November 1945, Nördlingen, Germany. Gerhard Müller, better known as Gerd, is **Germany**'s all-time leading scorer, with 68 goals in 62 games, including 14 goals in **FIFA World Cup** finals tournaments. Müller was a stocky, strong forward who depended on his power and nose for goals, a prolific scorer in club soccer with 365 goals in 427 games in the German Bundesliga, the vast majority for **Bayern Munich**. Playing alongside the legendary **Franz Beckenbauer**, Müller won three German championships and three **European Cup** titles between 1964 and 1979. Franz Beckenbauer went on to say, "Everything that FC Bayern has become is due to Gerd Müller and his goals." Müller won the **European Footballer of the Year** award in 1970, after scoring 10 goals for West Germany in the World Cup finals that year, where they were eliminated at the semifinal stage by **Italy**. Müller scored four goals in the 1974 World Cup finals, including an all-important strike in the final to put West Germany up 2-1 over the **Netherlands** as they went on to win the World Cup for the third time. Müller ended his playing career in 1981 after spending three years in the **United States** appearing in the **North American Soccer League**.

MUNICH AIR DISASTER. On 6 February 1958, the plane carrying the **Manchester United** club team, while taking off from Munich-Riem Airport in Munich en route back from a **European Cup** match, crashed from the runway in poor weather conditions, killing 23 of the 44 people on board, including eight Manchester United players. Two members of the plane's crew were killed along with three members of Manchester United's staff, eight journalists covering the team, and two other passengers. Many others on the flight, including future **England** star **Bobby Charlton**, were badly injured. The manager of Manchester United, **Sir Matt Busby**, was also severely hurt in the crash, though later made a full recovery. Busby's team, a young group who were England's most successful and best-known team at the time, were known as the "Busby Babes," and the disaster claimed the lives of some of England's greatest-ever talents, including the brilliant 21-year-old Duncan Edwards. The anniversary of the disaster is commemorated each year by Manchester United. The remarkable achievement by Sir Matt Busby of rebuilding the club following the tragic loss of so many players and staff members to eventually become champions of Europe in 1968 is considered to be one of the great feats in the history of English soccer.

NACIONAL. Based in the **Uruguayan** capital Montevideo, Nacional is the most successful club team in Uruguay, having claimed 42 domestic league championships (both amateur and professional), and boasting several titles in international competition. Nacional, founded on 14 May 1899 from a merger between Uruguay Atletica Club and Montevideo Football Club, is the oldest club in the country. The next year, Nacional began play at a new stadium, Gran Parque Central, which remains its official home base, though it plays many games at the larger, legendary **Estadio de Centenario**, also located in Montevideo, as does its fierce local rival, **Peñarol**. In international competition, Nacional has won the leading South American continental club tournament, the **Copa Libertadores**, on three occasions, in 1971, 1980, and 1988. Following each of those victories, Nacional went on to triumph over European opposition in the **Intercontinental Cup**, its three wins the joint best record in the history of the now defunct competition.

NAKATA, HIDETOSHI. B. 22 January 1977, Kōfu, Japan. Hidetoshi Nakata was **Japan**'s most famous player in the 1990s and 2000s, a talented midfield creator also known for his brash personality off the field. He played for Japan at the 1998, 2002, and 2006 **FIFA World Cup** finals tournaments, appearing 77 times for his country and scoring 11 goals. Nakata played much of his career in **Italy**, winning the 2001 Italian league championship with AS Roma. Nakata retired in 2006.

NASAZZI, JOSÉ. B. 24 May 1901, Montevideo, Uruguay. D. 17 June 1968. José Nasazzi was the first captain to lead his country's national team to glory at the **FIFA World Cup**, captaining **Uruguay** to victory at the inaugural tournament in 1930, held in Uruguay. Nasazzi was an ever-dependable and inspirational captain who led from defense at the right-back position. He had previously won both the 1924 and 1928 **Olympic Games Football Tournaments** with Uruguay and was referred to as "*El Gran Mariscal*" (the Grand Marshal) for his leadership skills. Nasazzi retired as a player in 1937, later managing the Uruguay national team during the Second World War.

NEDVĚD, PAVEL. B. 30 August 1972, Cheb, Czechoslovakia. Pavel Nedvěd, a gifted midfield player who earned Europe-wide fame playing for two clubs in **Italy**, Lazio (1996–2001) and **Juventus** (2001–2009), is one of the **Czech Republic**'s greatest-ever players. In 2003, he won the **European Footballer of the Year** award, a year that Nedvěd's Juventus won the Italian league championship for the second time in a row and reached the final of the **UEFA Champions League**, losing to **AC Milan** in a **penalty shoot-out**. Nedvěd also enjoyed a very successful career on the international stage playing for the Czech Republic, appearing 91 times for his country and finishing with a runners-up medal from the 1996 **UEFA European Football Championship**, where the Czech Republic lost to **Germany** in the final.

NEESKENS, JOHAN. B. 15 September 1951, Heemstede, Netherlands. Johan Neeskens appeared at the **FIFA World Cup** twice as a player for the **Netherlands**, a member of two of its strongest-ever national teams. They reached the final of the competition in both 1974 and 1978, though they lost on both occasions. A skillful attacking midfielder, he scored five goals in 12 games at those competitions, and a total of 17 goals in 49 games for his country. At club level, Neeskens starred for **Ajax Amsterdam** in his native Netherlands in the early 1970s. The team conquered European soccer, winning three successive **European Cup** competitions between 1971 and 1973. Neeskens then moved on to play for **Barcelona** in **Spain**, and then the New York Cosmos in the **United States**. Since retiring as a player, Neeskens has pursued a career in **coaching**.

NETHERLANDS. Soccer in the Netherlands is governed by the Royal Netherlands Football Association (in Dutch, *Koninklijke Nederlandse Voetbalbond*, or KNVB), founded in 1899. The KNVB was a founding member of the **Fédération Internationale de Football Association (FIFA)** in 1904 and, later, was a founding member of the **Union of European Football Associations (UEFA)**, in 1954. With a national population of a little more than 16 million, the Netherlands has an unusually high ratio of registered players, numbering more than one million according to FIFA. Dutch national and club teams have a rich history of success despite the relatively small size of the country. The national team has reached the **FIFA World Cup** final three times, in 1974, 1978, and 2010. They also achieved fourth place in 1998 but have yet to win the competition. The Dutch have appeared at nine World Cup tournaments, though they did not participate between 1938 and 1974.

The Netherlands' sole major international trophy came at the 1988 **UEFA European Football Championship** with an outstanding team led by **Ruud Gullit** and **Marco van Basten**. Dutch club teams have been very successful in European competition since the 1960s, with an unusually strong youth development system producing some of the world's top players, including **Johan Cruyff**, one of the greatest of all time. Cruyff led **Ajax Amsterdam** to three consecutive triumphs in the European Cup between 1971 and 1973, starting that run just a year after Feyenoord became the first Dutch team to win that competition in 1970. PSV Eindhoven won the same tournament in 1988, and Ajax Amsterdam claimed the **UEFA Champions League** in 1995, making the Netherlands one of the leading countries in the history of European club soccer. Dutch club teams play in the *Eredivisie* league, which has been dominated since its introduction in 1956 by Ajax Amsterdam (29 titles), PSV Eindhoven (21 titles), and Feyenoord (14 titles). *See also* MICHELS, RINUS; NEESKENS, JOHAN; RIJKAARD, FRANK.

NEW ZEALAND. Soccer in New Zealand is governed by New Zealand Football (NZF), founded in 1891 and one of the oldest national soccer associations in the world. The NZF affiliated with the **Fédération Internationale de Football Association (FIFA)** in 1948 and was a founding member of the **Oceania Football Confederation (OFC)** in 1966. Soccer is not the most popular sport in New Zealand due to the popularity of competing sports such as rugby and cricket, but the men's national team, known as the "All Whites," has shown considerable improvement in recent years. It is by far the strongest team in the OFC (in part, thanks to the departure of **Australia** to the **Asian Football Confederation**). New Zealand has won the continent's leading national team competition, the **OFC Nations Cup**, on three occasions, in 1973, 1998, and 2002, and finished runners-up in 2000. New Zealand has appeared at the **FIFA World Cup** twice, in 1982 and 2010. It exited in the first round on both occasions, but, at the 2010 FIFA World Cup in **South Africa**, New Zealand ended up as the only unbeaten team after exiting at the group stage with three ties, including a surprising draw with defending World Cup champions **Italy**. New Zealand's women's national team, commonly called the "Football Ferns" and who began play in 1975, have twice qualified for the **FIFA Women's World Cup**, failing to win a game in either 1991 or 2007. They have, however, been victorious in the OFC Women's Championship on three occasions.

The leading domestic league in New Zealand is the New Zealand Football Championship (NZFC), but the strongest club team in New Zealand, the Wellington Phoenix, play in Australia's A-League. In 2002, the NZFC founded the National Women's League, and Auckland teams have dominated play since then. *See also* WOMEN'S SOCCER.

NIGERIA. Nigerian soccer is organized by the Nigerian Football Federation (NFF), founded in 1945 and affiliated with the **Confederation of African Football (CAF)** in 1959 and with the **Fédération Internationale de Football Association (FIFA)** in 1960. The NFF has, however, been plagued in recent years by allegations of corruption, and a government investigation was launched in 2010. Nigeria's national team, nicknamed the "Super Eagles," has been one of the strongest-performing African national teams in international competition, appearing in the **FIFA World Cup** on four occasions, in 1994, 1998, 2002, and 2010. In 1994, Nigeria reached the last 16 of the World Cup, losing in extra time to eventual finalists **Italy**. Nigeria again reached the last 16 in the 1998 World Cup but lost in the first round on its two subsequent appearances in 2002 and 2010. Nigeria has twice won Africa's leading international competition, the **Africa Cup of Nations**, in 1980 and 1994, and has finished runners-up on four occasions, in 1984, 1988, 1990, and 2000. Nigeria has been particularly successful in global youth competitions, with three victories in the FIFA U-17 World Cup (in 1985, 1993, and 2007) and a gold medal at the **Olympic Games Football Tournament** (a competition mainly for players under 23 years old) in 1996. Nigeria's women's national team, known as the "Super Falcons," has been extremely successful in African competition and is the only African team to have qualified for all **FIFA Women's World Cup** tournaments held since 1991.

The NFF also organizes the leading domestic leagues in Nigeria. In men's soccer, the top professional division is the Nigerian Premier League, founded in 1973, and has been dominated in the past decade by Enyimba FC, from the southern Nigerian city of Aba. Enyimba FC won the African continent's leading club competition, the **CAF Champions League**, in 2003 and 2004, the only Nigerian team to do so. Nigeria does not have a professional women's league, slowing the development of the game, but does have a national Female Amateur League and a Female Challenge Cup organized by the NFF. *See also* CAF AFRICAN YOUTH CHAMPIONSHIP; CAF WOMEN'S AFRICAN CHAMPIONSHIP; ENYIMBA INTERNATIONAL FOOTBALL CLUB.

NORDAHL, GUNNAR. B. 19 October 1921, Hörnefors, Sweden. D. 15 September 1995. Gunnar Nordahl was the first professional **Swedish** soccer player. He joined **AC Milan** in **Italy** in 1949 at the age of 27 after a long and successful amateur career in Sweden, where he earned a living as a firefighter while playing. He was a major success at AC Milan, starring alongside two fellow Swedes who joined him at the club, Gunnar Gren and **Nils Liedholm**. Nordahl made 268 appearances for AC Milan, scored an impressive 221 goals, and was five times the top scorer in Italy's top division, in 1950, 1951,

1953, 1954, and 1955. He was a muscular, powerful forward able to drive past opponents. He linked up in superb fashion with his fellow Swedes, Gren and Liedholm, a combination that became popularly known as the Gre-No-Li forward line. He won two league championships with AC Milan, in 1951 and 1955. He left AC Milan in 1956 and continued to play in Italy for AS Roma until he retired in 1958. Nordahl was hugely effective at international level also, scoring 42 goals in 33 matches for Sweden and winning, with his country, the 1948 **Olympic Games Football Tournament** where he scored seven goals in four games. However, his international career was ended the next year, after his move to AC Milan, when the Swedish national association refused to include professional players on its national team. Nordahl took over a coaching role at AS Roma in 1958 and, later, managed clubs in his native Sweden.

NORTH AMERICAN SOCCER LEAGUE (NASL). The North American Soccer League (NASL) was the premier outdoor professional men's league in the **United States** from 1968 to 1984. A second-tier grouping of teams in the United States, also known as the "North American Soccer League," was founded in 2009. The original NASL reached a high point of popularity for professional soccer in the United States in the 20th century with the success of the New York Cosmos and their star player **Pelé** in the late 1970s. The team achieved national celebrity status, but overspending and unsuitable stadium situations doomed the league as a whole to bankruptcy by 1984. *See also* MAJOR LEAGUE SOCCER.

OCEANIA FOOTBALL CONFEDERATION (OFC). Founded in 1966, the Oceania Football Confederation is the smallest and youngest of the six regional confederations belonging to the **Fédération Internationale de Football Association (FIFA)**. It governs soccer in the South Pacific region from its headquarters in Auckland, **New Zealand**. The OFC currently has 11 full-member associations and five associate members, mostly small island nations with little soccer pedigree.

The impetus for the formation of the OFC came from the refusal of the **Asian Football Confederation (AFC)** to admit **Australia** and New Zealand as members in the early 1960s. Leaders of the Australian Soccer Federation and the New Zealand Football Association met with FIFA President **Sir Stanley Rous** to discuss forming a new confederation in the South Pacific. This was approved at the 1966 **FIFA Congress**, and Australia, Fiji, New Zealand, and Papua New Guinea became the founding members. The OFC later accepted American Samoa, Cook Islands, New Caledonia, Samoa, the Solomon Islands, Tahiti, Tonga, and Vanuatu as members.

A serious blow to the OFC's international stature came with the departure of the region's largest nation, Australia, who gave up their OFC membership to join the AFC in 2005, leaving the OFC without a nation with a fully professional domestic league. Currently, the winner of the OFC's **FIFA World Cup** qualifying competition takes on the fifth-ranked team in Asian qualifying for a berth in the World Cup finals. Australia qualified for the 2006 World Cup via this play-off, and New Zealand followed suit for the 2010 World Cup, defeating Bahrain in the play-off. The OFC also runs the premier continental competitions for the region's nations and clubs, including the **OFC Nations Cup**, held biennially, and the annual **OFC Champions League**, which determines the region's representative to the **FIFA Club World Cup**.

OFC CHAMPIONS LEAGUE. Organized by the **Oceania Football Confederation (OFC)**, the governing body of soccer in the Oceanic region, the OFC Champions League is the leading club competition in that confederation and is contested annually. The winning team earns the right to compete in a play-off for qualification to the **FIFA Club World Cup**. It was first played in 2007, replacing the previous premier OFC competition, the Oceania Club Championship, which itself began play in 1987. Teams from **New Zealand** and **Australia** have been the most successful in the history of the competition under its different formats since 1987, with four wins each, though Australian clubs can no longer enter the OFC Champions League, following Australia's move from the OFC to the **Asian Football Confederation (AFC)** in 2005.

OFC NATIONS CUP. The premier competition for nations in the **Oceania Football Confederation (OFC)**, the OFC Nations Cup was first contested in 1973 as the Oceania Cup and was won by **New Zealand**. It did not become a regular event until 1996, after which it was held every two years until 2004, **Australia** and New Zealand alternating as champions. The competition was weakened by Australia's departure from the OFC in 2006, and a four-year break was taken between the 2004 and 2008 competitions, the latter won by New Zealand. This earned them the OFC's place at the 2009 **FIFA Confederations Cup**.

OFFSIDE. The offside law, number 11 in the **Laws of the Game**, applies to all 11-a-side games worldwide played under the auspices of the international governing body, **Fédération Internationale de Football Association (FIFA)**. It was first applied in the 19th century and has gone through numerous changes made by the global authority on the Laws of the Game, the **International Football Association Board (IFAB)**. An attacking player is currently deemed to be in an offside position if he or she is closer to the opposing team's goal line than the ball and two players on the opposing team are when the ball is played (before 1925, it was three players on the opposing team). This attacking player may be penalized for being in an offside position if he or she is deemed by the **referee** to be actively involved in the play at the time the ball is played. The law states that a player is involved in active play if, in the opinion of the referee, he or she is interfering with play, interfering with an opponent, or gaining an advantage from being in that offside position. An exception given in the offside law is that a player cannot be offside when he or she is inside his or her own team's half of the field, or when play is restarted via a goal kick, throw-in, or corner kick. If an offside offense is called by the referee, an indirect free kick is awarded to the opposing team and taken from the spot of the infringement.

The offside rule serves the purpose of giving the game a structured form that leads the defending team to push up the field in a line (excluding the **goalkeeper**), thus keeping the opposing team from leaving attackers hanging near the opposing team's goal, because they would then be in an offside position. This prevents soccer from becoming immersed in speculative long-range passing to reach forwards holding their position by the goal line, encouraging, instead, a game of shorter passing and the use of creative skill to break past the defending team. Some teams, however, have taken the deployment of an "offside trap" to such lengths as to turn it into a defensive system of play of its own, generally considered a negative and unattractive style of play. The close calls needed to be made by **assistant referees** to determine if a player is in an offside position when the ball is played to him or her, and the interpretations of whether or not that player is actively involved in play, has added controversy and confusion to the game. The IFAB has subtly changed the offside law at various points to aid attacking teams in how **referees** apply the rule.

OLIMPIA FOOTBALL CLUB. Based in **Paraguay**'s capital city, Asunción, Olimpia Football Club has the best record in Paraguayan soccer and one of the strongest histories in continental South American competition. They were founded on 25 July 1902 by Dutch physical education teacher William Paats. He is the same man who first introduced soccer to Paraguay and who, with eight other men that day, decided upon the club's name and the use of distinctive black-and-white club colors. Olimpia has won 38 amateur and professional championships in Paraguayan domestic competition, along with three **Copa Libertadores** titles in South American competition, won in 1979, 1990, and 2002. The year 1979 proved to be Olimpia's greatest year, as they also won the **Intercontinental Cup**, defeating Malmö of **Sweden**.

OLYMPIC GAMES FOOTBALL TOURNAMENT. Men's international soccer has been played at the Summer Olympic Games as an official competition since 1904. It has been played in every Olympic Games except 1896 in Athens and 1932 in Los Angeles. In the first three decades of the 20th century, the Olympic Games soccer tournament was the world's leading international soccer competition. The establishment of the **FIFA World Cup** in 1930 by the **Fédération Internationale de Football Association (FIFA)** ended the Olympic Games soccer tournament's preeminent role in the global game.

The International Olympic Committee (IOC) was founded by Baron Pierre de Coubertin in 1892, and the first Olympic Games took place in Athens, Greece, in 1896. It remains a matter of historical controversy whether soccer was contested as an exhibition sport at the first Olympic Games, some suggesting both an Izmir XI and an Athenian XI played games. Soccer was an exhibition sport at the 1900 and 1904 Olympic Games. But with the growth of the sport internationally, it was only a matter of time before the Olympic Games hosted a serious soccer competition. The first official tournament, organized by **The Football Association** of **England**, was held at the London

Olympic Games of 1908 with the leading amateurs from six countries taking part. It was won by a team representing Great Britain that consisted solely of players from England. They defeated Denmark 2-0 in the final.

Considerable debate between the IOC and FIFA, the latter established in 1904 and growing in stature as the organizer of international soccer, took place over whether a soccer competition should be included at the 1912 Olympic Games in Stockholm, **Sweden**. The IOC eventually agreed that FIFA rules would be adopted and only national associations affiliated with FIFA would be allowed to participate. Following the First World War, soccer became the biggest-drawing event at the 1920 Olympics in Antwerp, **Belgium**, with 40,000 attending as Belgium defeated **Czechoslovakia** in the final. The 1920s were the high point of Olympic Games soccer tournaments, effectively serving as the world championship for the sport. The entrance of non-European teams for the first time in 1924 gave the tournament greater legitimacy as a global event. **Uruguay** won the competition at the Olympic Games in Paris in 1924, beating **Switzerland** in the final in front of 60,000 fans, with a reported 10,000 locked outside. In 1928, Uruguay beat Argentina in the final after a replay following a 1-1 draw.

In 1932, following the organization of the FIFA World Cup for the first time in 1930, no Olympic soccer tournament was held. The FIFA World Cup, a world championship that allowed professionals to play, was a growing problem for the competitions held at the amateur Olympic Games in the 1920s. In the decades after, as most of the world's best players became professionals, the issue of the Olympic Games' rule on amateur-only participation weakened the level of competition considerably when the soccer tournament returned to the Olympic Games from 1936 on. The IOC's amateurs-only rule also handed a considerable advantage to countries from the Communist bloc following the Second World War, whose athletes received state support but were not deemed to be professionals at the Olympic Games. Communist countries won every single Olympic Games soccer tournament contested between 1952 and 1980, **Hungary** becoming three-time champions.

As the Olympic movement's antipathy to professionalism declined and a desire to improve the level of competition in the tournament grew, the IOC made an agreement with FIFA to allow professionals to appear in the 1990s. But in order to prevent the Olympic Games' soccer tournament from operating as a competing world championship to the FIFA World Cup, the rules currently restrict the age of players competing to under 23 years old, with two exceptions for players over this age allowed per team.

Women's soccer began play at the Olympics in 1996 in Atlanta, the **United States** winning the competition on home soil. The United States claimed a silver medal for second place in Sydney in 2000, Norway winning the title, and then gold twice more, in 2004 in Athens and 2008 in Beijing, beating **Brazil** in the final both times. The women's tournament has consistently rivaled the **FIFA Women's World Cup** for its quality of play, with, unlike its male counterpart, no limitation on the age of the players involved.

OLYMPIQUE DE MARSEILLE. The southern French port city of Marseille is home to one of **France**'s most successful club teams, Olympique de Marseille, often known simply as "Marseille." It was founded in 1899 by a French sports official, René Dufaure de Montmirail, as part of a broader sports club and first achieved national prominence in the 1920s with three victories in the French Cup. In 1932, it was one of the founding members of France's first professional national league and won the competition for the first time in 1937. They won their second title in 1948 but then suffered disappointment (including a brief period in the second division) until the 1970s, when they won the league championship in both 1971 and 1972, the team sparked by its pair of foreign forwards, **Yugoslavian** Josip Skoblar and **Swede** Roger Magnusson. Marseille was relegated to the second division again in 1980 but returned to the top division in 1984 with a team brimming with young talent. In 1986, Marseille was purchased by multimillionaire Bernard Tapie, who brought in several highly paid star players, including Alain Giresse, **Jean-Pierre Papin**, Chris Waddle, **Enzo Francescoli**, and **Rudi Völler**. That gave the team more than enough ammunition to win five straight French league championships from 1989 to 1993. In May 1993, they became the first-and-still-only French club to win the **UEFA Champions League**, beating **AC Milan** 1-0 in the final.

However, controversy surrounded Marseille shortly after that triumph: a match-fixing scandal engulfed the club, which was stripped of its 1993 French league title but not its UEFA Champions League title. Further financial irregularities under Tapie's leadership led to Marseille's demotion from the French first division in 1994, and Tapie left the club and was later sentenced to two years in prison for corruption. Marseille returned to the top division in 1996 and, in 2010, won the French league championship for the first time since the Tapie era. Marseille plays its games at Stade Velodrome, opened in 1937 and a host to matches at both the 1938 and 1998 **FIFA World Cups**, with a current capacity of 60,000. *See also* DESAILLY, MARCEL; PELÉ, ABÉDI; WEAH, GEORGE.

ORLANDO PIRATES. The Orlando Pirates is a club team based in Johannesburg, **South Africa**, and is one of the most successful clubs on the African continent. They were founded in 1937 and have won the South African national league championship in its various incarnations on numerous occasions.

In 1995, the Orlando Pirates won Africa's leading competition, the African Cup of Champions Clubs, now known as the **CAF Champions League**. They play at Orlando Stadium, built in the 1950s and popularly known as the "Factory of Dreams."

OWEN, MICHAEL. B. 14 December 1979, Chester, England. Michael Owen was the **European Footballer of the Year** in 2001. At that time, he was at the peak of his career after bursting onto the world soccer stage three years earlier at the 1998 **FIFA World Cup** with a sensational goal against **Argentina** in the second round of the competition. That goal consisted of a long run and finish that showcased Owen's explosive pace playing as an out-and-out striker. He is one of England's all-time leading scorers, with 40 goals in 89 appearances. At club level, Owen began his career as a prolific goal scorer for **Liverpool Football Club** before moving to **Spain** in 2004 to play for **Real Madrid**. Owen returned to England in 2005 to play for Newcastle United, and then joined **Manchester United** in 2009. In recent years, Owen's goal-scoring record has receded as a series of serious injuries have hampered him physically.

P

PAISLEY, ROBERT. B. 23 January 1919, Hetton-le-Hole, England. D. 14 February 1996. No manager has led the famous English club team **Liverpool Football Club** to more championship victories than has Robert "Bob" Paisley. He took on the remarkable team built by his predecessor, Liverpool manager **Bill Shankly**, and led the team to even greater success. Paisley, a miner's son who signed on as a player for Liverpool in 1939, gave almost half a century of service to Liverpool. He won a championship playing with the team in 1947, and after he retired from playing, he served Shankly as a trainer and physiotherapist. Paisley was a trusted member of Shankly's infamous "boot room" backroom team, when Liverpool became the top team in England. But after Shankly's surprising departure in 1974, it would be left to a reluctant Paisley to take over the club and guide the team to the top of European club soccer. Under Paisley's management, Liverpool played 535 games, winning 308, drawing 131, and losing just 96. With stars such as **Kevin Keegan** and Kenny Dalglish, Liverpool won six English league championships in eight years, from 1976 to 1983, and, most famously, won the **European Cup** in 1977, 1978, and 1981, Paisley being the first English-born manager to lead his club to Europe's greatest club prize. Paisley retired in 1983, his success, in less than a decade in charge, yet to be equaled by any English club manager.

PAPIN, JEAN-PIERRE. B. 5 November 1963, Boulogne-sur-Mer, France. Jean-Pierre Papin, a forward with a remarkable goal-scoring record for his club teams and for **France**, is a former French star player. He was the **European Footballer of the Year** in 1991 while playing for **Olympique de Marseille** in France. He moved the following year to **Italian** giants **AC Milan**, with whom he won the **UEFA Champions League** in 1994, though he did not play in the final. Papin moved to **Germany** that year to play, without great success, for **Bayern Munich** and returned to spend the rest of his career at various French clubs before retiring in 2004. Papin enjoyed a successful national team career for France, scoring 30 goals in 54 games for his country, and appeared at the 1986 **FIFA World Cup**, where he scored twice in four games as France reached the semifinals, finishing in third place.

PARAGUAY. Soccer was introduced to Paraguay in the late 1890s by Dutch physical education instructor William Paats at a teachers' college in Asunción, the capital of the country. The interest was such that in 1902 he founded Paraguay's first club team, **Olimpia Football Club**, and in 1906, he was a founding member of the national Paraguayan Football Association (*Asociación Paraguaya de Fútbol* in Spanish), as it is called today. Paraguayan journalist Adolfo Riquelme was its first president, and the association started a league championship soon after. Olimpia has been the most successful club in Paraguayan soccer, with 38 domestic championship victories and three titles in the South American continental tournament, the **Copa Libertadores**, in 1979, 1990, and 2002. Olimpia also won the **Intercontinental Cup** in 1980. Paraguay's men's national team has achieved considerable success in international competition, twice winning the **Copa América**, in 1953 and 1979, and finishing as runners-up on five other occasions.

Paraguay's men's national team has appeared in the **FIFA World Cup** finals tournament eight times, its best performance coming in 2010 when it reached the quarterfinals of the competition in **South Africa**, losing at that point to eventual victors **Spain**. Soccer is now the most popular sport in Paraguay, and its capital, Asunción, is home to the headquarters of the **South American Football Confederation (CONMEBOL)**. **Women's soccer** has been slow to develop in Paraguay, and there is no domestic professional women's league. The Paraguay women's national team has never qualified for the **FIFA Women's World Cup** or the women's **Olympic Games Football Tournament**, though it did finish in fourth place at the 2006 Sudamericano Femenino competition, its best international result. *See also* ERICO, ARSENIO; ROMERO, JULIO CÉSAR.

PARR, LILY. B. 26 April 1905, St Helens, England. D. 24 May 1978. Lily Parr, a prolific goal scorer and prodigious talent, was one of the most popular female soccer players of the 20th century and one of the most well-known players of any gender at the peak of her popularity in 1920. She starred for **Dick, Kerr Ladies**, England's leading women's soccer team, who earned fame during and after the First World War for their outstanding performances. They drew record-breaking crowds, well into five figures, on numerous occasions. A ban on the use of **Football Association**–affiliated stadiums by women's soccer teams at the end of 1921 prevented the further development of the popularity of Parr and Dick, Kerr Ladies. However, she continued to play for the team, including extensive tours abroad, and, by her retirement in 1950, had scored more than 900 goals.

PASSARELLA, DANIEL. B. 25 May 1953, Chacabuco, Argentina. Daniel Passarella was the first captain of **Argentina** to lift the **FIFA World Cup**

Trophy. They won the competition in 1978 under his leadership, on home territory. He was a star defender for **River Plate** in his native Argentina at the time, playing for the club from 1974 to 1982 before moving to **Italy** and playing for Fiorentina and **Internazionale**. Passarella returned to Argentina to finish his career with River Plate in 1988 and retired the next year. He scored 143 goals in 486 appearances, an impressive total for a defender. Passarella also scored 22 goals in 70 games for Argentina, including three in his 12 games in FIFA World Cup finals tournaments (the 1982 World Cup as well as the 1978 competition). Following his retirement as a player, Passarella took up a career **coaching**, including a spell managing the Argentina national team in the 1990s. In 2009, he was elected as the president of his old club, River Plate.

PEDERNERA, ADOLFO. B. 18 November 1918, Avellaneda, Argentina. D. 12 May 1995. Adolfo Pedernera was part of the great **River Plate** team of the 1930s and 1940s in his native **Argentina** and was a key member of their magical forward line known as the "Machine." Pedernera orchestrated play from up and down the field. He roamed the field tirelessly to create chances and to score prolifically himself, scoring more than 100 goals for the club from 1933 to 1946. He moved to **Colombia** to play for **Club Deportivo Los Millonarios** from 1949 to 1953 and returned to Argentina to join Huracán for one final season before retiring in 1954. Pedernera played 36 games for Argentina, tallying 18 goals and winning the **Copa América** in both 1941 and 1945. *See also* LABRUNA, ÁNGEL; MORENO, MANUEL JOSÉ.

PELÉ. B. 23 October 1940, Três Corações, Brazil. Born Edison Arantes do Nascimento, but known universally as "Pelé," the Brazilian is the most legendary player in the history of soccer. Pelé won three **FIFA World Cups** with **Brazil** in his international career, from 1957 to 1971, scoring 77 goals in 92 games for his country. Pelé played most of his club career for **Santos Futebol Club** in Brazil, scoring 474 goals in just 438 games. In 2002, he was named joint winner of the FIFA Player of the Century Award, sharing the honor with **Argentina**'s **Diego Maradona**.

Pelé made his professional debut at the age of 15 for Santos and shot to worldwide fame with his international tournament debut for Brazil in the 1958 World Cup finals in **Sweden**. At the age of just 17, Pelé became the youngest scorer in World Cup history in Brazil's quarterfinal against Wales, then scored a **hat-trick** as Brazil beat **France** 5-2 in the semifinals. In the final against the hosts, Sweden, Pelé again scored twice, capping a mesmerizing tournament. Swedish player Sigge Parling said later, "After the fifth goal, I felt like applauding."

At club level, Pelé then led Santos to victorious **Copa Libertadores** campaigns in 1962 and 1963, followed by back-to-back **Intercontinental Cup** titles. In the 1962 World Cup finals, Pelé played in only two games due to a groin injury, Brazil winning the final without him. He was injured again in the group stage of the 1966 World Cup finals, Brazil departing early. The 1970 World Cup finals, though, would prove to be the crowning glory of Pelé's career: the first finals broadcast in Technicolor, Brazil's glorious run to the title included a legendary 4-1 mauling of **Italy** in the final, including Brazil's 100th FIFA World Cup goal through a powerful header by Pelé.

Pelé would not appear in another World Cup but did achieve further fame in the **United States** by joining the New York Cosmos in 1975 and playing three seasons in the **North American Soccer League** (NASL). Pelé retired from playing following the Cosmos' victory in the 1977 NASL Soccer Bowl championship. Unlike many other legendary players of his generation, Pelé has not taken up a **coaching** career in retirement and has instead pursued commercial activities and an ambassadorial role for world soccer.

PELÉ, ABÉDI. B. 5 November 1964, Accra, Ghana. Abédi Pelé, born Abédi Ayew but renaming himself after the legendary Brazilian star **Pelé**, was a three-time African Footballer of the Year and a key player for the **Ghana** national team. He won the **Africa Cup of Nations** with Ghana in 1983. Pelé played for a dozen clubs in his long career, from 1978 to 2000, his most significant success coming with **Olympique de Marseille** in **France**, with whom he won the 1993 **UEFA Champions League**.

PENALTY KICK. A penalty kick, awarded for a **foul** in the penalty area on the attacking team that is punishable by a direct **free kick**, is taken from 12 yards out with only the **goalkeeper** allowed to defend his **goal**. The penalty kick is taken after the **referee** blows his whistle, and all players, aside from the goalkeeper, must be at least 10 yards away from the ball at this point. The goalkeeper himself must stay on his goal line until the ball is kicked. The penalty kick taker cannot strike the ball a second time until another player has touched it. The penalty kick was introduced to the game in 1891 by the **International Football Association Board (IFAB)** as a way to punish fouls committed near the goal, though the penalty area itself was not marked out as it is presently until 1902. In recent times, penalty kicks have also been used in a **penalty shoot-out** as competitions to force a positive result after a tied game. *See also* LAWS OF THE GAME.

PENALTY SHOOT-OUT. In order to force a result that will eliminate one team following a tied game, penalty shoot-out competitions are sometimes used. Penalty shoot-outs usually consist of five kicks taken alternately by each team, with all players, except for the penalty kick taker and the opposing

goalkeeper, restricted to the center circle. The goalkeeper is required to stay on the **goal** line until the ball is kicked, in the same manner as a regular **penalty kick**, from a spot directly 12 yards out from the center of the goal line. The rules for penalty shoot-outs are provided for in the **Laws of the Game**. Each penalty kick taker may only strike the ball once and thus cannot score from a rebound. Each player may take only one penalty kick until all players on his team have also taken a kick, and only players on the field at the end of regular play are allowed to take a kick. The team with the most successful attempts on goal after five penalty kicks is the winner; if the shoot-out score is tied at this point, kicks proceed on a sudden-death basis, with as many further rounds of penalties taken as needed to determine a winner.

Penalty shoot-outs have been used in various competitions since the 1950s but only became particularly prominent in the 1970s, when they began to be used to break ties in European competitions, such as the **European Cup**. The first penalty shoot-out in a **FIFA World Cup** finals tournament came in 1982, with perhaps the most famous shoot-out of all time coming in the 1994 World Cup in the **United States**, **Brazil** defeating **Italy** on penalty kicks in the final of the competition. Penalty shoot-outs remain controversial and are often criticized for the seemingly arbitrary way in which they are used to determine a winner of the game outside the regular run of play. However, no alternate way of quickly settling the result of a tied game, in order to eliminate one team, has been generally agreed to be superior.

PEÑAROL. The oldest club in **Uruguay**, based in the capital, Montevideo, Peñarol has enjoyed considerable success, both domestically and on the international stage, with 36 professional national championships, five **Copa Libertadores** titles, and three **Intercontinental Cup** victories. It was founded as a sports club by a mainly British group of railway workers in 1891 and was originally known as "Central Uruguay Railway Cricket Club." But it has become best known for the soccer division of the club and has become commonly known simply as "Peñarol." Along with their city rivals, **Nacional**, Peñarol dominated Uruguayan football in the 20th century. The club won its first championship in 1905. The 1960s and 1980s were Peñarol's strongest decades in international play, winning the Copa Libertadores in 1960, 1961, 1966, 1982, and 1987. *See also* ESTADIO DE CENTENARIO; FIGUEROA, ELÍAS; GHIGGIA, ALCIDES; SCHIAFFINO, JUAN ALBERTO; VARELA, OBDULIO.

PERU. With a large expatriate British community playing the game at sporting clubs in the Peruvian capital, Lima, by the 1890s, Peru was one of the first South American countries to adopt soccer as a national sport. The game quickly spread to working-class urban communities, and Lima had an organized soccer league by the first decade of the 20th century. Peruvian soccer was semiprofessional by the 1930s, and this was reflected in its international emergence that decade, Peru reaching the quarterfinals of the 1936 **Olympic Games Football Tournament** and losing in a controversial replay to **Austria**, and then winning the 1939 **Copa América**. Peru has appeared in the **FIFA World Cup** on four occasions, though there was a long break between their first appearance in 1930, at the inaugural World Cup, and their next appearance in 1970, when their stylish team reached the quarterfinals, their best result to date. Peru also appeared at the 1978 and 1982 World Cups. In 1975, Peru won their second Copa América title, beating **Colombia** in the final.

Peruvian domestic soccer struggled to establish itself in the early decades of the 20th century, especially given the geographic difficulties and expense of navigating across the Andean nation. This was tragically illustrated in 1987 when a navy transport plane carrying the Alianza Lima club team crashed in the Pacific Ocean on approach to Lima. No Peruvian team has won South America's premier club competition, the **Copa Libertadores**, though Sporting Cristal of Lima reached the final in 1997, losing to Cruzeiro of **Brazil**, which matched the achievement of Peru's most successful club, Universitario, in 1972. *See also* CUBILLAS, TEÓFILO; LIMA NATIONAL STADIUM DISASTER.

PIOLA, SILVIO. B. 29 September 1913, Robbio Lomellina, Italy. D. 4 October 1996. Silvio Piola is perhaps the best striker ever produced by **Italy**. He is the all-time top scorer in the top Italian league, *Serie A*. He scored five goals at the 1938 **FIFA World Cup** for his country, as they won their second World Cup title. Piola scored twice in the final. He scored a total of 30 goals for Italy, using his height, speed, and athleticism to dominate defenders physically. Though Piola's career was interrupted by the Second World War, Piola's goal-scoring record in *Serie A* remains unbeaten, the bulk of his strikes coming for Lazio and Novara Calcio.

PITCH. *See* FIELD.

PLÁNIČKA, FRANTIŠEK. B. 2 June 1904, Prague, Austria-Hungary. D. 20 July 1996. František Plánička was a star **goalkeeper** for **Czechoslovakia** in the 1920s and 1930s. He was a one-club player, appearing almost 1,000 times for Slavia Prague. With that club, Plánička won eight Czech league titles and the **Mitropa Cup** in 1932. He played 76 times for Czechoslovakia and was their goalkeeper at the 1934 **FIFA World Cup**, earning a runners-up medal and losing to **Italy** in the final. He also played for his country at the 1938 World Cup. Though small of stature, Plánička was extremely agile and brave, and was known for his fair play on the field. He retired in 1939.

PLATINI, MICHEL. B. 21 June 1955, Jœuf, France. A French former national-team player and manager, Platini is now an administrator and the current president of the **Union of European Football Associations (UEFA)**. A midfielder blessed with considerable flair and a remarkable eye for goals, Platini played for **France** from 1976 to 1987, scoring 41 goals in 72 games. Platini was the **European Footballer of the Year** for three years straight, from 1983 to 1985. He captained France to the **UEFA European Football Championship** title in 1984, a tournament in which he was the top scorer with nine goals. France reached the **FIFA World Cup** semifinals twice with Platini, finishing fourth in 1982 and third in 1986.

Platini's club career was just as successful. He played for AS Nancy-Lorraine and AS Saint-Étienne in France, and moved to **Juventus** in **Italy** for the peak of his career, from 1982 to 1987. Platini captained Juventus to two Italian league championships and to victory in the **European Cup** in 1985, in a final overshadowed by the **Heysel Disaster**. Platini retired from playing in 1987.

After retirement, Platini managed the French national team for four years without great success before playing a key part in organizing the 1998 World Cup finals in France. This launched Platini's highly successful career as a soccer administrator: he joined the **FIFA Executive Committee** in 2002 and became the president of the Union of European Football Associations (UEFA) in 2007, defeating incumbent president Lennart Johansson in a tightly contested election. As UEFA president, Platini has attempted to spread European soccer's wealth to the eastern countries of the continent and has made strides to focus attention on the need for financial fair play among clubs.

POHANG STEELERS. Founded in 1973, Pohang Steelers have been, arguably, the leading club team in the **Republic of Korea** since the 1980s and one of the top teams in Asian continental club competition. They are based in the eastern Korean city of Pohang, in the province of North Gyeongsang, and their 25,000-capacity **stadium**, specifically built for Pohang Steelers in 1990, is known as "Steelyard Stadium." They were initially established as a company team by Park Tae-Joon, the president of Pohang Iron and Steel Company, and were known as the "POSCO Dolphins" and the "POSCO Atoms" before settling on their current name "Pohang Steelers" in 1997. That name change coincided with the start of a period of extraordinary success in Asian competition for the club, winning what is now known as the **AFC Champions League** in both 1997 and 1998, and again in 2009. Domestically, Pohang Steelers now have four league championships to their credit, won in 1986, 1988, 1992, and 2007, along with two Korean F.A. Cups won in 1996 and 2008. In 2009, Pohang Steelers finished in third place at the **FIFA Club**

World Cup, qualifying for the competition as a result of their 2007 AFC Champions League triumph and tying for the best finishing position by an Asian club in that competition.

POLAND. Soccer is now the most popular sport in Poland, but the sport came later to the country than to much of continental Europe due to the limited British presence in the country toward the end of the 19th century: the first teams were not formed until the first few years of the 20th century, with the strongest clubs emerging in the south of Poland in the city of Kraków. It would not be until the 1920s that a national structure for soccer was formed, with the formation of the Polish Football Association in 1919 (a year after Poland regained its independence), its affiliation with the **Fédération Internationale de Football Association (FIFA)** in 1923, and its joining the **Union of European Football Associations (UEFA)** in 1955.

In 1921, Poland crowned its first national league champions, KS Cracovia, and in 1927, Poland's top division, the *Ekstraklasa*, was founded. Poland's national team appeared for the first time at the **FIFA World Cup** in 1938, but did not fare well and did not appear again until 1974. The 1970s and 1980s proved to be a golden era for Polish soccer internationally: they finished in third place at the World Cup in both 1974 and 1982, and reached the last 16 in 1986 in **Mexico**. Poland would not qualify for another major tournament until the 2002 World Cup, where they exited at the first-round stage, which they did again at the same competition in 2006 in **Germany**. They did not qualify for the 2010 World Cup in **South Africa**. Poland will cohost the 2012 **UEFA European Football Championship**, a tournament they have only qualified for once in the past, the 2008 competition held in **Switzerland** and **Austria** at which they departed after the first round. *See also* BONIEK, ZBIGNIEW.

PORTO. *See* FUTEBOL CLUBE DO PORTO.

PORTUGAL. Soccer was introduced to Portugal in the late 19th century, brought back to the country by Portuguese students who had traveled to Britain. The first recorded game took place in October 1888. The governing body of soccer in Portugal, the Portuguese Football Federation (FPF, or *Federação Portuguesa de Futebol*, in Portuguese), was founded in 1914, formally affiliated with the **Fédération Internationale de Football Association (FIFA)** in 1923, and was a founding member of the **Union of European Football Associations (UEFA)** in 1954. Portugal's men's national team made its first appearance in a **FIFA World Cup** in 1966, where it reached the semifinals (losing to eventual champions **England**). Legendary forward **Eusébio** was the top scorer in the tournament with nine goals. They finished in third place. Portugal has appeared in four further World Cups with their best result since 1966 being fourth place in 2006. In 2004, Portugal hosted the **UEFA European Football Championship** and reached the final, surprisingly losing at that stage to Greece. Portugal has experienced considerable success at international youth level, winning the **FIFA U-20 World Cup** in both 1989 and 1991.

Portugal has developed some of Europe's best club teams since its national championship was first established in 1933. In the 1960s, **Benfica**, Sporting Lisbon, and **Futebol Clube do Porto** all built expansive stadiums and became serious forces in European competition. Benfica, in particular, dominated European soccer in the early 1960s, winning the European Cup (now the **UEFA Champions League**) in both 1961 and 1962, inspired by their star player, Eusébio. Portuguese soccer, though, was hampered by its authoritarian political regime under António de Oliveira Salazar, as foreign players were not allowed to be imported to the country, and Portuguese talent could not go abroad to develop further. Following the end of the Salazar regime in 1974, Portuguese clubs established themselves as serious contenders for European prizes again, culminating with victory by Futebol Clube do Porto in the 1987 European Cup. In 2004, FC Porto won the UEFA Champions League under head **coach** José Mourinho. The country also produced two **FIFA World Players of the Year**, **Luis Figo** (in 2001) and **Cristiano Ronaldo** (in 2008). **Women's soccer** has been slow to develop in Portugal, the Portuguese women's national team yet to appear in a **FIFA Women's World Cup** or **UEFA Women's Championship** tournament.

POZZO, VITTORIO. B. 2 March 1886, Piedmont, Italy. D. 21 December 1968. An Italian coach, Vittorio Pozzo most famously led **Italy** to successive **FIFA World Cup** victories in 1934 and 1938. In 97 games as manager of Italy, spanning from 1929 to 1948, the country won 64 games, drew 17, and lost 16, an outstanding record. An Anglophile, Pozza had learned the game as a student in **England**, then went on to play professionally for Grasshopper-Club Zürich in **Switzerland**. In 1906, Pozza went back to Italy to play for Torino, taking over as manager in 1912. He took charge of the Italian team at both the 1912 and 1924 **Olympic Games Football Tournaments**, winning a bronze medal at the latter. Five years later, Pozzo took charge of the Italian national team full time, and led Italy to victory in the second World Cup tournament, held in Italy in 1934. A gold medal followed for Italy at the 1936 Olympic Games Football Tournament, and Pozzo became the first-and-still-only coach to win a second World Cup title in 1938 in France, beating a renowned **Hungary** team in the final. Pozzo's reputation as a soccer manager was impeccable, but postwar Italy looked unkindly on his accommodation to Benito Mussolini's fascist regime. So Pozzo moved on to work in soccer journalism for some years before his death in 1968.

PREMIER LEAGUE. The Premier League, consisting of 20 club teams, is the leading soccer competition in **England**. The season runs from August to May, with each team playing each other once at their own stadium and once at their opponent's stadium. A system of promotion and relegation means that the three lowest-placed teams at the end of each season are replaced by three teams from the top of the **Football League** each year. The Premier League is currently the richest league in the world and has the largest global **television** audience of any national league, with teams such as **Manchester United** and **Liverpool Football Club** attracting substantial worldwide support. The Premier League was launched in 1992, as 22 of the top clubs from the Football League decided to break away and form their own league, increasing their share of the television revenue the games generated through a considerable television rights deal from the Sky Television satellite service. In 1995, the number of clubs in the league was reduced to 20, and by the end of the 2009/2010 season, 44 different clubs had competed in the Premier League for at least one season. *See also* ARSENAL FOOTBALL CLUB; CHELSEA FOOTBALL CLUB.

PRINZ, BIRGIT. B. 25 October 1977, Frankfurt am Main, West Germany. A German female player, Prinz won the **FIFA Women's Player of the Year** award three times in a row from 2003 to 2005 and is generally considered the finest European player of her generation. She is one of the most prolific goal scorers in the history of **women's soccer**. A natural athlete who played several sports at junior level, Prinz began professional play at the age of 16 for FSV Frankfurt, using her superior frame and technique to score prolifically. She moved to FFC Frankfurt in 1994 and has won nine German league championships with that club since, spending one summer season playing in the **United States** with the Carolina Courage and winning the professional WUSA Championship. Internationally, Prinz made her debut at the age of 16 and then led **Germany** to consecutive **FIFA Women's World Cup** victories in 2003 and 2007, along with five **UEFA Women's Championship** titles, making her one of the most successful players of all time.

PROFESSIONALISM. England was the first country to introduce professionalism to soccer, in the 19th century. English soccer's governing body, **The Football Association**, legalized professionalism for its affiliated clubs in July 1885 after 22 years of struggling to protect the **amateur** ethos it had followed since its founding in 1863. Its original rule forbade any player from receiving payment for participation in any Football Association match. The spread of the game among the working class in England and the increasingly larger paying crowds attending games made professionalism inevitable eventually, particularly in the northwest of England in the early 1880s, further from the conservative upper-class attitude of the southern-based Football Association. Clubs in that area frequently recruited working-class players from **Scotland** in a form of creeping, half-hidden professionalism, and social prejudice against this practice by the ruling southern elite fed into a bitter battle over the legalization of professionalism. Northern clubs threatened to break away and form their own British Football Association in 1884 in response to complaints in London about their payments to players for the time they missed from work.

The Football Association capitulated to the growing commercial tide in 1885, allowing professionalism under "certain restrictions," such as professionals wearing different colored shirts than did amateurs when representing England. These restrictions eventually disappeared as the game's rampant commercialism increasingly marginalized the obstinate amateur element. Those holdouts eventually formed their own Amateur Football Association in the early 20th century, and their ethos was epitomized by the gentleman's amateur club, **Corinthian Football Club**. Overseas, professionalism of the sport proceeded at wildly varying paces from country to country, with the French league turning entirely professional by 1933 but the German league not following suit until well after the Second World War, for example. But as the global game has grown, most countries now have professional men's leagues, and professional women's leagues such as **Women's Professional Soccer** (established in 2007) are also starting to appear.

PUSKÁS, FERENC. B. 2 April 1927, Kispest, Hungary. D. 17 November 2006. Ranked by most observers among the greatest players of all time, Ferenc Puskás' graceful play was at the heart of the success of his national team, **Hungary**, and his club team, **Real Madrid**, in the 1950s. Puskás grew up in poverty in Kispest, a town on the outskirts of Budapest, and made his debut for his local team, Kispest FC, as a teenager. His phenomenal talent was immediately recognized nationally, and he made his debut for Hungary at the age of just 18 in August 1945. Kispest FC won five league titles, and Puskás was the leading scorer in the domestic Hungarian championship several times between 1949 and 1956. Puskás was strong, yet immensely skilled and creative with the ball, blessed with a lethal goal-scoring ability. He then achieved international fame, as Hungary's fluid movement and incisive passing, under the coaching of the brilliant **Gusztáv Sebes**, became the envy of the world, Puskás at the heart of the team that went unbeaten for four years, from 1950 to 1954, and won the **Olympic Games Football Tournament** in 1952. In 1953, Hungary famously humiliated **England** at **Wembley Stadium**, destroying a country that still considered themselves the masters of the game 6-3 with Puskás playing a starring role.

Glory in the **FIFA World Cup** was denied Puskás and Hungary the next year, however, as they surprisingly lost in the final of the 1954 tournament to **West Germany**. Puskás received some blame for the defeat despite the fact he had not been fully fit for the final. Not long after the suppressed 1956 uprising in Hungary, Puskás fled to Spain, staying in Bilbao as his club team visited there for a game and receiving a 15-month suspension from the game as a result. He resumed his career in 1958 when he signed for Real Madrid in **Spain**. Alongside the brilliant **Alfredo di Stéfano**, Real Madrid went on a run of success never since matched in European club soccer, with five domestic championships from 1961 to 1965. The crowning moment for Puskás was his outstanding performance in the 1960 **European Cup** final against Eintracht Frankfurt, won 7-1 by Real Madrid. Puskás scored four goals. Puskás then appeared in the 1962 FIFA World Cup, this time for Spain. The team performed poorly and was eliminated at the first stage. His international career with Spain spanned just four games, with no goals scored, a pale comparison to his remarkable performances for Hungary, for whom he scored 83 goals in 84 games. Puskás retired from playing in 1967, took up a **coaching** career in Greece, and led Panathinaikos to two domestic league championships in 1971 and 1972, and a runners-up finish in the 1971 European Cup. He then moved on to coach **Colo Colo** in **Chile** from 1976 to 1978 before retiring to his native Hungary, where he has ever since been generally recognized as their greatest player of all time.

R

RACING CLUB. Based in Buenos Aires, **Argentina**, Racing Club de Avellane—commonly known simply as "Racing Club"—is one of the biggest and most successful clubs in South America. Founded in 1903, they have won seven Argentinean league titles. On the international stage, Racing Club won the **Copa Libertadores** in 1967 and, most famously, followed that triumph with victory in the **Intercontinental Cup**. A classic two-legged series against Celtic went to a third, deciding play-off game, a brutal affair won by Racing Club 1-0 in **Estadio de Centenario**, **Uruguay**. Since 1950, Racing Club has played at Estadio Juan Domingo Perón.

RAMSEY, SIR ALF. B. 22 January 1920, Dagenham, London, England. D. 28 April 1999. Sir Alf Ramsey remains the only man to have managed **England** to victory in the **FIFA World Cup**, winning on home soil in 1966. Ramsey was born to a working-class background in London, had a distinguished playing career for Southampton and Tottenham Hotspur, and retired in 1955. He then began his managerial career with Ipswich Town before moving on to the England job, replacing Walter Winterbottom in 1963. He became the first England manager to gain sole control of team selection and training, which previously had been subject to considerable interference from **The Football Association**'s committees. With England, Ramsey managed with discipline but also formed a bond with his players and was unafraid of tactical innovation, introducing a formation known as the "wingless wonders" that proved to be critical to England's success at the 1966 World Cup finals tournament. This was crowned with England's 4-2 win over West **Germany** at **Wembley Stadium** after extra time in the final of the World Cup. A small, but slow, decline followed in the subsequent years of Ramsey's tenure as England manager. They finished third at the 1968 **UEFA European Football Championship**, losing to **Yugoslavia**, and then lost 3-2 to West Germany in the quarterfinals of the 1970 World Cup. Ramsey's England would fall again to West Germany at the 1972 UEFA European Football Championship, in the qualifying tournament. Ramsey's tenure would be ended by England's failure to qualify for the 1974 World Cup; the crucial game was a failure to beat **Poland** at home. Ramsey's overall record as England manager was, however, exceptional: 113 games played, 69 won, 27 drawn, and only 17 lost. England, after considerable underachievement in the international game before Ramsey's tenure, established themselves as a world power under his guidance. In 2002, four years after his death, Ramsey was an inaugural inductee into the English Football Hall of Fame.

RANGERS FOOTBALL CLUB. Rangers, from Glasgow, have been one of the two dominant teams in the history of soccer in **Scotland**, along with their bitter local rivals, **Glasgow Celtic**, the two collectively known as the "Old Firm." Rangers were officially founded in January 1873, some months after their first informal game took place. An original member of the Scottish Football League in 1890, they won their first of 52 domestic League Championships in 1899, remarkably winning all 18 league games that season. In the 20th century, Rangers were long dogged by a common belief that they had an unofficial policy against signing Catholic players, and their Old Firm rivalry with Celtic, a historically Catholic club, was marked by religious tension. Rangers did not sign their first high-profile, openly Catholic player until Mo Johnston joined them in 1989. Rangers' stadium, Ibrox, has been their home since 1899 and holds the record for league attendance at a British stadium, 118,567 for a game against Celtic in January 1939. Two major disasters have taken place at the stadium: in 1902, during an **England** versus Scotland international game with 68,000 in attendance, part of the western stand collapsed, killing 25 people and injuring at least 500 more spectators. In 1971, 36 fans were killed on their way out of Ibrox after a Rangers versus Celtic game when crash barriers collapsed. The stadium has since been redeveloped, with a current capacity of a little more than 50,000. *See also* LAUDRUP, BRIAN.

REAL MADRID. One of the world's most famous clubs, **Real Madrid** has only **Barcelona** for serious competition as **Spain**'s most successful team. They have won the Spanish championship 31 times since their founding in March 1902, winning their first official title, the Madrid Championship, in 1905. The club's president from 1904 to 1908, Carlos Padrós, played a key role in the creation of that championship and was a key figure in the formation of global soccer's governing body, the **Fédération Internationale de Football Association (FIFA)** in 1904. In 1909, Real Madrid became founding members of the Spanish Football Association. Real Madrid was dominant in regional competition over the next two decades, winning 12 of the 18 Madrid Championships contested. They then joined the Spanish Championship, formed in 1929, going undefeated and winning the title in 1932, and triumphing again the next year, led by star player Ricardo Zamora, though they would not win it again until 1954.

The 1950s would establish Real Madrid's global fame with a decade of unparalleled success in European competition under club president Santiago Bernabéu. The turning point for the club had come in 1950 with the signing of **Alfredo di Stéfano**, the brilliant Argentinean player who, along with Hungarian **Ferenc Puskás**, led Real Madrid to continental glory as they remarkably won the first five iterations of the **European Cup**, founded in 1955. That unmatched fifth consecutive title in 1960 was marked by one of the greatest club performances of all time, when Real Madrid, wearing what was by then a world-famous all-white strip, crushed Eintracht Frankfurt 7-3 in the final at Hampden Park in Glasgow, **Scotland**. A few months later, Real Madrid won the inaugural **Intercontinental Cup**, defeating **Peñarol** of **Uruguay**. They won the European Cup for a sixth time in 1966, though they did not win it again until 1998. They had further European Cup triumphs in 2000 and 2002, featuring the remarkable talents of Raúl, **Zinedine Zidane**, and the Brazilian **Ronaldo** in this period. The club is now a marketing colossus, the world's richest club, and constantly competing with Barcelona in a heated rivalry known as *el clásico* on the field. *See also* BECKHAM, DAVID; BREITNER, PAUL; CANNAVARO, FABIO; ESTADIO SANTIAGO BERNABÉU; FIGO, LUIS; GENTO, FRANCISCO; GORDILLO, RAFAEL; KAKÁ; KOPA, RAYMOND; LAUDRUP, MICHAEL; OWEN, MICHAEL; RONALDO, CRISTIANO; SÁNCHEZ, HUGO; VALDANO, JORGE; ZAMORA, RICARDO; ZAMORANO, IVÁN.

RED STAR BELGRADE. Red Star Belgrade is a club from Serbia based in the capital, Belgrade, known as *Crvena Zvezda* in the Serbian language. They are the most successful club from the country and have often been highly successful in European competition, winning the **European Cup** and the **Intercontinental Cup** in 1991, the only **Yugoslavian** club to win those competitions before the country's breakup the following year. Red Star Belgrade is by far the most popular club in Yugoslavia, though it has a fierce rivalry with nearby FK Partizan. Red Star Belgrade plays in the 55,000-capacity **stadium** known as *Stadion Crvena Zvezda*.

REFEREE. The referee enforces the **Laws of the Game**. His duties, outlined in Law 5, include controlling the match in cooperation with his **assistant referees**; ensuring all equipment meets the stated requirements; acting as official timekeeper; taking disciplinary action; stopping the game for injuries; and stopping, suspending, or abandoning a match because of outside interference. According to the Laws of the Game, "The decisions of the referee regarding facts connected with play, including whether or not a goal is scored and the result of the match, are final."

RIJKAARD, FRANK. B. 30 September 1962, Amsterdam, Netherlands. Frank Rijkaard was a leading player for the **Netherlands** at international level and for clubs including **Ajax Amsterdam** and **AC Milan** during the 1980s and 1990s. Rijkaard appeared for the Netherlands at two **FIFA World Cup** tournaments, progressing to the second round in 1990 and the quarterfinals in 1994, but his greatest international success came starring for the great Dutch team at the 1988 **UEFA European Football Championship**, where the Netherlands won their first major international competition. At club level, Rijkaard won the Dutch league five times with his local club Ajax Amsterdam in two spells in the mid-1980s and mid-1990s, and won the **UEFA Champions League** in 1995 during his second period playing for the club. This followed considerable success playing in **Italy** for AC Milan with fellow Dutch stars **Ruud Gullit** and **Marco van Basten**, winning the European Cup and the **Intercontinental Cup** in both 1989 and 1990, later winning two Italian league championships, in 1992 and 1993. Rijkaard was an all-around talent who usually played in midfield, equally adept at defending or attacking. He took up a **coaching** career after his retirement from playing in 1995, going on, most notably, to manage the Netherlands and **Barcelona**, taking the **Spanish** club to UEFA Champions League glory in 2006.

RIMET, JULES. B. 14 October 1873, Theuley-les-Lavoncourt, France. D. 16 October 1956. The third president of the **Fédération Internationale de Football Association (FIFA)**, Rimet was the key figure behind the launch of the **FIFA World Cup** and its rise to become the leading global soccer tournament. Rimet was a grocer's son who won a scholarship to obtain his law degree in Paris. He never played soccer himself, but in 1897, along with several friends in **France**'s capital, he founded Red Star Football Club 93 and began his odyssey in world soccer administration. In 1911, Rimet was instrumental in the foundation of France's first national league and was its first president. In 1919, he also founded the *Fédération Française de Football* (FFF), French soccer's governing body, and remained its president until 1949. Rimet became heavily involved with FIFA's activities and was named temporary president of the organization during the **Olympic Games** of 1920. He was confirmed to the position permanently the next year, succeeding the late **Daniel Burley Woolfall**. Rimet began to push for FIFA to organize its own world championship for national teams, and the **FIFA Executive Committee** set up a special committee to study the possibility in 1926. Two years later at the **FIFA Congress** in Amsterdam, a 25-5 vote approved a World Cup competition to be held every four years. The **FIFA Congress** of 1929 determined the inaugural tournament should take place in 1930, and **Uruguay**—two-time Olympic champions in 1924 and 1928—was selected as the host nation, promising to build new stadiums and pay for the competing teams' travel expenses. Though the British associations refused to participate, the tournament was a success, won by hosts Uruguay, who defeated **Argentina** 4-2 in the final.

This set the stage for subsequent World Cup finals to be held in **Italy** (1934), France (1938), **Brazil** (1950), and **Switzerland** (1954) under Rimet's reign, leading him to be aptly called the "Father of the World Cup." In 1946, during Rimet's 25th year as president, the World Cup was renamed the **Jules Rimet Trophy** in recognition of his efforts in establishing the competition. Eight years later, Rimet stood down from the FIFA presidency after overseeing his fifth World Cup competition and was named FIFA's first honorary president for life.

RIVA, LUIGI. B. 7 November 1944, Leggiuno, Italy. A prolific goal scorer, Luigi Riva—often known as Gigi Riva—played for **Italy** on 42 occasions, scoring an impressive 35 goals between 1965 and 1974 for his country. He was on the Italian team that won the 1968 **UEFA European Football Championship** and scored three goals at the 1970 **FIFA World Cup** finals tournament, Italy finishing as runners-up to **Brazil**. He appeared again for Italy at the 1974 World Cup, but the competition proved to be a disappointment for the Italians. At club level, Riva played almost his entire career for Cagliari, leading the club to the 1970 Italian league championship, their only triumph in that competition to date. He scored a total of 164 goals in 315 games for Cagliari from 1962 until his retirement in 1976.

RIVALDO. B. 19 April 1982, Paulista, Brazil. Rivaldo, born Vitor Borba Ferreira but universally known by that single name, was the **FIFA World Player of the Year** and the **European Footballer of the Year** in 1999. He played his first game for **Brazil** in December 1993 and has made 74 appearances since, scoring 34 goals and last playing for his country in 2003. A tall, hugely talented, attacking midfielder, Rivaldo won the **FIFA World Cup** with Brazil in 2002 in the competition jointly hosted by the **Republic of Korea** and **Japan**. He played an important role in his country's winning run despite controversy in the first round, when he was fined for playacting after a dive against **Turkey**. At club level, Rivaldo's longest and most productive spell of play came for **Barcelona** in **Spain**, winning two Spanish league titles between 1997 and 2002, and scoring 136 goals in 253 games. Rivaldo also played for **AC Milan**, winning the **UEFA Champions League** with the **Italian** club in 2003.

RIVELINO, ROBERTO. B. 1 January 1946, São Paulo, Brazil. More commonly known simply as "Rivelino," the **Brazilian** starred for his country at three **FIFA World Cup** finals tournaments in the 1970s, scoring six goals in 13 games at those competitions. His crowning moment came in 1970 as Brazil won the World Cup in stylish fashion, with Rivelino linking up impressively with fellow star **Pelé** and the rest of an outstanding team, perhaps the greatest in World Cup history. Rivelino was an imaginative midfield player with an impressive passing range and was an excellent taker of **free kicks**. Rivelino played for Brazil a total of 92 times, between 1965 and 1978, scoring 26 goals. He played most of his career in his native country, mainly for **Corinthians Football Club**, but also appeared for Fluminese. He ended his career in **Saudi Arabia**, playing for **Al-Hilal** from 1978 to 1991.

RIVER PLATE. One of South America's most successful club teams, "Club Atlético River Plate," as they are formally known, or "River Plate," as they are commonly known, was founded in Buenos Aires, **Argentina**, in May 1901. They began life as a general sporting club and became best known for their soccer division, led by their first president, Leopoldo Bard. Their distinctive jersey design, all white with a diagonal red stripe, was inspired by a red ribbon pinned across their jersey in their early days. River Plate has won 33 domestic national league championships (the most in Argentina), two South American championships in the **Copa Libertadores**, and one **Intercontinental Cup**. They are based in the Núñez district of Buenos Aires and play at the Estadio Antonio Vespucio Liberti (usually known as "*El Monumental*" or the "Chocolate Box"), named after River Plate president Vespucio Liberti. El Monumental is also the home stadium for most of Argentina's national team games. The club has been home to many of Argentina's greatest-ever players, including the incomparable **Alfredo di Stéfano**. River Plate has a fierce rival in fellow Buenos Aires residents **Boca Juniors**, the two clubs playing in always-combustible contests each season known as the *Superclásico. See also* FRANCESCOLI, ENZO; LABRUNA, ÁNGEL; MORENO, MANUEL JOSÉ; PASSARELLA, DANIEL; PEDERNERA, ADOLFO; SÍVORI, OMAR.

RIVERA, GIANNI. B. 18 August 1943, Alessandria, Italy. One of **Italy**'s greatest-ever players, Gianni Rivera starred for his club team, **AC Milan**, and for his country in the 1960s and 1970s. In 1969, Rivera became the first Italian to win the **European Footballer of the Year** award. A playmaking midfielder, Rivera won a total of three Italian league championships with AC Milan, along with the **European Cup** title in both 1963 and 1969. He made a total of 658 appearances for AC Milan, scoring 158 goals. Rivera's international career with Italy was equally successful, winning the 1968 **UEFA European Football Championship**, and reaching the final of the 1970 **FIFA**

World Cup. Rivera appeared only briefly in Italy's defeat to **Brazil**. His last appearance for Italy came at the 1974 World Cup, Italy exiting in the first round. Rivera played a total of 60 games for Italy, scoring 14 goals.

ROMÁRIO. B. 29 January 1966, Rio de Janeiro, Brazil. Born Romário de Souza Faria but universally known solely as "Romário," he was a Brazilian forward blessed with a remarkable goal-scoring ability, scorer of 55 goals in 70 games for **Brazil**'s national team. He played on the Brazil team that won the 1994 **FIFA World Cup**, scoring five goals, and was named the tournament's best player. He was named **FIFA World Player of the Year** in 1994 following the World Cup. Romário's long career in club soccer spanned 1985 to 2009. He appeared for almost a dozen different club teams, most notably for Vasco de Gama in Brazil, PSV Eindhoven in the **Netherlands**, and a prolific spell for **Spanish** giants **Barcelona**, where he scored 53 goals in 82 games between 1993 and 1995. In the 1993–1994 season, Romário scored a remarkable 30 goals in 33 league games for Barcelona as the team won the Spanish league championship.

ROMERO, JULIO CÉSAR. B. 28 August 1960, Luque, Paraguay. Arguably **Paraguay's** greatest-ever player, Julio César Romero is sometimes known as "Romerito." His playing career lasted from 1977 to 1996, including spells with clubs in the **United States**, **Brazil**, and **Spain**, and he won the 1985 South American Footballer of the Year award. Romero was an attacking midfielder with a goal-scoring touch and appeared for Paraguay at the 1986 **FIFA World Cup**, scoring two goals in four games at the competition, Paraguay reaching the last 16.

RONALDINHO. B. 21 March 1980, Porto Alegre, Brazil. **Brazil**'s Ronaldinho was born Ronaldo de Assis Moreira, but is known universally as "Ronaldinho." He won both the **FIFA World Player of the Year** and **European Footballer of the Year** awards in 2005 while starring for **Barcelona in Spain**. He was also FIFA World Player of the Year in 2004. He played for Barcelona from 2003 to 2008, winning the Spanish league title twice and the **UEFA Champions League** in 2006. Ronaldinho moved to **AC Milan** in 2008 but has since struggled to reproduce the form of his years in Spain. He has also starred for Brazil's national team, making his debut at the age of 19 in 1999 against Latvia, and has scored 32 goals in 87 games since. He won the **FIFA World Cup** with Brazil in 2002 at the tournament held in the **Republic of Korea** and **Japan** and scored two goals in five games, though he also received a red card in Brazil's quarterfinal game against **England**.

RONALDO. B. 18 September 1976, Rio de Janeiro, Brazil. Commonly known simply as "Ronaldo," Ronaldo Luis Nazário de Lima is a Brazilian player and one of only two players to have twice won the **FIFA World Player of the Year** award. Ronaldo is regarded as one of the best goal scorers in the history of the game and has an unusual combination of pace, power, and finesse in his play. Ronaldo has twice won the **FIFA World Cup** playing with his native **Brazil**. He did not play in Brazil's victory in the 1994 World Cup in the **United States**, though he collected a winners' medal as a squad member. In the 2002 World Cup, he scored eight goals to win the Golden Shoe as the tournament's leading scorer, leading Brazil to their record fifth World Cup triumph. At the 2006 World Cup, Ronaldo tallied his 15th goal in World Cup play, setting a new record by passing the previous mark of 14 goals held by **Gerd Müller**. Between 1994 and 2006, Ronaldo scored a remarkable 62 goals in 97 games in his international career. Ronaldo began his professional club career with Brazilian team Cruzeiro before moving to Europe and starring for PSV Eindhoven in the **Netherlands**, **Barcelona** in **Spain**, **Internazionale** in **Italy**, **Real Madrid** back in Spain, **AC Milan** on a return to Italy, and from 2009, **Corinthians** in Brazil. In 2010, Ronaldo announced that he would retire from playing after the 2011 season in Brazil.

RONALDO, CRISTIANO. B. 5 February 1985, Madeira, Portugal. Born Cristiano Ronaldo dos Santos Aveiro but known the world over simply as "Cristiano Ronaldo," **Portugal**'s Ronaldo is one of the world's leading players and was the **FIFA World Player of the Year** and the **European Footballer of the Year** in 2008. Ronaldo had appeared 76 times for Portugal's national team as of August 2010, helping lead his country to fourth place at the 2006 **FIFA World Cup** and to the runners-up position at the 2004 **UEFA European Football Championship**. A dynamic winger and forward blessed with remarkable speed, athleticism, balance, and ball skills, Ronaldo has also enjoyed a very successful club career. He began his professional career with Sporting Club in his native Portugal in 2003, moving on to **Manchester United** in **England** that year and winning numerous trophies over the next five years, including three **Premier League** titles, one **Football Association Challenge Cup**, one **FIFA Club World Cup**, and the **UEFA Champions League** in 2008. Following that triumph, Ronaldo requested a move to **Real Madrid** in **Spain**. He departed in a controversial transfer with the Spanish club making him the most expensive player in the history of the sport. Ronaldo has yet to win a trophy with Real Madrid as of August 2010.

ROSSI, PAOLO. B. 23 September 1956, Prato, Italy. Italian forward Paolo Rossi was the star player for **Italy** at the **1982 FIFA World Cup**, the tournament's top scorer as his country won the World Cup for the third time. Rossi was also awarded the Golden Ball as the tournament's top player. Rossi's success at that World Cup came as a surprise to many, as he had only recently returned to play before the tournament after serving a two-year ban from soccer for his involvement in an Italian match-fixing scandal. Rossi had made his name at the previous World Cup tournament in 1978, scoring three goals as Italy finished in fourth place. In the 1982 World Cup, despite a slow start in the early matches, Rossi scored six goals to win the Golden Shoe as the tournament's top scorer, including scoring one in the final as Italy defeated West **Germany** 3-1 to win the World Cup for the third time. Following the tournament, Rossi won the 1982 **European Footballer of the Year Award**. At club level, Rossi then went on to achieve spectacular success playing for **Juventus**, with whom he won the Italian championship in 1982 and 1984, and the **European Cup** in 1985, playing alongside the brilliant Frenchman **Michel Platini**. Physically, Rossi was not endowed with outstanding pace or strength, but he was an intelligent goal-poaching striker, always ready to pounce on any opportunity around the **goal**. Rossi retired in 1987.

ROUS, SIR STANLEY. B. 25 April 1895, Watford, England. D. 18 July 1986. The sixth president of world soccer's governing body, **Fédération Internationale de Football Association (FIFA)**, Sir Stanley Rous oversaw the growth of the **FIFA World Cup** into an event of global significance with the finals held in **England** in 1966 and **Mexico** in 1970 during his tenure as FIFA president from 1961 to 1974.

Rous began his career in professional soccer as an elite referee after the First World War, taking charge of the 1934 **Football Association Challenge Cup** final. The same year, he was elected as the Secretary of **The Football Association**, a position he held until 1961. Rous was known for his patient and thoughtful diplomacy, leading revisions to the **Laws of the Game** as a member of the **International Football Association Board (IFAB)**, including the introduction of yellow and red cards and a modernization of **refereeing** in general. Rous spearheaded the return of the British national associations to FIFA membership in 1947. He became closely involved with FIFA, becoming the chairman of the FIFA referees' committee and helping draft updated FIFA statutes. He was knighted in Great Britain for his efforts in organizing the 1948 London Olympic Games and was the obvious choice to replace **Arthur Drewry** as FIFA president in 1961 after his fellow Englishman died in office. Under Rous, the FIFA World Cup reached a new level of prominence and exposure on **television** while FIFA's membership expanded considerably, and he continued the modernization of the Laws of the Game. Perhaps the most memorable moment of his FIFA presidency personally for

Rous came in 1966, when England won the World Cup for the first time, on home soil, at **Wembley Stadium** in London.

Rous' presidency was not without controversy. In 1966, all African member nations of FIFA boycotted the World Cup after FIFA refused to offer the **Confederation of African Football** a direct qualification spot for one of its member nations in the finals. Rous' failure to develop strong relations with the non-European members of FIFA proved to be the downfall of his regime and reflected his conservative attitude in an era of postcolonial development. There was continued controversy over his perceived support for the apartheid regime in **South Africa**. **João Havelange** outmaneuvered Rous in the elections for the FIFA presidency in the **FIFA Congress** of 1974, playing on Rous' unpopularity in Africa and Asia by promising to expand the World Cup finals to 24 teams and include more places for developing nations. Rous was further hurt by the Communist bloc's displeasure at the continued exclusion of **China** from FIFA membership, as he refused to expel Taiwan from FIFA. Rous' fate was sealed by his expulsion of the Soviet Union from the 1974 World Cup for refusing to play a qualifying tie in **Chile** at the notorious National Stadium, where Chilean dictator General Augusto Pinochet's forces had massacred many opposition figures. Rous also supported the continued FIFA membership of the racist South African Football Association (FASA), to the chagrin of many African nations pushing for exclusion of the apartheid-era regime from world sport. Havelange, meanwhile, traveled broadly to canvas support from outside the European establishment. The election for FIFA presidency at the FIFA Congress in Frankfort shortly before the 1974 World Cup finals saw Havelange defeat Rous by a count of 68 to 52 in the second round of voting. Upon leaving office, Rous was elected a lifetime FIFA honorary president.

ROYAL SPORTING CLUB ANDERLECHT. Usually known simply as "Anderlecht," this Brussels-based club is the most-storied team in **Belgium**, with a particularly notable period of success between 1976 and 1983. Anderlecht was founded on 27 May 1908 and began to dominate Belgian soccer following World War II, winning their 30th domestic league championship in 2010. They have also achieved considerable success in European competition, winning both the **UEFA Cup Winners' Cup** and the **UEFA Super Cup** in 1976 as well as in 1978, and the **UEFA Cup** in 1983. *See also* SCIFO, ENZO; VAN HIMST, PAUL.

RUMMENIGGE, KARL-HEINZ. B. 25 September 1955, Lippstadt, Germany. Karl-Heinz Rummenigge is best known as a star player for **Bayern Munich** at club level and for West **Germany** internationally. He has a goal-scoring record matched by very few in the European game. He was named **European Footballer of the Year** in both 1980 and 1981. He began his professional career with Bayern Munich in 1974, going on to score 162 goals in 310 appearances in the German league for the club and winning two **European Cup** titles and two German league championships. In 1984, Rummenigge moved to **Internazionale** in **Italy**, playing three seasons without winning a major honor. Rummenigge enjoyed extraordinary success playing for West Germany, scoring 45 goals in 95 international games, winning the **UEFA European Football Championship** in 1980 and twice finishing as runner-up with his country at **FIFA World Cup** finals tournaments, in 1982 in **Spain** and 1986 in **Mexico**. Following retirement from playing in 1987, Rummenigge entered a successful career in soccer administration and is currently the chairman of Bayern Munich and the European Clubs Association. He also sits on the board of the German Football League.

RUNGRADO MAY DAY STADIUM. The largest **stadium** in the world that regularly hosts soccer games is Rungrado May Day Stadium, located in the capital city of North Korea, Pyongyang. Its capacity is 150,000. It was built for the World Festival of Youth and Stadiums, opened on 1 May 1989, and hosts North Korean national team games among other events.

RUSSIA. Soccer is the most popular sport in Russia, with almost one million registered players. The sport in Russia is governed by the Football Union of Russia (RFS), formed in 1992 following the collapse of the Union of Soviet Socialist Republics (USSR), replacing the Football Federation of the USSR's (FFUSSR) role in organizing soccer in the country as a member of the game's global governing body, **Fédération Internationale de Football Association (FIFA)**. In international soccer, Russia is credited by FIFA with the results of the Soviet Union's international team during the period of its existence, 1922–1991, though many of its leading players were drawn from other nations within the Soviet Union. Combining the two periods, teams representing Russia have reached the **FIFA World Cup** finals tournament nine times. During this period, Russian soccer was at its strongest, particularly during the 1950s and 1960s. In 1960, the Soviet Union won the inaugural **UEFA European Football Championship**, inspired by legendary **goalkeeper Lev Yashin**. The year 1966 saw the best finish in a World Cup by a Russian or Soviet team, with the Soviet Union earning fourth place at the tournament in **England**. The Soviet Union also won the 1956 **Olympic Games Football Tournament** and finished runners-up in both the 1964 and 1972 UEFA European Football Championship. Another strong Soviet team emerged in the late 1980s, the Soviet Union losing again in the final of the UEFA European

Football Championship in 1988, this time to the **Netherlands**. The same year, the Soviet Union won the Olympic Games Football Tournament.

In 1992, following the breakup of the USSR, Russia competed as part of the Commonwealth of Independent States at the 1992 UEFA European Football Championship, incorporating most of the nations of the former Soviet Union. Since then, Russia has played independently, and its best international result has been reaching the semifinals of the 2008 UEFA European Football Championship held in **Austria** and **Switzerland** but losing at that stage to eventual victors **Spain**. Russia has produced three players who have won the **European Footballer of the Year** award: Lev Yashin, in 1963; **Oleg Blokhin**, in 1975; and **Igor Belanov**, in 1986. In domestic club soccer, the Russian Premier League is the leading division. Russian teams have enjoyed some success in pan-European competition in recent years, CSKA Moscow and Zenit St. Petersburg winning the **UEFA Cup** in 2005 and 2008, respectively.

S

SACCHI, ARRIGO. B. 1 April 1946, Fusignano, Italy. Arrigo Sacchi is an Italian soccer **coach** and is famous for leading **Italy** to the final of the 1994 **FIFA World Cup** and for managing **AC Milan** to two consecutive **European Cup** titles in 1989 and 1990. Unlike many coaches, Sacchi did not play professional soccer before beginning his managerial career, instead starting his career coaching at lower levels and working his way up to take over AC Milan in 1987. The following season, Sacchi led AC Milan to the *Serie A* domestic championship, preceding the two successive European Cup triumphs. He moved on to coach Italy from 1991 to 1996, losing the 1994 FIFA World Cup final on a **penalty shoot-out** after a 0-0 tie to **Brazil**.

SAMMER, MATTHIAS. B. 5 September 1967, Dresden, East Germany. Matthias Sammer was a leading player for **Germany** in the 1990s following the unification of the country, having previously played for East Germany in the 1980s. At club level, Sammer played for his hometown club, Dynamo Dresden, from 1985 to 1990, as a goal-scoring attacking midfielder. He then moved to Vfb Stuttgart in 1990 before a brief period at **Internazionale** in **Italy** in 1992 and 1993. He ended his career with a successful five-year spell back in Germany with **Borussia Dortmund**, where he was named the **European Footballer of the Year** in 1996 and won the **UEFA Champions League** with his club in 1997. Sammer also enjoyed substantial success playing for the German national team: he won the 1996 **UEFA European Football Championship** held in **England** that year, playing a creative role from a defensive position as a sweeper in a similar mold to his predecessor in that role for his country, **Lothar Matthäus**. Sammer played at the **FIFA World Cup** finals tournament on one occasion, reaching the quarterfinals of the competition with Germany in 1994 in the **United States**, the Germans exiting disappointingly early with a defeat to **Bulgaria**.

SAN SIRO. *See* STADIO GIUSEPPE MEAZZA.

SÁNCHEZ, HUGO. B. 11 July 1958, Mexico City, Mexico. Hugo Sánchez is best known for his outstanding performances as a striker for **Real Madrid**

in **Spain** and for the **Mexico** national team. For the latter, he appeared at the **FIFA World Cup** finals tournament on three occasions, in 1978, 1986, and 1994. He scored 29 goals in 74 games for Mexico. The peak of his career came playing for Real Madrid, where he played from 1985 to 1992, scoring 251 goals for the Spanish club and winning the league championship on five occasions. He was the top scorer in European soccer in 1990. Following his retirement from playing in 1997, he began a career in **coaching**, taking charge of the Mexico national team from 2006 to 2008, an unsuccessful tenure in charge for Sánchez.

SANTANA, TELÊ. B. 26 July 1931, Itabirito, Brazil. D. 21 April 2006. Telê Santana was a successful Brazilian player and even more successful **coach** in his later days, known for managing teams that won games while treating the sport as an art form to be played with style. He played a majority of his career in the 1950s for Fluminese of Rio de Janeiro and retired in 1963 after playing almost 600 games for three clubs. He began his managerial career with Fluminese in 1969, but after managing at three other Brazilian clubs in the 1970s, he made his name as **Brazil**'s head coach at both the 1982 and 1986 **FIFA World Cup** tournaments. Though neither team won the competition or even reached the final, Brazil's effective and stylish play won plaudits, especially Santana's 1982 team, which featured the brilliant **Zico**, **Sócrates**, and Falcao. They went out in the second round, however, following a surprising 3-2 defeat to **Italy**. Santana then coached in **Saudi Arabia** for two seasons before taking charge of Brazil again at the 1986 World Cup in **Mexico**. Brazil performed well and reached the quarterfinal stage, but heartbreakingly lost to **France** in a **penalty shoot-out**. Santana then coached Brazilian club teams for the rest of his career, first Flamengo and then, most successfully, **São Paulo Futebol Club**. In 1992, Santana was awarded the prestigious title of South American Coach of the Year by Uruguayan newspaper *El Pais*, following a season that saw São Paulo win both the **Copa Libertadores** and the **Intercontinental Cup**, the latter the most prestigious global club title at the time. Remarkably, Santana's team, led by the outstanding creative midfielder Rai, won the same impressive double the next season. In 1996, Santana was forced to retire from coaching after suffering from a stroke and passed away in 2006 from an intestinal infection. Santana is remembered as one of Brazil's most brilliant coaches, his teams embodying the flair his country's game is known for.

SANTOS FUTEBOL CLUB. Arguably **Brazil**'s most famous club team, Santos FC is based in the city of Santos in the state of São Paulo and plays in the first division of the Brazilian national league. They are best known for one of their players, **Pelé**, who spent the vast majority of his career at

Santos, scoring more than one thousand goals between 1956 and 1974. This period saw Santos shoot to fame as Pelé became the best-known player on the planet. Santos FC, originally named, in English, "Santos Foot-Ball Club," was founded on 14 April 1912 and joined the São Paulo Football League a year later. Brazilian clubs turned professional in the 1930s, and Santos won their first São Paulo state championship in 1935. They won the Brazilian national championship twice, and won both the **Copa Libertadores** and the **Intercontinental Cup** in 1962 as well as 1963, inspired by Pelé.

SANTOS, DJALMA. B. 27 February 1929, São Paulo, Brazil. Defender Djalmo Santos, who debuted at the age of just 16 and made 98 appearances for Brazil between 1952 and 1968, was a key part of **Brazil**'s winning teams at both the 1958 and 1962 **FIFA World Cup** tournaments. Playing an attacking right fullback position, he provided critical consistent support for the attack and coverage at the back for the superb Brazilian teams of that period, mirroring the excellent **Nílton Santos** on the left side (no relation). He also played at the 1954 and 1958 World Cups for Brazil. At club level, he played most of his career for Palmeiras in Brazil, winning three state championships. He retired in 1970.

SANTOS, NÍLTON. B. 16 May 1925, Rio de Janeiro, Brazil. Nílton Santos, a swashbuckling force who attacked from a left-back position and one of the first fullbacks to play the role in an offensive manner, was a critical component of **Brazil**'s winning teams at the 1958 and 1962 **FIFA World Cups**. Santos also appeared at the 1954 World Cup for Brazil. In total, he played 75 games for Brazil between 1949 and 1962, during which they won 55 games, tied 10, and lost 10. Santos played his entire club career for Botafogo in Brazil, making 716 appearances in 17 years and winning the state championship with his team on four occasions. *See also* SANTOS, DJALMA.

SÃO PAULO FUTEBOL CLUB. One of **Brazil**'s most successful clubs, São Paulo was originally founded in the country's largest city in 1930 and were refounded five years after the original incarnation went out of business. Within a decade, though, São Paulo had become one of the main forces in the state of São Paulo—catching up with rivals Palmeiras and **Corinthians**—by winning several Paulista State Championships in the 1940s with star player **Leônidas da Silva**, who scored a remarkable 140 goals in 211 games. The club continued to have consistent success in the following decades, apart from a barren period in the 1960s, and the 1990s saw São Paulo earn international fame. Victory in the 1991 national Brazilian championship earned the club entry to the 1992 **Copa Libertadores**, South America's leading international club tournament, São Paulo winning it for the first time that year. They followed this up shortly after, the same year, with victory in the **Intercontinental Cup** against European champions **Barcelona** with a 2-1 win in Tokyo. Impressively, São Paulo followed this up by winning both the Copa Libertadores and the Intercontinental Cup again the next year, this time beating **AC Milan** in the latter competition. Creative midfielder Rai was São Paulo's star player, under the savvy coaching of **Telê Santana**, who managed the club from 1990 to 1995. São Paulo fell into decline following Santana's departure but rose again in 2005 with a third triumph in the Copa Libertadores. They followed this up with a win at the second iteration of the **FIFA Club World Cup** (which had replaced the Intercontinental Cup), beating Liverpool 1-0 in the final in **Japan**. Further Brazilian national championship victories in 2006, 2007, and 2008 have cemented São Paulo's status as the country's leading club in the modern era. *See also* KAKÁ.

SAUDI ARABIA. The most successful men's national team in Asian continental competition is Saudi Arabia, with three victories in the **AFC Asian Cup** (1984, 1988, and 1996) and three runners-up finishes (1992, 2000, and 2007). Saudi Arabia has also appeared in four **FIFA World Cup** tournaments, in 1994, 1998, 2002, and 2006. Their best performance came at their first appearance in 1994 at the World Cup held in the **United States**, where they reached the second round after victories over Morocco and **Belgium** in the group stage before going out to **Sweden** with a 3-1 defeat. The Saudi Arabia Football Federation (SAFF), founded in 1956 and affiliated with the **Fédération Internationale de Football Association (FIFA)** in 1956 and with the **Asian Football Confederation (AFC)** in 1959, organizes the national team and governs the sport in Saudi Arabia.

The SAFF organizes the leading men's professional league in Saudi Arabia, the national Saudi Professional League, founded in 1976. The most successful club in domestic competition in Saudi Arabia is **Al-Hilal** based in the country's capital, Riyadh. Founded in 1957, Al-Hilal, an expensively bankrolled club that attracted well-known overseas names such as Brazil's legendary coach **Mário Zagallo** and star player **Rivelino**, has won 12 championships since the formation of the Saudi Professional League. Al-Hilal has also twice won Asia's leading continental club competition, now known as the **AFC Champions League**, with victories in 1992 and 2000. In recent years, Al-Hilal's great rivals Al-Ittihad have been notably more successful in the Saudi Professional League: they have six titles to their credit compared to Al-Hilal's three in the past decade.

SCARONE, HÉCTOR. B. 26 November 1898, Montevideo, Uruguay. D. 4 April 1967. Héctor Scarone was a key player for **Uruguay** in their victory at the inaugural **FIFA World Cup** in 1930, held in Uruguay. He was known as the "magician" in Uruguay for his ability to conjure up goals as both a creator and a scorer. He tallied 31 goals in 52 appearances for his country, including one at the 1930 World Cup tournament against Romania in the first round. Scarone, one of his country's most successful-ever players, also won the **Olympic Games Football Tournament** twice with Uruguay, in 1924 and 1928, along with four **Copa América** titles. At club level, Scarone played most of his career for Uruguayan team **Nacional**, racking up a prolific goal-scoring record while winning Uruguay's league championship on several occasions. He retired in 1939 and went on to coach Nacional and **Real Madrid** in **Spain** in 1951, the first non-European coach of the Spanish club. He stayed for only one season with Real Madrid, where he failed to win any trophies.

SCHIAFFINO, JUAN ALBERTO. B. 28 July 1925, Dundee, Uruguay. D. 13 November 2002. Juan Alberto Schiaffino was an outstanding **Uruguayan** player. He was an attacking forward whose most important goal came in the last game of the 1950 **FIFA World Cup** for Uruguay against **Brazil** when he assisted his country to an eventual victory that shocked the tournament's Brazilian hosts and gave Uruguay their second World Cup title. Schiaffino began his playing career for Uruguayan giants **Peñarol** before moving overseas to star for **AC Milan** in **Italy**. He played 171 total games for AC Milan, scoring 60 goals and helping them to win the Italian league championship on three occasions, in 1955, 1957, and 1959. He also played for AC Milan in the 1959 **European Cup** final, a game they lost to **Real Madrid**. He then moved on to play for fellow Italian club AS Roma in 1960 and retired two years later.

SCHIAVIO, ANGELO. B. 15 October 1905, Bologna, Italy. D. 17 April 1990. Angelo Schiavio was an Italian forward who played for Italy at the 1934 **FIFA World Cup**, where he scored four goals including the winning strike in the final against **Czechoslovakia** as his country won the World Cup for the first time. A strong and powerful forward, Schiavio scored 15 goals in 21 total games for Italy while playing his entire career for his hometown team Bologna Football Club 1909, scoring more than 200 goals for the club between 1922 and 1939, the year of his retirement.

SCHILLACI, SALVATORE. B. 1 December 1964, Palermo, Italy. Playing for his native **Italy**, Salvatore Schillaci was the top scorer, with six goals, at the 1990 **FIFA World Cup**, where Italy finished third. It was Schillaci's only appearance at the World Cup, and he played a mere six further times for Italy, finishing his national-team career with 16 appearances and seven goals.

His club career lasted from 1982 to 1999, notably playing for **Juventus** and **Internazionale** and earning a reputation as a potent poacher around the goal.

SCHMEICHEL, PETER. B. 18 November 1963, Gladsaxe, Denmark. Peter Schmeichel was a tall, dominant, and agile **goalkeeper** who won the 1992 **UEFA European Football Championship** playing for his native Denmark. He also appeared for Denmark at the 1998 **FIFA World Cup**, reaching the quarterfinal stage. Schmeichel played a record total of 129 games for Denmark between 1987 and 2001. He was a star player for **Manchester United** at club level during the 1990s, winning an impressive five **Premier League** titles with the **English** club and ending his career with the team by winning the final of the 1999 **UEFA Champions League**. He retired in 2003.

SCIFO, ENZO. B. 19 February 1966, Haine-Saint-Paul, Belgium. Scifo made his professional debut in 1983 at the age of 17 for Belgian giants **Royal Sporting Club Anderlecht**. He went on to play for eight different clubs before retirement in 2001. Scifo won the Belgian league four times with Anderlecht and the French league once with Monaco. From 1984 to 1998, Scifo played 84 times for **Belgium**, scoring 18 goals and winning acclaim for his technical ability as a midfield maestro. Since retirement, he has pursued a managerial career without notable success.

SCOTLAND. Scotland has the second-oldest national soccer association in the world, the Scottish Football Association (SFA), and the country's teams, players, coaches, and administrators played a crucial role in the formative decades of the sport in the late 19th century. Various archaic forms of soccer were played in Scotland dating back to the 15th century, though organized teams in a game using mainly the feet were not formed until 1867 when the Young Men's Christian Association (YMCA) created Queen's Park, the first club team in Scotland. Queen's Park played in the **Football Association Challenge Cup** in **England** and became the driving force behind the creation of the Scottish Football Association in 1873. Scotland's national team, which began playing regular international games against England in 1872, drew most of its players from Queen's Park in its early years. The SFA created the Scottish Cup in 1873, a tournament still played today, and the Scottish Football League was founded seven years later. The highest level of Scottish soccer is now the Scottish Premier League, formed in 1998 and dominated by two clubs from Glasgow, **Rangers Football Club** and **Glasgow Celtic**. In 1967, Celtic became the first British team, and is still the only Scottish team, to win the **European Cup**. Scotland's men's national team has reached the **FIFA World Cup** on eight occasions, though none since 1998, and has never advanced past the first round of the finals tournament. Scotland has twice appeared in the **UEFA European Football Championship,** where it reached the quarterfinals in 1992 in **Sweden.** *See also* BUSBY, SIR MATT; DALGLISH, KENNY; FERGUSON, ALEX; LAW, DENIS; SHANKLY, BILL.

SEBES, GUSZTÁV. B. 22 January 1906, Budapest, Hungary. D. 30 January 1986. A renowned coach and administrator, Gusztáv Sebes was best known as the tactical genius behind his native **Hungary**'s brilliant national team of the early 1950s. The "Magical Magyars," as they were nicknamed, transformed the future of world soccer with their visionary dynamic fluidity, presaging the Dutch mastery of "**Total Football.**" Hungary's most stunning international performance came in November 1953 in a much-hyped exhibition game against **England,** who had never been beaten on home soil by a national team from overseas. At **Wembley Stadium,** Sebes' Hungary outclassed and humiliated the English 6-3. Their graceful—yet incisive—play, especially from the unstoppable **Ferenc Puskás,** mesmerized their opponents and the crowd. A return match in Budapest the next year saw Hungary confirm their superiority with a 7-1 win over England. These famous victories came in the midst of a brilliant four-year unbeaten streak for Hungary under Sebes, the competitive highlight a gold medal at the 1952 **Olympic Games Football Tournament.** Sebes' Hungary continued the unbeaten streak into the 1954 **FIFA World Cup,** where they easily beat West **Germany,** the **Republic of Korea, Brazil,** and **Uruguay** on their way to the final. It was there that Hungary's unbeaten streak was finally broken and Sebes was denied his greatest triumph, when West Germany surprisingly took revenge on Hungary with a 3-2 win in a muddy, ugly game unsuited to the Hungarians' grace. Sebes went on to manage several Hungarian club teams. He played an important role as the vice president of the **Union of European Football Associations (UEFA)** from 1954 to 1960.

SEELDRAYERS, RODOLPHE WILLIAM. B. 16 December 1876, Düsseldorf, Germany. D. 7 October 1955. Elected as the fourth president of soccer's global governing body, the **Fédération Internationale de Football Association (FIFA),** in 1954, Seeldrayers died a little more than a year into his role, in October 1955. Seeldrayers still left an enormous contribution to FIFA, serving as a vice president of the organization for 27 years and operating as the right-hand man to visionary FIFA president **Jules Rimet.** Together, they oversaw the establishment of the organization itself and the institution of the **FIFA World Cup,** the inaugural tournament taking place in 1930. Seeldrayers first achieved prominence as an administrator as a founder of the Belgian Football Association and as a member of the International Olympic Committee. In the short period Seeldrayers served as FIFA president, the 1954 World Cup took place and the organization celebrated its 50th anniversary.

SEELER, UWE. B. 5 November 1936, Hamburg, Germany. Uwe Seeler was a star **German** forward who began his professional career at the age of just 16 for his local club Hamburg, in 1953. He went on to have an outstanding career for club and country, scoring 43 goals in 72 games for West Germany between 1954 and 1970. He was a stout, powerful striker with deceptively good ball skills and devastating acceleration that led to decisive and accurate finishing. Seeler is one of only a handful of men to have played in four **FIFA World Cup** finals tournaments for his country, scoring nine goals in 21 total games and reaching the World Cup final in 1966, where West Germany lost to **England**. He played almost his entire club career for Hamburg, scoring a total of 226 goals in 318 games for the club between 1953 and 1972. He later made a brief cameo appearance for Cork Celtic in Ireland before retiring for good in 1978.

SHANKLY, BILL. B. 2 September 1913, Glenbuck, Scotland. D. 29 September 1981. Most famous as the manager of **Liverpool Football Club** from 1959 to 1974, Shankly took the club from lower league obscurity in **England** to become the best team in the country. Under Shankly, Liverpool won three English League Championships, two **Football Association Challenge Cups**, and one **UEFA Cup**. He laid the groundwork for future domination in Europe by the club. His assistant, **Bob Paisley**, took the club to even greater heights in the years after, building on Shankly's success.

Born and raised in the Ayrshire mining village of Glenbuck, Shankly began his career in professional soccer as a player, spending most of his career with Preston North End and representing **Scotland** five times. He gained a reputation as a tough man and that would continue as he began his **coaching** career at the age of 34 with Carlisle, one of his former teams. He then spent short periods at Grimsby, Workington, and Huddersfield before taking over at Liverpool in 1959, who were then in the second division of the **Football League**. Shankly instituted a hard-but-farsighted fitness regime at the club, which helped win promotion for Liverpool back to the top flight in 1962, and, by 1964, Liverpool was champion of the country. They won the F.A. Cup the next year, the league championship again in 1966, and, in 1973, Liverpool claimed their first European title with victory in the UEFA Cup. In 1974, after winning the F.A. Cup again and finishing second in the league championship, Shankly surprisingly retired to spend more time with his family. Shankly died in September 1981, aged 67, and a statue of him, which marks his unparalleled contribution to Liverpool, stands outside Liverpool's stadium, Anfield.

SHEFFIELD FOOTBALL CLUB. Sheffield Football Club, which began play in 1857 and is commonly known as "Sheffield F.C.," is the oldest club team in the world. They are based in Sheffield, **England**, and currently play in England's Northern Premier League, a low level of the game. In 2004, Sheffield F.C. was awarded the FIFA Centennial Order of Merit by the sport's governing body, **Fédération Internationale de Football Association (FIFA)**, and FIFA President **Sepp Blatter** is the club's honorary president.

SHEVCHENKO, ANDRIY. B. 29 September 1976, Dvirkivschyna, Soviet Union. Andriy Shevchenko, a forward with an exceptional goal-scoring record in both club and international soccer, is one of the best Ukrainian players in the nation's history. He won the **European Footballer of the Year** award in 2004. His most successful period of play came with **AC Milan** in **Italy** from 1999 to 2006, winning the 2003 **UEFA Champions League** and scoring more than one hundred goals for the club. He appeared at the 2006 **FIFA World Cup** for Ukraine, scoring two goals in five games as they made it to the quarterfinal stage of the competition, their best-ever performance in the World Cup.

SIMONSEN, ALLAN. B. 15 December 1952, Vejle, Denmark. Allan Simonsen, a Danish forward who played most of his career outside Denmark, was the 1977 **European Footballer of the Year**. He had notable success for Borussia Mönchengladbach in **Germany** and for **Barcelona** in **Spain**. He also appeared on 56 occasions for Denmark's national team, scoring 21 goals, though he never appeared in a **FIFA World Cup** finals tournament. Simonsen retired from playing in 1989 and took up a career in **coaching**, which includes managing, in recent years, the small national teams of the Faroe Islands and Luxembourg.

SINDELAR, MATTHIAS. B. 10 February 1903, Kozlov, Austria-Hungary. D. 23 January 1939. Matthias Sindelar was an Austrian player. He was the leading performer for his country in the 1930s and perhaps its greatest player of all time. Sindelar played his entire senior-club career for FK Austria Wien in Vienna, **Austria**, and made his debut for the Austrian national team in 1926. In 1934, Sindelar starred for Austria as their exceptional team, nicknamed the "*Wunderteam*" and coached by the legendary **Hugo Meisl**, reached the semifinals of the **FIFA World Cup**, where they lost in controversial fashion to hosts **Italy**. Following the annexation of Austria by **Germany** in 1938, Sindelar refused to play for the combined national team of the two countries. He died just months later, officially of carbon monoxide poisoning, though unsubstantiated rumors continue to circulate that Sindelar was murdered by the Nazi regime for failing to play for and support the combined national team after the annexation of Austria.

SISSI. B. 2 June 1967, Esplanada, Brazil. Sissi was the joint top scorer at the 1999 **FIFA Women's World Cup**, where she scored seven goals to tie with **China**'s **Sun Wen** for the Golden Shoe award. Sissi was a pioneering female player for **Brazil**, which finished in third place at the 1999 Women's World Cup, their best-ever finish in a Women's World Cup to that date. Sissi also appeared at the 1995 Women's World Cup, where Brazil exited in the first round. Sissi overcame considerable prejudice against women playing soccer in her native Brazil. She eventually played professionally in the **United States** in the Women's United Soccer Association, from 2001 to 2003, and then in **Women's Professional Soccer** for FC Gold Pride in northern California, where she was also an assistant **coach**, in 2009. *See also* WOMEN'S SOCCER.

SÍVORI, OMAR. B. 2 October 1935, San Nicolás, Argentina. D. 17 February 2005. Omar Sívori was an extravagantly talented forward who played for both his native **Argentina** and for his adopted homeland **Italy**. He played the bulk of his club career in the latter country for **Juventus**. Sívori was small and fast, and an effective dribbler, at times humiliating defenders with his tricky play. He began his career in Argentina playing for **River Plate** in Buenos Aires and won the **Copa América** with the Argentinean national team in 1957. Sívori then moved to Italy to star for Juventus from 1957 to 1965, with whom he won three Italian league championships. He played for Italy's national team, including a brief appearance at the 1962 **FIFA World Cup**. He scored 135 goals in 215 games for Juventus, winning the **European Footballer of the Year** award in 1961. He ended his career playing with Italian club Napoli, retired from play in 1969, and went on to have a career in coaching that included a short period in charge of Argentina's national team during the 1970s.

SÓCRATES. B. 19 February 1954, Belém do Pará, Brazil. Sócrates was a star Brazilian player in the 1970s and 1980s. He was born Sócrates Brasileiro Sampaio de Souza Vieira de Oliveira, but is known around the world simply as "Sócrates." Sócrates made 60 appearances for **Brazil** beginning in 1979 and scored 22 goals. Along with his goal-scoring ability, he was perhaps even more valuable as an inventive passer of the ball from midfield. He captained Brazil at the 1982 **FIFA World Cup** and played for his country at the 1986 World Cup, though Brazil did not progress past the last-16 stage at either tournament. He played the bulk of his club career for **Corinthians** in his native Brazil, making almost 300 appearances. Sócrates retired from play in 1989.

SOUTH AFRICA. South Africa hosted the **FIFA World Cup** in 2010, the first nation on the African continent to do so. Such a scenario would have been unthinkable just a few decades ago under the apartheid regime, as South Africa's soccer community was divided by race along the lines of the broader divisions in the country, making it a pariah in the world of international sport. South African soccer has long been a reflection of the political state in the country, dating back to the game's origins in the 19th century under British colonial rule. The organized game dates back as far as 1862 when the first known soccer game took place between British soldiers and colonial administrators. Eventually, though, soccer became the most popular game with everyone in South Africa besides the white settlers, who instead focused on playing rugby and cricket. Under the apartheid regime instituted in South Africa following the Second World War, South Africa refused to field a mixed team in international competition and, as a result, was excluded from the first **Africa Cup of Nations** held in 1957 and eventually expelled from both the **Confederation of African Football (CAF)** and the **Fédération Internationale de Football Association (FIFA)**. Soccer continued to be played and to be an important part of communities excluded from white rule, and numerous clubs, leagues, and players survived, and even thrived, under difficult conditions during the apartheid years.

A new era began following the demise of the apartheid regime and the founding of the South African Football Association (SFSA) on 8 December 1991, which brought together four disparate soccer associations (reflecting the country's divided past), the Football Association of South Africa, the South African Soccer Association, the South African Soccer Federation, and the South African National Football Association. The SFSA became a member of the global soccer community again in June 1992, joining the global governing body, FIFA. South Africa's national team is known as *Bafana Bafana*, a Zulu term meaning "the boys, the boys" and has since then competed in three FIFA World Cup tournaments as well as winning the Africa Cup of Nations in 1996 and finishing as runners-up in the same competition two years later. In 2010, South Africa successfully staged the FIFA World Cup, with 64 games played from 11 June to 11 July in 10 venues across nine South African cities, a total of 3,178,856 fans attending the tournament won by **Spain**. *See also* ORLANDO PIRATES.

SOUTH AMERICAN YOUTH CHAMPIONSHIPS. Known in Spanish as *Juventud de América*, the South American Youth Championships is the premier men's junior competition in South America and is organized by the region's governing **FIFA confederation**, the **South American Football Confederation (CONMEBOL)**. It features teams from all 10 of its member nations and is contested biennially. The age limit for players in the tournament is 20, and it serves as a qualifying competition for both the **Olympic Games Football Tournament** and the **FIFA U-20 World Cup**. The competition is structured into a first-round group stage and a final-round group stage, with no elimination round. **Brazil** has been the most successful team in the history of the tournament with 11 wins, followed by **Uruguay** with seven, and **Argentina** with four.

SOUTH KOREA. *See* KOREA, REPUBLIC OF.

SOVIET UNION. *See* RUSSIA.

SPAIN. Spain has produced some of the world's best players and teams on a consistent basis since the sport first became popular in the country in the late 19th century. In July 2010, they won their first **FIFA World Cup** title in their 13th appearance at a World Cup finals tournament. Until 2010, Spain's best finish at a World Cup was fourth place, at the 1950 World Cup held in **Brazil**, and Spain had earned a reputation in recent decades for underachievement given the plethora of talented Spanish players. But this spell was broken at World Cup level with victory in 2010 by a team, managed by Vicente del Bosque, that played a short-passing game and dominated possession in every game of the tournament. Spain has also twice won the **UEFA European Football Championship**, in 1964 and in 2008, and finished as runners-up in the tournament in 1984. Spain won the men's **Olympic Games Football Tournament** in 1992 and has a very successful **futsal** team, twice winners of the FIFA Futsal World Cup.

Spanish soccer is governed by the Royal Spanish Football Federation, known in Spanish as *Real Federación Española de Fútbol* (RFEF), founded in 1909 and affiliated with the **Fédération Internationale de Football Association (FIFA)** in 1913. (Madrid Football Club originally represented Spain at the founding of FIFA in May 1904.) The RFEF was also a founding member of the **Union of European Football Associations (UEFA)** in 1954. The RFEF governs the game at all levels from the top tier, known as La Liga, one of the world's leading domestic club leagues, on down to amateur levels, with the assistance of 19 regional affiliated federations. In Spain, according to FIFA's count in 2006, there are more than two million players, 653,190 of them registered with 18,190 club teams. Between them, those clubs have won a total of 12 European Cup and **UEFA Champions League** titles, a record in Europe. The most famous of these clubs have been among the most successful in the history of world soccer: **Barcelona**, founded in 1899, were winners, in 2009, of an unprecedented collection of domestic, continental, and global trophies including victories in La Liga, the Spanish Cup, the Spanish Super Cup, the **UEFA Super Cup**, the UEFA Champions League, and the **FIFA Club World Cup**, a set of achievements never before done in one calendar year. Their great rival for recognition as the strongest team in Spanish club soccer, **Real Madrid**, was named the most successful club of the 20th century by FIFA and has now won a total of 31 La Liga championships, 17 Spanish Cups, and a record nine European Cup and UEFA Champions League titles, including a run of five straight victories from 1955 to 1959. Both Barcelona and Real Madrid count millions of fans each and are among the richest clubs in the world, dominating Spanish soccer with vast commercial income. The RFEF also runs the women's elite soccer competition, the *Superliga*, founded in 1988, and the women's Spanish national team, who have never won a senior major international competition. *See also* ESTADIO SANTIAGO BERNABÉU; GENTO, FRANCISCO; SUÁREZ, LUIS; ZAMORA, RICARDO.

STÁBILE, GUILLERMO. B. 17 January 1905, Buenos Aires, Argentina. D. 27 December 1966. Guillermo Stábile was a leading player and **coach** from **Argentina** and was the top scorer at the inaugural **FIFA World Cup**, held in 1930, finishing with eight goals in four games. Argentina reached the final of that competition, where Stábile scored once in a 4-2 defeat to Uruguay. Stábile played the first half of the 1930s at club level in **Italy** for Genoa and Napoli before retiring in 1939 after spending three years in **France** playing for Red Star Paris, and even appearing for the French national team. Stábile then began a very successful coaching career. He coached Argentina from 1939 to 1960 and won an impressive six **Copa América** titles in that period.

STADIO GIUSEPPE MEAZZA. Better known commonly as the "San Siro," Stadio Giuseppe Meazza is a famous stadium in Milan, **Italy**. It is home to two of Italy's top club teams, **Internazionale** and **AC Milan**. The stadium, opened in 1926, has also played host to games at two different **FIFA World Cup** tournaments held in Italy, in 1934 and 1990. The 1934 tournament included a famous game at the San Siro that saw hosts Italy defeat tournament favorites **Austria** in a legendary semifinal game. It underwent significant renovation before the 1990 tournament and currently has a capacity of a little more than 80,000. The stadium's original official name was *Nuovo Stadio Calcistico San Siro* (in English, the San Siro New Football Stadium). In 1980, it was renamed Stadio Giuseppe Meazza in honor of **Giuseppe Meazza**, a star Italian player who appeared for both Internazionale and AC Milan.

STADIUMS. Soccer games are played in a variety of styles of stadium around the world, from ultramodern, billion-dollar structures like **Wembley**

Stadium in **England**, which accommodates tens of thousands of spectators, to ramshackle constructions that hold only dozens of fans. They are found in one form or another in most countries worldwide. The era of modern soccer that began in the 19th century in Great Britain saw the first teams play in stadiums borrowed from cricket clubs in the 1860s and 1870s. The oval shape of the cricket field was ill fitted for soccer and the structures were ill prepared for the large crowds soccer was to attract. The growing popularity of soccer in the late 19th century led to a boom in stadium construction in England in the 1880s and 1890s. The rise of professional soccer and the growing income from gate receipts facilitated major investment projects by soccer clubs. Large grandstands were built to accommodate spectators, and more-comfortable locker room facilities were built for players. Architects such as Scotsman Archibald Leitch led the creation of ever-more ambitious structures, such as the famous Ibrox Park stadium built for **Rangers Football Club** in **Scotland**. But with larger stadiums and growing crowds, and with only rudimentary health and safety precautions taken, came new dangers: in 1902, hastily rebuilt terracing at Ibrox Park collapsed, sending dozens of men to their deaths. It was the first major disaster at a soccer game, with dozens since occurring worldwide, whether due to poor construction, extreme weather conditions, violence in the stadium, or poor crowd-control management.

Of course, the vast majority of soccer stadiums have safely hosted hundreds of games. In recent decades, safety measures have been implemented to minimize the risks of **hooliganism** and to provide comfortable and safe facilities for spectators and players in most stadiums used at the highest levels of the leading leagues. Many stadiums have become iconic worldwide for their aesthetic appearance or the atmosphere generated during games, especially those hosting major FIFA World Cup games. Some of the most famous include the **Estadio de Centenario** in **Uruguay**, host of the first-ever **FIFA World Cup** final in 1930; the **Estadio Azteca** in **Mexico**, the only stadium to host two World Cup finals (in 1970 and 1986) and known for its challenging altitude conditions; and the **Maracanã** in **Brazil**, which accommodated almost 200,000 fans for the final game of the 1950 World Cup. Various stadiums of well-known clubs, such as the **Estadio Santiago Bernabéu** belonging to **Spain**'s **Real Madrid**, or **Manchester United**'s Old Trafford stadium in northern England, have become globally renowned and attract tourists who merely tour the stadiums on nongame days. *See also* HEYSEL STADIUM DISASTER; HILLSBOROUGH STADIUM DISASTER; LIMA NATIONAL STADIUM DISASTER; RUNGRADO MAY DAY STADIUM; STADIO GIUSEPPE MEAZZA.

STOICHKOV, HRISTO. B. 8 February 1966, Plovdiv, Bulgaria. Hristo Stoichkov is a former star player for **Bulgaria** and was named **European Footballer of the Year** in 1994. Combining a combustible temper with formidable power and skill, Stoichkov was a prolific goal scorer and creative forward for his country and for his clubs. His peak came in the early 1990s when he led Bulgaria to fourth place at the 1994 **FIFA World Cup** in the **United States**, won the Spanish league with **Barcelona** in **Spain** on five occasions, and had one **UEFA Champions League** victory, in 1992. He formed an impressive and productive striking partnership at Barcelona with **Brazil**'s Romário. Stoichkov ended his playing career in the United States, where he played in **Major League Soccer** for the Chicago Fire and DC United, before embarking on a peripatetic **coaching** career, which was less successful than was his playing career.

SUÁREZ, LUIS. B. 2 May 1935, La Coruña, Spain. Perhaps the greatest Spanish player of his generation in the 1950s and 1960s, Luis Suárez was born Luis Suárez Miramontes, but is commonly known only by his first two names. He was the **European Footballer of the Year** in 1964, when he starred for **Spain** as they won their first major tournament, the **UEFA European Football Championship**. Suárez was an elegant and creative midfielder with an eye for goals, scoring 14 goals for Spain in 32 appearances between 1957 and 1974. His long club career saw him star most notably for **Barcelona** in Spain, where he won the Spanish league championship three times, and **Internazionale** in **Italy**, where he won the Italian league twice. He also won the **European Cup** with Internazionale in 1964 and 1965. Following his retirement from playing in 1973, Suárez managed several club teams and then the Spanish national team at the 1990 **FIFA World Cup**, where Spain exited in the second round following a defeat to **Yugoslavia**. Suárez left the position shortly after.

SUPERGA AIR DISASTER. On May 4 1949, a flight carrying the Torino A.C. soccer club from Turin in **Italy** crashed into a hill called "Superga" not far from Turin, killing all 31 people onboard. The plane had flown into a thunderstorm, and bad weather and poor navigation was ultimately determined by the Italian authorities to be the cause of the crash. At the time, Torino had won five successive Italian league championships and were generally considered to be the best team in all of Europe. Most of their team also played for the Italian national team. The crash devastated the club, killing 18 players and almost the entire first team. Unlike **Manchester United** following their own tragic **Munich Air Disaster**, Torino was unable to rebuild successfully and has since played second fiddle in Turin to their rivals **Juventus**.

SWEDEN. Soccer is the most popular sport in Sweden, which has a strong record in international competition in both the men's and women's games. The sport was first played in Gothenburg in the late 1880s, and a city championship was started there in 1896. The governing Swedish Football Association was founded in 1904 and, in time, became one of the seven founding members of the **Fédération Internationale de Football Association (FIFA)**. Sweden played its first international game in 1908 and soon made a mark in global competition, winning a bronze medal at the 1924 **Olympic Games Football Tournament** and later, in 1948, winning gold in the same competition. Sweden made its debut at the **FIFA World Cup**, in 1934, and finished in fourth place in 1938. Its best performance to date in the World Cup, out of 11 total appearances, came in 1958, when Sweden hosted the World Cup and finished runners-up, losing to **Brazil** in the final. Sweden also finished in third place in 1950 and in 1994. Sweden's women's team, drawing on a strong base of participation for the sport in the country, has equaled the achievement of the men's team, finishing runners-up at the 2003 **FIFA Women's World Cup**. Sweden's women's national team also won the **UEFA Women's Championship** in 1984 and has finished runners-up on three occasions, in 1987, 1995, and 2001. Sweden has one of the strongest women's clubs in the world, **Umeå IK**, twice winners of the UEFA Women's Champions League. *See also* LIEDHOLM, NILS; NORDAHL, GUNNAR.

SWITZERLAND. The Swiss Football Association (ASF-SFV) was founded in 1895 and was a founding member of the **Fédération Internationale de Football Association (FIFA)** in 1904 and the **Union of European Football Associations (UEFA)** in 1954. Both organizations have their headquarters in Switzerland. Switzerland hosted the **FIFA World Cup** in 1954, reaching the quarterfinals of that tournament and matching its previous best performances, in the 1934 and 1938 World Cups. It has appeared in nine total World Cups and has not advanced past the second round since 1954. Switzerland's best performance in senior international competition came as runners-up in the 1924 men's **Olympic Games Football Tournament**, before the founding of the World Cup. Switzerland has enjoyed success at youth level in recent years, winning the 2009 FIFA U-17 World Cup and the 2002 UEFA European Under-17 Championship. The highest level of domestic club soccer in Switzerland is the Swiss Super League, the successor to the first professional league established in Switzerland in 1897. The most successful club in Swiss soccer is Grasshopper Club Zürich. Founded by an English student, it has been a general sports club dating back to 1886 and is winner of 27 national championships. *See also* BLATTER, JOSEPH S.

T

TELEVISION. The number of spectators viewing a top-level soccer game on television in most countries now considerably outstrips the number of spectators physically at the stadium. This is particularly true for major international competitions like the **FIFA World Cup** and the **UEFA Champions League**, which are watched by hundreds of millions worldwide and draw in billions of dollars of revenue for the governing bodies and participating teams. These television-rights fees, which have risen massively in recent decades, have become increasingly important to the income of governing bodies and club and international teams, and have fueled the rampant inflation of players' salaries since the 1970s, when soccer was first televised internationally in color broadcasts. Soccer was first broadcast on television when the British Broadcasting Corporation (BBC) televised an international game between **England** and **Scotland** in 1938, and the **Football Association Challenge Cup** final between Huddersfield Town and Preston North End the same year.

The FIFA World Cup was not shown on television until the 1954 event in **Switzerland**. Extensive coverage of the next three events was especially prominent on European television, and worldwide satellite broadcasting began in 1966. The World Cup was broadcast in color for the first time in 1970, which considerably increased its appeal, and audiences have continued to rise rapidly. The World Cup is now the most-watched sporting event in the world on television, above even the Olympic Games. FIFA claimed a cumulative audience of 26.3 billion people for the 64 games played at the 2006 FIFA World Cup in **Germany**, shown in 214 countries. Television and marketing rights for the tournament in 2006 were sold for $2.1 billion, and $3.2 billion was raised for the 2010 World Cup in **South Africa**.

Numerous national soccer competitions also sell their domestic and international television broadcasting rights for hundreds of millions of dollars annually, with the most lucrative rights being for the **Premier League** in England. For the 2007 to 2010 period, the Premier League raised almost $4 billion in domestic television-rights income, the bulk coming from Sky Television, and raised nearly a further $1 billion for overseas rights. The most-watched single club game each season is now the UEFA Champions League

235

final, with a total global audience of 206 million viewers in 2010, which beat America's Super Bowl for the most-watched annual sports event on world television. The growing ease of the availability of soccer on television internationally has greatly increased the revenue for leading clubs and has directly contributed to spiraling transfer fees and salaries paid at the highest levels of the game for players. However, it has also led to some concern for the viability of lower-level soccer leagues, since many armchair fans prefer to watch games at home rather than support their local teams now that they are able to follow clubs in overseas countries on television every weekend via satellite broadcasts. The leading English Premier League teams now claim large followings in most countries around the world.

The promise of greater television-revenue returns has led to significant changes being made to traditional competitions by the sport's governing bodies. The FIFA World Cup expanded to 32 teams, the 22 original clubs in the English Premier League broke away from the original **Football League** in 1992 in order to keep more of the television revenue available for themselves, and the formation of the UEFA Champions League allowed more teams into the competition than did its predecessor, the European Cup. The scheduling of games in leagues around the world is now largely dictated by the demands of television companies rather than tradition or convenience for fans attending the game in person. And the ties between soccer and television are continuing to expand as media companies exploit new technology. High-definition broadcasts and even 3-D transmissions are now becoming commonplace in countries around the world.

TESSEMA, YDNEKATCHEW. B. 11 September 1921, Jimma, Ethiopia. D. 19 August 1987. Ydnekatchew Tessema was an Ethiopian soccer player, **coach**, and administrator. A prolific goal-scoring forward, he played for Santa-George SA in Ethiopia from 1943 to 1958, and appeared for the Ethiopian national team. He then coached various Ethiopian clubs and the Ethiopia national team, leading them to their first-and-still-only major title, the 1962 **Africa Cup of Nations**, hosted that year by Ethiopia. By this time, Tessema's active role behind the scenes in sports administration had already made him a prominent figure in African soccer, as he played a key role in the founding of the **Confederation of African Football (CAF)** in 1957. Tessema became the fourth president of CAF in 1972, remaining in that role overseeing African soccer until his death in 1987. Tessema also served on the International Olympic Committee and was the head of the Ethiopian Olympic Committee. Under his leadership, CAF modernized its operations, introduced numerous new junior and club competitions, and improved the marketing of African soccer. Earlier, as general secretary of

CAF during the 1960s, Tessema successfully lobbied for the **Fédération Internationale de Football Association (FIFA)** to increase the number of **FIFA World Cup** finals places awarded to African national teams. Tessema died of cancer in 1987.

THROW-IN. A throw-in is used to restart play by the opposing team of the player who last touched the ball before it crossed the touchline. It is the only time an outfield player is allowed to handle the ball. A specific set of rules laid out in Law 15 of the **Laws of the Game** define the procedure that must be followed when a throw-in is taken. At the moment of throwing the ball, the player must

- face the field of play,
- have both feet placed on or behind the touchline,
- hold the ball with both hands,
- throw the ball from behind and over his or her head, and
- throw the ball from the point where the ball had previously crossed the touchline.

If any of these requirements are not met, an **infringement** is called, commonly known as a "foul throw," and a throw-in is awarded to the opposing team from the same spot on the touchline. All opposing players must be at least two yards away when the ball is thrown, and the thrower may not touch the ball again until another player has done so first. A goal cannot be scored directly from a throw-in, but a long throw-in is often used as an effective tactic to attack the opposing team's goal, by launching the ball into the penalty area. Various alternative methods of restarting play from the touchline have been tried, including kick-ins, but throw-ins remain the simplest way to restart the game with the least disruption to the flow of play.

TIFO. *Tifo*, an Italian word, is the name commonly used to refer to choreographed displays of support by organized groups of fans, large in-**stadium** arrangements usually performed before games that can involve considerable numbers of flags, banners, streamers, cards, and other materials sometimes coordinated around the entire arena. Tifo is usually organized and paid for by supporters' groups, especially hardcore fan groups known as **ultras**, and is most commonly found in European and South American stadiums, though it is also now increasingly evident in North American games. Tifo originated in **Italy** and comes from the Italian word *tifosi*, meaning supporters of the team, and supporters' groups of Italian teams have long had one of the strongest traditions of performing significant tifo displays.

TIGANA, JEAN. B. 23 June 1958, Bamako, French Sudan. Jean Tigana was born in what was French Sudan and is now Mali and went on to become a star player for **France** at international level. He also enjoyed a highly successful club career. Tigana played for France at both the 1982 and 1986 **FIFA World Cups**, with the French finishing in third place at the latter tournament, Tigana forming part of a superb French attacking force that also included **Michel Platini** and Alain Giresse. That trio containing Tigana had been at the heart of France's victory two years earlier in the 1984 **UEFA European Football Championship**. Tigana played his entire club career in France, winning three league titles with an expensively assembled Bordeaux team in the 1980s. Since retiring in 1991, he has been a **coach** at several European clubs.

TOSTÃO. B. 25 January 1947, Belo Horizonte, Brazil. Tostão was born Eduardo Gonçalves de Andrade but is universally known as "Tostão." He was a leading Brazilian forward in the 1960s and 1970s. He played for **Brazil** at the 1970 **FIFA World Cup**. He scored twice in the tournament as the Brazilians won the competition while playing some of the best soccer ever seen, Tostão playing an important role as a creative link in the attack. He also appeared at the 1966 World Cup in **England**, where Brazil exited in the first round. In total, he scored 32 goals in 54 games for Brazil. At club level, Tostão starred for Brazilian club Cruzeiro, for whom he scored more than 200 league goals. Tostão retired in 1973.

TOTAL FOOTBALL. "Total Football" is the name given to a style of play most notably popularized by the brilliant **Netherlands** team in the 1970s, which built on the tactical innovations of **Ajax Amsterdam**. Both teams were coached by **Rinus Michels**. Total Football depends on players being able to fluidly switch positions, according to the flow of play, rather than operating in rigid, fixed positions. A wide defender, for example, would, in this system, frequently roam forward and attack from deep positions, a midfielder dropping back to cover the defender defensively when necessary. It is a system that demands a high level of technical ability from all players to be able to switch positions. These Dutch tactical innovations were not entirely new in the 1970s. Many aspects of Total Football were evident much earlier in the superb **Hungarian** national team of the 1950s.

TURKEY. Soccer was brought to Turkey in the late 19th century by British immigrants, though, at first, the ruling Ottoman emperor attempted to stem the game's spread to Turkey's Muslim population. But by 1913, the game had become popular in Turkish urban areas, and a league had been established in Istanbul with more than 5,000 regular players. In 1923, the Turkish Football

Federation (*Türkiye Futbol Federasyonu*) was founded and affiliated with the **Fédération Internationale de Football Association (FIFA)** the same year. The amateur Istanbul Football League remained Turkey's leading league until 1959, when the professional Turkish Super League was formed, which remains the top level of Turkish soccer today. Turkey's national team struggled in international play, reaching the **FIFA World Cup** only once in the 20th century, in 1954, and exiting in the first round after a win over **Republic of Korea** and two heavy defeats to West **Germany**. Turkish domestic clubs continued to develop and, following entrance to the **Union of European Football Associations (UEFA)** in 1962, began to make an impact on European competition. In 1989, **Galatasaray** reached the semifinals of the European Cup (now the **UEFA Champions League**) and famously defeated **Manchester United** in the same competition in 1993 and 1996. In 2000, Galatasaray became the first Turkish club to win a European competition, with victory in the UEFA Cup (now the **UEFA Europa League**). The Turkish national team has also showed improvement in recent decades, reaching their first major international tournament in 40 years in 1996 at the **UEFA European Football Championship**, held in **England**. They reached the quarterfinals of the 2000 UEFA European Football Championship and then the semifinals of the **2002 FIFA World Cup**, held in the Republic of Korea and **Japan**. Turkey then reached the semifinals of the UEFA European Football Championship in 2008, though did not qualify for the 2010 FIFA World Cup in **South Africa**. *See also* FENERBAHÇE SPOR KULÜBÜ.

U

UEFA CHAMPIONS LEAGUE. The UEFA Champions League, an annual tournament open to the top teams in each nation affiliated with the **Union of European Football Associations (UEFA)**, is the most prestigious international competition for clubs in Europe. The UEFA Champions League is the most-watched televised annual sporting event in the world. The winning team qualifies for the **FIFA Club World Cup**. Until 1992, when the tournament's branding and structure was significantly changed by UEFA, the competition was known as the "European Cup." It was first contested in 1955, a year after the founding of UEFA, though it was not initially organized by UEFA. The winners of the UEFA European Champions League are awarded the UEFA European Champions Clubs' Cup trophy.

The main competition in the UEFA Champions League begins with 32 teams playing in eight groups of four teams, each team playing each other once at home and once away. Twenty-two teams qualify directly for the group stage and for the 2009/2010 season. Qualification to the competition at this stage was determined for clubs in the countries with the best past records in UEFA competitions as assessed by their coefficient ranking. Its rules state: "The three national associations with the highest UEFA coefficient ranking will each have three teams who gain automatic entry to the group stage, with the countries ranked 4 to 6 in the standings having two automatic qualifiers and the associations ranked 7 to 13 having one." Preliminary rounds of competition determine the other 10 entrants to make up the field of 32 teams for the group stage. The top two teams in the standings of each group then qualify for the knockout elimination stage, played in home-and-away two-legged ties, until the 16 remaining teams have been reduced to two for the final, a single game played at a neutral venue chosen in advance by UEFA.

Counting winners of both the UEFA Champions League and the European Cup, clubs from **Spain** have been the most successful in the tournament's history, with 12 victories, including the most successful individual team, **Real Madrid**, with nine victories. Real Madrid set the standard for the competition in its early years, cementing their fame Europe-wide by winning the first five iterations of the competition, between 1955 and 1960, led by their star midfield player **Ferenc Puskás**. Teams from England and Italy have each won the tournament a total of 11 times.

UEFA CUP. *See* UEFA EUROPA LEAGUE.

UEFA CUP WINNERS' CUP. The UEFA Cup Winners' Cup, as it was known for most of its existence between 1960 and 1999, was an annual tournament organized by the **Union of European Football Associations (UEFA)** for the winners of national cup competitions from each UEFA member association. The first unofficial tournament, in 1960–1961, featured 10 teams and was won by Fiorentina, who defeated **Rangers Football Club** in the final. The tournament was competed under UEFA auspices from 1961–1962 onward, with **Barcelona** winning it four times and proving to be the most successful team in the tournament's history. UEFA disbanded the tournament as part of the expansion of the **UEFA Champions League**. The last iteration of the tournament, in 1999, was won by Lazio in Villa Park, Birmingham, England.

UEFA EUROPA LEAGUE. The UEFA Europa League, organized by the **Union of European Football Associations (UEFA)**, ranks behind only the **UEFA Champions League** in importance as an international club competition in Europe. The origins of the tournament date back to 1955 and the establishment of the Inter-Cities Fairs Cup, a pioneering tournament pitting teams from European cities with trade fairs against each other. In 1971, the tournament came under the auspices of the UEFA, and it was renamed the UEFA Cup. Qualification for the tournament has usually been for the best-placed teams in each UEFA national association's domestic league who have not qualified for the UEFA Champions League. In 1999, it merged with the **UEFA Cup Winners' Cup**, and domestic cup winners now qualified for the enlarged competition as well. A reorganization and rebranding of the tournament took place in 2009, and a new name, the "UEFA Europa League," was introduced. There was also an increase in the number of group-round games played. Now 48 teams play in 12 groups of four in the first stage, with the top two in each group qualifying for the second round. They are joined at this stage by the eight teams who finished third in the UEFA Champions League group stage (and were thus eliminated from that competition), to create an even field of 32 teams. A knockout tournament then takes place, with three rounds of two-legged matchups leading to a single-game final at a neutral location, the showpiece game of the tournament. Three teams are tied with the most wins across all the iterations of the tournament under UEFA's official organization: **Juventus**, **Internazionale**, and **Liverpool** have each won it three times.

UEFA EUROPEAN CHAMPION CLUBS' CUP. *See* UEFA CHAMPI-ONS LEAGUE.

UEFA EUROPEAN FOOTBALL CHAMPIONSHIP. The UEFA European Football Championship is the premier soccer competition for men's teams from the member nations of the **Union of European Football Associations (UEFA)**. First contested in 1960, it is held every four years in a host nation or joint host nations selected by UEFA. The hosts automatically qualify for the competition, with all other member nations competing in preliminary rounds of qualifying that begin almost two years before the tournament itself. For the last competition in 2008, the format of the tournament allowed for 16 teams to take part in the final competition. UEFA has since announced that the tournament will be expanded to 24 teams in 2016. The winners of the tournament claim the Henri Delaunay Trophy, named after Henri Delaunay, the first general secretary of UEFA, who had advocated the creation of a competition for European nations from the 1920s until his death in 1955. In 1957, UEFA approved the formation of what was initially known as the "European Nations' Cup" and was later renamed the "UEFA European Football Championship." Since 1996, each competition is also known by the abbreviation "Euro" along with the year of the tournament, such as UEFA Euro 2008.

The first staging of the competition in 1960 was won by the **Soviet Union**. Of the 17 original entrants who participated in the preliminary rounds (around half the membership of UEFA), four teams competed in the finals competition held in **France**. **England**, West **Germany**, and **Italy** were notable absentees from the competition. The 17 original entrants played home and away games from September 1958 to May 1960 to determine which four teams would go to France for the tournament that would see two semifinals leading to a final. The first semifinal featured **Czechoslovakia** and the Soviet Union, the latter comfortably winning 3-0 with two goals coming from Valentin Ivanov. The second semifinal was a remarkable game between hosts France and **Yugoslavia** with nine goals scored in what remains to date the highest scoring game in the tournament's history. Yugoslavia won 5-4 and moved on to the final, where they faced the imposing defensive force of the Soviet Union led by legendary **goalkeeper Lev Yashin**. The Soviets won the game in extra time with a headed goal from Viktor Ponedelnik giving them a 2-1 win and the right to be called the first country to be champions of Europe.

The second staging of the tournament took place in Spain in 1964 and was won by the hosts, who beat the defending champions, the Soviet Union, 2-1 in the final. As in 1960, a qualifying tournament led to a four-team finals competition, though, this time, 29 countries entered at the initial stage, an increase of 12 from 1960. The four qualifiers to the semifinal stage were **Spain**, **Hungary**, Denmark, and the Soviet Union. The first game on 17 June 1964 at

Santiago Bernabéu Stadium in Madrid pitted Spain against the Hungarians, a tight encounter won 2-1 by the Spanish after extra time. The second semifinal was held the same day at Camp Nou in **Barcelona**, with the Soviet Union crushing Denmark 3-0. The final took place on 21 June in front of 79,115 at the Santiago Bernabéu Stadium; a partisan home crowd witnessed a 2-1 victory for Spain that saw the country earn their first major international title. The winner came from Marcelino with six minutes left in the game.

The third edition of the UEFA European Football Championship, now known by that name for the first time rather than the "European Nations' Cup," was held in Italy in 1968. The tournament took on a new form: the qualifying competition was revamped from a straight knockout system to a group format. In the qualifiers, the decisive game between **Scotland** and England at Hampden Park, Scotland, drew 130,711 spectators, still the largest crowd for any UEFA European Football Championship match to date. There, England earned the draw that would take them through to the tournament finals for the first time. They were joined in the final four by Yugoslavia, hosts Italy, and the Soviet Union. Italy progressed past the Soviet Union at the semifinal stage after a 1-1 draw at the end of extra time was settled by a coin toss in their favor, which was the method UEFA then used to settle tied games in the competition. England lost to Yugoslavia 1-0 after suffering their first sending off in senior competition when Alan Mullery was shown the red card.

In 1972, the fourth staging of the UEFA European Football Championship was held in West Germany from 14 to 18 June, and the hosts claimed their first European title when they beat the Soviet Union in the final. As in the previous tournament in 1968, four teams qualified for the final stage. West Germany was picked ahead of **Belgium**, Hungary, and the Soviet Union to host the semifinals and final. The semifinals began with West Germany defeating Belgium 2-1; the West German team was led by the imperious midfielder **Franz Beckenbauer** and the prolific forward **Gerd Müller**, both of whom would be central to their victory two years later in the 1974 **FIFA World Cup**. Müller scored twice in the game. In the other semifinal, the Soviet Union defeated Hungary to reach their third UEFA European Football Championship final out of the four held since the first edition in 1960. In the final, though, the Soviets could not match the strength, speed, and skill of the West German team, who cruised to a 3-0 victory, Müller scoring twice again and Herbert Wimmer claiming the other goal.

The fifth edition of the UEFA European Football Championship was hosted by Yugoslavia from 16 to 20 June 1976. The final tournament featured four teams who made it through the qualifying rounds: Czechoslovakia, the **Netherlands**, defending champions West Germany, and Yugoslavia. The first semifinal took place on 16 June in Zagreb, with Czechoslovakia beating the Netherlands 3-1 thanks to two goals in extra time, the Dutch losing two players during the game to red cards. In the second semifinal on 17 June, also in Zagreb, Yugoslavia took a 2-0 lead against West Germany only to see that lead evaporate. They lost 4-2 after extra time, Dieter Müller scoring a late **hat-trick** for the West Germans. In the final, on 20 June in Belgrade, West Germany again fell behind 2-0, with goals from Ján Švehlík and Karol Dobiaš for the Czechs. West Germany fought back once more, though, with another goal from Müller and an equalizer from Bernd Hölzenbein a minute before the end of time tying it up. No goals were scored in extra time, and, for the first time, the UEFA European Football Championship winner was determined by a penalty shoot-out. Uli Hoeness missed the critical fourth kick for the West Germans, and Czechoslovakia scored all theirs to win the UEFA European Football Championship for the first time.

The 1980 UEFA European Football Championship was the sixth staging of the competition and was held in Italy from 11 to 22 June. The tournament was expanded from its previous setup of four finalist teams to include eight who came through the qualifying competition, with hosts Italy automatically qualifying. The first round was a group stage, the eight teams divided into two groups of four, each team playing each other once, with the winners of each group advancing to play each other in the final. Group A was won by a West German team inspired by midfielder Bernd Schuster and finishing ahead of Czechoslovakia, the Netherlands, and Greece. Group B saw Belgium go on to the final, with hosts Italy (missing star striker **Paolo Rossi**), England, and Spain going out. A third place play-off between the two second-place teams in the groups was won by Czechoslovakia over Italy on a **penalty shoot-out**. The final on 22 June took place in Rome's Olympic Stadium, a tight game won 2-1 by West Germany thanks to a second goal from Horst Hrubesch just before the end of 90 minutes. West Germany thus claimed their second UEFA European Football Championship title.

The 1984 edition of the UEFA European Football Championship was hosted by France and took place from 12 June to 27 June, featuring eight teams. The hosts, France, had automatically qualified to be one of the eight teams at the final tournament, along with a further seven who had come through a qualifying competition featuring 32 nations from UEFA. The eight teams were divided into two groups of four, with the top two advancing to the semifinal stage. France won group A with **Denmark** in second place, while Spain won group B with **Portugal** in second place. France, inspired by the midfield trio of **Michel Platini**, Alain Giresse, and **Jean Tigana**, played Portugal in their semifinal, an exciting game won by the French 3-2 after extra time due to a winning goal from Platini in the 119th minute. The other semifinal was decided by penalty kicks after a 1-1 tie between Spain and

Denmark, the Spanish going through to meet France. The final was held in Paris, and, there, France won their first major international tournament, when an inspired Platini, who scored nine goals in five games during the competition, led them to a 2-0 win over Spain.

The eighth staging of the tournament was held in West Germany in June 1988, and was won by the Netherlands, claiming their first major international trophy. Seven countries qualified to join West Germany in the eight-team finals tournament, title-holders France surprisingly failing to do so. The eight teams were divided into two groups in the first round, with the top two from each heading to the semifinals. Group A was won by West Germany, with Italy in second place, and both Spain and Denmark were eliminated. The Soviet Union won group B, and the Netherlands came in second to qualify for the next stage, the Republic of Ireland and England both heading home. The strength and skill of the Dutch team, centered around **Ruud Gullit**, **Frank Rijkaard**, and lethal striker **Marco van Basten**, was demonstrated in the first semifinal in Hamburg, when they defeated the host nation West Germany 2-1 thanks to a winning goal from van Basten just two minutes from the end of the game. At the other semifinal in Stuttgart, a young-but-talented Italy was beaten 2-0 by the Soviet Union. In the final, held in Munich's Olympic Stadium, the Netherlands were unstoppable. Ruud Gullit scored the first goal with a header in the first half, and a scorching volleyed goal from van Basten in the second half sealed the game for a 2-0 win for the Dutch and their first European title.

In 1992, the ninth edition of the UEFA European Football Championship was held in **Sweden**, with eight teams again taking part. The tournament was surprisingly won by Denmark, who only qualified for the tournament as a replacement for Yugoslavia, who dropped out due to the outbreak of their civil war. Denmark had just two weeks to prepare for the tournament and did not perform especially well in the first round, finishing second in group A behind hosts Sweden, though this was enough to qualify for the semifinal stage. In group B, the Netherlands and Germany went through to the semifinals. Host Sweden was defeated by Germany in the first semifinal, thanks mainly to two goals by German forward Karl-Heinz Riedle. In the second semifinal, Denmark upset reigning European champion, the Netherlands, after a 2-2 tie was settled by penalty kicks in favor of the Danes. Germany was favored to win the final, but Denmark took an early lead with an 18th minute goal from John Jensen and, with a second goal from Kim Vilfort in the 78th minute, secured a 2-0 win and the championship.

The 1996 tournament, the 10th edition of the UEFA European Football Championship, was hosted by England in June of that year and won by Germany. The finals were expanded to include 16 teams, up from the previous eight, broken down in the first round into four groups of four teams, with the top two in each progressing to the quarterfinal stage. In the first round, group A was won by England with the Netherlands also moving on; France topped group B with Spain in second place; Germany won group C ahead of the **Czech Republic**; and Portugal headed group D, Croatia qualifying as well. In the quarterfinals, Germany advanced over Croatia, England defeated Spain on penalty kicks, the Czech Republic beat Portugal 1-0, and France went through following a penalty shoot-out victory over the Netherlands. Hosts England failed to fulfill their hopes of winning the tournament on home soil, losing on penalty kicks to Germany in the first semifinal. The second semifinal was also decided by a penalty shoot-out, with France losing to the Czech Republic following a 0-0 tie. The final at **Wembley Stadium** saw the Czech Republic take the lead from a goal by Patrick Berger, but Germany found an equalizer from substitute Oliver Bierhoff, who then scored a winner in extra time to give Germany their third UEFA European Football Championship title.

In 2000, two nations, the Netherlands and Belgium, jointly hosted the 11th staging of the UEFA European Football Championship. France won the competition for the second time, inspired by their star player **Zinedine Zidane**, just two years after winning the **1998 FIFA World Cup**. As in 1996, 16 teams competed in the tournament, with four groups of four teams, the top two in each qualifying for the quarterfinals. Portugal and Romania qualified from group A, Italy and **Turkey** from group B, Spain and Yugoslavia from group C, and the Netherlands and France from group D. In the quarterfinals, Portugal comfortably beat Turkey 2-0 in Amsterdam, Italy defeated Romania by the same score line in Brussels, a rampant Dutch team crushed Yugoslavia 6-1 in Rotterdam, and France won a high-quality game with Spain 2-1. France then defeated Portugal in the first semifinal, winning 2-1 thanks to a Zidane goal from a penalty late in extra time. The second semifinal saw the Netherlands fail to capitalize on their opponents' mistakes: Italy had a man sent off in the first half and gave up two penalties, which the Dutch missed. The Italians held on for a scoreless tie and then beat the Netherlands on a penalty shoot-out, after three Dutch misses. The final saw further drama: Italy seemed set for victory thanks to a goal by Marco Delvecchio in the 55th minute, giving them a 1-0 lead, which they held until the fourth minute of stoppage time at the end of the game. France then leveled the score with a goal by Sylvain Wiltord. In extra time, France sealed victory and the European title by two goals to one with a strike by David Trezeguet in the 103rd minute.

The 12th edition of the UEFA European Football Championship took place in 2004, held in Portugal from 12 June to 4 July. It was surprisingly won by Greece, who claimed their first-ever major international tournament victory.

Sixteen teams again took part in the final competition, with the first round consisting of a group stage featuring four groups of four teams, the top two in each progressing to the quarterfinals. In those quarterfinals, hosts Portugal defeated England on a penalty shoot-out following a 2-2 tie. Netherlands advanced past Sweden, also via penalty kicks. Greece shocked France by beating them 1-0 and the Czech Republic won 3-0 against Denmark. Greece's hard-working but unspectacular team, coached by German Otto Rehhagel, then beat the Czech Republic to advance to the final. There, they faced Portugal, who had beaten the Netherlands 2-1 in the other semifinal. At the final in Lisbon, held in front of 62,865 at Estádio da Luz, the hosts and favored Portugal were unable to get a grip on the game, and a single goal from Angelos Charisteas in the 57th minute decided the result, Greece winning 1-0 to claim the championship.

In 2008, the 13th iteration of the UEFA European Football Championship was jointly hosted by **Austria** and **Switzerland** from 7 to 29 June, with 16 teams participating in the finals competition. It was won by Spain, who claimed their second European title. The two hosts qualified automatically, and the other 14 teams came through a qualifying competition that ran through 2006 and 2007. In the finals tournament, the 16 teams were divided into four groups of four teams, with the top two in each group qualifying for the quarterfinals. In that stage, Germany beat Portugal 3-2, Turkey won on a penalty shoot-out against Croatia, **Russia** beat the Netherlands 3-1 after extra time, and Spain defeated Italy on penalty kicks. The first semifinal saw Germany again win 3-2, this time defeating Turkey, while Spain illustrated their quality with a 3-0 victory over Russia. The final saw Spain crowned as European champions for the second time after a 1-0 win over Germany, thanks to a 33rd minute goal from forward Fernando Torres.

UEFA EUROPEAN UNDER-19 CHAMPIONSHIP. The longest-running junior competition in world soccer, the UEFA European Under-19 Championship is an annual tournament for national teams composed of players under the age of 19 from the European member nations of the **Union of European Football Associations (UEFA)**. The tournament, played a year before the biennial **FIFA U-20 World Cup** takes place, is used as a qualification campaign for that event. It began play in 1948, organized by the international governing body of soccer, **Fédération Internationale de Football Association (FIFA)**, and was known as the "FIFA Junior Tournament" until 1955, when it was taken over by UEFA, formed in 1954. In 1981, UEFA changed the age eligibility level for the tournament, reducing it to 18, but, in 2002, it became an under-19 event again. **England** is the most successful nation in the history of the competition, with nine victories.

UEFA EUROPEAN UNDER-21 CHAMPIONSHIP. Soccer's governing confederation in Europe, the **Union of European Football Associations (UEFA)**, organizes the UEFA European Under-21 Championship for its members' national associations' representative teams with an age limit of 21. It is contested every two years, and UEFA also uses it as a qualifying competition to determine its entrants for the **Olympic Games Football Tournament**. UEFA has organized the competition since 1984; prior to that, an under-23 challenge competition existed in Europe from 1967 to 1976. It became an under-21 event that year. **Italy** is the most successful country in the competition, with five victories.

UEFA SUPER CUP. Organized by the **Union of European Football Associations (UEFA)**, the UEFA Super Cup is an annual game held between the reigning champions of Europe's two most-prestigious international club competitions, currently the **UEFA Champions League** and the **UEFA Europa League**. It began unofficially in 1973 as a contest between two Dutch teams at the top of the European game, with that year's European Cup (as the UEFA Champions League was then known) winner **Ajax Amsterdam** taking on that year's **UEFA Cup Winners' Cup** victor Feyenoord, the former winning the first title with a 3-1 victory over two games. UEFA began sanctioning the tournament in 1975, adding considerably to its prestige, and it has been contested every year since. Its scheduling, usually at the start of the European season, though, has limited its visibility compared to other major competitions. In 1999, the UEFA Cup Winners' Cup was disbanded by UEFA, so the winners of what was then the UEFA Cup and is now the UEFA Europa League have taken their place in the contest. Up to 2010, **AC Milan** has been the most successful team in the tournament, with five titles.

UEFA WOMEN'S CHAMPIONSHIP. The leading continental competition for European women's national teams is the UEFA Women's Championship, which began play in 1984, then known as the "UEFA European Competition for Representative Women's Teams." Scandinavian teams won the first two editions of the competition, in 1984 and 1987, and the competition was contested every two years until 1997, when it switched to taking place every four years. **Germany** has dominated it since 1989, winning six of the last seven competitions, the exception being a second win for Norway in 1993. The tournament has grown in size over the past three decades, reflecting the development of **women's soccer** in Europe: 12 teams entered the qualification process for the inaugural 1984 competition, while 45 teams attempted to qualify for the 2009 tournament.

ULTRAS. Many hardcore supporters of club teams, especially in continental Europe, call themselves "ultras," meaning fans willing to support their teams in an extreme fashion. This can involve being part of a fanatic supporters' group committed to organizing spectacular, elaborate, and expensive choreographed *tifo* displays in the **stadium** to show support for the team. Ultras typically stand and sing for the duration of the game, and they generally stand together in groups at one end of the stadium. Ultras typically travel large distances to follow their teams wherever they play. Ultras are sometimes associated with **hooliganism**, and, though violence has been associated with some ultras groups, the vast majority of ultras are not violent. Rivalries between some ultras group can, however, become bitter and result in regular confrontations.

UMEÅ IK. One of the world's leading women's club teams, Umeå IK is based in the city of Umeå, **Sweden**, and is part of a broader sports club. **Women's soccer** began play at Umeå IK in 1985, and they have since been enormously successful in domestic and European competition, winning seven Swedish national league championships and winning the **UEFA Women's Championship** on two occasions, in 2003 and 2004. Their star players have included the four-time **FIFA World Player of the Year**, **Marta**.

UNION OF EUROPEAN FOOTBALL ASSOCIATIONS (UEFA). UEFA is the governing administrative body of European soccer, one of six continental confederations recognized by the **Fédération Internationale de Football Association (FIFA)**. UEFA currently consists of 53 member nations operating as a representative democracy and is headquartered in Nyon, Switzerland. The UEFA president at present is **Michel Platini**, who defeated incumbent president Lennart Johansson in 2007. The riches of the European game ensure that UEFA is the most powerful confederation within FIFA. It has the largest representation at the **FIFA World Cup**, with 14 entrants of the 32 finalists at the 2010 tournament in **South Africa**. UEFA's stated mission is "to create the right conditions for the game in Europe to prosper and develop."

Though it was the second confederation to affiliate with FIFA, UEFA was founded in 1954, several decades after its South American equivalent, the **South American Football Confederation (CONMEBOL)**. Frenchman Henri Delaunay was selected as UEFA's first general secretary, and its headquarters were in Paris until 1959, when they were moved to Switzerland. The year before, UEFA organized its first continental competition for national teams, the **UEFA European Football Championship** (called the "UEFA European Nations Cup" until 1968), which has been held every four years since 1960. The trophy awarded to the winning team is named after Delaunay. In 1984, the **UEFA Women's Championship** began play, and it is held every four years for women's national teams.

UEFA also oversees club football in Europe, where it organizes the world's richest club tournament, the **UEFA Champions League** (formerly the European Cup), along with the **UEFA Europa League** (formerly the UEFA Cup), **UEFA Super Cup**, UEFA Intertoto Cup, the **UEFA Women's Champions League** (originally founded as the UEFA Women's Cup in 2000), as well as many youth tournaments. UEFA also governs European **futsal**. *See also* UEFA CUP WINNERS' CUP.

UNITED STATES. Soccer in the United States is governed by the U.S. Soccer Federation (USSF), often known simply as U.S. Soccer. The USSF is recognized by the **Fédération Internationale de Football Association (FIFA)** as the governing body of soccer at all levels in the United States and is headquartered in Chicago, Illinois. Its mission is "to make soccer, in all its forms, a preeminent sport in the United States and to continue the development of soccer at all recreational and competitive levels." The USSF was fully affiliated with FIFA in 1914, just a year after its founding in 1913, when it was originally called the "United States Football Association." The organization of soccer in the United States would be troubled for the next 80 years after that, the sport failing to take root as a professional sport to the same extent as it developed in many other countries, particularly further south in the Americas. Administrative infighting, a lack of funding, and rival league competitions doomed many efforts to form a lasting national professional league in the United States until the 1990s, when **Major League Soccer (MLS)** was formed.

The most serious and longest-lasting attempt at forming a professional league before the establishment of MLS was the **North American Soccer League (NASL)**, which lasted from 1968 to 1984 and attracted major global stars, such as **Pelé**, **Johan Cruyff**, and **Franz Beckenbauer**. Pelé's club, the New York Cosmos, achieved global notoriety and large crowds. However, many clubs in the NASL struggled to attract significant crowds, and overspending doomed the league, as did competition from **indoor soccer**, which became particularly popular in the United States in the 1980s. Despite this, the popularity of soccer in the United States has been demonstrated by attendance at major international events that have been held there: the 1984 **Olympic Games Football Tournament**, held in Los Angeles, attracted a crowd of more than 90,000 to the Rose Bowl for the final game and, in part, led FIFA to award the 1994 **FIFA World Cup** to the United States, in an attempt to aid the development of the sport there. The World Cup was a considerable success, with an all-time record of 3,387,538 fans attending at an average of 68,991 per game, a record for the World Cup that still stands today.

The principal legacy of the 1994 World Cup was the formation of a new outdoor professional league, Major League Soccer, which fulfilled a promise made to FIFA and built off the financial success of the World Cup for U.S. Soccer. It began play in 1996 with 10 teams, and has since established itself as a lasting presence in American soccer. It expanded to 16 teams by 2010, including one in **Canada**, and is expected to reach 19 total teams by 2012. Numerous famous players have played in MLS since 1996, including **Lothar Matthäus**, **David Beckham**, and Cuauhtémoc Blanco. The top American teams in Major League Soccer each year enter the **CONCACAF Champions League**. A professional women's league, **Women's Professional Soccer**, was founded in 2007 and is composed of seven teams as of August 2010. It succeeded the previous women's professional league, the Women's United Soccer Association (WUSA), which ran from 2000 to 2003.

At the international level, the U.S. men's national team achieved some success in the early years of World Cup competition, finishing in third place at the first World Cup in 1930, held in **Uruguay**, and surprisingly defeating **England** at the 1950 World Cup in **Brazil**. But the United States did not again qualify for a World Cup until 1990, a long barren period that reflected the parlous state of the sport domestically. Since then, the United States is one of a handful of countries to have appeared at every World Cup held after 1990. It qualified for the second round at the World Cup held in the United States in 1994, reached the quarterfinals of the 2002 World Cup jointly hosted by the **Republic of Korea** and **Japan**, and won its group in the first round of the 2010 World Cup in **South Africa**, but lost to **Ghana** in the second round in extra time. The United States has also, along with **Mexico**, dominated continental competition, winning the **CONCACAF Gold Cup** on four occasions, in 1991, 2002, 2005, and 2007.

The U.S. women's national team has been more successful than its men's counterpart. It has consistently been one of the best countries in the women's game globally since the 1990s, taking advantage of the large number of youth soccer and college participants in women's soccer. The U.S. women's team has won two **FIFA Women's World Cup** titles, in 1991 and 1999, the latter competition held in the United States in front of large crowds with the U.S. team coached by **Tony DiCicco**, and turning stars, such as **Kristine Lilly**, **Michelle Akers**, and **Mia Hamm** into national celebrities. The U.S. women's team has also won the **Olympic Games Football Tournament** on three of the four occasions on which it has been contested, 1996, 2004, and 2008. *See also* DONOVAN, LANDON; DORRANCE, ANSON; GAETJENS, JOE; MCBRIDE, BRIAN.

URUGUAY. Soccer is the most popular sport in Uruguay. Despite a relatively small national population numbering at around three-and-a-half-million people, Uruguay's men's national team has been one of the leading performers in international soccer since the 1920s. In that decade, Uruguay won gold medals for winning both the 1924 and 1928 **Olympic Games Football Tournaments**, at the time the world's leading international soccer competition. Uruguay followed this with victory in the inaugural **FIFA World Cup** held in 1930 in Uruguay, who had won the hosting rights from the **Fédération Internationale de Football Association (FIFA)**, in part, because of the country's promises to stage a fittingly grand event and pay for the travel and accommodation of the competing teams. The 1930 World Cup coincided with the celebration of the 100th anniversary of the adoption of Uruguay's first constitution. The spectacular **Estadio de Centenario** venue was built in the capital, Montevideo, to commemorate this and host the bulk of the World Cup games, including the final. A total of 10 games were played there. Since then, Uruguay has appeared in 10 further World Cup finals tournaments and won the tournament again in 1950 in **Brazil** with an upset victory over the hosts, forever remembered as the *Maracanazo*, referencing the shock caused when Uruguay defeated the favorites Brazil in the final game at the legendary **Maracanã Stadium**. Uruguay has also finished fourth at the World Cup on three occasions since, in 1954, 1970, and 2010. The latter success followed a long fallow period for Uruguay's national team in the World Cup and surprised many observers. Uruguay's national team has also performed very well in South America's continental international competition, the **Copa América**, with 14 victories, a record only matched by **Argentina**. Uruguay's national women's team has enjoyed little success, failing to appear at any editions of the **FIFA Women's World Cup**. The development of **women's soccer** in Uruguay is stunted by the lack of a national women's league.

Domestic men's club soccer in Uruguay is, like the national teams, controlled by the country's national association, the *Asociación Uruguaya de Fútbol*, founded in 1900. Since 1932, it has organized the professional *Campeonato Uruguayo de Fútbol*, the country's league system. Two clubs from Montevideo, **Peñarol** and **Nacional**, have dominated the league, with the former having won 37 professional titles, and the latter 31. Both have also been very successful in continental club competition, particularly in South America's premier cup competition, the Copa Libertadores: Nacional has won it three times, in 1971, 1980, and 1988, and Peñarol has taken five **Copa Libertadores** titles, in 1960, 1961, 1966, 1982, and 1987. *See also* ANDRADE, JOSÉ LEANDRO; FRANCESCOLI, ENZO; GHIGGIA, ALCIDES; NASAZZI, JOSÉ; SCARONE, HÉCTOR; SCHIAFFINO, JUAN ALBERTO; VARELA, OBDULIO.

V

VALDANO, JORGE. B. 4 October 1955, Las Parejas, Argentina. Jorge Valdano was a significant driving force in **Argentina**'s 1986 **FIFA World Cup** victory, scoring four goals for his country as they won the tournament, including a goal in the final against West **Germany**. Valdano also briefly appeared in the 1982 World Cup, but his competition was ended just 24 minutes into the first game due to injury. At club level, Valdano began his career playing for Newell's Old Boys in Argentina. He moved to Spain in 1975 and played for Alaves, Real Zaragoza, and then, most successfully, **Real Madrid**. With the latter club, Valdano won four Spanish league championships and won the **UEFA Cup** in both 1985 and 1986. Valdana retired in 1987 and **coached** Real Madrid from 1994 to 1996. *See also* MARADONA, DIEGO.

VALDERRAMA, CARLOS. B. 2 September 1961, Santa Marta, Colombia. Carlos Valderrama, an imaginative passer of the ball from deep in midfield, played for **Colombia** at three **FIFA World Cup** finals tournaments in the 1990s and is one of his country's most creative-ever talents. Valderrama played for Colombia a total of 111 times, scoring 11 goals. He was the South American Footballer of the Year in both 1987 and 1993 and remains the only Colombian to win the award.

VAN BASTEN, MARCO. B. 31 October 1964, Utrecht, Netherlands. One of the greatest European strikers of the 20th century, the **Netherlands**' Marco van Basten's career was cruelly curtailed in his prime due to serious ankle injuries. He retired at the age of just 29 in 1993. Only the previous year, van Basten had been named **FIFA World Player of the Year**, adding to his accolade as **European Footballer of the Year** the same year, a title he had also won in 1988 and 1989. Van Basten's lethal finishing was first seen at **Ajax Amsterdam** in his native Netherlands, where he began his professional club career in 1982. He played there until 1987 and scored an average of more than one goal every game. In 1988, now playing at **AC Milan** in **Italy**, his international career peaked for the Netherlands. He played a starring role in leading his country to their first international title at the **UEFA European Football**

Championship. Van Basten scored five goals to finish as the tournament's top scorer, including a remarkable long-range volleyed goal against the **Soviet Union** in the final. The next year was van Basten's best in club soccer, scoring 19 goals in *Serie A* and helping AC Milan win the **European Cup** when he scored twice in the final against Steaua Bucharest in an emphatic 4-0 victory. AC Milan repeated as champions the next year, with van Basten appearing in the final, a 1-0 win over **Benfica**. Ankle injuries, however, continued to dog van Basten even as Milan won further domestic titles. He made his last professional appearance in 1993.

After a considerable break from soccer, van Basten began a **coaching** career with Ajax Amsterdam in 2003, then taking over as national team manager for the Netherlands in 2004. He led them to the second round of the 2006 **FIFA World Cup**, losing to **Portugal** 1-0 in a bitterly contested game. His team then reached the quarterfinals of the 2008 UEFA European Football Championship but lost to **Russia**. Leaving his post after the tournament without having achieved great success in charge of the Netherlands, van Basten returned again to Ajax Amsterdam, this time as head coach, only to resign from the post in May 2009.

VAN HIMST, PAUL. B. 2 October 1943, Sint-Pieters-Leeuw, Belgium. Paul van Himst was an outstanding **Belgian** attacking player. He was a prolific goal scorer at club level, mainly with **Royal Sporting Club Anderlecht**, for whom he scored more than 200 goals from 1959 to 1975. Van Himst appeared for Belgium's national team a total of 81 times, scoring 30 goals, and was named Belgium's player of the century in awards given by the **Union of European Football Associations (UEFA)** in 2003. Following his retirement from playing in 1977, van Himst pursued a successful career **coaching** at both club and international levels and managed Belgium at the 1994 **FIFA World Cup**.

VARELA, OBDULIO. B. 20 September 1917, Paysandú, Uruguay. D. 2 August 1996. Obdulio Varela was the captain of **Uruguay** when they won the 1950 **FIFA World Cup**, upsetting **Brazil** on home soil in the crowning moment of Varela's exceptional career. A decisive and determined midfielder or center back, Varela played for Uruguay from 1939 to 1954. He also won the **Copa América** with his country in 1952 and appeared at the 1954 World Cup in **Switzerland**, where Uruguay finished in fourth place. At club level, Varela played most of his career for Peñarol in Uruguay and won the national championship with his club on six occasions before his retirement from playing in 1955.

VOGTS, BERTI. B. 30 December 1946, Büttgen, West Germany. Berti Vogts is a German **coach** and former star defender for his national team. Vogts played for West **Germany** at three **FIFA World Cup** finals tournaments in the 1970s. He collected a winners' medal at the 1974 competition, playing a key defensive role in the West German victory over the **Netherlands** in the final that year. He also won the 1972 **UEFA European Football Championship** with his country. Vogts' entire playing career was spent playing for Borussia Mönchengladbach in Germany's Bundesliga, winning five league titles and two **UEFA Cup** winners' medals. Following his retirement, he coached Germany for most of the 1990s and won the 1996 **UEFA European Football Championship**, though he failed to advance beyond the quarterfinal stage at either the 1994 or the 1998 World Cup finals tournaments. In 2008, he became the coach of Azerbaijan.

VÖLLER, RUDI. B. 13 January 1960, Hanau, West Germany. **Germany**'s Rudi Völler played in three **FIFA World Cup** finals tournaments for his country, in 1986, 1990, and 1994. West Germany won the 1990 World Cup with Völler scoring three goals in the competition. Völler was a predatory striker who also scored prolifically in Germany, **Italy**, and **France** at club level between 1977 and 1996. He won the **UEFA Champions League** with French club **Olympique de Marseille** in 1993. Since retiring from playing, Völler has managed at club level and **coached** Germany's national team at the 2002 World Cup, where he led his country to the final of the competition, losing there to **Brazil**. He resigned from the post in 2004 after a disappointing performance at the **UEFA European Football Championship** that year. *See also* KLINSMANN, JÜRGEN; MATTHÄUS, LOTHAR.

WALTER, FRITZ. B. 31 October 1920, Kaiserslautern, Germany. D. 17 June 2002. Fritz Walter captained West **Germany** to their surprising 1954 **FIFA World Cup** triumph, earning himself legendary status in German soccer for all time. He was a creative attacker and prolific scorer, known for his work rate and strong technical ability with the ball. Walter began his professional playing career with his hometown club, FC Kaiserslautern, making his debut at the age of 17. Two years later, he was picked to play for West Germany for the first time, in July 1940, and scored a **hat-trick** against Romania. The Second World War interrupted Walter's career, as he was conscripted into the army and taken prisoner in the **Soviet Union**. He was fortunate to return home in 1945. There, he began his career again, returning to play for FC Kaiserslautern at club level and to captain Germany shortly after they rejoined international play in 1951. Walter led Kaiserslautern to West German championship honors in both 1951 and 1953. The next year, he achieved everlasting fame by leading his country, under **Sepp Herberger**'s inspirational coaching, to a surprising victory in the 1954 World Cup held in **Switzerland**. West Germany defeated **Turkey** and **Austria** en route to the final, where they faced **Hungary**, a team unbeaten in the tournament and who had already easily defeated West Germany in the first-round group stage. But Walter led West Germany's inspirational performance as they won 3-2 to claim the World Cup for the first time, a triumph that was also seen as crucial in reviving West German confidence in the reconstruction era following World War II. Walter again led West Germany at the 1958 World Cup in **Sweden**, where they exited at the semifinal stage, losing 3-1 to the hosts. Walter's playing career ended the next year, with a total of 33 goals in 61 appearances for West Germany, due to an injury in that game against Sweden. He was awarded the FIFA Order of Merit in 1996 and passed away in 2002.

WEAH, GEORGE. B. 1 October 1966, Monrovia, Liberia. In 1995, George Weah, a prolific and powerful goal scorer, became the first African player to receive the **FIFA World Player of the Year** award, following an outstanding season representing **AC Milan**. The same year, he was also named **European Footballer of the Year** and African Footballer of the Year, an unprecedented set of achievements. Weah's career took some time to reach such a peak: he played most of his younger years in African soccer before joining Monaco in 1988, after Cameroon's national team coach Claude le Roy spotted him playing for Tonnerre of Yaoundé and recommended him to the club. With Monaco, Weah scored freely and led the club to success in numerous cup competitions, including reaching the final of the **UEFA Cup Winners' Cup** in 1992. He moved on to Paris Saint-Germain that year and won the French league championship in 1994 before a transfer to AC Milan the next season. Though tasked with replacing the outstanding **Marco van Basten** as Milan's main goal scorer, Weah showed no hesitation in adapting to Italy and quickly became the most-feared striker in the Italian league, eventually scoring 60 goals in 114 games for the club. At national level, though, Weah had less success with a weak Liberia team and is, so far, the only FIFA World Player of the Year never to appear in a **FIFA World Cup** finals tournament. Weah played out his final seasons with less notable success in **England** (for Manchester City and **Chelsea**), France (for **Olympique de Marseille**), and the United Arab Emirates (for Al-Jazira) before retiring in 2003 and taking up a prominent career as a politician and humanitarian ambassador. He ran unsuccessfully for the presidency of Liberia in 2005.

WEMBLEY STADIUM. Located in London, **England**, Wembley Stadium is the 90,000 all-seater capacity home of England's national team and all other flagship events of its owner, **The Football Association**, including the **Football Association Challenge Cup** final and semifinals. It is arguably the most famous soccer stadium in the world. Wembley Stadium is a multipurpose venue that has also hosted rugby, American football, motor racing, and musical concerts. The current **stadium** was opened in 2007 after a long and expensive rebuilding project. The stadium was designed by acclaimed architect Sir Norman Forster, its most striking feature being a 133-meter-tall arch above the northern half of the stadium.

The original Wembley Stadium, built in just 300 days, was opened on 23 April 1923. It was initially known as the "Empire Stadium," as it was built for the British Empire Exhibition in the Wembley Park Leisure Grounds. The stadium quickly became famous for its distinctive "Twin Towers" at its entrance. The first event at the stadium was the 1923 F.A. Cup final between Bolton Wanderers and West Ham United, which became infamously known as the "White Horse Final." This name came about because the stadium's 127,000 capacity was massively overrun, with an estimated 200,000 fans cramming in for the first F.A. Cup final held in London, causing scenes of considerable disorder and danger. Order was successfully restored and the final played following intervention by mounted police. One light-gray horse was immortalized due to the black-and-white photos of the event published afterward, and it has become known forever in popular imagination as the White Horse Final. F.A. Cup finals and England internationals have produced the most memorable moments in the stadium's history, including the 1966 World Cup final, where hosts England defeated West Germany 4-2 after extra time.

WEN, SUN. B. 6 April 1973, Shanghai, China. Sun Wen, a retired **Chinese** player, was named, along with American **Michelle Akers**, the women's co-player of the century in 2002 by the sport's global governing body, **Fédération Internationale de Football Association (FIFA)**. Wen played for China at four **FIFA Women's World Cup** finals tournaments, scoring a total of 11 goals in 20 games. She played in the final of the 1999 FIFA Women's World Cup, with China losing in a **penalty shoot-out** to the **United States** after a 0-0 tie. She also played in two **Olympic Games Football Tournaments**, winning the silver medal with China in 1996. *See also* WOMEN'S SOCCER.

WEST GERMANY. *See* GERMANY.

WOMEN'S PROFESSIONAL SOCCER (WPS). Women's Professional Soccer is the top level of women's professional soccer in the **United States** and is arguably the highest quality professional women's league in the world. It was founded in 2007 and began play in 2009. The league is currently composed of six teams who play a regular-season league format before play-offs to determine the champions. The inaugural winners of WPS in 2009 were Sky Blue FC from New Jersey, and the 2010 champions were FC Gold Pride.

WOMEN'S SOCCER. Women's soccer is an embedded part of the global game, with participants numbering in the millions worldwide. Soccer is the fastest-growing women's team sport in the world. In 1991, the **FIFA Women's World Cup** was established, and it now features hundreds of professionals who play in top-tier leagues, such as **Women's Professional Soccer** in the **United States** and the Bundesliga in **Germany**. Historically, women's soccer was long actively discriminated against by male-dominated authorities in most parts of the world, its growth stunted by deliberate obstacles placed in its way until recent decades. Only since the 1970s has that changed, although women's soccer players, fans, and administrators still face challenges based on prejudice against women's participation in sports that lingers to this day around the world.

The first recorded women's soccer game in **England** took place in 1895, following a game organized in **Scotland** three years earlier. But, as with the sport in general, women played forms of the game recognizable as antecedents to modern soccer much earlier than the 19th century organization of the sport: Chinese paintings from the Han dynasty (206 BC—220 AD) era depict women playing a ball game played with the feet. In 19th century Britain, as Association Football became increasingly popular, women regularly played the game at colleges. It remained, though, a sport hardly accessible practically or culturally to lower-class women.

The outbreak of the First World War in 1914 kick-started women's club teams into existence in England, the first place that women's soccer became a popularly known pursuit. With women joining the workforce in new ways due to the needs of the war, they took on jobs that before had not been open to them, such as at munitions factories. And, like their male-worker colleagues, women began playing soccer on their breaks. Soon enough, games between teams from different factories were organized in 1916, and the most famous team of all emerged from one factory in Preston, Lancashire: the Dick, Kerr factory, run by W. B. Dick and John Kerr. On Christmas Day in 1917, female workers from the Dick, Kerr factory played a charity match in Preston that drew more than 10,000 spectators and raised a large sum of money for donations to a local hospital. On Boxing Day in 1920, a crowd of 53,000 watched **Dick, Kerr Ladies** defeat St. Helen's Ladies 4-0 at Goodison Park in Liverpool. The team became famous nationwide, their quality of play highly commended by the press, and, with other teams springing up around the country, a Women's Football Association was formed.

Just a year later, though, the ruling male-dominated **Football Association** made a decision that set back the development of women's soccer in Britain for decades, with a ripple effect around the world. At a time when English soccer was still seen to set the example in the global game, women were banned from playing at any **Football League** stadiums in England, the council of The Football Association stating, "Complaints having been made as to football being played by women, the Council feel impelled to express their strong opinion that the game of football is quite unsuitable for females and ought not to be encouraged." This blocked the development of women's soccer in its stride. With similar bans in place elsewhere in Europe, the Dick, Kerr Ladies were forced to play abroad in order to find stadiums that would fit the crowds keen to see them play. Thus, in 1922, the Dick, Kerr Ladies toured the United States, where they were feted by the president of the country himself. Female stars such as the iconic **Lily Parr**, a prolific goal-scoring prodigy for Dick, Kerr Ladies, would never again play in front of the kind of crowds she had seen early in her career in England. It was only in 1971 that The Football Association finally lifted the ban on women's soccer teams using stadiums of clubs affiliated with The Football Association, but the game had spent decades languishing, and women's soccer in England would not even begin to approach its former popularity until the 1990s.

Elsewhere, though, women's soccer had begun to take serious leaps forward, aided by the shifting gender politics of the 1960s that saw women's participation in sport generally escape many of its previous pejorative associations. Informal women's World Cup tournaments were organized in Europe in the 1970s, while **China** became a stronghold for women's soccer, and the enactment of Title IX in the United States in 1972 led to the rapid development of women's soccer in the American educational system. Unprecedented new opportunities for women's teams began to develop in schools and colleges. Internationally, independent women's clubs and leagues began to organize competitions outside the structures regulating men's soccer. The governing authorities of men's soccer, such as the **Fédération Internationale de Football Association (FIFA)**, the **Union of European Football Associations (UEFA)**, and the U.S. Soccer Federation (USSF) took note and began to incorporate women's soccer competitions under their auspices, albeit in an initially often-haphazard and, at times, careless way.

In November 1991, the first FIFA Women's World Cup took place, in China, featuring teams from 12 nations, with more than half a million fans attending the 26 games staged. A crowd of 65,000 at Tianhe Stadium in Guangzhou watched the final between Norway and the United States, the Americans winning the inaugural competition thanks to a goal in extra time by **Michelle Akers**, the top scorer in the tournament. Four years later, the second Women's World Cup was held in **Sweden**, 12 teams again taking part. On this occasion, two European nations reached the final, where Germany—a perennial powerhouse in women's soccer—lost to Norway by two goals to none.

The 1999 FIFA Women's World Cup proved to be a watershed for the sport's development: held in the United States in large stadiums and with considerable national media coverage, record crowds attended the 32 games, with 1,194,215 total attendees. A record crowd of 90,185 fans came to the Rose Bowl in Southern California for the final game between the United States and China, a game that was decided by a **penalty shoot-out** in the host nation's favor. The game attracted 17.9 million viewers on **television** in the United States, and star players, such as **Mia Hamm**, became household names in the country.

Four years later, in 2003, the Women's World Cup was again staged in the United States in front of large crowds, though the tournament had originally been scheduled to be hosted in China. The outbreak of Severe Acute Respiratory Syndrome (SARS) in China in early 2003 forced FIFA to move the competition at short notice. Germany defeated the United States in the semifinals to face fellow-European competition from Sweden, the Germans defeating the Swedes 2-1 at the final in the Home Depot Center, just outside Los Angeles, in front of a crowd of 26,137.

The Women's World Cup was eventually played in China four years later, in 2007, with almost one million fans attending the 32 games that took place. Germany successfully defended its title, defeating **Brazil** 2-0 despite the latter featuring **Marta**, a star forward on her way to four consecutive **FIFA World Player of the Year** awards. FIFA also runs world championship competitions for women at junior levels, including the **FIFA U-20 Women's World Cup**, first contested in 2002 and held biennially. All **FIFA confederations** now run international women's competitions, the oldest and most closely contested being the **UEFA Women's Championship** in Europe, dominated by Germany.

The growth of the women's game over the past two decades is illustrated further at club-team level by the establishment of new leagues in numerous countries, the strongest consistent league being Germany's Bundesliga. The first entirely professional women's league was founded in the United States in 2000, the Women's United Soccer Association, though it folded in 2003 after overambitious spending doomed the league financially. A new professional league, Women's Professional Soccer, was founded in 2007 and began play in 2009. The league is currently composed of five teams who play a regular season league format before play-offs to determine the champions. The inaugural winners of WPS in 2009 were Sky Blue FC from New Jersey, and the 2010 champions were FC Gold Pride. *See also* DORRANCE, ANSON.

WOOLFALL, DANIEL BURLEY. B. 15 June 1852, Blackburn, England. D. 24 October 1918. The second president of soccer's global governing body, the **Fédération Internationale de Football Association (FIFA)**, Woolfall took over from Frenchman **Robert Guérin** just two years into the organization's existence and oversaw its solidification as the international governing body of soccer. A former administrator of **The Football Association**, Woolfall was well placed to improve the relationship between England and FIFA. Under Woolfall's leadership, the **Laws of the Game** were developed as a uniform set agreed to by all members of FIFA, a critical development for the international growth of the sport. During his 12-year tenure as FIFA president, membership of the organization more than doubled, expanding its reach outside Europe for the first time, to countries including **South Africa**, **Argentina**, and the **United States**. International competition also began during Woolfall's tenure, with FIFA overseeing the **Olympic Games Football Tournaments** in 1908 and 1912. The eruption of the First World War in 1914 made international cooperation and competition extremely difficult, however, and when Woolfall died in the year war ended in 1918, FIFA faced a considerable task to continue the progress made in the early years of his presidency.

WORLD CUP. *See* FIFA WORLD CUP.

Y

YASHIN, LEV. B. 22 October 1929, Moscow, Russia. D. 20 March 1990. Lev Yashin's significance as one of the best **goalkeepers** of the 20th century extends beyond his considerable acrobatic abilities: his dominance of the penalty area and beyond altered the way the game was approached by players in his position. His command of the penalty area was on view at three successive **FIFA World Cup** finals tournaments, from 1958 to 1966, appearing for what was then the **Soviet Union**.

Yashin began playing on an organized team during the Second World War, for the works team of a munitions factory, as a young worker at the age of just 12. After the war, when the Soviet league again began, following the devastation to the country, Yashin signed on for Dinamo Moscow, one of its leading clubs. He would play there for his entire career, from 1949 to 1971, making more than 300 appearances in **goal** and playing a key role in five Soviet league championship victories for the team. Yashin's glowing international reputation was built from his performance for the Soviet team, making his first appearance in 1954. Two years later, he would keep goal as the Soviet Union won their first international tournament, the 1956 **Olympic Games Football Tournament**, in **Australia**. Garbed all in black, earning him the nickname the "Black Spider," he made his mark worldwide at the 1958 World Cup finals in **Sweden**, where the Soviets reached the quarterfinal stage. Two years later, Yashin played a critical role defensively as the Soviets won the 1960 **UEFA European Football Championship**, defeating **Yugoslavia** 2-1 in a hard-fought final. With Yashin still keeping goal, the Soviet Union again reached the quarterfinal stage of the World Cup in 1962, this time in **Chile**. The next year, Yashin became the first-and-still-only goalkeeper to be given the **European Footballer of the Year** award. He again kept goal for the Soviet Union in the 1966 World Cup final in **England**, where the Soviets produced their best World Cup result in their existence, reaching the semifinal stage. Yashin traveled with the Soviet Union team but did not play at the 1970 World Cup in Mexico and ended his international career that year after 78 appearances. Following retirement from playing, Yashin took up an administrative role with Dinamo Moscow and passed away in 1990. The regard in which Yashin is held internationally is reflected by the decision of the **Fédération Internationale de Football Association (FIFA)** in 1994 to name the new award for best goalkeeper at the World Cup after him.

YUGOSLAVIA. During the existence of Yugoslavia as a country in the 20th century until its breakup in 1992, it produced some extraordinarily successful soccer teams and players. Yugoslavia appeared at the **FIFA World Cup** on eight occasions, its best finish being fourth place in both 1930 and 1962. Yugoslavia also twice reached the final of the **UEFA European Football Championship**, in 1960 and 1976. Several club teams in constituent parts of Yugoslavia, such as **Red Star Belgrade** in present-day Serbia, winners of the **European Cup** and the **Intercontinental Cup** in 1991, shortly before the breakup of the country, also enjoyed success in European competition. *See also* DINAMO ZAGREB; MITROPA CUP.

Z

ZAGALLO, MÁRIO. B. 9 August 1931, Maceió, Brazil. An enormously successful Brazilian player and **coach**, Mário Zagallo played a key role in four of **Brazil**'s first five **FIFA World Cup** triumphs. As a player, Zagallo won several titles with Flamengo and Botafogo in his native Brazil. Zagallo played for Brazil in the 1950s and 1960s, making 37 appearances and scoring four goals, including a goal against **Sweden** in the 1958 World Cup final, which Brazil went on to win. Again featuring Zagallo, Brazil won the next World Cup in 1962, held in **Chile** as well.

After retirement from playing, Zagallo took over coaching at Brazilian club Botafogo in the late 1960s before becoming the Brazilian national team manager in 1970. Zagallo inherited a team with remarkable talent, and he molded them into one of the greatest attacking teams the world has ever seen. With **Pelé** playing a starring role, Brazil romped to their third World Cup victory in the 1970 finals in **Mexico**, winning all six games, Zagallo becoming the first man to win a World Cup as both a player and a manager. Brazil was less successful at the next World Cup in 1974, finishing fourth in West **Germany** under Zagallo's guidance. He then had a peripatetic career as both a club and international coach, with spells in Kuwait, **Saudi Arabia**, and the United Arab Emirates at international level, and with several clubs, his most notable success being a Brazilian national championship with Flamengo in 1986.

Zagallo won his fourth FIFA World Cup medal as an assistant coach for Brazil at the 1994 tournament in the **United States**. He then took over as head coach of Brazil once again, leading them to victory in the 1997 **Copa América**, and then to a runners-up spot at the 1998 World Cup in **France**. Despite some success, his second spell in charge of Brazil did not live up to his first, and Brazil's pragmatic approach received some criticism in contrast to the fluid style of the 1970s team Zagallo coached. After further short managerial spells at Portugesa and Flamengo, Zagallo appeared again on the Brazil bench at the 2006 World Cup in Germany, this time as a technical director, but on this occasion, they got no further than the quarterfinals.

ZAMALEK SPORTING CLUB. One of the most successful African clubs of all time, Zamalek Sporting Club (commonly known as "Al-Zamalek") from Cairo, **Egypt**, have won five **CAF Champions League** titles and 11 Egyptian league championships. The club was founded as Kasr El-Nil in 1911 by British expatriates and was changed to its current name, Zamalek Sporting Club, in 1952 after the Egyptian revolution. They currently play at Cairo International Stadium, a 74,000-capacity venue, opened in 1960 and significantly renovated in 2009, and located in the northeast of Cairo.

ZAMORA, RICARDO. B. 21 January 1901, Barcelona, Spain. D. 8 September 1978. During the interwar period, from 1918 to 1939, Ricardo Zamora was commonly regarded as the best **goalkeeper** in the world. At club level, he played most of his career in his native **Spain**, for Espanyol, **Barcelona**, and **Real Madrid**. An intimidating, giant force in the **goal**, Zamora became nationally famous in Spain not merely for his abilities as a goalkeeper but also for his charisma and personality off the field, where he lived an indulgent celebrity lifestyle. Zamora played for Spain on 46 occasions between 1920 and 1936, appearing at both the **FIFA World Cup** and **Olympic Games Football Tournament** for his country. He moved to **France** in 1936 and played for Nice before retiring in 1938. He later **coached** several teams across Europe.

ZAMORANO, IVÁN. B. 18 January 1967, Santiago, Chile. Iván Zamorano starred for **Chile** in the 1980s and 1990s and was one of the leading South American players of his generation. A lethal striker known in particular for his heading ability, he scored 34 goals in 69 games for Chile and played at the 1998 **FIFA World Cup** for his country, though he failed to score a goal. At the 2000 **Olympic Games Football Tournament**, Zamorano scored six goals in just five games as Chile finished third, winning a bronze medal. The peak of Zamorano's career came in the 1990s, when he won the Spanish league title with **Real Madrid** in 1995 and the **UEFA Cup** with **Internazionale** in **Italy** in 1998. He retired in 2003.

ZICO. B. 3 March 1953, Rio de Janeiro, Brazil. Perhaps the greatest Brazilian player of his generation, Zico's international career did not result in the same triumphs as did his predecessor's (**Brazil**'s best, **Pelé**), but some still whisper his name in the same breath when considering the respective talents of the two. Born Arthur Antunes Coimbra, he began his career with local club Flamengo in 1971, staying with the Brazilian club until 1983 and earning a reputation as one of Brazil's best attacking players. He was a goal scorer who was particularly deadly at taking **free kicks**. In that period, Flamengo claimed six São Paulo state titles, three national Brazilian championships, and, in 1981, won both the **Copa Libertadores** and the **Intercontinental Cup**.

Zico made his international debut for his country in 1976 and represented Brazil at the 1978, 1982, and 1986 **FIFA World Cup** tournaments. Zico was unfortunate to play for Brazil during a period of frustrating underachievement: despite their flowing, fantastic play—with Zico as the fulcrum of the team—they failed to live up to the impossible standard set by the previous generation of Brazilians, who had won three World Cup victories between 1958 and 1970. Zico came closest to glory with Brazil in the 1978 World Cup, reaching the semifinal stage. The 1982 Brazil team, though it did not go as far in the competition, is regarded as one of the best in World Cup history. Brazil won all three of its group-stage games, Zico scoring three goals. In the second-group stage, Brazil beat reigning champions **Argentina** 3-1, with Zico scoring again, but exited the tournament after a surprising defeat to hosts **Italy**. The next year, Zico moved to Italy to play for Udinese in *Serie A*, a successful sojourn that ended in 1985 with a return to Flamengo in Brazil, where he retired from play in 1994. He went on to have an impressive managerial career in **Japan**.

ZIDANE, ZINEDINE. B. 23 June 1972, Marseille, France. Zinedine Zidane's only rival for recognition as **France**'s greatest-ever player is **Michel Platini**, though Zidane went a step further than his predecessor from the 1980s by leading his country to their first-and-only **FIFA World Cup** triumph in 1998, on home soil. Zidane also led France to victory in the 2000 **UEFA European Football Championship** in the midst of a five-year period of glory that saw him named as **FIFA World Player of the Year** three times. At club level, he reached the pinnacle of the game starring for **Real Madrid** in their victorious 2002 **UEFA Champions League** run.

Born in Marseille in southern France, Zidane's Algerian heritage and leadership of France's multicultural '98 team saw him become a national icon for reasons beyond his phenomenal talent with the ball. Still, it was his magical mastery of the ball that took him out of poverty in childhood to a professional career with Cannes, where he made his debut in 1988 before moving on to Girondins de Bordeaux in 1992. Zidane's impressive play turned Bordeaux into a title contender and led to a move to Italian giants **Juventus** in 1996, where he won the league championship in his first season with the club. This was followed by impressive runs to, but disappointing defeats in, two consecutive UEFA Champions League finals, in 1997 and 1998. It was following a world-record transfer fee move to Real Madrid that Zidane finally won the UEFA Champions League, scoring the winning goal for his **Spanish** club with a superb volley in a 2-1 win over Bayer Leverkusen from **Germany**.

At international level, the 1998 World Cup finals in Zidane's native France saw him earn worldwide fame as the creative hub of his country's first World Cup victory. Zidane scored twice in the final against **Brazil** in a

3-0 victory for France. He then led his country to an unprecedented back-to-back sequence of victories in international tournaments, scoring two goals in France's winning run in the 2000 UEFA European Football Championship. But struggling with injury, Zidane was able to do little to help his country defend their World Cup title in 2002, where France exited in the first round of the finals tournament. The 2004 UEFA European Football Championships was almost as disappointing, with France losing to Greece in the quarterfinals. Zidane briefly retired from international soccer before returning in time for the 2006 World Cup tournament in Italy. He earned the FIFA Golden Ball as player of the tournament as he drove France to the final once again. Yet, it was there that Zidane would earn global infamy for the wrong reasons and despite his seventh-minute goal from the penalty spot. Taunted by Italian midfielder Marco Materazzi in extra time and with the score tied at 1-1, Zidane head butted him in the chest in response and was sent off. France went on to lose the game in a **penalty shoot-out**. That moment illustrated most vividly that behind Zidane's placid appearance, a temperamental passion flamed. Zidane retired following the final, a controversial ending to one of the greatest careers in the game's history.

ZOFF, DINO. B. 28 February 1942, Mariano del Friuli, Italy. Dino Zoff is widely regarded as the greatest **goalkeeper** in the history of **Italy**'s national team. He was a **FIFA World Cup** winner with his country at the 1982 competition held in **Spain**. A rock-solid and reliable goalkeeper, he played for Italy over a period of 15 years, making his debut in 1968 and racking up 111 total appearances. He also played for Italy at the 1974 and 1978 World Cups and won the **UEFA European Football Championship** with his country in 1968. At club level, Zoff's best run of success came playing for **Juventus**, with whom he won the Italian national league championship six times and with whom he won the **UEFA Cup** in 1977. Following retirement from playing in 1983, Zoff began a career as a coach, eventually managing Italy from 1998 to 2000. He reached the UEFA European Football Championship final in 2000, though lost there to **France**.

Appendix A

Presidents of the Fédération
Internationale de Football Association (FIFA)

1904–1906	Robert Guérin, France
1906–1918	Daniel Burley Woolfall, England
1921–1954	Jules Rimet, France
1954–1955	Rodolphe William Seeldrayers, Belgium
1955–1961	Arthur Drewry, England
1961–1974	Sir Stanley Rous, England
1974–1998	João Havelange, Brazil
1998–	Joseph S. Blatter, Switzerland

Appendix B

FIFA World Player of the Year Award (Men)

1991	Lothar Matthäus (Germany)
1992	Marco van Basten (Netherlands)
1993	Roberto Baggio (Italy)
1994	Romário (Brazil)
1995	George Weah (Liberia)
1996	Ronaldo (Brazil)
1997	Ronaldo (Brazil)
1998	Zinedine Zidane (France)
1999	Rivaldo (Brazil)
2000	Zinedine Zidane (France)
2001	Luis Figo (Portugal)
2002	Ronaldo (Brazil)
2003	Zinedine Zidane (France)
2004	Ronaldinho (Brazil)
2005	Ronaldinho (Brazil)
2006	Fabio Cannavaro (Italy)
2007	Kaka (Brazil)
2008	Cristiano Ronaldo (Portugal)
2009	Lionel Messi (Argentina)
2010	Lionel Messi (Argentina)

Appendix C

FIFA World Player of the Year Award (Women)

2001	Mia Hamm (United States)
2002	Mia Hamm (United States)
2003	Birgit Prinz (Germany)
2004	Birgit Prinz (Germany)
2005	Birgit Prinz (Germany)
2006	Marta (Brazil)
2007	Marta (Brazil)
2008	Marta (Brazil)
2009	Marta (Brazil)
2010	Marta (Brazil)

Appendix D

FIFA World Cup:
Dates, Hosts, Winners, and Runners-Up

	Host Nation	Dates	Winners	Runners-Up
1930	Uruguay	13–30 July	Uruguay	Argentina
1934	Italy	27 May–10 June	Italy	Czechoslovakia
1938	France	4–19 June	Italy	Hungary
1950	Brazil	24 June–16 July	Uruguay	Brazil
1954	Switzerland	16 June–4 July	West Germany	Hungary
1958	Sweden	8–29 June	Brazil	Sweden
1962	Chile	30 May–17 June	Brazil	Czechoslovakia
1966	England	11–30 July	England	West Germany
1970	Mexico	31 May–21 June	Brazil	Italy
1974	West Germany	13 June–7 July	West Germany	Netherlands
1978	Argentina	1–25 June	Argentina	Netherlands
1982	Spain	13 June–11 July	Italy	West Germany
1986	Mexico	31 May–29 June	Argentina	West Germany
1990	Italy	8 June–8 July	West Germany	Argentina
1994	United States	17 June–17 July	Brazil	Italy
1998	France	10 June–12 July	France	Brazil
2002	Republic of Korea/Japan	31 May–30 June	Brazil	West Germany
2006	Germany	9 June–9 July	Italy	France
2010	South Africa	11 June–11 July	Spain	Netherlands

Appendix E

FIFA Women's World Cup:
Dates, Hosts, Winners, and Runners-Up

	Host Nation	*Dates*	*Winners*	*Runners-Up*
1991	China	16–30 November	United States	Norway
1995	Sweden	5–18 June	Norway	Germany
1999	United States	19 June–10 July	United States	China
2003	United States	20 September–12 October	Germany	Sweden
2007	China	23 September–13 October	Germany	Brazil

Appendix F

Olympic Games Football Tournament: Dates, Hosts, Winners, and Runners-Up

Men's Competition

	Host City	Dates	Winners	Runners-Up
1908	London, England	19–24 October	Great Britain	Denmark
1912	Stockholm, Sweden	29 June–4 July	Great Britain	Denmark
1920	Antwerp, Belgium	28 August–6 September	Belgium	Spain
1924	Paris, France	25 May–9 June	Uruguay	Switzerland
1928	Amsterdam, Netherlands	27 May–13 June	Uruguay	Argentina
1936	Berlin, Germany	3–15 August	Italy	Austria
1948	London, England	31 July–13 August	Sweden	Yugoslavia
1952	Helsinki, Finland	15 July–2 August	Hungary	Yugoslavia
1956	Melbourne, Australia	24 November–8 December	Soviet Union	Yugoslavia
1960	Rome, Italy	26 August–10 September	Yugoslavia	Denmark
1964	Tokyo, Japan	11–23 October	Hungary	Czechoslovakia
1968	Mexico City, Mexico	13–26 October	Hungary	Bulgaria
1972	Munich, West Germany	26 August–10 September	Poland	Hungary
1976	Montreal, Canada	18–31 July	East Germany	Poland
1980	Moscow, Soviet Union	20 July–2 August	Czechoslovakia	East Germany
1984	Los Angeles, United States	29 July–11 August	France	Brazil
1988	Seoul, Republic of Korea	17 September–1 October	Soviet Union	Brazil
1992	Barcelona, Spain	24 July–8 August	Spain	Poland
1996	Atlanta, United States	20 July–3 August	Nigeria	Argentina
2000	Sydney, Australia	13–30 September	Cameroon	Spain
2004	Athens, Greece	11–28 August	Argentina	Paraguay
2008	Beijing, China	7–23 August	Argentina	Nigeria

Women's Competition

	Host City	Dates	Winners	Runners-Up
1996	Atlanta, United States	21 July–1 August	United States	China
2000	Sydney, Australia	13–30 September	Norway	United States
2004	Athens, Greece	11–29 August	United States	Brazil
2008	Beijing, China	6–21 August	United States	Brazil

Appendix G

UEFA European Football Championship: Dates, Hosts, Winners, and Runners-Up

	Host Nation(s)	Dates	Winners	Runners-Up
1960	France	6–10 July	Soviet Union	Yugoslavia
1964	Spain	17–21 June	Spain	Soviet Union
1968	Italy	5–8 June	Italy	Yugoslavia
1972	Belgium	14–18 June	West Germany	Soviet Union
1976	Yugoslavia	16–20 June	Czechoslovakia	West Germany
1980	Italy	11–22 June	West Germany	Belgium
1984	France	12–27 June	France	Spain
1988	West Germany	10–25 June	Netherlands	Soviet Union
1992	Sweden	10–26 June	Denmark	Germany
1996	England	8–30 June	Germany	Czech Republic
2000	Belgium and the Netherlands	12 June–2 July	France	Italy
2004	Portugal	12 June–4 July	Greece	Portugal
2008	Austria and Switzerland	7 June–29 June	Spain	Germany

Appendix H

Copa América: Dates, Hosts, Winners, and Runners-Up

	Host Nation	Dates	Winners	Runners-Up
1916	Argentina	2–12 July	Uruguay	Brazil
1917	Uruguay	30 September–14 October	Uruguay	Brazil
1919	Brazil	11–29 May	Brazil	Argentina
1920	Chile	11 September–3 October	Uruguay	Brazil
1921	Argentina	2–30 October	Argentina	Uruguay
1922	Brazil	17 September–22 October	Brazil	Uruguay
1923	Uruguay	29 October–2 December	Uruguay	Paraguay
1924	Uruguay	12 October–2 November	Uruguay	Paraguay
1925	Argentina	29 November–25 December	Argentina	Paraguay
1926	Chile	12 October–3 November	Uruguay	Chile
1927	Peru	30 October–27 November	Argentina	Peru
1929	Argentina	1–17 November	Argentina	Uruguay
1935	Peru	6–27 January	Uruguay	Peru
1937	Argentina	27 December 1936–1 February 1937	Argentina	Paraguay
1939	Peru	15 January–12 February	Peru	Paraguay
1941	Chile	2 February–4 March	Argentina	Chile
1942	Uruguay	10 January–7 February	Uruguay	Brazil
1945	Chile	14 January–28 February	Argentina	Chile
1946	Argentina	12 January–10 February	Argentina	Paraguay
1947	Ecuador	30 November–31 December	Argentina	Uruguay
1949	Brazil	3 April–11 May	Brazil	Peru
1953	Peru	22 February–1 April	Paraguay	Uruguay
1955	Chile	27 February–30 March	Argentina	Peru
1956	Uruguay	21 January–15 February	Uruguay	Argentina
1957	Peru	7 March–6 April	Argentina	Uruguay
1959	Argentina	7 March–4 April	Argentina	Paraguay
1959	Ecuador	5–25 December	Uruguay	Brazil
1963	Bolivia	10–31 March	Bolivia	Argentina
1967	Uruguay	17 January–2 February	Uruguay	Chile
1975	*	17 July–28 October	Peru	Brazil
1979	*	18 July–11 December	Paraguay	Brazil
1983	*	10 August–4 November	Uruguay	Paraguay
1987	Argentina	27 June–12 July	Uruguay	Colombia
1989	Brazil	1–16 July	Brazil	Argentina
1991	Chile	6–21 July	Argentina	Chile
1993	Ecuador	15 June–4 July	Argentina	Colombia
1995	Uruguay	5–23 July	Uruguay	Colombia
1997	Bolivia	11–29 June	Brazil	Mexico
1999	Paraguay	29 June–18 July	Brazil	Mexico
2001	Colombia	11–29 July	Colombia	Honduras
2004	Peru	6–25 July	Brazil	Uruguay
2007	Venezuela	26 June–15 July	Brazil	Mexico

*The tournament had no single host nation, with games alternating on a home-team and visiting-team basis.

Appendix I

Africa Cup of Nations: Dates, Hosts, Winners, and Runners-Up

	Host Nation	*Winners*	*Runners-Up*
1957	Sudan	Egypt	Ethiopia
1959	Egypt	Egypt	Sudan
1962	Ethiopia	Ethiopia	Egypt
1963	Ghana	Ghana	Sudan
1965	Tunisia	Ghana	Tunisia
1968	Ethiopia	Congo-Kinshasa	Ghana
1970	Sudan	Sudan	Ghana
1972	Cameroon	Congo-Brazzaville	Mali
1974	Egypt	Zaire	Zambia
1976	Ethiopia	Morocco	Zambia
1978	Ghana	Ghana	Uganda
1980	Nigeria	Nigeria	Algeria
1982	Libya	Ghana	Libya
1984	Ivory Coast	Cameroon	Nigeria
1986	Egypt	Egypt	Cameroon
1988	Morocco	Cameroon	Nigeria
1990	Algeria	Algeria	Nigeria
1992	Senegal	Ivory Coast	Ghana
1994	Tunisia	Nigeria	Zambia
1996	South Africa	South Africa	Tunisia
1998	Burkina Faso	Egypt	South Africa
2000	Ghana & Nigeria	Cameroon	Nigeria
2002	Mali	Cameroon	Senegal
2004	Tunisia	Tunisia	Morocco
2006	Egypt	Egypt	Ivory Coast
2008	Ghana	Egypt	Cameroon
2010	Angola	Egypt	Ghana

Appendix J

AFC Asian Cup: Dates, Hosts, Winners, and Runners-Up

	Host Nation	Winners	Runners-Up
1956	Hong Kong	Republic of Korea	Israel
1960	Republic of Korea	Republic of Korea	Israel
1964	Israel	Israel	India
1968	Iran	Iran	Burma
1972	Thailand	Iran	Republic of Korea
1976	Iran	Iran	Kuwait
1980	Kuwait	Kuwait	Republic of Korea
1984	Singapore	Saudi Arabia	China
1988	Qatar	Saudi Arabia	Republic of Korea
1992	Japan	Japan	Saudi Arabia
1996	United Arab Emirates	Saudi Arabia	United Arab Emirates
2000	Lebanon	Japan	Saudi Arabia
2004	China	Japan	China
2007	Indonesia, Malaysia, Thailand, and Vietnam	Iraq	Saudi Arabia

Appendix K

OFC Nations Cup: Dates, Hosts, Winners, and Runners-Up

	Host Nation	Winners	Runners-Up
1973	New Zealand	New Zealand	Tahiti
1980	New Caledonia	Australia	Tahiti
1996	*No host nation**	Australia	Tahiti
1998	Australia	New Zealand	Australia
2000	Tahiti	Australia	New Zealand
2002	New Zealand	New Zealand	Australia
2004	Australia	Australia	Solomon Islands
2008	*No host nation***	New Zealand	New Caledonia

*The competition was played as a round-robin group stage tournament with no fixed host nation.

**The competition was played on a home and away basis with no fixed host nation.

Appendix L

CONCACAF Gold Cup: Dates, Hosts, Winners, and Runners-Up

	Host Nation	Winners	Runners-Up
1991	United States	United States	Honduras
1993	Mexico and United States	Mexico	United States
1996	United States	Mexico	Brazil U-23
1998	United States	Mexico	United States
2000	United States	Canada	Colombia
2002	United States	United States	Costa Rica
2003	Mexico and United States	Mexico	Brazil U-23
2005	United States	United States	Panama
2007	United States	United States	Mexico
2009	United States	Mexico	United States

Appendix M

UEFA Champions League:
Dates, Hosts, Winners, and Runners-Up

Men's Competition

Season	Final Host City	Winners	Runners-Up
1955–1956	Paris	Real Madrid (ESP)	Stade Reims (FRA)
1956–1957	Madrid	Real Madrid (ESP)	Fiorentina (ITA)
1957–1958	Brussels	Real Madrid (ESP)	AC Milan (ITA)
1958–1959	Stuttgart	Real Madrid (ESP)	Stade Reims (FRA)
1959–1960	Glasgow	Real Madrid (ESP)	Eintracht Frankfurt (GER)
1960–1961	Berne	Benfica (POR)	Barcelona (ESP)
1961–1962	Amsterdam	Benfica (POR)	Real Madrid (ESP)
1962–1963	London	AC Milan (ITA)	Benfica (POR)
1963–1964	Vienna	Internazionale (ITA)	Real Madrid (ESP)
1964–1965	Milan	Internazionale (ITA)	Benfica (POR)
1965–1966	Brussels	Real Madrid (ESP)	Partizan Belgrade (SRB)
1966–1967	Lisbon	Glasgow Celtic (SCO)	Internazionale (ITA)
1967–1968	London	Manchester United (ENG)	Benfica (POR)
1968–1969	Madrid	AC Milan (ITA)	Ajax Amsterdam (NED)
1969–1970	Milan	Feyenoord (NED)	Glasgow Celtic (SCO)
1970–1971	London	Ajax Amsterdam (NED)	Panathinaikos (GRE)
1971–1972	Rotterdam	Ajax Amsterdam (NED)	Internazionale (ITA)
1972–1973	Belgrade	Ajax Amsterdam (NED)	Juventus (ITA)
1973–1974	Brussels	Bayern Munich (GER)	Atlético Madrid (ESP)
1974–1975	Paris	Bayern Munich (GER)	Leeds United (ENG)
1975–1976	Glasgow	Bayern Munich (GER)	AS Saint-Étienne (FRA)
1976–1977	Rome	Liverpool (ENG)	Borussia Mönchengladbach (GER)
1977–1978	London	Liverpool (ENG)	Club Brugge KV (BEL)
1978–1979	Munich	Nottingham Forest (ENG)	Malmö FF (SWE)
1979–1980	Madrid	Nottingham Forest (ENG)	Hamburg (GER)
1980–1981	Paris	Liverpool (ENG)	Real Madrid (ESP)
1981–1982	Rotterdam	Aston Villa (ENG)	Bayern Munich (GER)
1982–1983	Athens	Hamburger SV (GER)	Juventus (ITA)
1983–1984	Rome	Liverpool (ENG)	Roma (ITA)
1984–1985	Brussels	Juventus (ITA)	Liverpool (ENG)
1985–1986	Seville	Steaua Bucharest (ROU)	Barcelona (ESP)
1986–1987	Vienna	Porto (POR)	Bayern Munich (GER)
1987–1988	Stuttgart	PSV Eindhoven (NED)	Benfica (POR)
1988–1989	Barcelona	AC Milan (ITA)	Steaua Bucharest (ROU)
1989–1990	Vienna	AC Milan (ITA)	Benfica (POR)
1990–1991	Bari	Red Star Belgrade (SRB)	Olympique de Marseille (FRA)

Season	Final Host City	Winners	Runners-Up
1991–1992	London	Barcelona (ESP)	Sampdoria (ITA)
1992–1993	Munich	Olympique de Marseille (FRA)	Olympique de Marseille (FRA)
1993–1994	Athens	AC Milan (ITA)	Barcelona (ESP)
1994–1995	Vienna	Ajax Amsterdam (NED)	AC Milan (ITA)
1995–1996	Rome	Juventus (ITA)	Ajax Amsterdam (NED)
1996–1997	Munich	Borussia Dortmund (GER)	Juventus (ITA)
1997–1998	Amsterdam	Real Madrid (ESP)	Juventus (ITA)
1998–1999	Barcelona	Manchester United (ENG)	Bayern Munich (GER)
1999–2000	Paris	Real Madrid (ESP)	Valencia (ESP)
2000–2001	Milan	Bayern Munich (GER)	Valencia (ESP)
2001–2002	Glasgow	Real Madrid (ESP)	Bayer Leverkusen (GER)
2002–2003	Manchester	AC Milan (ITA)	Juventus (ITA)
2003–2004	Gelsenkirchen	Porto (POR)	Monaco (FRA)
2004–2005	Istanbul	Liverpool (ENG)	AC Milan (ITA)
2005–2006	Saint–Denis	Barcelona (ESP)	Arsenal (ENG)
2006–2007	Athens	AC Milan (ITA)	Liverpool (ENG)
2007–2008	Moscow	Manchester United (ENG)	Chelsea (ENG)
2008–2009	Rome	Barcelona (ESP)	Manchester United (ENG)
2009–2010	Madrid	Internazionale (ITA)	Bayern Munich (GER)
2010–2011	London	Barcelona (ESP)	Manchester United (ENG)

Women's Competition

Season	Host City/Cities	Winners	Runners-Up
2001–2002	Frankfurt, Germany*	FFC Frankfurt (GER)	Umeå IK (SWE)
2002–2003	Umeå, Sweden, and Hjørring, Denmark	Umeå IK (SWE)	Fortuna Hjørring (DEN)
2003–2004	Umeå, Sweden, and Frankfurt, Germany	Umeå IK (SWE)	FFC Frankfurt (GER)
2004–2005	Stockholm, Sweden, and Potsdam, Germany	FFC Turbine Potsdam (GER)	Djurgården/Älvsjö (SWE)
2005–2006	Potsdam, Germany, and Frankfurt, Germany	FFC Frankfurt (GER)	FFC Turbine Potsdam (GER)
2006–2007	Umeå, Sweden, and Borehamwood, England	Arsenal L.F.C. (ENG)	Umeå IK (SWE)
2007–2008	Umeå, Sweden, and Frankfurt, Germany	FFC Frankfurt (GER)	Umeå IK (SWE)
2008–2009	Kazan, Russia, and Duisburg, Germany	FCR 2001 Duisburg (GER)	Zvezda 2005 Perm (RUS)
2009–2010	Getafe, Spain	FFC Turbine Potsdam (GER)	Olympique Lyonnais (FRA)
2010–2011	London, England	Olympique Lyonnais (FRA)	FFC Turbine Potsdam (GER)

*The 2002 edition of the competition was the only time the competition had a single game final; later editions were played on a home and away basis.

Appendix N

Copa Libertadores:
Dates, Winners, and Runners-Up

Men's Competition

Season	Winners	Runners-Up
1960	Peñarol (URU)	Olimpia (PAR)
1961	Peñarol (URU)	Palmeiras (BRA)
1962	Santos (BRA)	Peñarol (URU)
1963	Santos (BRA)	Boca Juniors (ARG)
1964	Independiente (ARG)	Nacional (URU)
1965	Independiente (ARG)	Peñarol (URU)
1966	Peñarol (URU)	River Plate (ARG)
1967	Racing Club (ARG)	Nacional (URU)
1968	Estudiantes (ARG)	Palmeiras (BRA)
1969	Estudiantes (ARG)	Nacional (URU)
1970	Estudiantes (ARG)	Peñarol (URU)
1971	Nacional (URU)	Estudiantes (ARG)
1972	Independiente (ARG)	Universitario (PER)
1973	Independiente (ARG)	Colo Colo (CHI)
1974	Independiente (ARG)	São Paulo FC (BRA)
1975	Independiente (ARG)	Unión Española (CHI)
1976	Cruzeiro (BRA)	River Plate (ARG)
1977	Boca Juniors (ARG)	Cruzeiro (BRA)
1978	Boca Juniors (ARG)	Deportivo Cali (COL)
1979	Olimpia (PAR)	Boca Juniors (ARG)
1980	Nacional (URU)	Internacional (BRA)
1981	Flamengo (BRA)	Cobreloa (CHI)
1982	Peñarol (URU)	Cobreloa (CHI)
1983	Grêmio (BRA)	Olímpico (URU)
1984	Independiente (ARG)	Grêmio (BRA)
1985	Argentinos Juniors (ARG)	América (COL)
1986	River Plate (ARG)	América (COL)
1987	Peñarol (URU)	América (COL)
1988	Nacional (URU)	Newell's Old Boys (ARG)
1989	Atlético Nacional (COL)	Olimpia (PAR)
1990	Olimpia (PAR)	Barcelona SC (ECU)
1991	Colo Colo (CHI)	Olimpia (PAR)
1992	São Paulo (BRA)	Newell's Old Boys (ARG)
1993	São Paulo (BRA)	Universidad Católica (CHI)
1994	Vélez Sarsfield (ARG)	São Paulo FC (BRA)
1995	Grêmio (BRA)	Atlético Nacional (COL)

Season	Winners	Runners-Up
1996	River Plate (ARG)	América (COL)
1997	Cruzeiro (BRA)	Sporting Cristal (PER)
1998	Vasco da Gama (BRA)	Barcelona SC (ECU)
1999	Palmeiras (BRA)	Deportivo Cali (COL)
2000	Boca Juniors (ARG)	Palmeiras (BRA)
2001	Boca Juniors (ARG)	Cruz Azul (MEX)
2002	Olimpia (PAR)	São Caetano (BRA)
2003	Boca Juniors (ARG)	Santos (BRA)
2004	Once Caldas (COL)	Boca Juniors (ARG)
2005	São Paulo (BRA)	Atlético Paranaense (BRA)
2006	Internacional (BRA)	São Paulo (BRA)
2007	Boca Juniors (ARG)	Grêmio (BRA)
2008	LDU Quito (ECU)	Fluminense (BRA)
2009	Estudiantes (ARG)	Cruzeiro (BRA)
2010	International (BRA)	CD Guadalajara (MEX)

Women's Competition

Season	Winners	Runners-Up
2009	Santos (BRA)	Universidad Autónoma (PAR)
2010	Santos (BRA)	Everton (CHI)

Appendix O

AFC Champions League:
Dates, Winners, and Runners-Up

Season	Winners	Runners-Up
1967	Hapoel Tel-Aviv (ISR)	Selangor (MAS)
1969	Maccabi Tel-Aviv (ISR)	Yangzee (KOR)
1970	Esteghlal (IRA)	Hapoel Tel-Aviv (ISR)
1971	Maccabi Tel-Aviv (ISR)	Al-Shorta (IRQ)
1972–1985	*Not contested*	
1986	Daewoo Royals (KOR)	Al-Ahli Jeddah (KSA)
1987	Furukawa (JPN)	Al-Hilal (KSA)
1988	Yomiuri (JPN)	Al-Hilal (KSA)
1989	Al-Sadd (QAT)	Al-Rasheed (IRQ)
1990	Liaoning (CHN)	Nissan FC (JPN)
1991	Esteghlal (IRA)	Liaoning FC (CHN)
1992	Al-Hilal (KSA)	Esteghlal (IRA)
1993	PAS Tehran (IRA)	Al-Shabab (KSA)
1994	Thai Farmers Bank (THA)	Omani Club (OMA)
1995	Thai Farmers Bank (THA)	Al-Arabi (QAT)
1996	Ilhwa Chunma (KOR)	Al-Nasr (KSA)
1997	Pohang Steelers (KOR)	Ilhwa Chunma (KOR)
1998	Pohang Steelers (KOR)	Dalian Wanda (CHN)
1999	Jubilo Iwata (JPN)	Esteghlal (IRA)
2000	Al-Hilal (KSA)	Jubilo Iwata (JPN)
2001	Suwon Samsung Bluewings (JPN)	Jubilo Iwata (JPN)
2002	Suwon Samsung Bluewings (JPN)	Anyang LG Cheetahs (KOR)
2003	Al-Ain (UAE)	BEC Tero Sasana (THA)
2004	Al-Ittihad (KSA)	Seongnam Ilhwa Chunma (KOR)
2005	Al-Ittihad (KSA)	Al-Ain (UAE)
2006	Chonbuk Hyundai Motors (KOR)	Al-Karama (SYR)
2007	Urawa Red Diamonds (JPN)	Sepahan (IRA)
2008	Gamba Osaka (JPN)	Adelaide United (AUS)
2009	Pohang Steelers (KOR)	Al-Ittihad (KSA)
2010	Seongnam Ilhua Chunma (KOR)	Zob Ahan (IRA)

Appendix P

CAF Champions League:
Dates, Winners, and Runners-Up

Season	Winners	Runners-Up
1965	Oryx Douala (CMR)	Stade Malien (MLI)
1966	Stade (CIV)	Real Bamako (MLI)
1967	Tout Puissant Englebert (CGO)	Asante Kotoko (GHA)
1968	Tout Puissant Englebert (CGO)	Étoile Filante de Lom (TOG)
1969	Ismaily Sporting Club (EGY)	Tout Puissant Englebert (CGO)
1970	Asante Kotoko (GHA)	Tout Puissant Englebert (CGO)
1971	Canon Yaoundé (CMR)	Asante Kotoko (GHA)
1972	Hafia FC (GUI)	Simba FC (UGA)
1973	AS Vita Club (CGO)	Asante Kotoko (GHA)
1974	CARA Brazzaville (CGO)	Ghazl El-Mehalla (EGY)
1975	Hafia FC (GUI)	Enugu Rangers (NGA)
1976	MC Algiers (ALG)	Hafia FC (GUI)
1977	Hafia FC (GUI)	Hearts of Oak (GHA)
1978	Canon Yaoundé (CMR)	Hafia FC (GUI)
1979	Union Douala (CMR)	Hearts of Oak (GHA)
1980	Canon Yaoundé (CMR)	AS Bilima (CGO)
1981	JE Tizi-Ouzou (ALG)	AS Vita Club (CGO)
1982	Al-Ahly (EGY)	Asante Kotoko (GHA)
1983	Asante Kotoko (GHA)	Al-Ahly (EGY)
1984	Zamalek Sporting Club (EGY)	Shooting Stars (NGA)
1985	FAR Rabat (MAR)	AS Dragons (CGO)
1986	Zamalek Sporting Club (EGY)	Africa Sports National (CIV)
1987	Al-Ahly Sporting Club (EGY)	Al-Hilal (SUD)
1988	EP Sétif (ALG)	Iwuanyanwu Owerri (NGA)
1989	Raja CA Casablanca (MAR)	MP Oran (ALG)
1990	JS Kabylie (ALG)	Nkana Red Devils (ZAM)
1991	Club Africain (TUN)	Nakivubo Villa SC (UGA)
1992	Wydad AC (MAR)	Al-Hilal (SUD)
1993	Zamalek Sporting Club (EGY)	Asante Kotoko (GHA)
1994	Espérance Sportive de Tunis (TUN)	Zamalek Sporting Club (EGY)
1995	Orlando Pirates (RSA)	ASEC Mimosas (CIV)
1996	Zamalek Sporting Club (EGY)	Shooting Stars (NGA)
1997	Raja CA Casablanca (MAR)	Obuasi Goldfields (GHA)
1998	ASEC Mimosas (CIV)	Dynamos Football Club (ZIM)
1999	Raja CA Casablanca (MAR)	Espérance Sportive de Tunis (TUN)
2000	Hearts of Oak (GHA)	Espérance Sportive de Tunis (TUN)

Season	Winners	Runners-Up
2001	Al-Ahly Sporting Club (EGY)	Mamelodi Sundowns (RSA)
2002	Zamalek Sporting Club (EGY)	Raja CA Casablanca (MAR)
2003	Enyimba (NGA)	Ismaily Sporting Club (EGY)
2004	Enyimba (NGA)	Étoile Sportive du Sahel (TUN)
2005	Al-Ahly Sporting Club (EGY)	Étoile Sportive du Sahel (TUN)
2006	Al-Ahly Sporting Club (EGY)	CS Sfaxien (TUN)
2007	Étoile Sportive du Sahel (TUN)	Al-Ahly Sporting Club (EGY)
2008	Al-Ahly Sporting Club (EGY)	Cotonsport Garoua (CMR)
2009	Tout Puissant Mazembe (CGO)	Heartland (NGA)
2010	Tout Puissant Mazembe (CGO)	ES Tunis (TUN)

Appendix Q

OFC Champions League:
Dates, Winners, and Runners-Up

Season	Winners	Runners-Up
1987	Adelaide FC (AUS)	University-Mount Wellington (NZL)
1999	South Melbourne FC (AUS)	Nadi FC (FIJ)
2001	Wollongong Wolves (AUS)	Tafea FC (VAN)
2005	Sydney FC (AUS)	AS Magenta (NCL)
2006	Auckland City FC (NZL)	AS Pirae (TAH)
2007	Waitakere United (NZL)	Ba FC (FIJ)
2007–2008	Waitakere United (NZL)	Kossa FC (SOL)
2008–2009	Auckland City FC (NZL)	Koloale FC (SOL)
2009–2010	PRK Hekari United (PNG)	Waitakere United (NZL)
2010–2011	Aukland City FC (NZL)	Amicale FC (VAN)

Appendix R

CONCACAF Champions League:
Dates, Winners, and Runners-Up

Season	Winners	Runners-Up
1962	CD Guadalajara (MEX)	CSD Comunicaciones (GUA)
1963	Racing Club Haiten (HAI)	CD Guadalajara (MEX)
1964–1966	*Tournament not contested*	
1967	Alianza FC (SLV)	Jong Colombia (ANT)
1968	CD Toluca* (MEX)	
1969	CD SC Cruz Azul (MEX)	CSD Comunicaciones (GUA)
1970	CD SC Cruz Azul (MEX)**	
1971	CD SC Cruz Azul (MEX)	LD Alajuelense (CRC)
1972	CD Olimpia (HON)	SV Robinhood (SUR)
1973	SV Transvaal (SUR)***	
1974	CSD Municipal (GUA)	SV Transvaal (SUR)
1975	Atlético Español (MEX)	SV Transvaal (SUR)
1976	CD Aguila (SLV)	SV Robinhood (SUR)
1977	Club América (MEX)	SV Robinhood (SUR)
1978	*No overall winner declared*	
1979	CD F.A.S. (SLV)	Tigres UANL (MEX)
1980	Pumas UNAM (MEX)	Universidad NAH (HON)
1981	SV Transvaal (SUR)	Atletico Marte (SLV)
1982	Pumas UNAM (MEX)	SV Robinhood (SUR)
1983	Atlante FC (MEX)	SV Robinhood (SUR)
1984	Violette AC (HAI)****	
1985	CD Olimpia (HON)	Club América (MEX)
1986	LD Alajuelense (CRC)	SV Transvaal (SUR)
1987	Club América (MEX)	Defence Force (TRI)
1988	CD Olimpia (HON)	Defence Force (TRI)
1989	Pumas UNAM (MEX)	Pinar del Rio (CUB)
1990	Club América (MEX)	Pinar del Rio (CUB)
1991	Puebla (MEX)	Police FC (TRI)
1992	Club América (MEX)	LD Alajuelense (CRC)
1993	Deportivo Saprissa (CRC)	Leon (MEX)
1994	CS Cartagines (CRC)	Atlante FC (MEX)
1995	Deportivo Saprissa (CRC)	CSD Municipal (GUA)
1996	CD SC Cruz Azul (MEX)	CID Necaxa (MEX)
1997	CD SC Cruz Azul (MEX)	Los Angeles Galaxy (USA)
1998	D.C. United (USA)	CD Toluca (MEX)
1999	CID Necaxa (MEX)	LD Alajuelense (CRC)
2000	Los Angeles Galaxy (USA)	CD Olimpia (HON)
2001	*Tournament not completed*	

(continued)

Season	Winners	Runners-Up
2002	Pachuca CF (MEX)	Monarcas Morelia (MEX)
2003	CD Toluca (MEX)	CA Monarcas Morelia (MEX)
2004	LD Alajuelense (CRC)	Deportivo Saprissa (CRC)
2005	Deportivo Saprissa (CRC)	Pumas UNAM (MEX)
2006	Club América (MEX)	CD Toluca (MEX)
2007	Pachuca CF (MEX)	CD Guadalajara (MEX)
2008	Pachuca CF (MEX)	Deportivo Saprissa (CRC)
2008–2009	Atlante (MEX)	CD SC Cruz Azul (MEX)
2009–2010	Pachuca CF (MEX)	Cruz Azul (MEX)
2010–2011	Monterrey (MEX)	Real Salt Lake (USA)

*CD Toluca were declared champions as the remaining team in the competition after the disqualification of Aurora FC (GUA) and SV Transvaal (SUR).

**CD SC Cruz Azul (MEX) were declared winners after withdrawal of Deportivo Saprissa (CRC) and SV Transvaal (SUR).

***SV Transvaal (SUR) were declared winners after withdrawal of Deportivo Saprissa (CRC) and LD Alajuelense (CRC).

****Violette AC (HAI) were declared winners following the disqualification of CD Guadalajara (MEX) and New York Pancyrian-Freedoms (USA).

Appendix S

FIFA Club World Cup: Dates, Hosts, Winners, and Runners-Up

Year	Host Nation	Winners	Runners-Up
2000	Brazil	Corinthians (BRA)	Vasco de Gama (BRA)
2005	Japan	São Paulo FC (BRA)	Liverpool (ENG)
2006	Japan	Internacional (ARG)	Barcelona (SPA)
2007	Japan	AC Milan (ITA)	Boca Juniors (ARG)
2008	Japan	Manchester United (ENG)	LDU Quito (ECU)
2009	United Arab Emirates	Barcelona (SPA)	Estudiantes (ARG)
2010	United Arab Emirates	Internazionale (ITA)	TP Mazembe (CGO)

Appendix T

Intercontinental Cup:
Dates, Winners, and Runners-Up

Season	Winners	Runners-Up
1960	Real Madrid (ESP)	Peñarol (URU)
1961	Peñarol (URU)	Benfica (POR)
1962	Santos (BRA)	Benfica (POR)
1963	Santos (BRA)	AC Milan (ITA)
1964	Internazionale (ITA)	Independiente (ARG)
1965	Internazionale (ITA)	Independiente (ARG)
1966	Peñarol (URU)	Real Madrid (ESP)
1967	Racing Club (ARG)	Glasgow Celtic (SCO)
1968	Estudiantes (ARG)	Manchester United (ENG)
1969	AC Milan (ITA)	Estudiantes (ARG)
1970	Feyenoord (NED)	Estudiantes (ARG)
1971	Nacional (URU)	Panathinaikos (GRE)
1972	Ajax Amsterdam (NED)	Independiente (ARG)
1973	Independiente (ARG)	Juventus (ARG)
1974	Atlético Madrid (ESP)	Independiente (ARG)
1975	*Not contested*	
1976	Bayern Munich (GER)	Cruzeiro (BRA)
1977	Boca Juniors (ARG)	Borussia Mönchengladbach (GER)
1978	*Not contested*	
1979	Olimpia (PAR)	Malmö (SWE)

From 1980 forward, the competition was known as the "Toyota Cup" and was played in Tokyo, Japan.

Season	Winners	Runners-Up
1980	Nacional (URU)	Nottingham Forest (ENG)
1981	Flamengo (BRA)	Liverpool (ENG)
1982	Peñarol (URU)	Aston Villa (ENG)
1983	Grêmio (BRA)	Hamburg (GER)
1984	Independiente (ARG)	Liverpool (ENG)
1985	Juventus (ITA)	Argentinos Juniors (ARG)
1986	River Plate (ARG)	Steaua Bucharest (ROM)
1987	Porto (POR)	Peñarol (URU)
1988	Nacional (URU)	PSV Eindhoven (NED)
1989	AC Milan (ITA)	Atlético Nacional (COL)
1990	AC Milan (ITA)	Olimpia (PAR)
1991	Red Star Belgrade (SRB)	Colo Colo (CHI)
1992	São Paulo (BRA)	Barcelona (ESP)
1993	São Paulo (BRA)	AC Milan (ITA)
1994	Vélez Sarsfield (ARG)	AC Milan (ITA)
1995	Ajax Amsterdam (NED)	Grêmio (BRA)

Season	Winners	Runners-Up
1996	Juventus (ITA)	River Plate (ARG)
1997	Borussia Dortmund (GER)	Cruzeiro (BRA)
1998	Real Madrid (ESP)	Vasco de Gama (BRA)
1999	Manchester United (ENG)	Palmeiras (BRA)
2000	Boca Juniors (ARG)	Real Madrid (ESP)
2001	Bayern Munich (GER)	Boca Juniors (ARG)
2002	Real Madrid (ESP)	Olimpia (PAR)
2003	Boca Juniors (ARG)	AC Milan (ITA)
2004	Porto (POR)	Once Caldes (COL)

Bibliography

CONTENTS

INTRODUCTION

The number of books written on world soccer has increased enormously in the past two decades, with broad narratives of the global game, monographs on the history of soccer in specific countries, and a spate of academic works on aspects of the game's sociology much more widely available than ever before. The best single history of the global game is David Goldblatt's *The Ball Is Round*, a monumental and learned account of the history of soccer worldwide. A briefer, polemical book covering the same history from a perspective focused on the balance between the joy of the game and the growing business of the sport over the 20th century can be found in Eduardo Galeano's classic *Soccer in Sun and Shadow*. Further diverse perspectives on the sport as a culture are in the excellent compendium edited by John Turbull, *The Global Game: Writers on Soccer*. On the field, the strongest account of the game's evolution tactically is in Jonathan Wilson's *Inverting the Pyramid: A History of Football Tactics*.

Soccer as a global sport has generated a new genre in the past two decades, the travelogue, with Simon Kuper's early *Soccer against the Enemy* the best of those, with Kuper traveling from Serbia to Scotland to investigate the passion and politics interweaved into soccer culture. The story of the FIFA World Cup is told well in Brian Glanville's *The Story of the World Cup*. Though largely focused on Britain, Neil Carter's *The Football Manager: A History* is an excellent overview of the development of soccer coaching as a profession. From an academic perspective, numerous works cover the game using primary sources in valuable ways, such as Adrian Harvey's *Football, the First Hundred Years: The Untold Story*. The majority of the literature on soccer today is written by journalists: this can range from outstanding inside stories of specific teams, such as Hunter Davies' classic account of Tottenham Hotspur in the 1970s with *The Glory Game*, to Andrew Jennings' investigative account of the corruption surrounding the highest levels of soccer administration globally, in *Foul! The Secret World of FIFA: Bribes, Vote Rigging and Ticket Scandals*. Fan-driven accounts have also become popular since the 1990s: there is a large range of books produced by former soccer hooligans barely worth mentioning, while Nick Hornby's *Fever Pitch*, the story of a young man's obsession with soccer and Arsenal Football Club in the context of his life growing up in London, became a popular culture hit in the early 1990s. How the business of soccer, and its growing rapaciousness and commercialization, has impacted on fans and the clubs they support in Britain is particularly well covered in David Conn's *The Beautiful Game?* Women's soccer has been largely neglected in soccer literature, but two teams' stories are well told with larger lessons drawn on the fight women have had to wage to play the game: Barbara Jacobs' *The Dick, Kerr's Ladies* on an English women's soccer club in the pre–World War II era and Jere Longman's *The Girls of Summer*, on the victorious 1999 U.S. Women's World Cup team.

In recent years, numerous monographs on the history of the sport in specific countries have been produced: some of the best include *Brilliant Orange* by David Winner on the Netherlands; *Tor!* by Ulrich Hesse-Lichtenberge on Germany; *Calcio*, by John Foot on Italian soccer; *Morbo*, Phil Ball's history of Spanish soccer; *Futebol*, Alex Bellos' book on soccer in Brazil; and on North American soccer, David Wangerin's *Soccer in a Football World*. Broader regional coverage can be found for Eastern Europe and Russia in Jonathan Wilson's *Behind the Curtain*, for the Far East in John Horne and Wolfram Manzenreiter's *Football Goes East*, and for Africa in Filippo Maria Ricci's *Elephants, Lions and Eagles*, among others.

Photography and design have inspired several excellent volumes: a look below the spotlights of the top tiers of European soccer can be found in Hans van der Meer's *European Fields: The Landscape of Lower League Football*, and graphic design is well covered in Jeremy Leslie and Patrick Burgoyne's *FC Football Graphics*. Soccer has even inspired some splendid fiction, albeit based on a true story: David Peace's novel, *The Damned Utd*, on the career of English soccer manager Brian Clough.

This bibliography covers works mainly in the English language and is thus skewed toward coverage of Great Britain, which has the largest soccer literature of any English-speaking country due to the origins and popularity of the game there. A fairly extensive literature does now exist on soccer in the United States, with several recent single-volume studies on various aspects of the game's history, sociology, and economics having been released in the past decade. Coverage of the sport in non-English speaking countries in the English language has also improved greatly, with a select few works in other languages also provided. The works are divided by region. A separate bibliographic section also details the growing number of works on women's soccer. Useful reference works, magazines, and websites on world soccer are also listed.

WORLD SOCCER HISTORY AND SOCIOLOGY

Armstrong, Gary, and Richard Giulianotti. *Fear and Loathing in World Football*. Oxford: Berg, 2001.

Brown, Adam. *Fanatics! Power, Identity and Fandom in Football*. London: Routledge, 1998.

Darby, Paul, Martin Johnes, and Gavin Mellor, eds. *Soccer and Disaster: International Perspectives*. New York: Routledge, 2005.

Foer, Franklin. *How Soccer Explains the World: An Unlikely Theory of Globalization*. New York: HarperCollins, 2004.

Galeano, Eduardo. *Soccer in Sun and Shadow*. London: Verso, 1998.

Giulianotti, Richard. *Football: A Sociology of the Global Game*. Cambridge: Polity Press, 1999.

Giulianotti, Richard, Norman Bonney, and Mike Hepworth. *Football, Violence, and Social Identity*. London: Routledge, 1994.

Goldblatt, David. *The Ball Is Round: A Global History of Soccer*. New York: Viking, 2006.

Harvey, Adrian. *Football: the First Hundred Years—The Untold Story*. New York: Routledge, 2005.

Hough, Peter. "'Make Goals Not War': The Contribution of International Football to World Peace." *International Journal of the History of Sport* 25, no. 10 (2008): 1287–1305.

Jennings, Andrew. *Foul! The Secret World of FIFA: Bribes, Vote Rigging and Ticket Scandals*. London: HarperCollins, 2007.

Kuper, Simon. *Soccer against the Enemy: How the World's Most Popular Sport Starts and Fuels Revolutions and Keeps Dictators in Power*. New York: Nation Books, 2006.

Lanfranchi, Pierre, Christiane Eisenberg, Tony Mason, and Alfred Wahl, eds. *100 Years of Football: The FIFA Centennial Book*. London: Weidenfeld & Nicolson, 2004.

Martinez, D. P., and Projit Bihari Mukharji. *Football: From England to the World*. London: Routledge, 2009.

McIlvanney, Hugh. *McIlvanney on Football*. London: Mainstream Publishing, 1999.

Merrill, Christopher. *The Grass of Another Country: A Journey through the World of Soccer*. New York: H. Holt, 1993.

Morris, Desmond. *The Soccer Tribe*. London: Cape, 1981.

Murphy, Patrick, John Williams, and Eric Dunning. *Football on Trial: Spectator Violence and Development in the Football World*. London: Routledge, 1990.

Murray, Bill. *The World's Game: A History of Soccer*. Urbana: University of Illinois Press, 1998.

Rous, Stanley. *Football Worlds: A Lifetime in Sport*. London: Faber and Faber, 1978.

Sugden, John Peter, and Alan Tomlinson. *Badfellas: Fifa Family at War*. Edinburgh: Mainstream Publishing, 2003.

——. *FIFA and the Contest for World Football: Who Rules the People's Game*. Cambridge: Polity, 1998.

Taylor, Matthew. *The Association Game: A History of British Football*. Harlow, England: Pearson Longman, 2008.

Turnbull, John, Thom Satterlee, and Alon Raab, eds. *The Global Game: Writers on Soccer*. Lincoln: University of Nebraska Press, 2008.

Vinnai, Gerhard. *Football Mania: The Players and the Fans: The Mass Psychology of Football*. London: Orbach and Chambers, 1973.

Wagg, Stephen. *Giving the Game Away: Football, Politics, and Culture on Five Continents*. London: Leicester University Press, 1995.

Weiland, Matt, and Sean Wilsey, eds. *The Thinking Fan's Guide to the World Cup*. London: Harper Perennial, 2006.

Wilson, Jonathan. *Behind the Curtain: Travels in Eastern European Football*. London: Orion, 2006.

——. *Inverting the Pyramid: A History of Football Tactics*. London: Orion, 2008.

THE FIFA WORLD CUP

Crouch, Terry. *The World Cup: The Complete History*. 3rd ed. London: Aurum, 2010.

Freddi, Cris. *Complete Book of the World Cup 2006*. London: HarperSport, 2006.

Glanville, Brian. *The Story of the World Cup*. London: Faber and Faber, 1997.

Jawad, Hyad. *Four Weeks in Montevideo: The Story of World Cup 1930*. London: Seventeen Media, 2009.

Lisi, Clemente Angelo. *A History of the World Cup: 1930–2006*. Lanham, Maryland: Scarecrow Press, 2007.

McIlvanney, Hugh, and John Arlott. *World Cup '66*. London: Eyre & Spottiswood, 1966.

Spurling, John. *Death or Glory: The Dark History of the World Cup*. London: Vision Sports Publishing, 2010.

Sugden, John Peter, and Alan Tomlinson. *Hosts and Champions: Soccer Cultures, National Identities and the USA World Cup*. Aldershot, UK: Arena, 1994.

Tomlinson, Alan, and Christopher Young. *National Identity and Global Sports Events: Culture, Politics, and Spectacle in the Olympics and the Football World Cup*. Albany: State University of New York Press, 2006.

WOMEN'S SOCCER

Araton, Harvey. *Alive and Kicking: When Soccer Moms Take the Field and Change Their Lives Forever*. New York: Simon & Schuster, 2001.

Brennan, Patrick. *The Munitionettes: A History of Women's Football in North East England during the Great War*. Rowlands Gill, UK: Donmouth Publishing, 2007.

Crothers, Tim. *The Man Watching: A Biography of Anson Dorrance, the Unlikely Architect of the Greatest College Sports Dynasty Ever*. Ann Arbor, Michigan: Sports Media Group, 2006.

Davies, Pete. *I Lost My Heart to the Belles*. London: Heinemann, 1996.

Fan, Hong, and J. A. Mangan. *Soccer, Women, Sexual Liberation Kicking Off a New Era*. London: F. Cass, 2004.

Fozooni, Babak. "Iranian Women and Football." *Cultural Studies* 22, no. 1 (2008): 114–33.

Jacobs, Barbara. *The Dick, Kerr's Ladies*. London: Robinson Publishing, 2004.

Lee, James F. *The Lady Footballers: Struggling to Play in Victorian Britain*. London: Routledge, 2008.

Longman, Jere. *The Girls of Summer: The U.S. Women's Soccer Team and How It Changed the World*. New York: HarperCollins, 2000.

Newsham, Gail J. *In a League of Their Own! The Dick, Kerr Ladies' Football Club*. London: Scarlet Press, 1997.

Owen, Wendy. *Kicking against Tradition: A Career in Women's Football*. Stroud, UK: Tempus, 2005.

Rudd, Alyson. *Astroturf Blonde: Up Front and Onside in a Man's Game*. London: Headline, 1998.

Smale, David. *Nothin' Finer Carolina: The History of the University of North Carolina Women's Soccer*. Virginia Beach, Virginia: The Donning Company, 1995.

Williams, Jean. *A Beautiful Game: International Perspectives on Women's Football.* New York: Berg Publishers, 2008.

———. *A Game for Rough Girls? A History of Women's Football in Britain.* London: Routledge, 2003.

Williamson, David J. *Belles of the Ball.* Devon, England: R&D Associates, 1991.

Woodhouse, Donna, and John Williams. *Offside? The Position of Women in Football.* Reading: South Street, 1999.

AFRICA

General

Alegi, Peter. *African Soccerscapes: How a Continent Changed the World's Game.* Athens: Ohio University Press, 2010.

Armstrong, Gary, and Richard Giulianotti, eds. *Football in Africa: Conflict, Conciliation, and Community.* New York: Palgrave Macmillan, 2004.

Bloomfield, Steve. *Africa United: Soccer, Passion, Politics, and the First World Cup in Africa.* London: Harper Perennial, 2010.

Darby, Paul. *Africa, Football, and FIFA: Politics, Colonialism, Resistance.* London: Routledge, 2002.

Hawkey, Ian. *Feet of the Chameleon: The Story of African Football.* London: Portico, 2010.

Kapuściński, Ryszard. *The Soccer War.* New York: Knopf, 1991.

Pannenborg, Arnold. *How to Win a Football Match in Cameroon: An Anthropological Study of Africa's Most Popular Sport.* Leiden: African Studies Centre, 2008.

Ricci, Filippo Maria. *Elephants, Lions, and Eagles: A Journey through African Football.* London: WSC Books, 2008.

Ghana

"Win the Match and Vote for Me: The Politicisation of Ghana's Accra Hearts of Oak and Kumasi Asante Kotoko Football Clubs." *The Journal of Modern African Studies* 47, no. 1 (2009): 19–39.

Nigeria

Akpabot, Samuel Ekpe. *Football in Nigeria.* London: Macmillan Publishers, 1985.

Vasili, Philip. "The Right Kind of Fellow: Nigerian Football Tourists as Agents of Europeanization." *The International Journal of the History of Sport* 11, no. 2 (August 1994): 191–211.

South Africa

Alegi, Peter. *Laduna! Soccer, Politics and Society in South Africa.* Scottsville, South Africa: University of Kwazulu Natal Press, 2004.

Bolsmann, Chris. "White Football in South Africa: Empire, Apartheid and Change, 1892–1977." *Soccer & Society* 11, no. 1–2 (2010): 1–2.

Collins, Neal. *A Game Apart: The Real Story behind the World Cup in South Africa, 2010*. Milton Keynes, UK: AuthorHouse, 2009.

Korr, Chuck, and Marvin Close. *More Than Just a Game: Football v Apartheid, The Most Important Football Story Ever Told*. London: HarperCollins, 2008.

Latakgomo, Joe. *Mzansi Magic: Struggle, Betrayal and Glory: The Story of South African Soccer*. Cape Town: Tafelberg, 2010.

Thabe, George Andries Lesitsi, and M. Mutloatse. *It's a Goal! 50 Years of Sweat, Tears, and Drama in Black Soccer*. Johannesburg: Skotaville Publishers, 1983.

ASIA

General

Dimeo, Paul, and James Mills. *Soccer in South Asia: Empire, Nation, Diaspora*. London: F. Cass, 2001.

Far East (Japan, Republic of Korea, China)

Horne, John, and Wolfram Manzenreiter, eds. *Football Goes East: The People's Game in China, Japan, and Korea*. London: Routledge, 2004.

——, eds. *Japan, Korea and the 2002 World Cup*. London: Routledge, 2002.

Moffett, Sebastian. *Japanese Rules: Japan and the Beautiful Game*. London: Yellow Jersey Press, 2003.

Perryman, Mark. *Going Oriental: Football after World Cup 2002*. Edinburgh: Mainstream Publishing, 2002.

India

Basu, Jaydeep. *Stories from Indian Football*. New Delhi: UBS Publishers' Distributors, 2003.

Bhattacharya, Nalinaksha. *Hem and Football*. London: Secker & Warburg, 1992.

Majumdar, Boria. "Ghati-Bangal on the Maidan: Subregionalism, Club Rivalry and Fan Culture in Indian Football." *Soccer and Society* 9, no. 2 (2008): 286–99.

Majumdar, Boria, and Kausik Bandyopadhyay. *A Social History of Indian Football*. London: Routledge, 2006.

——. *Goalless: The Story of a Unique Footballing Nation*. New Delhi: Viking, 2006.

Mason, Tony. "Football on the Maidan: Cultural Imperialism in Calcutta." *The International Journal of the History of Sport* 8, no. 1 (May 1990): 85–96.

Mitra, Soumen. *In Search of an Identity: The History of Football in Colonial Calcutta*. Kolkata: Dasgupta & Co., 2007.

Iraq

Freeman, Simon. *Baghdad FC: Iraq's Football Story: A Hidden History of Sport and Tyranny.* London: John Murray, 2006.

EUROPE

General

Ahlstrom, F., ed. *Fifty Years of European Club Football.* Nyon: UEFA.
Gehrmann, Siegfried. *Football and Regional Identity in Europe.* Münster: Lit-Verlags-Gesellschaft, 1997.

Denmark

Christensen, Peter, and Frederik Stjernfelt. *Fodbold! Forfattere om fænomenet fodbold.* Copenhagen: Gyldendal, 2003.

France

Dauncey, Hugh, and Geoff Hare, eds. *France and the 1998 World Cup: The National Impact of a World Sporting Event.* London: Frank Cass, 1999.
Dubois, Laurent. *Soccer Empire: The World Cup and the Future of France.* Berkeley: University of California Press, 2010.
Hare, Geoff. *Football in France: A Cultural History.* New York: Berg, 2003.
Rühn, Christov. *Le Foot: The Legends of French Football.* London: Abacus, 2000.

Germany

Downing, David. *The Best of Enemies: England v. Germany, a Century of Football Rivalry.* London: Bloomsbury, 2001.
Eisenberg, Christiane. "Football in Germany: Beginnings, 1900–1914." *The International Journal of the History of Sport* 8, no. 3 (September 1991): 205–20.
Hesse-Lichtenberger, Ulrich. *Tor! The Story of German Football.* London: WSC Books, 2003.
Tomlinson, Alan, and Christopher Young. *German Football: History, Culture, Society.* New York: Routledge, 2006.
Wangerin, David. *Fussball Book: German Football since the Bundesliga.* Perton, Staffordshire: D. Wangerin, 1993.

Great Britain

Bains, Jas, and Sanjiev Johal. *Corner Flags and Corner Shops: The Asian Football Experience.* London: Victor Gollancz, 1998.

Beck, Peter. *Scoring for Britain: International Football and International Politics, 1900–1939.* (Series: Sport in the Global Society). London: F. Cass, 1999.

Carter, Neil. *The Football Manager: A History.* New York: Routledge, 2006.

Collins, Tony, and Wray Vamplew. *Mud, Sweat, and Beers: A Cultural History of Sport and Alcohol.* New York: Berg Publishers, 2002.

Conn, David. *The Beautiful Game? Searching for the Soul of Football.* London: Yellow Jersey Press, 2005.

Crampsey, Robert A. *The Game for the Game's Sake: The History of Queen's Park Football Club, 1867–1967.* Glasgow: Queen's Park Football Club, 1967.

Davies, Hunter. *Boots, Balls, and Haircuts: An Illustrated History of Football from Then to Now.* London: Cassell Illustrated, 2003.

Dunning, Eric, Patrick Murphy, and John Williams. *The Roots of Football Hooliganism: An Historical and Sociological Study.* London: Routledge & Kegan Paul, 1988.

Farnsworth, Keith. *Sheffield Football: A History.* Sheffield: Hallamshire Press, 1995.

Fishwick, Nicholas. *English Football and Society, 1910–1950.* Manchester: Manchester University Press, 1989.

Fynn, Alex, Lynton Guest, and Peter Law. *The Secret Life of Football.* London: Queen Anne Press, 1989.

Harding, John. *Behind the Glory: A History of the Professional Footballers Association—100 Years of the PFA.* Derby, UK: Breedon, 2009.

Hickey, Colm, and J. A. Mangan, eds. *Soccer, Schoolmasters, and the Spread of Association Football.* London: Routledge, 2005.

Hill, Dave. *"Out of His Skin": The John Barnes Phenomenon.* London: Faber, 1989.

Hopcraft, Arthur. *The Football Man: People and Passions in Soccer.* London: Aurum Press, 2006.

Hornby, Nick. *Fever Pitch.* London: Penguin Books, 1992.

Hunter, Davies. *The Glory Game: The New Edition of the British Football Classic.* Edinburgh, Scotland: Mainstream Publishing, 2000.

Imlach, Gary. *My Father and Other Working-Class Football Heroes.* London: Yellow Jersey, 2005.

Inglis, Simon. *Engineering Archie: Archibald Leitch—Football Ground Designer.* London: English Heritage, 2005.

———. *Soccer in the Dock: A History of British Football Scandals, 1900–1965.* London: Willow Books, 1985.

Murray, William James. *Bhoys, Bears and Bigotry: Rangers, Celtic and the Old Firm in the New Age of Globalised Sport.* Edinburgh: Mainstream Publishing, 2003.

Peace, David. *The Damned Utd.* London: Faber, 2006.

Russell, Dave. *Football and the English: A Social History of Association Football in England, 1863–1995.* Preston, UK: Carnegie Publishing, 1997.

Sanders, Richard. *Beastly Fury: The Strange Birth of British Football.* London: Bantam, 2009.

Stubbs, David. *Send Them Victorious: England's Path to Glory 2006–2010.* London: O Books, 2010.

Tischler, Steven. *Footballers and Businessmen: The Origins of Professional Soccer in England.* New York: Holmes & Meier, 1981.

Thornton, Phil. *Casuals: The Story of Terrace Fashion.* Preston, UK: Milo Books, 2004.

Walvin, James. *The People's Game: The History of Football Revisited.* Edinburgh: Mainstream Publishing, 2000.

Wilson, Jonathan. *The Anatomy of England: A History in Ten Matches.* London: Orion, 2010.

Winner, David. *Those Feet: A Sensual History of English Football.* London: Bloomsbury UK, 2005.

Greece

Tzanelli, Rodanthi. "'Impossible Is a Fact': Greek Nationalism and International Recognition in Euro 2004." *Media, Culture & Society* 28, no. 4 (2006): 483–503.

Hungary

Szöllősi, György. *Puskás.* Budapest: Ringier, 2005.

Ireland

Coyle, Padraig. *Paradise Lost and Found: The Story of Belfast Celtic.* Edinburgh: Mainstream Publishing, 2001.

Cullen, Donal. *Freestaters: The Republic of Ireland Soccer Team, 1921–1939.* Southend, UK: Desert Island Books, 2007.

O'Callaghan, Conor. *Red Mist: Roy Keane and the Football Civil War, a Fan's Story.* London: Bloomsbury, 2004.

Tuohy, Mark. *Belfast Celtic.* Belfast: Blackstaff Press, 1989.

West, Patrick. *Beating Them at Their Own Game: How the Irish Conquered English Soccer.* Dublin, Ireland: Liberties, 2006.

Israel

Ben-Porat, Amir. *From Game to Commodity: Football in Israel 1948–1999.* Beer Sheva: Ben Gurion Univ. of the Negev Press, 2002.

Sorek, Tamir. *Arab Soccer in a Jewish State: The Integrative Enclave.* Cambridge: Cambridge University Press, 2007.

Italy

Agnew, Paddy. *Forza Italia: A Journey in Search of Italy and Its Football.* London: Ebury, 2006.

Edgerton, Paul. *William Garbutt: The Father of Italian Football*. Cheltenham, UK: SportsBooks, 2009.

Foot, John. *Calcio: A History of Italian Football*. London: Fourth Estate, 2006.

———. *Winning at All Costs: A Scandalous History of Italian Soccer*. New York: Nation Books, 2007.

Manna, Alexandra, and Mike Gibbs. *The Day Italian Football Died: Torino and the Tragedy of Superga*. Derby, UK: Breedon, 2000.

Martin, Simon. *Football and Fascism: The National Game under Mussolini*. Oxford: Berg, 2004.

McGinniss, Joe. *The Miracle of Castel Di Sangro*. Boston: Little, Brown, 1999.

Parks, Tim. *A Season with Verona: Travels around Italy in Search of Illusion, National Character and—Goals!* New York: Arcade Publishing, 2002.

Testa, Alberto. *Football, Fascism and Fandom: The Ultras of Italian Football*. London: A&C Black, 2010.

Vialli, Gianluca, and Gabriele Marcotti. *The Italian Job: A Journey to the Heart of Two Great Footballing Cultures*. London: Transworld Publishers, 2007.

Liechtenstein

Connelly, Charlie. *Stamping Grounds: Exploring Liechtenstein and Its World Cup Dream*. London: Abacus, 2005.

Malta

Armstrong, Gary, and Jon P. Mitchell. *Global and Local Football: Politics and Europeanization on the Fringes of the EU*. London: Routledge, 2008.

The Netherlands

Cruyff, Johan, Frits Barend, and Henk van Dorp. *The Best of Ajax, Barcelona, Cruyff: The ABC of an Obstinate Maestro*. London: Bloomsbury, 1997.

Kuper, Simon. *Ajax, the Dutch, the War: Football in Europe during the Second World War*. London: Bloomsbury, 2000.

Winner, David. *Brilliant Orange: The Neurotic Genius of Dutch Soccer*. Woodstock, New York: Overlook Press, 2002.

Russia/Former Soviet Union

Dougan, Andy. *Dynamo: Defending the Honour of Kiev*. London: Fourth Estate, 2001.

Downing, David. *Passovotchka: Moscow Dynamo in Britain, 1945*. London: Bloomsbury, 1999.

Edelman, Robert. *Serious Fun: A History of Spectator Sports in the USSR*. New York: Oxford University Press, 1993.

———. *Spartak Moscow: A History of the People's Team in the Workers' State.* Ithaca, New York: Cornell University Press, 2009.

Riordan, James. *Comrade Jim: The Spy Who Played for Spartak.* London: Fourth Estate, 2008.

———. *Sport in Soviet Society: Development of Sport and Physical Education in Russia and the USSR.* Cambridge: Cambridge University Press, 1977.

Spain

Ball, Phil. *Morbo: The Story of Spanish Football.* London: WSC Books, 2001.

———. *White Storm: 100 Years of Real Madrid.* Edinburgh: Mainstream Publishing, 2002.

Burns, Jimmy. *Barça: A People's Passion.* London: Bloomsbury, 2000.

NORTH AMERICA

Canada

Amis, John Matthew. *The History of Soccer in Nova Scotia.* Nova Scotia: John Matthew Amis, 1997.

Jose, Colin. *Keeping Score: The Encyclopedia of Canadian Soccer.* Vaughan, Ontario: Soccer Hall of Fame and Museum, 1998.

———. *On-Side: 125 Years of Soccer in Ontario.* Vaughan: Ontario Soccer Association in conjunction with the Soccer Hall of Fame and Museum, 2001.

Jose, Colin, and William F. Rannie. *The Story of Soccer in Canada.* Lincoln, Ontario: W. F. Rannie, 1982.

Mexico

Magazine, Roger. *Golden and Blue Like My Heart: Masculinity, Youth, and Power among Soccer Fans in Mexico City.* Tucson: University of Arizona Press, 2007.

United States of America

Allaway, Roger. *Corner Offices & Corner Kicks: How Big Business Created America's Two Greatest Soccer Dynasties, Bethlehem Steel and the New York Cosmos.* Haworth, New Jersey: St. Johann Press, 2009.

———. *Rangers, Rovers and Spindles: Soccer, Immigration and Textiles in New England and New Jersey.* Haworth, New Jersey: St. Johann Press, 2005.

Bondy, Filip. *Chasing the Game: America and the Quest for the World Cup.* New York: De Capo Press, 2010.

Cirino, Tony. *U.S. Soccer vs. the World: The American National Team in the Olympic Games, the World Cup, and Other International Competition.* Leonia, New Jersey: Damon Press, 1983.

Douglas, Geoffrey. *The Game of Their Lives.* New York: H. Holt and Co., 1996.

Jenkins, Garry. *The Beautiful Team: In Search of Pelé and the 1970 Brazilians.* London: Simon & Schuster, 1998.

Lacey, Josh. *God Is Brazilian: Charles Miller, the Man Who Brought Football to Brazil.* Stroud, UK: Tempus Publishing, 2005.

Lever, Janet. *Soccer Madness: Brazil's Passion for the World's Most Popular Sport.* Long Grove, Illinois: Waveland Press, 1995.

PHOTOGRAPHY AND DESIGN

Hoon, Will. *Football Days: Classic Football Photographs by Peter Robinson.* London: Mitchell Beazley, 2003.

Kuper, Simon. *Magnum Soccer.* New York: Phaidon Press, 2005.

Leslie, Jeremy, and Patrick Burgoyne. *FC Football Graphics.* London: Korinsha Press, 1998.

Meer, Hans van der. *European Fields: The Landscape of Lower League Football.* Göttingen, Germany: SteidlMack, 2006.

REFERENCES

Allaway, Roger, Colin Jose, and David Litterer. *The Encyclopedia of American Soccer History.* Lanham, Maryland: Scarecrow Press, 2001.

Bestard, Miguel Angel, Michael Robinson, and Mike Ross. *International Football in South America, 1901–1991.* Cleethorpes, UK: Soccer Book Publishing, 1992.

Cox, Richard William, Dave Russell, and Wray Vamplew. *Encyclopedia of British Football.* London: F. Cass, 2002.

Hollander, Zander. *The American Encyclopedia of Soccer.* New York: Everest House Publishers, 1980.

Seddon, Peter J., C. McKinley, and A. E. Cunningham. *A Football Compendium: An Expert Guide to the Books, Films and Music of Association Football.* Boston, UK: British Library, 1999.

When Saturday Comes: The Half Decent Football Book. London: Penguin, 2005.

JOURNALS, MAGAZINES, AND PERIODICALS

Champions. The official magazine of the UEFA Champions League, *Champions* covers elite European soccer. Published bimonthly.

F.C. Business Magazine. Publication for the soccer industry in Great Britain. Trade magazine focusing on the business of running a soccer club. Published eight times a year.

FIFA World Magazine. Official publication of the sport's governing body, Fédération Internationale de Football Association (FIFA).

Four Four Two. A leading London-based soccer magazine with coverage focused on Great Britain. Published monthly.

She Kicks. Successor to *Fair Game* magazine, *She Kicks* is the world's leading magazine focused on women's soccer, based in Great Britain.

Soccer America. The leading soccer magazine in the United States since the 1970s, *Soccer America* currently offers four special issues a year, with most of its coverage now online only.

Soccer and Society. An academic journal based in England covering the historical, sociological, political, and economic aspects of soccer.

Welsh Football. Independent magazine covering Welsh soccer, published in Wales.

When Saturday Comes. Published in London, *When Saturday Comes* is Great Britain's leading independent soccer magazine. Published monthly.

World Soccer. *World Soccer*, published in Great Britain, is the leading magazine covering global soccer in the English language. Published monthly.

WEBSITES OF INTEREST

www.cafonline.com—official website of the African Football Confederation (CAF), the FIFA confederation responsible for overseeing soccer on the African continent.

www.conmebol.com—official website of the South American Football Confederation (CONMEBOL), the FIFA confederation responsible for overseeing soccer in South America.

www.fifa.com—official website of the sport's global governing body, Fédération Internationale de Football Association (FIFA).

www.oceaniafootball.com—official website of the Oceania Football Confederation (OFC), the FIFA confederation responsible for overseeing soccer in the Oceanic region.

www.rsssf.com—website of the Rec.Sport.Soccer Statistics Foundation (RSSSF), an extremely useful reference website. Features results and statistics on numerous competitions.

www.ssbra.org/html/laws/ifab.html—website of the South Bay Referee Association. Usefully contains the archives, including meeting minutes, of the International Football Association Board (IFAB).

www.the-afc.com—official website of the Asian Football Confederation (AFC), the FIFA confederation responsible for overseeing soccer in Europe.

www.uefa.com—official website of the Union of European Football Associations (UEFA), the FIFA confederation responsible for overseeing soccer in Europe.

About the Author

Tom Dunmore is a soccer writer and executive living in Chicago, Illinois. He is originally from Brighton, England, and moved to the United States in 2001. Tom has since pursued a doctoral degree in international history at the University of Chicago and, in 2010, was appointed vice president of the Chicago Riot Soccer Club of the Major Indoor Soccer League. He publishes an award-winning global soccer-culture blog, www.pitchinvasion.net, winner of a gold-medal award from *When Saturday Comes* magazine in 2009. Tom was an international soccer columnist for the *Chicago Sports Weekly* from 2007 to 2008. He is also the chairman of Section 8 Chicago, the Independent Supporters' Association for the Chicago Fire Soccer Club, and is a longtime fan of Brighton and Hove Albion in his native England. Tom is an avid amateur soccer player for his team, Seawolves.

Dure, Beau. *Long-Range Goals: The Success Story of Major League Soccer.* Washington, D.C.: Potomac Books, 2010.

Foulds, Sam, and Paul E. Harris. *America's Soccer Heritage: A History of the Game.* Manhattan Beach, California: Soccer for Americans, 1979.

Gardner, Paul, and Pelé. *The Simplest Game: The Intelligent Fan's Guide to the World of Soccer.* New York: Macmillan, 1996.

Haner, Jim. *Soccerhead: An Accidental Journey into the Heart of the American Game.* New York: North Point Press, 2006.

Hopkins, Gary. *Star-Spangled Soccer: The Selling, Marketing and Management of Soccer in the USA.* Basingstoke, UK: Palgrave Macmillan, 2010.

Jose, Colin. *American Soccer League, 1921–1931: The Golden Years of American Soccer.* Lanham, Maryland: Scarecrow Press, 1998.

Markovits, Andrei, and Steven Hellerman. *Offside: Soccer and American Exceptionalism.* Princeton, New Jersey: Princeton University Press, 2001.

Newsham, Gavin. *Once in a Lifetime: The Incredible Story of the New York Cosmos.* New York: Grove Press, 2006.

Simonson, Mark. *Soccer in Oneonta.* Charleston, South Carolina: Arcadia Publishing, 2004.

Smith, Melvin I. *Evolvements of Early American Foot Ball: Through the 1890/91 Season.* Bloomington, Indiana: AuthorHouse, 2008.

Szymanski, Stefan, and Andrew S. Zimbalist. *National Pastime: How Americans Play Baseball and the Rest of the World Plays Soccer.* Washington, D.C.: Brookings Institution Press, 2005.

Tossell, David. *Playing for Uncle Sam: The Brits' Story of the North American Soccer League.* Edinburgh: Mainstream Publishing, 2003.

Toye, Clive. *A Kick in the Grass: The Slow Rise and Quick Demise of the NASL.* Haworth, New Jersey: St. Johann Press, 2006.

Ungrady, Dave. *Unlucky: A Season of Struggle in Minor League Professional Soccer.* New Market, Maryland: Sports Publishing International, 1999.

Wahl, Grant. *The Beckham Experiment: How the World's Most Famous Athlete Tried to Conquer America.* New York: Crown Books, 2009.

Wangerin, David. *Soccer in a Football World: The Story of America's Forgotten Game.* London: WSC Books, 2006.

OCEANIA

Australia

Please note that although Australia is part of Oceania, since 2005 it has been a member of the Asian Football Confederation (AFC) rather than the Oceania Football Confederation (OFC).

Solly, Ross, and Jeff Kennett. *Shoot Out: The Passion and the Politics of Soccer's Fight for Survival in Australia.* Milton, Qld: John Wiley & Sons, 2004.

Thompson, Trevor. *One Fantastic Goal: A Complete History of Football in Australia.* Sydney: ABC Books for the Australian Broadcasting Corporation, 2006.

New Zealand

Hilton, Tony, and Barry Smith. *An Association with Soccer: The NZFA Celebrates Its First 100 Years*. Wellington: New Zealand Football Association, 1991.

Little, Charles. 2002. "The Forgotten Game? A Reassessment of the Place of Soccer within New Zealand Society, Sport and Historiography." *Soccer and Society* 3, no. 2: 38–50.

Matheson, John, and Sam Malcolmson. *All Whites '82*. Auckland: Hodder Moa, 2007.

Small, John. *Canterbury Soccer, 1903–2003*. Christchurch: Mainland Soccer, 2003.

SOUTH AMERICA

General

Arbena, Joseph. *Sport and Society in Latin America: Diffusion, Dependency, and the Rise of Mass Culture*. (Contributions to the study of Popular Culture, no. 20). New York: Greenwood Press, 1988.

Mason, Tony. *Passion of the People? Football in South America*. London: Verso, 1995.

Miller, Rory, and Liz Crolley. *Football in the Americas: Fútbol, Futebol, Soccer*. London: Institute for the Study of the Americas, 2007.

Taylor, Chris. *The Beautiful Game: A Journey through Latin American Football*. London: Indigo, 1999.

Argentina

Alabarces, Pablo, Ramiro Coelho, and Juan Sanguinetti. "Treacheries and Traditions in Argentinian Football Styles: The Story of Estudiantes de La Plata." In *Fear and Loathing in World Football*, edited by Gary Armstrong and Richard Giulianotti. Oxford: Berg, 2001.

Alabarces, Pablo, and María Graciela Rodríguez. *Cuestión de pelotas: Fútbol, deporte, sociedad, cultura*. Cap. Federal, Argentina: Atuel, 1996.

"Generals and *Goles*: Assessing the Connection between the Military and Soccer in Argentina." *The International Journal of the History of Sport* 8, no. 1 (May 1990): 120–30.

Brazil

Bellos, Alex. *Futebol: The Brazilian Way of Life*. London: Bloomsbury, 2002.

Castro, Ruy. *Garrincha: The Triumph and Tragedy of Brazil's Forgotten Footballing Hero*. London: Yellow Jersey, 2005.

Hamilton, Aidan. *An Entirely Different Game: The British Influence on Brazilian Football*. Edinburgh: Mainstream Publishing, 1998.

CPSIA information can be obtained at www.ICGtesting.com
Printed in the USA
269308BV00004B/3/P